P9-CFH-135

The
Whole Foods Market
COOKBOOK

The Whole Foods Market® COOKBOOK

A GUIDE TO NATURAL FOODS
WITH 350 RECIPES

Steve Petusevsky and
Whole Foods Market Team Members

Illustrations by David Watts

CLARKSON POTTER / PUBLISHERS
NEW YORK

Copyright © 2002 by Whole Foods Market Services, Inc.
Whole Foods Market® is a registered trademark of Whole Foods Market, Inc.

All rights reserved. No part of this book may be reproduced or transmitted in any form or by any means, electronic or mechanical, including photocopying, recording, or by any information storage and retrieval system, without permission in writing from the publisher.

Published by Clarkson Potter/Publishers, New York, New York.
Member of the Crown Publishing Group, a division of Random House, Inc.
www.randomhouse.com

CLARKSON N. POTTER is a trademark and POTTER and colophon are registered trademarks of Random House, Inc.

Printed in the United States of America

Design by Maggie Hinders
Illustrations by David Watts

Library of Congress Cataloging-in-Publication Data
Petusevsky, Steve.
    The Whole Foods Market cookbook / by Steve Petusevsky and Whole Foods Market Team Members.
    1. Cookery (Natural foods).   2. Natural foods.   3. Whole Foods Market.   I. Title.
TX741.P47   2002
641.5'63—dc21   2001050032

ISBN 0-609-80644-0 (paper)
ISBN 0-609-60713-8

10   9   8   7   6

First Edition

The Team Members of Whole Foods Market
would like to dedicate this cookbook to everyone who has
a passion for fresh, great-tasting food.
We especially appreciate our customers, who help bring
Whole Foods Market store communities to life.

We hope this book helps nourish your body, mind, and soul.

Acknowledgments

THIS COOKBOOK reflects the culmination of a long journey involving hundreds of personalities and an incredible team effort. We would like to take this occasion to thank the many people responsible for this book:

Christopher Adams, Ciro Alfieri, Amy Archinal, Chaz Armstrong, Lesli Baily, Melissa Barnes, Nick Bell, David Berenson, Andrew Bickle, Donna Blagdan, Paige Brady, Marla Camp, Jeff Campbell, Janet Chaykin, Doe Coover, Bebe Cotton, Cindy Cuomo, Charlotte Davis, Rashne Desai, Mary Diedrich, Michelle Di Pietro, Joe Dobrow, Karen Doyle, George Eckrich, Becky Foulk, Bonnie Frechette, Susannah Frishman-Phillips, Tanya Fuqua, Yvette Giraud, Stephen Goldberg, Jane Goode, H. Jeane Griggs, Amy Hopfensperger, Marc Jonna, Pat Kauffman, Edmund Lamacchia, Polly Lanning, Kate Lowery, Lenore Lustig, Donna Macartney, Matt Mason, John Mitchell, Cat Mondello, Rita Neal, Julia Obici, Erin O'Hagan, Benjamin Orphan, Kirsten Osolind, Denis Ring, Lori Rockenstyre, Gabrielle Rosi, Christopher Ryding, Bruce Silverman, David Smith, Honey Smith, Laurie Stern, Shari Stern, Judith Stocks, Cathy Strange, David Watts, and Margaret Wittenberg. We would also like to thank Katie Workman and the entire team at Clarkson Potter.

Contents

Foreword

THINKING BACK to more than twenty-one years ago when we opened the doors to the first Whole Foods Market store, we set out with a pretty simple mission: to provide a more natural alternative to what we eat than the options the food supply chain was typically offering at the time. Our Team Members and customers alike have shared intense enthusiasm for the freshest, highest quality, and most flavorful natural and organic foods. Together we have helped instigate the transformation of the food industry back to "naturalness" and the support of small local farmers and food artisans. Though our Whole Foods Market family has now grown to more than 23,000 team members, thousands of vendor partners and millions of customers in the United States and Canada, we remain as committed as ever to our founding ideals.

This cookbook, with its hundreds of recipes and useful tips from our team members, is our attempt at capturing a bit of the essence of what the Whole Foods Market experience is all about. Our team members work with fresh, vibrant foods every day and proudly bring great, pure food to each of the communities we serve. They are passionate about sharing with our customers the highest quality foods and gourmet products as well as unique recipes and entertaining ideas. Many created and contributed their favorite recipes from our kitchens and from their own homes.

We hope that in sharing our mission, passion, and culinary creations with you, day in and day out, in our stores and within these pages, we can help you to quench your desires for great taste sensations from the freshest, highest quality ingredients bursting with the purest, most natural flavors. From our kitchens to yours, may you enjoy our collection of recipes and take pleasure in the warmth of breaking bread with family and friends.

—John Mackey
Cofounder and CEO of Whole Foods Market

Introduction

The Whole Foods Market

WHOLE FOODS MARKET stores feature an exciting choice of thousands of products and a unique shopping experience. Our stores are filled with healthful ingredients, abundant samples, open kitchens where our in-store chefs conjure up ever-changing selections of prepared foods, scratch bakeries, hand-stacked produce, take-out food stations, gourmet cheese displays, European-style charcuterie departments, and pristine seafood cases that bring fresh product up to eye level. To enrich your cooking at home, there are also recipe cards to take with you, entertaining ideas, and the latest information on emerging food issues.

From the beginning, Whole Foods Market emerged as a true innovator, transforming food shopping from a chore into a dynamic experience that enlivens all the senses. The wondrous sights, sounds, smells, and activity make each shopping trip a true experience of discovery. Like the public markets of years past, Whole Foods Market stores play a unique role as a community meeting place where friends can gather, interact, and learn, while at the same time discover the many joys of eating and sharing food.

Whole Foods, Whole People, Whole Planet™

WE believe in a virtuous circle entwining the food chain, human beings, and Mother Earth: Each is reliant upon the others through a beautiful and delicate symbiosis.

Whole Foods: We obtain our products locally and from all over the world—often from small, uniquely dedicated food artisans. We strive to offer the highest quality, least processed, most flavorful, and naturally preserved foods. Why? Because food in its purest state—unadulterated by artificial additives, sweeteners, colorings, and preservatives—is the best tasting and most nutritious food available.

Whole People: We recruit the best people we can to become part of our team. We empower them to make their own decisions, creating a respectful workplace where people are treated fairly and are highly motivated to succeed. We look for people who are passionate about food. Our Team Members are also well-rounded human beings. They play a critical role in helping build the store into a profitable and beneficial part of its community. Also, our customers are the lifeblood of our business, and we celebrate the fact that this knowledgeable consumer group turns to us for the very best, most natural food and nutritional products available. We go to extraordinary lengths to serve our customers competently, efficiently, knowledgeably, and with flair.

Whole Planet: We believe companies, like individuals, must assume their share of responsibility as tenants of Planet Earth. On a global basis, we actively support organic farming—the best method for promoting sustainable agriculture and protecting the environment and the farmworkers. On a local basis, we are actively involved in our communities by supporting food banks, sponsoring neighborhood events, compensating our Team Members for community service work, and contributing at least 5 percent of total net profits to not-for-profit organizations.

Our Vision and Philosophy

As a pioneer of the natural foods movement, Whole Foods Market was part of a small but vocal group concerned with how the raw ingredients that ultimately ended up on our dinner tables and in our children's lunch boxes were grown, processed, and sold. Through the years, many of our foods had lost much of their true flavor due to the advent of modern farming practices, the disappearance of the small family farm, and the increased use of synthetic chemicals in production. Operating against the mainstream view over two decades ago, this group shared a simple vision: The purity of our food and the health of our bodies are directly related to the purity and health of our environment. The vitality and well-being of each individual is a microcosm of a much larger culture, global in stature.

When we opened our first store in 1980, the seeds that represent Whole Foods Market's unique core values and commitment to "Whole Foods, Whole People, Whole Planet™" were first planted. In fact, this commitment has become our motto and today expresses our philosophy: The planet's health and human health are inextricably linked with how we grow our food and what we eat. We have since cultivated those seeds to grow into the world's largest organic and natural foods supermarket—a company of "heart and soul."

We carry natural and organic products because we believe that food in its purest state— unadulterated by artificial additives, sweeteners, colorings, and preservatives—is the best tasting and most nutritious food available. We actively support organic farming because we believe it is the best method for promoting sustainable agriculture as well as protecting the environment and farmworkers. By seeking out farmers and food artisans from around the corner as well as all around the world, Whole Foods Market searches for not only the purest but also the freshest and most flavorful foods available.

Sharing Our Knowledge

We realize that, as the leader in the movement away from processed foods and artificial flavors and back to taste and whole foods, we have another major responsibility. We are committed to helping teach consumers about natural foods . . . and hence about cooking. We are committed to staying on the forefront of new ingredients and emerging food trends, stocking our shelves with natural food ingredients that nurture our health and well-being as well as our appetites. Natural and organic foods are minimally processed and as such may have the purest flavor and the maximum nutritive value.

Whole Foods Market shoppers know that not only are we driven to find the best quality and safest selection of ingredients, but we are also enthusiastic about sharing our knowledge with customers. Walk through a store and invariably you'll hear a customer asking a Team Member, "How should I cook this?" More people are turning to natural and organic products to improve their health and lifestyle, but they need a bit of help in the transition. Whole Foods Market appreciates and celebrates the difference whole foods can make in the quality of one's life. By helping people understand how to prepare and cook foods that are as close to their natural state as possible, we are in turn supporting the well-being and health of both people and the planet.

We hope the recipes and information provided in this cookbook will inspire our customers and readers to embrace the pleasures associated with making or eating delicious food, while also fulfilling their aspirations for total wellness.

Quality Standards

OUR business is to sell the highest quality foods we can find at the most competitive prices possible. We evaluate quality in terms of nutrition, freshness, appearance, and taste. Historically, our Quality Standards have differentiated Whole Foods Market from other grocery stores, served as an educational tool, and formed the basis for consumer and Team Member trust.

WHOLE FOODS MARKET QUALITY STANDARDS

- We carefully evaluate each and every product we sell.
- We feature foods that are free from artificial preservatives, colors, flavors, and sweeteners.
- We are passionate about great-tasting food and the pleasure of sharing it with one another.
- We are committed to foods that are fresh, wholesome, and safe to eat.
- We seek out and promote organically grown foods.
- We provide food and nutritional products that support health and well-being.

A Basic Approach to Natural Foods

Cooking with natural foods offers a distinct advantage: Simplicity produces elegant and rewarding results. Natural foods ingredients are grown and produced with care and great attention, yielding tremendous flavor, which merely needs to be enhanced by other uncomplicated ingredients, not camouflaged. Natural foods menus reflect balance and a variety of choices. First, you need to understand the basics of natural foods and how they relate to your kitchen at home. Simply put, here are the elements of natural foods cooking:

- Cook with ingredients as close as possible to their natural state with a minimum amount of processed foods.
- Avoid foods with artificially based flavors, colors, preservatives, and sweeteners.
- Use whole grains and unbleached and unbromated flours.
- Serve mostly seasonal fruits and vegetables with an emphasis on organically grown produce.
- Purchase poultry and beef raised without the use of growth stimulants and antibiotics.
- Avoid hydrogenated fats.

Before You Get Started

The most important time-saving tip is having all your ingredients in front of you before you begin to cook. Read the whole recipe all the way through before starting to cook. Organize your work area before the stove begins to heat up. When all your necessary ingredients are prepped and ready to go, it's called your *mise-en-place*, which translates to "everything in its place." Have all your dicing and slicing done and all liquid and dry ingredients measured before you start cooking. Always prepare your produce items separately from fresh meats, seafood, and poultry to prevent the potential risk of bacterial cross-contamination. Leave your meat, poultry, and seafood in the refrigerator while preparing the other ingredients in your recipe. Try to use two cutting boards, one for vegetables and one for meat, poultry, or seafood.

POTS AND PANS

You don't need to have a large set of pots and pans to cook with. There are some great selections in department stores, but here's a word of advice: Buy a good set that will last a lifetime. It's worth investing the money in the beginning; you will rarely have to replace anything down the road. Purchase pots and pans with flexible cooking function more in mind. As we discuss cooking methods like sautéing, steaming, braising, searing, and so forth, you will see that the kind of pot and pan you own is more important to you than the brand. Generally look for these qualities in cookware: good conductivity, heavy gauge, ease of cleanup, and a variety of sizes. You also don't want pots and pans that are going to be too heavy or uncomfortable to handle and lift. Here's a good list to start with:

- Sauté pans
- Sauce pots
- Wok-style pan
- Steamer pan set
- Cast-iron pan
- Roasting pan
- Cookie sheet with raised sides

Caring for Cast-Iron Pans

UNLIKE pans made from other materials, cast-iron pans need to be seasoned before their first use to create an almost nonstick surface. After purchasing the pan, wash it well and dry it. Add ¼ cup of vegetable oil to the pan and place the pan in a 325°F. oven for about 1 hour. Turn the oven off, and allow the pan to cool until it can be handled. Discard the oil, and wipe the pan clean. You may have to repeat this process a few times, but it will be worth it. The cooking surface will have a glossy sheen, and cooked foods will come out of the pan easily. After cooking with your cast-iron pan, wash it well and rub a thin layer of oil into the pan as it sits on a low-heat burner for about 10 minutes. A properly seasoned cast-iron pan will last a lifetime.

ESSENTIAL UTENSILS

There is a gadget and tool for everything. In fact, there are many more gadgets than any cook ever has need for. What did our forefathers and foremothers of cooking use, and how did they turn out such incredible food from scratch before the onslaught of machinery? Modern cooks need not stockpile every "new, improved" device. Here are some utensils we find handy:

- Spoons—regular and slotted, made from any number of materials, including wood, plastic, stainless steel, and hard rubber
- Spatulas—both rubber scrapers and heavy-handled metal and plastic spatulas for turning foods in a pan
- Wire whips for whisking
- Ladles of various sizes, for soups, sauces
- Cook's fork, for lifting roasts from pans
- Vegetable peeler
- Kitchen tongs
- Pastry brush
- Stainless-steel mixing bowls
- Handheld immersion blender—great for soups, sauces, dressings, and marinades
- Asian-style vegetable mandolin—inexpensive and indispensable for julienned and very thinly sliced vegetables; serves many of the same functions that a two-hundred-dollar stainless-steel mandolin does
- Meat thermometer

- Colanders—a small handheld one and a larger double-handled colander for draining pasta and vegetables
- Grater
- Measuring cups (dry and liquid) and spoons
- Rolling pin
- Meat mallet
- Kitchen timer

KNIVES

If you invest in a good set of knives and take care of it, you will own it for life. It's normally less expensive to buy a set that includes a chef's knife, carving knife, a serrated slicing knife, a paring knife, and a steel for honing the edge. Truth is, if you are looking for just the essentials, you need a chef's knife, a utility knife, and a paring knife with a steel. Consider a cleaver, as well.

Cooking with Natural Foods

Many methods of classical and modern cooking are used in the preparation of natural foods. Generally speaking, there is a definitive sensitivity to preserve the natural flavors and textures along with the nutritional profile of raw ingredients. There is also a whole new universe of ingredients to explore (see "Whole Foods Glossary," page 395). When you combine these ingredients with a fresh appreciation for basic cooking principles and add some contemporary flair and educated choices to the mix, your cooking will become surprisingly simple and deliciously rewarding.

Cooking Methods

Baking and *roasting* are interchangeable terms, though roasting is most often used in association with meat, poultry, fish, and vegetables and when cooking with higher temperatures. Essentially this is a basic method of dry-heat cooking. It's important to preheat the oven so whatever is placed in the oven begins to cook immediately. This is especially critical when you wish to brown or seal the outside of the food you're cooking, meat, fish, and especially poultry. Searing the outside surface keeps the natural juices inside, producing a moist and succulent end product. Although baking and roasting are normally associated with cooking meats and poultry items, this dry-heat method is a unique way to flavor vegetables, bringing out and caramelizing their natural sugar content. Baking is also a term used to describe the oven-cooking of desserts and breads.

Sautéing comes from the French word *sauter*, which means "to jump." Sautéed dishes usually incorporate ingredients that are cut small so they may "jump" in the pan. When sautéing foods, use as little oil or fat as possible and try to cook the ingredients as quickly as possible over high heat. The high temperature seals the ingredients rapidly. It's important to use the right oil for this cooking method so the oil doesn't burn before the food is cooked (see "Whole Foods Glossary," page 395). When sautéing, food should be as dry as possible and left uncrowded in the pan. This prevents the formation of a layer of steam while cooking, which would lower the cooking temperature and inhibit browning. A sauté pan usually has slanted sides that allow the food to be tossed up and back into the pan. *Stir-frying* in a wok is somewhat related. A wok has slanted sides, not unlike a sauté pan, and ingredients are tossed over very high temperatures until cooked through. Ingredients that are wok-cooked are normally sliced on the bias or diagonally to increase the surface area and make them cook more quickly.

Water sautéing is similar to sautéing, except with little or no oil. You may spray a sauté pan with a fine mist of oil and heat the pan over moderate heat before adding ingredients. Just as the ingredients begin to cook, add water or another liquid such as stock, fruit juice, or vegetable juice to prevent sticking and burning in the pan. If you prefer no fat in your dish, you may begin the cooking process using the liquid and leave the oil mist out.

Pan-frying is similar to sautéing, except more oil or fat is used, and the vegetables or cuts of meat, poultry, or fish are larger. It is especially important to achieve the right oil temperature before pan-frying or the results will be greasy and unappealing. Sometimes when pan-frying meats or poultry, if the cut is thick (a thick chicken breast or turkey steak, for example), you may have to finish cooking the dish in the oven.

Searing is browning an ingredient quickly over high heat, in order to seal in the flavor. Searing can be done in a pan or under a broiler. The term *blackening*, normally associated with Cajun cooking, is essentially searing with a layer of spices on the outside

Expanding the Flavor of Dried Spices

TO intensify the flavor of dried spices, many recipes begin with heating a small amount of oil and adding some onion and spices. This initial sautéing process concentrates the flavor of dried spices and makes them ring through later in the recipe. You may also heat a small dry nonstick pan and add spices to the pan over medium heat, stirring often for 1 to 2 minutes to toast the spices and increase their natural flavor.

About Oils

TO use less oil, purchase an inexpensive mister used for plants at any department store. Fill the mister with either canola, olive, or a mixture of several oils (see "Whole Foods Glossary," page 395). You can then merely spray oil onto your sauté pan or saucepot and cook while using much less oil than before with the same results. After all, sauté literally means to cook quickly in a small amount of fat.

Try mixing 1 part sesame oil and 2 parts canola oil for cooking Asian recipes. Use 1 part extra-virgin olive oil and 2 parts canola oil for a great all-purpose blend.

You may also season your oils to add a subtle underlying flavor element to your dishes. Adding dried chilies, lemon peel, fresh herb sprigs, bay leaves, or whole garlic cloves works well. Just heat the oil, add the flavoring ingredients when the oil is almost to a boiling point, and then allow it to cool to room temperature. Refrigerate. After a few days the flavors will have infused your oil with added taste. Use within 1 month.

Lemon Oil: Heat 2 tablespoons of lemon zest with 1 cup of extra-virgin olive oil until it barely bubbles, then turn off the flame and allow the flavors to infuse.

surface. Cast-iron skillets are one of the best pans in which to sear food. *Pan-searing* normally refers to cooking ingredients solely in a sauté pan or skillet, rather than finishing them in the oven.

Braising is a mixture of both searing and cooking in a liquid. Usually meats or vegetables are first browned in a small amount of oil; then a liquid is added to the pan. The pan is then covered, and the ingredient is cooked at a simmer (185°F.) until done. This process develops pronounced flavor and is also effective when cooking less tender cuts of meat, since they become tender from the slow cooking in liquid. You must use a pan with a tight-fitting lid to prevent the liquid from evaporating.

Steaming produces a quick cooking action, which involves placing foods on a rack or plate over boiling or simmering water in a covered pot. If you've ever gotten burned by opening a simmering pot, you know that steam is much hotter than plain boiling water. There are steamer baskets made of wood that you may also use. Steaming is a good way to preserve the nutritional profile, color, and texture of many foods.

Simmering, simply put, is cooking gently in liquid that reaches about 185°F. The bubbles should barely break the surface. Simmering temperature is critical when making soups and stocks. Boiling is rapid simmering and is the method most commonly used to cook pasta, and foods like vegetables are often added to boiling water or other liquid; then the temperature is lowered.

Poaching is cooking in a simmering liquid that is normally flavored with herbs, vegetables, wine, lemon, and seasonings. Poaching produces a juicy, moist result, especially if the liquid simmers at 185°F. Although poultry may be poached, seafood is especially delicious when poached because the low moist heat prevents the delicate seafood from breaking apart. Seafood is cooked when it is opaque.

Broiling is a method of cooking with radiant heat. The extremely hot temperatures generated by a broiler are recommended for more tender cuts of meat, poultry, and seafood. Vegetables and firm tofu can be cut into steaks and broiled, as well. Broiled foods turn out better when the broiler is preheated first, which promotes even browning and proper caramelization of the natural juices. A good method to broil foods is first to brush the ingredients with a seasoned oil, which helps to conduct the heat, allows the food to brown faster, and adds flavor. Most of our marinades can be used for this purpose.

Grilling is more popular now than it has ever been. Once relegated to homeowners with backyards, grilling has become a favored cooking method with devotees who consider it an art form. Grilling, an intuitive cooking method, takes time and experience to master. There is nothing like the smoky, sweet flavor of food cooked on a grill. The high-temperature dry heat of a grill sears the outside of the food being cooked and seals the juices inside. One of the best benefits that grilling affords is that leftover grilled foods can be tossed into salads, soups, and stews, giving a whole new flavor to other foods.

Making Roasted Garlic

THE flavor of roasted garlic is almost indescribable. The strong garlic flavor mellows as the natural sugar caramelizes and the clove becomes creamy and tender. Whole heads of garlic may be roasted by cutting off the top ⅓ inch of the head. Rub the surface with olive oil, sprinkle with a bit of salt, and roast in a preheated 375°F. oven on a baking pan for 20 to 25 minutes, until the head is tender. These delicious whole cloves can be detached from the core and squeezed onto bread or vegetables, into soup or pasta, or eaten on crackers. They are dreamy and comforting to eat. Whole peeled cloves may be tossed in a little olive oil, sprinkled with salt, and roasted on a baking pan in a 375°F. oven for 20 minutes, until golden brown and tender. These softened cloves may be tossed into any dish, especially pasta or steamed vegetables, where they become precious culinary gems just waiting to be inhaled.

Barbecuing is a form of grilling normally associated with foods cooked over hardwoods. In most cases a barbecue sauce or marinade is used to flavor and coat the food being cooked. In fact, a personal, often closely held secret sauce is what distinguishes good barbecue from great barbecue. Some wood varieties used in barbecues burn hotter than others and produce different flavors. Fruit woods, such as apple and cherry, impart their own mild taste, while other woods, such as hickory, maple, and mesquite, offer a more pronounced flavor and somewhat hotter cooking temperature.

Cooking Basics

SOUPS AND STOCKS

For details on making soups and stocks, please see pages 53 to 56.

PASTA

For details on cooking pasta and couscous, please see pages 179 to 181.

GRAINS AND BEANS

For information and charts on cooking grains and beans, please see pages 155 to 158.

VEGETABLES
Prepping Cut Vegetables

Most vegetables may be precut and stored for later use. Hearty vegetables, such as carrots, onions, celery, broccoli, and cauliflower, may be diced or sliced and kept for up to three days without sacrificing any quality. Peppers may be cut or sliced the day prior to cooking. *Do not wash vegetables after cutting.* This will rinse off valuable water-soluble vitamins and also make the cut vegetables perish rapidly. Always rinse the whole vegetable, dry well with a kitchen towel or paper towels, and then cut. Keep the cut vegetables in resealable plastic bags, ready for use.

Whiter Whites, Brighter Brights

There's a bit of nature's chemistry in every pot of simmering vegetables. Here's how to preserve the personality and color of your favorite vegetables.

Using acidulated water. Certain cut fruits and vegetables should be kept in water with lemon juice added to it in order to preserve the white color. Artichokes, apples, celery root, pears, and fennel should be plunged into about 2 quarts water with about $1/3$ cup lemon juice. Keep the ingredients in acidulated water just while you are prepping for immediate use. When vegetables are left in water with acid, they start to break down and look a bit weary.

Keeping potatoes white before cooking. Potatoes should be peeled and plunged directly into cold water to prevent browning. Potatoes can be stored in water for a few hours, but it's best to keep them in water just until you are ready to cook them.

How to keep your green vegetables bright green. There is nothing better than crisp, bright green vegetables that burst with individuality, impart subtle sweetness, and glow with plate appeal. Here's how you do that:

Bring enough water to barely cover the vegetables to a boil. Because nutrients and vitamins in the vegetables are water soluble, add a minimum amount to cook. Add a bit of salt to the water. Kosher salt is what many chefs use to add a more delicate flavor to the vegetables. Add the green vegetables, bring the water back to a full boil as quickly as possible, and simmer just until the vegetable is crisp to the bite or al dente. *Immediately* drain the cooked vegetables and plunge into ice water until the vegetables are completely chilled. Vegetables such as broccoli, green beans, spinach, collard greens, kale, and asparagus will look amazingly bright green on your dinner plate when you use this method.

Remember, any acid (such as lemon juice or vinegar) will destroy the chlorophyll and cause the green vegetable to turn yellow. Many of us grew up thinking that green vegetables were supposed to be yellow green and were meant to fall apart without putting up a fight. This will never be the case again.

After cooking the vegetable and chilling it in ice water, drain well and store it in a covered container for later use. You may use the vegetables immediately or create meals later by sautéing them in butter or olive oil or stir-frying or dipping them into boiling water when you are ready to eat.

How to keep a red vegetable red. Red vegetables are a different story. When such acids as lemon or lime juice, vinegar, or certain fruit juices are added to the cooking liquid, they

Plumping Sun-Dried Tomatoes

PLACE the sun-dried tomatoes in a pot covered with cold water. Bring the water to a boil and simmer for 5 minutes. Allow the tomatoes to sit in the water as it cools for about half an hour. You will see them plump up. Drain them, and then you may either use them as is or marinate them for future use. Use a good-quality extra-virgin olive oil for the best flavor. You may also add fresh herb sprigs such as rosemary, thyme, or oregano. Dried herbs are also fine to use. Try using some dried Italian herb mix. For 1 cup of plumped sun-dried tomatoes, add 1 tablespoon of dried herbs. If you want some heat, try adding a minced jalapeño pepper or a teaspoon of dried red chili flakes.

Roasting and Peeling Peppers

PEPPERS can be skinned using several methods. The key to easily slipping the skin off a pepper is to char the outer skin and then quickly cover the peppers either in a bowl with a towel placed over the top or in a paper bag so the warm pepper steams, which loosens the burnt outer skin. You may broil the pepper in the oven, brown on a grill, or place directly on an open flame or electric burner (which really makes lots of smoke but works well). The grill produces a mellow, smoky flavor. Any way you choose, the skin must be blackened before it will loosen. After cooling slightly, peel the outer skin off under running water. You may now use the skinned pepper for cooking, or marinate it with your favorite vinaigrette or olive oil.

keep red vegetables red and preserve the natural pigment. Acids are helpful in brightening the red color. That's why red cabbage is normally cooked with vinegar or apples. Beets are also treated in the same manner. Try a little raspberry vinegar in the cooking water.

How to keep white vegetables white. Cauliflower and other white vegetables contain pigments called flavones. When exposed to acids (such as citrus juice or vinegar) the pigments stay white. When these vegetables are cooked in an alkaline medium, they yellow. Try adding a bit of lemon juice and salt to cauliflower for a whiter white.

Preparing Root Vegetables

Root vegetables, such as turnips, carrots, potatoes, and parsnips, do not need to be plunged into ice water after cooking (as they will absorb the water like a sponge). Allow them to cool at room temperature.

Caramelizing Vegetables

Caramelizing a vegetable is the process of bringing the natural sugar to the vegetable's surface and turning it to caramel. This is normally done in a saucepan or in the oven. The procedure involves heating a pan over moderate heat and adding oil or butter. The fat must be almost smoking hot when the vegetables are placed into the pan. Once the vegetable is added, it must not be disturbed for a few minutes, allowing the sugar to begin the browning process. A common cook's mistake is to immediately begin stirring the vegetables, which whips oxygen into the pan, lowers the temperature, and impedes the caramelizing process.

Chili Tips

What to look for when you buy fresh chilies. A fresh chili, regardless of which variety, should be glossy, shiny, and smooth skinned. Cracks and crevices, wrinkles and soft spots are signs of age. Fresh chilies are available all year round, although summer is officially chili season.

How to store them. Don't wash them first. Any excess moisture tends to make chili peppers decay. Keep fresh chilies dry, and store them in a paper bag in your refrigerator. They can keep for up to a week. If you see any soft spots or darkened areas, try to use that pepper immediately.

Dried chilies. These should be glossy and whole. If they appear broken or severely cracked, they are old. Dried chilies can be stored in a tightly covered container for a few months or, if you need to store them longer, you may freeze them. This takes away some of their chili fire, however.

Chili lore. Many chili heads say that most of the heat of the chili is located along the fine rib that runs down the length of a pepper, which holds the seeds. If you want to lighten up on the capsaicin content, then remove this rib along with the seeds. Remember, it might be wise to wear gloves as the natural substance capsaicin is so strong it can cause burning and irritation to any part of your body that it comes in contact with.

How to quell the heat. There are several ways to help douse the fire of freshly eaten chilies. Bread, rice, milk, yogurt, and sour cream are some. However, the best method is a little-known cure: Sugar or some kind of sugar syrup swirled around a mouth in flames immediately spells relief.

Why do we love the pain of really hot chilies? Several theories exist. The most common has to do with our brains releasing endorphins that create a sense of well-being not unlike the "high" a marathon runner may experience.

Chili oddity. Northeastern University in Boston conducted a nationwide study of antacid usage in more than two hundred cities across the United States. El Paso, Texas, a community that eats more than its share of spicy food and chilies, came out the lowest of all. You figure it out.

ALTERNATIVE PROTEINS

Foods such as tofu, tempeh, and seitan (wheat gluten), when properly cooked, can taste wonderful and offer delicious and nutritionally balanced alternatives to red meat. There are a few simple things to know about alternative proteins.

Tofu

Although there are several kinds of tofu or bean curd available, tofu basically comes in hard and soft textures. You will see firm and extra-firm blocks of bean curd; however, there is little difference. They both lend themselves toward slicing or dicing. Use firm tofu when you want the tofu to hold its shape, such as for Griddled Sesame and Garlic Tofu with Wilted Bok Choy (page 226) or Braised Five-Spice Tofu (page 228). You may cook firm tofu using several methods. These include sautéing, grilling, broiling, or braising. Marinating tofu overnight noticeably enhances the flavor. Marinated tofu can be grilled, broiled, or baked, allowing you to enjoy the taste of tofu without spending a lot of time in the kitchen.

There are several varieties of soft tofu or silken tofu. Silken tofu is like custard and has a creamy, delicate texture and flavor. It is best used in making sauces, desserts, dressings, and soups. Many stocks or broths make a simple and rewarding meal when silken tofu is added. You may only need to add a few spoonfuls to the hot broth.

Freezing tofu. Tofu may also be frozen and then thawed to change its texture. This freezing process makes the tofu chewier and more meaty. The tofu takes on a fork-and-knife texture. Freeze the whole block of tofu or cut it into 1-inch-thick slices and freeze on a plate overnight. The following day, defrost and use in any tofu recipe.

Pressing tofu. Tofu contains a good deal of water. You may press the tofu for 20 minutes or overnight in your refrigerator by placing it in a colander atop a bowl. Top the tofu with a plate and weight it down with a jar or can. The excess water will drain off, producing bean curd with a firm texture.

Tempeh

Tempeh comes in several flavors, combining soybeans with a variety of grains, seeds, and nuts. Tempeh can be marinated like tofu before it is cooked. Tempeh is extremely versatile and may be sautéed, grilled, broiled, used in stir-fries, or simmered in a flavored broth. It may be used in entrées, soups, stews, casseroles, or sandwiches instead of beef or poultry. Crumbled, it makes great chili or meat sauce for pasta.

Seitan or Wheat Meat

Seitan is not a soy-based food. It is made from gluten—the protein found in wheat—and it provides a flavorful alternative to meat. With a meatlike texture, seitan may be sliced, chopped, or cut into medallions, cutlets, and steaks. It is best when marinated overnight. The porous wheat meat absorbs flavors easily and may be sautéed, baked, grilled, stir-fried, or braised. It takes on a very meatlike consistency in all dishes. Seitan works well in chili, stew, shepherd's pie, and casserole dishes. It's also quite good when grilled and served like a Philly cheese steak sandwich.

GRAIN-BASED MILKS

Milk beverages are made from many grains and nuts: soy, oat, rice, and almonds. All these beverages may be used to make shakes and smoothies. Although soy milk and rice milk may be used in cooking, oat milk is preferable since it won't break down when exposed to heat. Oat milk is especially creamy in soups and sauces, where it has a tendency to reduce and thicken. Always use unflavored milk when cooking. Vanilla and other flavored milks are great when making desserts and hot cereals. Dressings, mashed potatoes, sauces, and gravies may also be prepared using grain-based milks in place of dairy products.

MEAT, POULTRY, AND SEAFOOD

There is an artistry to perfect meat cooking. Now that many home cooks own meat thermometers, it is easier to produce more predictable results. There is more involved than sticking a roast or bird in the oven and setting the timer. Here's some information to help you make the perfect roast, poach the perfect salmon, or stuff the perfect chicken.

All meat, including beef, lamb, and pork, must be cooked by using dry or moist heat cookery. This goes for poultry, as well.

Dry Heat

Generally, larger cuts of meat are roasted, which sears the outside and seals in the natural juices. *Roasting* and *baking* are terms that are used interchangeably. They refer to cuts of meat that are cooked uncovered in a pan. For a better flavor and to help in making a pan gravy, a mixture of carrots, celery, and onion (called a mirepoix) is added during the cooking process. A mixture of dried or fresh herbs and seasonings is also rubbed onto the surface of the meat to add flavor. There are many premixed spice rubs from which to choose, making it simple to flavor roasts without lots of extra work. For additional flavor, you may marinate your meat and poultry before cooking with a premade or homemade marinade. Other methods of dry heat cooking are broiling, pan-searing, and grilling.

Searing. The outer crust of meat, poultry, seafood, vegetables, or tofu takes on a rich flavor because the high heat used to sear food acts to caramelize the natural juices and concentrate the taste. In the case of meat, poultry, or seafood, this seared crust prevents the natural juices from running out. Sometimes cooks use a light dusting of flour to assist in the

A Golden Crust

EVERYONE knows the best part of the roast is the well-browned surface containing all the seasonings, herbs, and caramelized pan drippings. The best way to achieve a crispy browned crust and juicy interior is to preheat your oven to 450° to 475°F. before placing your roast pan in the oven. Once the oven's hot, place the roast in the oven and bake for the first 20 minutes at this higher temperature. After browning the roast, lower the temperature to 325° to 350°F. for the remaining cooking time.

searing process. In either case, a hot pan with very hot oil is needed to sear food successfully. For more information, see pages 8–9.

Salt. Remember to add salt after the surface of the roast has begun to brown, because the salt draws moisture to the roast surface; if salt is added too early, the roast will actually take longer to brown.

Doneness. Red meat (including beef, lamb, pork) can be cooked to the desired level of doneness and tested with a meat thermometer. Here are the proper temperature ranges for doneness: For safety, the USDA recommends cooking beef hamburgers and ground-beef mixtures (such as meat loaf) to 160°F. on a meat thermometer. However, whole muscle meats such as steaks and roasts may be cooked to 145°F. (medium rare), 160°F. (medium), or 170°F. (well done). The USDA offers the chart on page 18 for approximate beef cooking times.

The USDA recommends cooking ground-pork patties and ground-pork mixtures (such as meat loaf) to 160°F., or until juices are clear. Whole muscle meats such as chops and roasts should be cooked to 160°F. (medium) or 170°F. (well done). Internal temperature of safely cooked pork should reach 160°F. when measured with a meat thermometer. Sometimes pork will have a pink appearance even after cooking. This is normal and as long as you have fully cooked pork to the proper internal temperature, it's perfect to enjoy.

Moist Heat Cooking

Less tender cuts of meat are braised using a combination of dry- and moist-heat cooking principles. Stew beef, beef chuck, shoulder, or shanks (like the classic Italian dish osso buco) are normally cooked using moist-heat methods. Shrinkage is greater with meats that are cooked in a liquid since the cooking process is longer. Braising, pot roasting, stewing, boiling, and poaching are all methods of moist-heat cooking. Meats that are cooked using moist heat are done when they are tender; insert a fork or skewer into the meat—it should be tender when the fork slides out easily.

APPROXIMATE BEEF COOKING TIMES (°F)

TYPE	SIZE	COOKING METHOD	COOKING TIME	INTERNAL TEMPERATURE
Rib roast, bone in	4 to 6 lbs.	Roast 325°	23 to 25 min./lb. 27 to 30 min./lb. 32 to 34 min./lb.	Medium rare 145° Medium 160° Well done 170°
Rib roast, boneless rolled	4 to 6 lbs.	Roast 325°	Add 5 to 8 min./lb. to times above	Same as above
Chuck roast, brisket	3 to 4 lbs.	Braise 325°	2 to 3 hours	Medium 160°
Round or rump roast	2½ to 4 lbs.	Roast 325°	30 to 35 min./lb. 35 to 40 min./lb.	Medium rare 145° Medium 160°
Tenderloin; whole, half	4 to 6 lbs. 2 to 3 lbs.	Roast 425°	45 to 60 min. total 35 to 45 min. total	Medium rare 145° Medium 160°
Steaks	¾ in. thick	Broil/Grill	4 to 5 min. per side 6 to 7 min. per side	Medium rare 145° Medium 160°
Stew or shank cross cuts	1 to 1½ in. thick	Cover with liquid; simmer	2 to 3 hours	Medium 160°
Short ribs	4 in. long and 2 in. thick	Braise 325°	1½ to 2½ hours	Medium 160°

Poultry

Most of our poultry dishes are made with whole chickens, chickens that have been cut into portion sizes, or boneless skinless chicken breasts. Any chicken part may be cooked using dry- or moist-heat cooking methods. Bone-in chicken parts lend themselves especially well to moist-heat cookery because they produce a flavorful sauce when braised in liquid. An example is Thai-Style Green Curry Chicken (page 273). Most of our marinades work well with boneless skinless chicken breasts.

The USDA recommends minimum endpoint cooking to ensure food is safe to eat. For whole chickens and turkeys, the USDA recommends 180°F. for thigh meat, 170°F. for breast meat, and 165°F. for stuffing, whether cooked alone or in the bird. When using a thermometer, always make sure to place it in the thickest part of the thigh or breast. Although it's the best way to tell if your poultry is cooked, if you don't have a thermometer, another method for testing doneness is to pierce the thickest part of the chicken with a sharp knife or skewer. If the juice runs pink, the chicken is not cooked yet. If it runs clear, the chicken should be fully cooked.

How to Roast a Perfect Chicken

ROAST chicken will always be a mainstay of American cooking. You don't really need any special gadgets to make the perfect chicken. We've seen chickens roasted vertically, horizontally, and diagonally. However, the best way to cook a chicken is up on a rack inside a roast pan so it doesn't sit in its own fat. A 350°F. oven is a perfect temperature for the entire duration of cooking. There are several premade seasoning and herb mixtures to flavor your chicken.

It is also important to allow a roast chicken to rest for 15 minutes after roasting and before cutting, which allows the natural juices to redistribute themselves back through the chicken. This will give you a much more moist result.

Seafood

Most fish varieties may be cooked with dry or moist heat. A general rule to follow is that fattier fish varieties work best with dry-heat methods, such as grilling, broiling, or roasting. The natural fat content bastes the fish while cooking and aids in browning, as well. Thin, flat fish species such as tilapia, sole, and flounder work well as sautéed items, especially if they are coated with egg or a flavored crust, which helps seal in the natural juices of the fish. Steaklike fish are excellent when marinated and grilled.

 Tip from the Team: Having trouble deboning your fish? To pinbone a fish—such as salmon, trout, walleye, or whitefish—run your finger over the flesh side of the fillet until you find the line of bones. Use a strawberry huller or small needle-nose pliers to remove the bones as you move your fingers down the fillet. For fish with bigger bones, such as grouper or snapper, use "elbow" pliers, with a small crook at the end.

SHRIMP

Shrimp are easy to clean. They can simply be rinsed well before and after shelling. They must also be deveined unless they are very small, as medium to large shrimp always house the intestinal tract, which is sandy and gritty, and not too appetizing. Shrimp are often overcooked, and the results can be tough and rubbery. Here's the best way to cook shrimp: Boil a quart of water with a good pinch of salt. Add some crab-boil spices or your favorite seasoning mixture, and include some hot chilies and some lemon slices. Add a pound of shrimp with the shell on, cover the pot, return to a boil, and simmer for 3 minutes, until just cooked. Shrimp should immediately be plunged into ice water to stop the cooking process and keep them tender. Unless you are making a pan-sautéed dish like scampi, shrimp are usually juicier and more flavorful when cooked with the shell on. The paper-thin shell holds the juice in and adds flavor to the shrimp. The shell helps hold the shape and natural curvature of the shrimp, as well. The cooked shrimp can then be peeled and warmed through in a sauce or added to the final dish.

OTHER SHELLFISH

All shellfish must be cleaned well before cooking.

Bivalves such as mussels, oysters, and clams must be scrubbed well: They have a tendency to hold dirt. Remember that bivalves are alive when purchased. Look for clean, whole shellfish that are not chipped, broken, and smashed. The shells should be tightly shut and not gaping open, which indicates they were most likely dead. There should be no noticeable odor, either. Shellfish need to be kept cold and moist, but they must still be able to breathe up until the time you cook them. Store them in a large bowl with a wet paper towel over the top. Although scallops are technically bivalves, they are normally sold without shells. They can simply be rinsed before sautéing, broiling, or grilling.

Mussels. Because mussels tend to be gritty, they need a bit of special cleaning. Place the mussels in a clean sink or a large bowl of cold water. Add a few tablespoons of cornmeal, which forces the mussels to take in fresh water and expel excess dirt and salt, acting as sort of a filtering process. You must then remove the mussels' "beards." The beard is a stringy group of fibers that is located between the shells. Gently pull the beard from the mussel before cooking. After removing the beard, gently rinse the mussels in a colander, and you are ready to cook. Large green New Zealand mussels, normally sold frozen and fully cleaned, are readily available in most markets. They need no special handling.

Clams. Although they arrive in the market already cleaned, they must still be handled in the same way mussels are for a truly grit-free result. Soak them in cold water for about 20 minutes. You don't need to add the cornmeal.

 Tip from the Team: To open clams without a knife, wash the clams, place in a freezer for 5 to 10 minutes, and then they will open on their own but should be eaten or cooked shortly thereafter.

Oysters. Oysters are normally shucked using an oyster knife for eating raw.

Best way to cook mussels and clams. There is nothing better than pan-steaming mussels or clams with fresh herbs, onion, garlic, and white wine. Here's how you do it: Heat 1 tablespoon of olive oil or butter in a large 5½-quart saucepot. Add 1 cup of minced onion and

Toasting Nuts for Added Flavor

NUTS have a much more intense, rich flavor when they are toasted before adding to a recipe. In almost all cases except when the nut needs to be puréed raw for thickening purposes, the recipes contained in this book call for toasted nuts. There are a few ways to toast them.

Place them on a baking dish in a preheated 350°F. oven for 6 to 10 minutes, until golden brown (time varies, depending on the size of the nut). Don't leave them unattended—they turn quickly from golden brown to black. Nuts continue to cook after they are removed from the pan, so remove them when they're light golden brown. Another method of toasting seeds preferred by some home cooks is to sauté them in either a dry pan or a pan sprayed lightly with vegetable oil. Stir continually over medium heat for 5 to 7 minutes, until golden brown.

2 cloves of garlic. Sauté this mixture for 2 minutes, and place 2 pounds of mussels or clams in the pot. Add 1 cup of dry white wine and a few sprigs of your favorite herbs such as thyme, tarragon, oregano, or basil. If you like spicy food, add a minced chili pepper or a half teaspoon of crushed red chili flakes. Place a lid over the pot, and bring to a boil. Lower the pot to a simmer and steam the shellfish for 6 to 8 minutes, until all the shells open. Discard any shellfish with unopened shells.

For a change of pace, try grilling shellfish. Place cleaned mussels, clams, or oysters on the grill directly or on a screen so they don't fall through the grill. Close the grill, and cook over high heat for 10 minutes, until the shells open fully. Dip the shellfish in melted butter or your favorite dipping sauce.

Lobster. Lobster must be cooked live, even though most people like to leave this task to someone else. There are two schools of thought when it comes to cooking lobster. Some cooks feel that it is better to place live lobsters in cold water with some vegetables and herbs to flavor the cooking liquid. Diced onions, carrots, celery, and leeks all work well with this method. Adding some herb sprigs such as parsley, thyme, or even bay leaves will complement the cooking liquid, as well. A good handful of salt should be added, too. The water is then brought to a boil, and the lobsters should be simmered until cooked through. A 1 1/4- to 1 1/2-pound lobster will take 12 to 15 minutes to cook. Some cooks feel the meat is more tender when cooked in this manner.

The other method of cooking lobster is to plunge the lobster into rapidly boiling water.

You may add the same vegetables and herbs. A good handful of salt also adds flavor to the cooked lobster.

Ingredient Guidelines

Cooking is an intuitive skill that can end up producing a spectrum of results. Giving two cooks the same recipe doesn't necessarily mean you'll get identical dishes. Even cooking from the best written recipes can result in varying flavors. You may be missing a required ingredient or decide to be creative and add a little of your own touch as you gain confidence. This cookbook is meant to be a practical guide, a book that will never leave your kitchen counter. Here are some general ingredient rules that may help you when you are using this book:

Water—We've listed water as an ingredient only when it's actually part of the recipe. For example, if you need to add 6 quarts of water to a soup recipe, the water is listed. Unless otherwise specified, always use cold water.

Lemon juice and lime juice—We recommend using fresh-squeezed lemon juice and lime juice when possible. They're simple to squeeze and taste superior to frozen or bottled juices. If you decide to go with processed, read the labels first. Some citrus juices contain preservatives and other chemicals, which leave a bitter aftertaste.

Scallions—Use both the white part and the greens. Just trim off the root and the last 1 inch of the greens. Most of the flavor is concentrated in the white bulb end.

Leeks—Trim off the root end. Cut off the dark green end where it begins to turn pale green. Save for stock or discard.

Fresh herbs and dried herbs—Fresh herbs are used at the end of a recipe to take full advantage of the volatile herb fragrance. The aromatic oils are destroyed by long cooking. Dried herbs are best for simmering and lengthy cooking processes. There are some occasions when dried herbs and spices can't really be substituted for fresh. Some examples are fresh ginger, parsley, and dill. If you don't have these, just omit them from a recipe. Dried or granulated garlic is really a personal decision; we always use fresh.

Ginger—Always peel the ginger before using, unless otherwise specified.

Salting—Our recipes are made with sea salt or kosher salt. They have a mild flavor and enhance the natural flavor of recipes rather than making food taste salty.

Pepper—When we say freshly ground pepper, it may be black or white peppercorns. White is a bit more mild and is normally used when you don't want to see the freshly milled little black specks in your dish, as for light-colored foods or cream sauces. You may also use cayenne pepper, if you wish, although it's hotter.

Peppers—Peppers are normally seeded before chopping. You may remove the fine white veins from the inside of the pepper if they bother you or if you're making a really fancy dish and you want to achieve culinary perfection. When we use hot peppers, the choice to seed or not is up to you. Remember that most of the heat is in the seeds or close to them along the veins.

Dairy products—If you are concerned about keeping fat content down in your meals, we recommend low-fat as opposed to fat-free for dairy products such as cheese, sour cream, ricotta, yogurt, and milk. Low-fat products still taste good and act the same way as their full-fat counterparts in most recipes.

Flour—We use only unbleached, unbromated white flour for all our cooking recipes. Flour is essentially finely milled wheat berries. We don't use standard white flour, because it may be artificially bleached or treated with certain chemicals as a quicker, less expensive way to whiten and condition the flour. Bromated flour normally has certain dough conditioners added, as well. We prefer just plain flour in our recipes.

Vegetarian and Vegan Options

TO help you choose recipes based on varying dietary concerns, we have noted recipes that are comprised of vegetarian ingredients and those comprised of vegan ingredients on the leaf icon near the recipe title.

While there are many different types of vegetarians, for purposes of recipe identification we have used the following:

= *Vegan*—A diet excluding all animal products (such as honey or dairy products) and meats, fish, or fowl.

= *Vegetarian*—A diet including plant foods and animal products, such as dairy and eggs, but no meats, fish, or fowl.

Many recipes provide a choice of ingredients in order to make the resulting dish vegetarian or vegan. In these instances, we have marked the recipe with the appropriate notation.

Using tomatoes—You may use the most seasonal, ripe tomatoes for any recipe. The smaller oval Roma or plum tomatoes or round plump vine tomatoes are just fine.

Cooking with oil—For sautéing regular dishes we normally use pure olive oil and in uncooked dishes we prefer extra-virgin olive oil, which has more flavor. If you wish, you may also use extra-virgin olive oil in cooking; though it's more expensive it offers more taste, as well. When we want to let other flavors speak in a dish, we use a neutral oil like canola oil. (See "About Oils," page 9.)

Pasta—All the recipes were tested using dried semolina pasta, unless otherwise specified.

Guide to Boxes, Bonuses, and Tips

THROUGHOUT this book you will find special advice, hints, and insightful information that we hope will help make your cooking experience more fun and enjoyable. Here is a guide to these special bonus sections:

SIDEBARS—These boxes provide supplementary details about an ingredient, cooking process, or recipe. Sometimes we may highlight technical information about specific cooking methods or procedures. In other instances we share anecdotes, interesting food facts, or trivia you can share with your family and friends while dining.

RECIPE BONUSES AND VARIATIONS—You will find these ideas at the end of many recipes. It's our way of offering you more choices. Recipe bonuses may suggest uses for leftovers, offer a timesaving hint, or provide ideas for ingredient substitutions. They may also offer options such as using an entrée recipe as a sandwich filling.

TIPS FROM THE TEAM—Here you will find personal favorite kitchen tips from numerous Whole Foods Market Team Members (employees) across the country. We share with you some old family secrets as well as some from our commercial kitchens that save time, make cooking more enjoyable, or, in some cases, are simply amusing to ponder while preparing your meal.

NUTRITIONAL PROFILES—At the end of each recipe, you will find nutritional information. Please note that this data is based upon using low-fat dairy products, low-fat mayonnaise and low-sodium soy sauce. If you choose to use standard versions of these items, the nutritional profile will vary.

Hand to Mouth

BAKED FALAFEL BALLS ● GARDEN OF EVA SUMMER ROLLS ● SPICY CHICKPEA PATTIES WITH CILANTRO, LIME, AND CHILIES ● GRILLED MARINATED ARTICHOKE HEARTS ● RASPBERRY-STUFFED BRIE WRAPPED IN PHYLLO ● CRISPY GARLIC TOFU BITES ● FRIED GREEN TOMATOES ● SAMOSAS ● CHILI CHEESE TAMALES ● PIQUILLO PEPPERS WITH GOAT CHEESE ● TOMATO BRUSCHETTA ● FRAGRANT GINGER-LIME CHICKEN FINGERS ● BARBADIAN CHICKEN FINGERS ● CRUNCHY SESAME FIVE-SPICE CHICKEN ● TERIYAKI CHICKEN WINGS ● TURKEY, SAGE, AND PINE NUT MEATBALLS ● SATÉ CHICKEN SKEWERS ● TANDOORI STUFFED LETTUCE LEAF CUPS ● ASIAN TUNA DUMPLINGS WITH SOY DIPPING SAUCE ● SHRIMP AND SCALLOP CHALUPAS

At one time, appetizers were merely a menu item served in small portions that preceded a larger entrée course. Traditionally, we think of them as a prelude to things to come—a little something to stimulate our taste buds before the real show begins. Although some of this tradition still holds true, much of the world's appetite and eating habits have changed.

It's not uncommon, when dining out, to simply select a few items from the appetizer menu and skip the entrée altogether. This can be especially fun when eating with a group and sharing a selection of dishes. This flexible kind of meal is perfectly suited to your own dining table and can be a lively, eclectic way to entertain.

Most of these varied hand-to-mouth dishes reflect a growing interest in ethnic foods from around the globe. They're our American versions of Spanish tapas or Chinese dim sum. Variety is the common denominator that truly exemplifies global cuisine and acts as the thread throughout this chapter. From Fried Green Tomatoes (page 35) to Asian Tuna Dumplings with Soy Dipping Sauce (page 48) and on to the even more unusual Samosas (page 36), these recipes reflect Whole Foods Market's broad diversity and wealth of authentic cultural cuisine. Don't be afraid to mix and match. Try choosing items by menu category —select a chicken recipe, a seafood recipe, and two vegetable recipes (unless, of course, you are a vegetarian). Most important, have fun and remember, this chapter places no borders on good taste.

Serving sizes are based on appetizer portions.

Baked Falafel Balls

¾ cup water

½ cup bulgur

1 tablespoon olive oil

1 medium red onion, minced

2 cloves garlic, minced (1 teaspoon)

¼ teaspoon crushed red chili flakes

1¼ teaspoons cumin

1¼ teaspoons coriander

1½ cups cooked chickpeas

1½ tablespoons lemon juice

¼ cup plus 2 tablespoons dried bread
crumbs

⅛ cup minced fresh cilantro

⅛ cup minced parsley

Salt to taste

Olive oil for spraying falafel

Lemon Tahini Sauce (page 311)

FALAFEL are little Middle Eastern croquettes made from ground dried chickpeas (also known as garbanzo beans), spices, and parsley. Our falafel are continents away from the traditional deep-fried version, but with all the flavor and crunch intact. They are usually stuffed inside pita bread and served with a tahini sauce made from ground sesame seeds. Plan on making large quantities; they are so addictive. Don't worry, you can stop eating them anytime—really.

If you choose to serve without Lemon Tahini Sauce, these falafel balls are vegan.

Bring the water to a boil and remove from the heat. Mix in the bulgur. Cover well with a lid or plate. Allow the bulgur to sit until all the water is absorbed, about 20 minutes. Heat the olive oil in a small sauté pan. Sauté the onion and garlic over medium heat until the onion is translucent. Add the red chili flakes, cumin, and coriander, and sauté for 1 minute. Combine the chickpeas and bulgur in the bowl of a food processor; add the lemon juice, bread crumbs, cilantro, parsley, and salt, and process until just mixed. Preheat the oven to 400°F. Allow the mixture to rest for 15 minutes before forming into 2-inch balls. Place the balls onto a lightly oiled sheet pan. Spray the balls with olive oil. Bake for 25 to 30 minutes, until golden, turning the pan once during baking.

Serve the falafel with the Lemon Tahini Sauce.

PER SERVING: CALORIES 160; CALORIES FROM FAT 70; CALORIES FROM SATURATED FAT 10; PROTEIN 4 G; CARBOHYDRATE 20 G; TOTAL FAT 8 G; SATURATED FAT 1 G; CHOLESTEROL 0 MG; SODIUM 160 MG; 44% CALORIES FROM FAT

vegan

Garden of Eva Summer Rolls

SERVES 6

THESE rolls are beautiful, and refreshing to eat. Dampened sheets of rice paper turn translucent, allowing colorful edible blossoms and crisp vegetables to peek through. Also try Thai Dipping Sauce (page 316) instead of the Creamy Peanut Sauce, but note that the dish will no longer be vegan or vegetarian.

1 (7-ounce) package rice stick or bean thread noodles
4 cups thinly sliced Napa cabbage
2 cups baby spinach leaves, washed and thinly sliced
¼ cup thinly sliced fresh Thai or regular basil leaves
3 tablespoons chopped fresh cilantro
¼ cup chopped fresh mint
2 scallions, sliced thinly and diagonally
1½ cups edible flowers, stems removed
18 spring roll wrappers
Creamy Peanut Sauce (page 312) to serve

Bring 2 quarts of water to a boil, add the noodles, and cook for 3 minutes. stirring often. Drain well, rinse under cold water until chilled, then drain well again.

In a large bowl, combine the sliced Napa cabbage, spinach, basil, cilantro, mint, scallions, and edible flowers to make the greens for the filling.

To assemble the spring rolls, fill pan large enough to hold a spring roll wrapper 4 inches deep with very hot water. Immerse one spring roll wrapper in the water until it is soft and flexible, about 30 seconds.

Lay the wrapper out on a cutting board, table, or counter. Place ½ cup of the greens mixture and ¼ cup of the noodles in the center of the wrapper. Roll the edge closest to you over the top of the ingredients and gently pull back to lock ingredients in place. Fold the left and right sides into the center and roll up tightly to form the spring roll. Place seam side down in a sealable container; cover the rolls with wet lettuce leaves or a damp paper towel so they don't dry out. Continue rolling remaining spring rolls.

Spring rolls will keep for 2 days in the refrigerator if covered with a damp paper towel in a tightly sealed container. When displaying spring rolls on a buffet for guests, cover with wet lettuce leaves to keep them from drying out. Serve with Creamy Peanut Sauce.

PER 3 ROLLS: CALORIES 320; CALORIES FROM FAT 15; CALORIES FROM SATURATED FAT 0; PROTEIN 11 G; CARBOHYDRATE 65 G; TOTAL FAT 1.5 G; SATURATED FAT 0 G; CHOLESTEROL 10 MG; SODIUM 570 MG; 5% CALORIES FROM FAT

How to Use Rice Paper Wrappers

RICE paper wrappers are very delicate and frail. They must be handled very carefully so that the brittle round or square rice paper doesn't crack.

To soften the wrappers for stuffing, fill a large bowl or baking pan with warm water. Place the rice paper in the warm water and make sure it's submerged. The paper will soften in about 30 seconds. You may place 2 or 3 wrappers in at a time, but just make sure they stay separated. Remove them one at a time to fill.

To fill, place a clean kitchen towel on your counter or work space. Gently place the softened rice paper on the towel and top with the filling ingredients before rolling up. The roll will automatically seal itself because of the natural starch in the rice paper.

NOTE: If you are using square wrappers, place the wrapper before you with one corner pointing away from you.

vegan

Spicy Chickpea Patties with Cilantro, Lime, and Chilies

SERVES 10

WHEN the comforting texture of chickpeas combines with vibrant curry, aromatic ground cumin, jalapeños, and fresh cilantro, the flavors explode in your mouth. These little patties may be served as small as silver-dollar size or in larger entrée portions. Try them with the soothing Cucumber Raita or Onion Chutney.

⅛ cup canola or olive oil
½ medium red onion, minced
2 cloves garlic, minced (1 teaspoon)
1 jalapeño pepper, minced
2 teaspoons curry powder
1 teaspoon cumin
1 (15¾-ounce) can chickpeas, rinsed and drained
¼ cup chickpea flour
½ cup dried bread crumbs
½ cup minced fresh cilantro
3 scallions, minced
Juice of 2 limes
Salt to taste

Chickpea flour for dusting cakes
Vegetable oil for spraying pan
Cucumber Raita to serve (page 340), or Onion Chutney (page 338)

In a large nonstick pan, heat the canola or olive oil over medium heat. Sauté the onion, garlic, jalapeño, curry powder, and cumin for 3 minutes, until the onion is softened. Transfer the spice mixture to the bowl of a food processor fitted with a standard S blade, and process for 20 seconds, until coarsely chopped. Add the chickpeas, chickpea flour, bread crumbs, cilantro, scallions, lime juice, and salt.

Continue to process for 20 seconds more, until the mixture is coarsely chopped, well combined, and has formed a thick paste. The paste should be firm enough to be scooped and shaped into small patties. After making the patties, lightly dust them with chickpea flour.

Heat a large nonstick pan over medium heat and spray it with the vegetable oil. Sauté the patties for 4 minutes on each side, until they are golden brown and heated through. For an even crispier patty, place one on a sheet pan for 10 minutes in the center of a 375°F. oven. Serve with Cucumber Raita or Onion Chutney.

PER SERVING: CALORIES 110; CALORIES FROM FAT 40; CALORIES FROM SATURATED FAT 0; PROTEIN 3 G; CARBOHYDRATE 15 G; TOTAL FAT 4.5 G; SATURATED FAT 0 G; CHOLESTEROL 0 MG; SODIUM 150 MG; 36% CALORIES FROM FAT

Grilled Marinated Artichoke Hearts

vegan

1 (14-ounce) can artichoke hearts, whole in brine, drained

¼ cup Italian Herb Vinaigrette (page 329) or your favorite herb dressing

SIMPLE with a mild smoky flavor and lemony aftertaste, these little packages are extremely versatile in the kitchen. They may be used as an appetizer, on a pizza, or in a sandwich or omelette.

Cut the artichoke hearts in half. Marinate in the refrigerator for at least 1 hour or overnight in the Italian Herb Vinaigrette.

Prepare a charcoal or gas barbecue. Grill the artichokes for 2 minutes on each side until lightly browned. You may also broil them on a sheet pan approximately 3 inches from the heating element of your broiler for 5 minutes on each side.

PER SERVING: CALORIES 110; CALORIES FROM FAT 60; CALORIES FROM SATURATED FAT 10; PROTEIN 3 G; CARBOHYDRATE 9 G; TOTAL FAT 7 G; SATURATED FAT 1 G; CHOLESTEROL 0 MG; SODIUM 410 MG; 54% CALORIES FROM FAT

Raspberry-Stuffed Brie Wrapped in Phyllo

KILO BRIE WHEEL SERVES 30; 10-OUNCE BRIE WHEEL SERVES 10

ONE of the world's great cheeses, brie has an edible, fluffy white rind that envelops a cream-colored, buttery-soft interior. A wheel of brie is natural party food because of its size and elegant reputation (see Note). Delicious on its own, brie takes on even greater character when wrapped in either puff pastry or delicate phyllo dough and baked. Stuffing brie with sweet fruit preserves before wrapping adds another flavor surprise and cuts the richness of the cheese.

1 kilo brie wheel

¾ cup raspberry, apricot, or cherry preserves

6 13 x 18-inch sheets frozen phyllo dough, defrosted

Vegetable oil for spraying phyllo dough or ⅛ cup butter, melted, for brushing dough

P reheat the oven to 375°F. Slice the wheel of brie cheese in half so that you have two circles of cheese. Spread the preserves evenly over the entire surface of one brie circle. Top with the remaining brie to make a sandwich and gently press the halves together. Place the brie sandwich in the freezer on a plate while you get the phyllo dough ready.

Lay the phyllo sheets on a clean work surface and cover snugly with damp paper towels or plastic wrap. Take out one sheet and spray lightly with the vegetable oil or brush with melted butter. Repeat this process, stacking up the phyllo sheets to form a single pile.

Place the brie wheel on the stack and wrap the edges up around the wheel, twisting the phyllo around the top of the brie wheel. Spray the stuffed wheel with the vegetable oil or brush with remaining melted butter and place on a baking dish in the center of the preheated oven.

Bake for about 25 minutes, or until the brie is heated through and the phyllo dough is golden brown. Allow to cool before serving.

NOTE: For a smaller party, use 4 sheets phyllo dough, a 10-ounce brie wheel, and ¼ cup preserves.

PER ⅛-CUP SERVING: CALORIES 140; CALORIES FROM FAT 90; CALORIES FROM SATURATED FAT 60; PROTEIN 7 G; CARBOHYDRATE 5 G; TOTAL FAT 10 G; SATURATED FAT 6 G; CHOLESTEROL 35 MG; SODIUM 230 MG; 64% CALORIES FROM FAT

Brie Wheel Variations

- As an alternative to preserves, you may stuff the center of the brie with the same quantity of pesto or olive tapenade. Sprinkle ½ cup chopped sun-dried tomatoes over the stuffing.

- Sprinkle 1 cup of the following on the cheese (with or without preserves): chopped toasted pecans, hazelnuts, pine nuts, sun-dried cranberries, chopped figs, or chopped walnuts.

- Instead of phyllo dough, you may use one sheet of puff pastry. They usually come 2 sheets to a 17.3-ounce package. Thaw the pastry sheet at room temperature for 20 to 30 minutes before unfolding. Preheat the oven to 400°F. Lightly beat one egg. Roll out the dough gently on a lightly floured surface into a 12-inch square. Place the brie in the center and bring the edges of the pastry sheet up around and over the stuffed brie. Join the edges together and seal with some of the beaten egg. Make a decorative design over the top if you wish. Brush the puff pastry with the rest of the egg and bake in the center of the oven for 20 minutes, until the brie is heated through and the center is melted.

hand to mouth

33

Crispy Garlic Tofu Bites

SERVES 4

EVEN if you are not a tofu fan, these crispy nuggets are hard to keep out of your mouth. Tamarind is indigenous to India and has been cultivated for its pungent acidic flavor since prehistoric times. It can be found as a frozen paste, a liquid concentrate, or fresh in pods. The porous tofu soaks up the tamarind's bittersweet flavor and together with tamari, ginger, and garlic forms a caramelized crust around each little bite. The crunchy roasted sunflower seeds add contrasting texture. These are excellent hot from the oven or chilled.

⅛ cup tamari

6 cloves garlic, minced (3 teaspoons)

2½ tablespoons lemon juice

⅛ cup orange juice concentrate

⅛ cup tamarind paste

⅛ cup ketchup

1 tablespoon minced fresh ginger
  (1-inch piece)

½ teaspoon curry powder

½ teaspoon garam masala (see Note)

1½ tablespoons molasses

4 teaspoons cornstarch

1 tablespoon cold water

1 pound extra-firm tofu, pressed
  (see page 15)

1 cup sunflower seeds, toasted

Vegetable oil for spraying pan

Combine the tamari, garlic, lemon juice, orange juice, tamarind paste, ketchup, ginger, curry powder, garam masala, and molasses in a small saucepan. Bring to a rolling simmer. Combine the cornstarch and cold water. With the sauce simmering slowly, whisk in the diluted cornstarch. Simmer the sauce for 1 minute; remove the pan from the heat. When the tofu is ready, cut it into 1-inch squares, coat it in marinade, and marinate it for 2 hours in the refrigerator. Preheat the oven to 400°F.

Roll the tofu in sunflower seeds until well coated. Place the tofu on a lightly oiled baking pan. Bake for about 25 minutes, or until deep golden brown, turning the pan once during the cooking process.

NOTE: If you wish to make your own garam masala, see Tandoori Stuffed Lettuce Leaf Cups (page 47).

PER SERVING: CALORIES 330; CALORIES FROM FAT 190; CALORIES FROM SATURATED FAT 20; PROTEIN 16 G; CARBOHYDRATE 23 G; TOTAL FAT 21 G; SATURATED FAT 2.5 G; CHOLESTEROL 0 MG; SODIUM 670 MG; 57% CALORIES FROM FAT

Fried Green Tomatoes

SERVES 4

2 green tomatoes, sliced ¼ inch thick

½ teaspoon salt, plus more to taste

½ plus ¼ cup unbleached all-purpose flour

I cup cornmeal

Freshly ground pepper to taste

I cup buttermilk

½ cup canola oil

THIS is a lighter version of a favorite Southern classic. This recipe will work with firm red or yellow tomatoes, as well. Tomatoes are the third most popular vegetable eaten by Americans, behind potatoes and processed tomato foods like juice, purée, and—you guessed it—ketchup.

Season the tomato slices with the salt. Combine the ¼ cup flour, cornmeal, and salt and pepper. Set up a breading station: In three separate bowls, place the remaining ½ cup flour, buttermilk, and cornmeal mixture. Coat each tomato slice in the flour, tap off the excess, submerge in the buttermilk, and then coat well in the cornmeal. Bread all of the tomato slices; refrigerate for at least 1 hour. (You may prepare the tomatoes several hours ahead of cooking.) When the tomatoes are ready, heat the canola oil in a skillet over medium-high heat, until a single drop of water makes the oil sizzle. Cook the tomato slices until they are golden brown on each side, turning them once. Remove the tomatoes to a plate lined with paper towels for a few moments. Serve them immediately.

PER SERVING: CALORIES 380; CALORIES FROM FAT 260; CALORIES FROM SATURATED FAT 20; PROTEIN 6 G; CARBOHYDRATE 26 G; TOTAL FAT 28 G; SATURATED FAT 2.5 G; CHOLESTEROL 5 MG; SODIUM 910 MG; 68% CALORIES FROM FAT

hand to mouth

Samosas

SERVES 20

THE WHOLE FOODS MARKET COOKBOOK

THIS authentic Himalayan recipe is made with spiced potato filling. Plan on making many and freezing them.

TO PREPARE THE SPICED POTATO FILLING

Boil the potatoes in enough water to cover them, until fully cooked. Cool potatoes slightly, place them in a large bowl, and mash them. In a small skillet, heat the canola oil and sauté the onion, garlic, ginger, and fresh pepper until the onion is translucent. Add the garam masala, curry powder, cumin, and turmeric to the skillet. Sauté for 30 seconds; remove the pan from the heat. Add the onion, cilantro, lemon juice, salt and pepper, and peas; mix well.

TO PREPARE THE DOUGH In a large bowl, combine the flour, salt, and butter until the mixture resembles a coarse meal. Add cold water to the mixture and gently blend until the water is fully incorporated; roll the dough into a ball. Knead the dough gently on a smooth surface no more than 5 times to form into a ball. Lightly dust the dough with flour, wrap the dough, and chill it in the refrigerator for 1 hour.

Preheat the oven to 400°F.

To assemble the samosas, roll the dough out on a lightly floured surface to ⅛-inch thickness. Cut the dough into 4-inch squares. Place 2 tablespoons of filling in the center of each square. Brush the edges with the egg wash. Fold the samosas in half to form a triangle, and press the edges together to seal them. Place the samosas on a baking sheet and brush the tops with the egg wash. Bake for about 25 minutes, or until golden.

The Spiced Potato Filling

1 pound russet potatoes, peeled and diced
1 tablespoon canola oil
1 cup diced red onion
2 cloves garlic, minced (1 teaspoon)
4 teaspoons minced fresh ginger
1 serrano or jalapeño pepper, seeded and minced
1 teaspoon garam masala
1 teaspoon curry powder
1 teaspoon cumin
⅛ teaspoon turmeric
⅛ cup minced fresh cilantro
⅛ cup lemon juice
Salt and freshly ground pepper to taste
¾ cup frozen peas, thawed

The Dough

6 cups unbleached all-purpose flour
1 teaspoon salt
¼ pound (1 stick) butter
½ cup cold water

The Egg Wash

1 large egg beaten with 1 tablespoon water

PER SERVING: CALORIES 220; CALORIES FROM FAT 50; CALORIES FROM SATURATED FAT 30; PROTEIN 5 G; CARBOHYDRATE 35 G; TOTAL FAT 6 G; SATURATED FAT 3 G; CHOLESTEROL 25 MG; SODIUM 130 MG; 23% CALORIES FROM FAT

Chili Cheese Tamales

vegetarian

SERVES 4

The Masa

½ cup corn flour

1 teaspoon baking powder

1 teaspoon salt

⅓ cup corn oil

4 tablespoons (½ stick) butter at
   room temperature

1 cup plus 2 tablespoons hot water

4 large corn husks

1 cup Tomatillo-Chipotle Salsa
   (page 339)

8 ounces Monterey Jack cheese,
   grated

THESE little handcrafted corn packages, steamed in their own husks, are a labor of love. Corn husks may be found in most Mexican grocery stores. If corn husks are unavailable, you may use small squares of tinfoil. The corn dough, which becomes the filling for the softened husks, is called masa.

TO PREPARE THE MASA Place the corn flour, baking powder, and salt in the bowl of an electric mixer fitted with a paddle attachment. Add the corn oil and butter to the dry ingredients and beat slowly together for 2 minutes, until mixed well. Add the hot water and continue to mix for 2 minutes longer. Intermittently stop the mixer to scrape down the sides of the bowl. Transfer the dough to a plate and cover loosely with plastic wrap; allow the masa to rest for about 30 minutes before filling the husks.

Soak the dried corn husks in very warm water for at least 30 minutes. Weigh them down in a bowl of water with a can or other heavy object until they are pliable.

To prepare the filling, combine the Tomatillo-Chipotle Salsa with the Monterey Jack cheese.

For each tamale, measure ½ cup of masa and roll into a ball. Press and semiflatten the masa ball onto a softened corn husk, spreading the masa dough into the husk in an even layer. Place ¼ cup filling in the center of the husk and bring the sides of the husk together, pressing the dough around the filling so it is enclosed in the dough. Fold the corn husks to wrap them tightly around the tamale, and fold the ends under the tamale. Twist the tamale ends or fasten them with strips of husk like a little package to seal.

In a bamboo steamer, in a saucepan with a vegetable steamer, or in a sauce pot fitted with a tight lid containing a colander over boiling water, steam all the tamales for 45 to 60 minutes.

Serve with some of the additional Tomatillo-Chipotle Salsa.

PER SERVING: CALORIES 580; CALORIES FROM FAT 460; CALORIES FROM SATURATED FAT 190; PROTEIN 16 G; CARBOHYDRATE 18 G; TOTAL FAT 51 G; SATURATED FAT 21 G; CHOLESTEROL 80 MG; SODIUM 1,110 MG; 79% CALORIES FROM FAT

hand to mouth

37

Piquillo Peppers with Goat Cheese

SERVES 6

IN this recipe the creamy texture and sharp flavor of goat cheese is complemented by piquant piquillo peppers. That's hard to pronounce—easy to eat. Handle these peppers gently, gingerly, and tenderly, as they are indeed delicate. The results are inspired and as attractive as they are delicious.

1 (7-ounce) jar piquillo peppers

2 ounces prosciutto, very thinly sliced

8 fresh basil leaves

1 (3.5-ounce) log mild firm goat cheese

1 teaspoon dried Italian herbs

Drain the whole peppers and slice vertically, opening them gently and removing any seeds. Lay the peppers on a clean kitchen towel or paper towels to dry. Press the surface with another paper towel to remove any excess liquid.

Place a 20-inch-long piece of waxed paper or parchment paper on the kitchen countertop. Unfold the peppers gently one at a time and lay them skin side down onto the parchment paper, overlapping them to form a rectangle about 5 × 16 inches long. Place the prosciutto slices over the peppers, overlapping them. Place the basil leaves over the prosciutto. Evenly crumble the goat cheese over the surface of the peppers. Sprinkle evenly with Italian herbs.

Using the waxed paper, from the end closest to you, fold up the roll carefully into a pinwheel until it is closed. Press gently and evenly to compact the roll as much as possible. To get a really firm pinwheel, use a ruler or straightedge and press the roll to compact it. Twist the ends together and refrigerate to firm up. If you refrigerate the roll overnight, it will be easier to cut into thin slices. Enjoy with crackers or baguette slices and serve as an appetizer.

PER SERVING: CALORIES 110; CALORIES FROM FAT 60; CALORIES FROM SATURATED FAT 40; PROTEIN 8 G; CARBOHYDRATE 3 G; TOTAL FAT 7 G; SATURATED FAT 4.5 G; CHOLESTEROL 20 MG; SODIUM 220 MG; 54% CALORIES FROM FAT

Piquillo Peppers

PIQUILLO peppers are a very specific variety of pepper grown in the Navarre region of Spain. These triangle-shaped peppers are harvested when fully red, when they are no longer than 4 inches and the moisture content does not exceed 3 percent. This careful monitoring ensures a consistent deep, rich, and complex flavor with a slight spicy bite. Their unique taste pairs well with strong flavors (anchovies, hard cheeses, olives, seafood), and their uniform size makes them ideal for stuffing.

vegan

Tomato Bruschetta

SERVES 4

AH, the simplicity of ripe seasonal ingredients in harmony with one another on the same piece of crusty bread. From the Italian *bruscare,* meaning "to roast over coals," this garlic bread was traditionally made by rubbing fresh garlic over peasant bread and drizzling it with fruity extra-virgin olive oil. The bread was then baked in a brick wood-fired oven until crisp and golden brown. Here's an updated version you can make at home.

1 pound plum tomatoes, chopped
2 cloves garlic, minced (1 teaspoon)
1 small red onion, minced
⅛ cup minced parsley
3 tablespoons chopped fresh basil
¼ teaspoon salt
¼ teaspoon freshly ground pepper
⅛ cup extra-virgin olive oil
4 teaspoons balsamic vinegar
1 tablespoon red wine vinegar
Half baguette, sliced ¼ inch thick

Preheat the oven to 400°F.

Combine the tomatoes, garlic, onion, parsley, basil, salt, pepper, olive oil, and vinegars in a large mixing bowl to make the bruschetta. Place the baguette slices on a baking pan in a single layer. Bake the slices until just golden, remove them from the oven, flip them, and return to the oven until golden. Serve the warm baguette slices topped with the bruschetta.

PER SERVING: CALORIES 130; CALORIES FROM FAT 70; CALORIES FROM SATURATED FAT 10; PROTEIN 2 G; CARBOHYDRATE 14 G; TOTAL FAT 8 G; SATURATED FAT 1 G; CHOLESTEROL 0 MG; SODIUM 160 MG; 54% CALORIES FROM FAT

Peeling and Seeding Tomatoes

TOMATOES may be peeled when you're making a more upscale or special-occasion dish. First bring a sauce pot of water to a boil. Make sure the water is at least 6 to 8 inches deep. Remove the stem end of the tomato with a small paring knife or tomato shark, which is a tool specifically designed to remove the core. Make a crisscross mark on the bottom of the tomato. Plunge the tomato into the boiling water and keep it in the hot water for about 1 minute. Remove the tomato from the water with a slotted spoon and rinse under cold water immediately. The skin should just peel off easily. To seed, cut the tomato in half or into quarters and squeeze out the seeds. The tomato is now ready to be chopped or diced.

Fragrant Ginger-Lime Chicken Fingers

SERVES 4

1 clove garlic, minced ($\frac{1}{2}$ teaspoon)

$\frac{1}{4}$ cup lime juice

6 tablespoons plus 2 tablespoons
  minced fresh ginger

$1\frac{1}{2}$ tablespoons tamari

1 tablespoon toasted sesame oil

1 teaspoon cornstarch

$\frac{1}{8}$ cup water

1 pound boneless skinless chicken
  breasts, cut into 1-inch-wide strips

$2\frac{1}{2}$ cups dried bread crumbs

$\frac{1}{8}$ cup black sesame seeds

$\frac{3}{4}$ cup unbleached all-purpose flour

2 large eggs whisked with $\frac{1}{2}$ cup
  water

Canola or vegetable oil for spraying

WHOEVER created the chicken finger probably never realized it would become a culinary icon. Once you get a taste of the tart lime and fragrant ginger, we'll have you wrapped around the flavor of these fingers. They are "oven-fried" with hardly any oil. Oven-frying produces many of the same taste attributes of deep-frying—a crunchy flavorful coating with moist chicken underneath—because the crust seals in the natural juices.

In a large bowl, combine the garlic, lime juice, the 2 tablespoons ginger, tamari, sesame oil, cornstarch, and water to make the marinade. Marinate the chicken strips at least 4 hours in the refrigerator. In another large bowl, combine the bread crumbs, the remaining 6 tablespoons ginger, and the sesame seeds.

Preheat the oven to 450°F. Set up an area for breading the chicken: the flour in one bowl, the beaten eggs in a second bowl, and the bread crumb mixture in a third container. Coat the chicken in flour; tap off the excess. Then coat the chicken in the egg mixture, and finally coat with the bread crumb mixture. Place the chicken on a lightly oiled sheet pan. Spray the chicken with canola oil. Bake for 20 to 25 minutes, until the chicken is golden brown.

PER SERVING: CALORIES 190; CALORIES FROM FAT 45; CALORIES FROM SATURATED FAT 10; PROTEIN 15 G; CARBOHYDRATE 21 G; TOTAL FAT 5 G; SATURATED FAT 1 G; CHOLESTEROL 60 MG; SODIUM 310 MG; 24% CALORIES FROM FAT

hand to mouth

41

Barbadian Chicken Fingers

SERVES 6

FOR this Caribbean-inspired finger food, allspice, ginger, chilies, and lime create a fantastic flavor combination typical of island cuisine. This version is oven-fried, which uses less fat than traditional fried fingers. Save some of the Jamaican Jerk Sauce to use as a dipping sauce. Or try them with Cucumber Raita (page 340). These chicken fingers are also excellent as a sandwich topped with Creole Remoulade Sauce (page 314), field greens, and sliced dill pickles. Adventurous kids enjoy these as much as grown-ups do.

Marinate the chicken in the jerk sauce and buttermilk for at least 1 hour in the refrigerator.

TO PREPARE THE CRUST Preheat the oven to 400°F. In a small bowl, combine all ingredients for the crust. Gently dip the marinated fingers one at a time in the crumb mixture, shaking off any excess crumbs. Line up the lightly breaded fingers on a sheet pan, spray them lightly with the vegetable oil, and bake for 20 to 25 minutes, turning once, halfway through, to brown them evenly on both sides. Serve immediately.

PER SERVING: CALORIES 240; CALORIES FROM FAT 45; CALORIES FROM SATURATED FAT 15; PROTEIN 37 G; CARBOHYDRATE 10 G; TOTAL FAT 5 G; SATURATED FAT 1.5 G; CHOLESTEROL 100 MG; SODIUM 240 MG; 19% CALORIES FROM FAT

1½ pounds chicken tenders or boneless skinless chicken breasts cut into 1-inch-wide strips
½ cup Jamaican Jerk Sauce (page 307) or your favorite bottled brand
½ cup buttermilk or plain yogurt

The Crust
¼ cup dried bread crumbs
¼ cup fine cornmeal, white or yellow
½ teaspoon dried thyme
⅛ teaspoon allspice
Pinch of cayenne pepper
Salt and freshly ground pepper to taste

Vegetable oil for spraying chicken fingers

Crunchy Sesame Five-Spice Chicken

SERVES 4

¼ cup plus 2 tablespoons teriyaki sauce (see Note)

2 teaspoons five-spice powder

⅛ cup teaspoons tamari

2 teaspoons toasted sesame oil

3 tablespoons honey

1 pound boneless skinless chicken breast, cut into 1-inch strips

1 cup shredded unsweetened coconut

1 cup yellow cornmeal

⅛ cup minced parsley

⅛ to ¼ cup canola oil

THESE chicken strips are a good example of the five-flavor principle. This ancient Asian flavor philosophy notes that our taste buds detect only five flavors: sour, salty, sweet, bitter, and spicy. This principle certainly holds true with each bite. The crunchy coconut and sesame crust is baked, not fried as so many coconut chicken dishes are.

To prepare the marinade, combine the teriyaki sauce, five-spice powder, tamari, sesame oil, and honey. Marinate the chicken strips in the refrigerator for at least 4 hours.

Preheat the oven to 450°F.

In a large bowl, combine the coconut, cornmeal, and parsley—this will be the breading. Remove the chicken from the marinade; save the marinade. Roll the chicken in the breading to coat all sides. Dip the chicken in the remaining marinade and then in the breading again. Place the chicken strips on a lightly oiled sheet pan. Spray the chicken with the canola oil. Bake for 15 to 20 minutes, until golden.

NOTE: You may use our Teriyaki Chicken Wings marinade on page 44, or use your favorite bottled brand.

PER SERVING: CALORIES 510; CALORIES FROM FAT 180; CALORIES FROM SATURATED FAT 70; PROTEIN 39 G; CARBOHYDRATE 46 G; TOTAL FAT 21 G; SATURATED FAT 8 G; CHOLESTEROL 85 MG; SODIUM 1,630 MG; 35% CALORIES FROM FAT

Teriyaki Chicken Wings

SERVES 10

THESE are the perfect hand-to-mouth snack with their own built-in handles. Fresh citrus juice, wild blossom honey, and grated ginger caramelize over these wings to form a delicate glaze and to seal in the natural juices of the wings.

TO PREPARE THE TRIPLE CITRUS TERIYAKI MARINADE Pulse the soy sauce, ginger, cilantro, garlic, vinegar, honey, sesame oil, and the citrus juices in a blender for 1 minute, until well combined.

Place the chicken wings in a container small enough so that the wings are completely covered with 1 cup of the marinade, and marinate in the refrigerator for at least 1 hour or preferably overnight for 12 hours (see Note).

Preheat the oven to 450°F. Line a baking pan with foil for easy cleanup. Discard the marinade. Place the wings on the pan and bake for 8 minutes, until well browned—they will be a mahogany color. Remove the pan from the oven, baste the wings with additional fresh marinade, and sprinkle with sesame seeds. Return the wings to the oven and continue baking for 5 more minutes.

NOTE: This marinade recipe will make more than you need for the wings. The marinade will keep for 1 month in your refrigerator and may be used for grilling your favorite meat, poultry, tofu, or vegetables. It may also be used as a dipping sauce for the chicken wings.

PER SERVING: CALORIES 310; CALORIES FROM FAT 180; CALORIES FROM SATURATED FAT 50; PROTEIN 25 G; CARBOHYDRATE 5 G; TOTAL FAT 20 G; SATURATED FAT 5 G; CHOLESTEROL 75 MG; SODIUM 430 MG; 58% CALORIES FROM FAT

The Triple Citrus Teriyaki Marinade

1 cup soy sauce or tamari

¼ cup minced fresh ginger

⅛ cup minced fresh cilantro

8 cloves garlic, minced (4 teaspoons)

3 tablespoons white wine vinegar

½ cup honey

½ cup toasted sesame oil

½ cup orange juice

½ cup lime juice

½ cup lemon juice

2 pounds chicken wings

⅛ cup sesame seeds

Turkey, Sage, and Pine Nut Meatballs

SERVES 8

2 teaspoons olive oil

1 medium onion, minced

2 stalks celery, minced

2 cloves garlic, minced (1 teaspoon)

3 tablespoons fresh oregano, or
    1 tablespoon dried

1/8 cup minced fresh sage, or
    1 tablespoon dried

6 sun-dried tomatoes, plumped in
    boiling water and chopped
    (see page 12)

1 pound ground turkey

1/2 cup pine nuts, toasted

1/2 cup dried bread crumbs

Lemon pepper to taste

Salt to taste

SAGE, once used as a medicinal herb, is derived from the Latin *salvus*, which means "healthy." Mixed with lean ground turkey, sun-dried tomatoes, and toasted pine nuts, sage carries the flavor of these meatballs to a new level. We know they promote healthy appetites. A cooling raita (page 340) partners these perfectly.

In a large pan, heat the olive oil over medium heat. Sauté the onion, celery, garlic, and oregano for 3 minutes, until the vegetables are tender. Place the sautéed vegetables in a large mixing bowl and allow them to cool. Add the sage, sun-dried tomatoes, turkey, pine nuts, bread crumbs, lemon pepper, and salt to the bowl. Mix all the ingredients by hand or with a large spoon until well combined. Using a 2-ounce scoop to measure, roll the turkey mixture into balls and place on a large baking pan. Bake at 350°F. for about 25 minutes, or until the turkey is cooked through.

PER SERVING: CALORIES 180; CALORIES FROM FAT 100; CALORIES FROM SATURATED FAT 20; PROTEIN 13 G; CARBOHYDRATE 9 G; TOTAL FAT 11 G; SATURATED FAT 2 G; CHOLESTEROL 45 MG; SODIUM 160 MG; 55% CALORIES FROM FAT

Saté Chicken Skewers

SERVES 8

SATÉS or satays are a favorite Indonesian street food snack and may be served as an appetizer, a quick bite, or a main dish. Satés may be made from marinated cubes or long strands of poultry, beef, lamb, or seafood. Seasonal vegetables may also be used as long as they have the same cooking time. The marinade is usually heavily spiced and full of vibrant flavor, which goes well with palate-cooling peanut sauce. To prevent the wooden skewers from burning, soak them in water for at least 30 minutes before grilling. You may also wrap the skewer ends in foil.

14 (6-inch) bamboo skewers
½ cup plus ¼ cup Curry Coconut Peanut Sauce (page 313)
1½ teaspoons coriander
¼ teaspoon turmeric
2 cloves garlic, minced (1 teaspoon)
5 teaspoons lemon juice
½ teaspoon ground fennel seeds
3 small shallots, minced
2 teaspoons sugar
2 teaspoons tamari
Pinch of cayenne pepper
1 pound boneless skinless chicken breast cut into 1-inch-wide strips, 2 to 3 inches long

To assemble the chicken skewers, soak the bamboo skewers in water for 30 minutes. In a large bowl, combine the ½ cup of the Curry Coconut Peanut Sauce with the coriander, turmeric, garlic, lemon juice, fennel, shallots, sugar, tamari, and cayenne pepper to make the marinade. Skewer the chicken strips, one per skewer. Coat the chicken with the marinade and marinate for at least 2 hours or overnight, if possible.

To grill, cook the skewers 4 minutes on each side over a medium-hot fire until golden brown. Baste with some of the remaining ¼ cup sauce after turning the skewers; reserve the rest of the sauce for serving.

To cook in the oven, preheat the oven to 450°F. Place the chicken skewers on a foil-lined baking pan. Bake for 7 minutes; then remove the chicken from the oven. Turn the skewers over, baste them with some of the remaining ¼ cup sauce, and bake for 7 more minutes, until golden brown on both sides.

Serve with the remaining sauce.

PER SERVING: CALORIES 130; CALORIES FROM FAT 40; CALORIES FROM SATURATED FAT 15; PROTEIN 18 G; CARBOHYDRATE 5 G; TOTAL FAT 4.5 G; SATURATED FAT 2 G; CHOLESTEROL 45 MG; SODIUM 190 MG; 31% CALORIES FROM FAT

Tandoori Stuffed Lettuce Leaf Cups

SERVES 4

**The Tandoori Spices
(Garam Masala)**

1 teaspoon cumin

1 teaspoon coriander

½ teaspoon cardamom

½ teaspoon whole cloves

½ teaspoon freshly ground pepper

⅛ teaspoon cayenne pepper

⅛ teaspoon cinnamon

½ teaspoon turmeric

¾ cup plain yogurt

1 teaspoon salt

3 tablespoons minced fresh cilantro

1 pound medium shrimp, peeled and
chopped

1 mango or papaya, peeled, pitted and
diced

½ head of iceberg or leaf lettuce,
left in whole leaves

MASALA means "spice" in Indian cuisine. You may easily find powdered or spice paste mixtures in many Whole Foods Market stores and in most Indian grocery stores. The dried spice mixture here, our own garam masala recipe, may be used for shrimp, seafood, poultry, tofu, or vegetables. The filling in this recipe is fabulous stuffed into fresh, cool lettuce leaves or wrapped in flat bread.

TO PREPARE THE TANDOORI SPICES Combine the cumin, coriander, cardamom, cloves, black pepper, cayenne pepper, cinnamon, and turmeric in a small bowl. If you prefer, use 2 tablespoons of premade garam masala spices instead of this spice mixture.

To prepare the marinade, heat the tandoori spices in a dry skillet over a medium flame for 2 minutes, stirring frequently until the spices are fragrant and lightly toasted. Place the spices into a medium bowl and let them cool to room temperature. Mix the yogurt, salt, and cilantro with the spice mixture. Add the shrimp to the bowl, coat well with the marinade, and refrigerate for at least 30 minutes.

Preheat the broiler. For easy cleanup, line a baking pan with foil. Lay the shrimp in a single layer on the baking pan. Place the pan of shrimp 4 inches from the broiler; broil for 6 to 8 minutes, until lightly browned. Chill the shrimp. When the shrimp are chilled, combine them with the mango. To serve the shrimp, make small lettuce leaf holders by gently separating leaves from their core. You may also remove the core from a head of iceberg lettuce and then separate it into leaves. Serve the shrimp in lettuce cups or use the leaves as wrappers for the shrimp mixture.

PER SERVING: CALORIES 210; CALORIES FROM FAT 35; CALORIES FROM SATURATED FAT 10; PROTEIN 27 G; CARBOHYDRATE 19 G; TOTAL FAT 4 G; SATURATED FAT 1 G; CHOLESTEROL 175 MG; SODIUM 690 MG; 17% CALORIES FROM FAT

hand to mouth

47

Asian Tuna Dumplings with Soy Dipping Sauce

SERVES 12

LITTLE dumplings are like tiny holiday gifts or birthday presents. There is much expectation over the edible treat inside before you get through the tender outer wrapper. These packages are excellent pan-fried or steamed. Dip each of them with the anticipation of popping the next in your mouth. You may use firm tofu in place of tuna for a vegetarian version.

The Tuna Filling

1 1/2-inch-thick slice fresh ginger

2 cloves garlic

1/8 teaspoon crushed red chili flakes

1/2 small yellow onion, minced

1/2 red pepper, roasted, peeled, and minced

3/4 cup washed and chopped spinach

4 teaspoons tamari

1/3 pound fresh tuna steak, diced

24 wonton wrappers

6 lettuce leaves (for steaming, optional)

1 recipe Soy Dipping Sauce (page 315)

TO PREPARE THE TUNA FILLING Combine the ginger, garlic, red chili flakes, onion, pepper, spinach, and tamari in the bowl of a food processor; pulse until finely chopped. Add the tuna to the food processor and pulse until roughly chopped. Transfer this mixture to a small bowl.

To assemble the dumplings, you will need a small cup or bowl with 1/4 cup water, the wonton wrappers, tuna filling, and a slightly damp paper towel. Place 2 wonton wrappers at a time on the counter with one corner of each wrapper pointing away from you. (The wrappers will dry out quickly when uncovered.) Place 1/2 tablespoon of the filling in the center of each wrapper. Moisten the 2 edges of the wrapper farthest from you with water, using your finger or a brush. Fold the dry edges of the wrapper over onto the moistened ones to make a triangle. Place the wontons on a plate and keep them covered with the slightly moist paper towel. Continue until all the dumplings are made.

To steam the dumplings, set a bamboo steamer or plate over water in a large pot or wok; bring the water to a simmer. Line the steamer basket with lettuce leaves, allowing some space for the steam to travel up through the steamer or over the plate. The lettuce will keep the dumplings from sticking to the steamer or plate. Lay the dumplings on top of the lettuce; cover the steamer. Allow the dumplings to steam for about 5 minutes, or until they are cooked through.

Serve the dumplings with the Soy Dipping Sauce.

PER SERVING: CALORIES 80; CALORIES FROM FAT 0; CALORIES FROM SATURATED FAT 0; PROTEIN 7 G; CARBOHYDRATE 12 G; TOTAL FAT 0 G; SATURATED FAT 0 G; CHOLESTEROL 10 MG; SODIUM 880 MG; 0% CALORIES FROM FAT

Variation: To fry the dumplings, while holding the point of the triangle, shape each dumpling so that it can sit up on its own. Heat ¼ cup toasted sesame oil in a large skillet over high heat until the oil just starts to smoke. Holding by the point, carefully place the dumplings into the hot oil. Fry them until the dumplings are deep golden brown on the bottom. Reduce the heat to low. Very carefully add ¼ cup water to the pan. Cover immediately. Continue cooking for 2 to 3 minutes, until the dumplings are cooked through.

hand to mouth

Shrimp and Scallop Chalupas

SERVES 4

CHALUPA is Spanish for "boat." Serve these tortilla rafts, inspired by the foods of Mexico's interior, for a light appetizer or brunch dish. The contrasting textures of this dish work well with one another and seem to be perfectly balanced. You may make chalupas with crumbled firm tofu if you prefer. The boats are made from flour tortillas, which are more pliable than corn tortillas and hold every seafood morsel intact.

1 (16-ounce) can refried black beans

1 (10-ounce) jar prepared green salsa

½ pound sea scallops, cut into ½-inch pieces

¾ pound medium shrimp, peeled, split in half

½ yellow onion, very thinly sliced

3 cups Napa cabbage, very thinly sliced

1 tablespoon chili powder

¼ cup canola oil

4 (6-inch) flour tortillas

¼ cup grated Monterey Jack cheese

¼ cup grated queso fresco (any mild white Mexican cheese will work fine)

1 cup Pico de Gallo (page 339)

1 ripe avocado, sliced

Combine the beans and green salsa in a saucepan and cook over medium-low heat, stirring often as you continue to prepare the recipe. The bean mixture will thicken slightly.

In a large bowl, combine the scallops, shrimp, onion, cabbage, and chili powder; set these aside. Heat the canola oil over medium-high heat in a medium skillet until almost smoking. Lightly pan-fry the tortillas one at a time, cooking both sides until the tortilla is crisp and golden (see Note). Keep the tortillas warm in a 200°F. oven while you continue.

Heat a large sauté pan until very hot; then quickly sear the shrimp mixture until the shrimp are pink and turn opaque. The scallops will become opaque, as well.

To assemble the chalupas, place one crisp tortilla on each plate. Spread one quarter of the bean mixture over each tortilla. Top the beans with one quarter of the shrimp mixture. Sprinkle on one quarter of the cheeses and one quarter of the Pico de Gallo, and finish with one quarter of the avocado slices.

NOTE: To oven-fry the tortillas, preheat the oven to 450°F. Brush both sides of the tortilla lightly with oil and bake until it is crisp and golden.

PER SERVING: CALORIES 830; CALORIES FROM FAT 310; CALORIES FROM SATURATED FAT 50; PROTEIN 50 G; CARBOHYDRATE 75 G; TOTAL FAT 35 G; SATURATED FAT 6 G; CHOLESTEROL 180 MG; SODIUM 1,290 MG; 37% CALORIES FROM FAT

Stocks, Soups, and Chilis

STOCKS ◆ VEGETABLE STOCK ◆ CHICKEN STOCK ◆ ASIAN STOCK ◆ MISO BROTH ◆ ROASTED THREE-ONION STOCK ◆ TERRA-COTTA STOCK ◆ AROMATIC BROTH ◆ **SOUPS** ◆ CHILLED STRAWBERRY AND RHUBARB SOUP ◆ GAZPACHO ◆ CHILLED GREEK EGGPLANT SOUP ◆ SWEET POTATO, CORN, AND KALE CHOWDER ◆ CREOLE RICE AND BEAN SOUP ◆ PANANG GREEN PEA SOUP ◆ WHITE BEAN AND SWISS CHARD SOUP ◆ SPICY MUNG BEAN SOUP ◆ CHIPOTLE BLACK BEAN SOUP ◆ ROASTED CORN POBLANO CHOWDER ◆ BUTTERNUT SQUASH BISQUE ◆ TRIPLE-MUSHROOM BISQUE ◆ CREAMY SPINACH BISQUE ◆ CARROT GINGER SOUP ◆ COUNTRY VEGETABLE SOUP WITH BARLEY AND OATS ◆ RED BEANS AND RICE ◆ FRENCH ONION SOUP FOR EVERYONE ◆ HUNGARIAN SWEET 'N' SOUR CABBAGE SOUP ◆ MISO VEGETABLE CHOWDER ◆ *THE* CHICKEN SOUP ◆ SPICY CHICKEN AND TORTILLA SOUP ◆ CHICKEN AND WILD RICE SOUP ◆ LENTIL, SAUSAGE, AND RICE SOUP ◆ BAHAMIAN CONCH CHOWDER ◆ **CHILI** ◆ SWEET POTATO CHILI ◆ CHUNKY GARDEN VEGETABLE CHILI ◆ CHILI BLANCO WITH CHICKEN ◆ **SOUP GARNISHES**

There is a bit of genius in every ladle of soup.

Walking into a kitchen filled with the aroma of simmering soup can comfort you even on the most stressful day. No other type of food seems to evoke nostalgic memories and the sense of family more. The essence of soup is filled with emotional power.

There is a reason why time-honored soup is ever popular and unchanging in its appeal. Soup has always been a warm and welcoming symbol of sustenance, one that invites communal dining and nurtures both our appetite and our spirit. Did you ever wonder how many pressing issues and vital matters were resolved (or disappeared) over a bowl of creamy and robust soup?

There is an old Spanish proverb, "Between soup and love, the first is better."

Soup is a friendly food that can be served as a first course or a complete nutritious meal. How ironic that an age-old food lends itself to our modern hectic lifestyle. Most of these soups can be prepared in under an hour and yield enough to serve for several meals. Soup may be frozen and enjoyed over a period of several months. Soup also provides a good medium for kitchen experimentation. In general, soup recipes are forgiving and adding a pinch of one spice or some vegetable trimmings from another meal can sometimes give rise to a fabulous new soup tradition of your own.

Making Soup from Scratch

Now that we've discussed the various methods and philosophy of natural foods cooking (pages 7 to 11), we want to apply this information to the kitchen. Soups and stocks are a good place to start; they embody the soul of the kitchen.

Although soups have a richer flavor when made from homemade stock, it's not necessary. Most soups can be made with clean, pure water as a liquid base. There is also a wealth of packaged broths, stock pastes, and nondairy beverages, such as oat, soy, rice, and nut milks, that may be used to make soups. Making stock at home is simple, yet it is clearly a time commitment.

Vegetable and chicken stocks form the foundation of most soups. There are, of course, several variations of each. The terms *stock, broth,* and *bouillon* all describe the remaining liquid after cooking vegetables, meats, poultry, or seafood in a flavored water. Typically, the solids are strained out and discarded, and the flavored water is used as a base for soups. *Broth* is used interchangeably with the word *bouillon,* which comes from the French word *bouillir,* "to boil."

How to Make Great Stock

- Always start with cold water. Clean filtered or bottled water is preferable, but cold is a must. Cold water encourages the flavor of vegetables or bones to infuse the liquid, producing complex flavors and rich color. Conversely, hot water seals the outside of the stock ingredients and results in a much weaker broth. The stock or broth should be brought to a boil and then immediately lowered to a simmer of 185°F., which temperature becomes evident when the surface of the liquid bubbles gently. Stock or broth must simmer slowly in order to produce a crystal-clear end result. If you cook over high temperatures, your stock will be cloudy and murky.
- Never use vegetables that are old or distressed. It's okay if they are past their prime a bit; however, fresh seasonal vegetables at their peak produce the best flavor.
- Herbs are added in two stages. Add dried herbs at the beginning of the cooking process—the flavor of dried herbs expands and increases in the stock or broth. Add fresh herbs during the last 15 minutes of cooking—the essential oils of fresh herbs are fleeting and will be degraded by extended heating.
- Peppercorns must be added during the last 15 to 20 minutes or they will become bitter. When added at the end, a spicy, peppery taste permeates and enhances the stock or broth.

- Vegetable stocks should be simmered for at least 1 hour. Poultry and beef stocks need at least 2½ to 3 hours to extract a strong flavor.
- Never turn stock into a garbage pot for all vegetable trimmings. You may use a variety of vegetables for a basic vegetable stock; however, some guidelines follow.
  - Vegetable trimmings such as tomato ends, carrot peels, mushroom stems, scallions, any herb fronds, ginger peel, leeks, and fennel are always welcome.
  - When you want to create more body in your stock, add a peeled diced potato. Natural potato starch acts to very slightly thicken the liquid.
  - Due to their strong flavor, stay away from broccoli and broccoli stems, cabbage, turnips, rutabagas, beets, asparagus (unless you're making asparagus soup), cauliflower, eggplant, parsnips (unless you're making chicken soup), and entire heads of old garlic.
- When the stock is cooked, strain the liquid through a colander or, if you want a very clear stock, through cheesecloth or a coffee filter. Press out all the flavored liquid with a ladle or the back of a spoon. You may season the broth with sea salt or kosher salt and pepper after it is strained. There is not much you can do with the cooked vegetables other than contributing them to the compost bin.

 Tip from the Team: For light broths, sauces, and vinaigrettes blend tomato ends, cores, and scraps with a pinch of salt until smooth. Pour into a double coffee filter and let strain overnight in the refrigerator. The result is a crystal-clear full-flavored tomato "consommé."

- Stock vegetables don't need to be peeled, but should be roughly chopped in a large dice.
- When making poultry and beef stocks, cover the bones with cold water and bring to a simmer. After foamy suds appear on the surface (this is called a raft), skim and simmer at least 30 minutes before adding the vegetables.

The Basics of Making Great Soup

Many of us remember our mothers simply throwing a variety of ingredients in a large pot and boiling it to make soup. We've learned, though, that there is a more premeditative art involved. There are essentially two families of soup—thin broth soups containing lots of garnish and thick, hearty soups. Thick and hearty soups are typically made with beans, legumes, vegetables, or a combination of all three. Included in this family are cream soups enriched with cream and butter or thickened with a roux—a cooked mixture containing

Thickening Agents

THERE was a time when, in order to get a thick creamy soup, you had to use a roux. While this mixture of fat and flour cooked together is traditional in dishes such as authentic Cajun stews and gumbos, it is quite heavy and a bit out of step with the modern diet. We prefer to thicken soups with puréed cooked beans, with legumes, or with the starch from grains such as short-grain rice, couscous, or bulgur. Other creative thickeners include roasted chunks of starchy vegetables (like winter squash) and rich liquids, such as oat and soy milk. Puréed nut meats, such as cashews, sesame seed, or sunflower seeds, are also very flavorful and offer additional nutritional benefits.

equal parts of flour and fat. As a healthier alternative, we show you new ways to make hearty thick soups without using a traditionally heavy roux.

Thin broth-based soups can be vegetarian or seafood-, beef-, or poultry-based and contain noodles, grains, sliced vegetables, pieces of chicken, tofu, or other protein sources.

Many of our soups are made without dairy products. Some of our creamy chowders are made with alternatives to cow's milk, such as soy, oat, or rice milk, which makes soup velvety rich while providing nutritional benefits.

Here are some basic soup-making steps to help you achieve a consistently flavorful bowl of soup: Start with a soup pot large enough to hold all the ingredients with plenty of bubbling room. A 5½-quart pot is good if you want to make 2 quarts of finished soup.

Unless you are making a fat-free soup, most soups start by heating some type of fat in the pot. The most common fats we use are olive oil, canola oil, butter, or a mixture of both oil and butter.

The basic foundation for many soup recipes is a mirepoix—a mixture of carrots, celery, and onion. Sometimes just a bed of onions or leeks is used to start a soup. This mirepoix bed is normally sautéed in the heated fat to begin the soup-making process. Typically thyme, bay leaves, rosemary, or other aromatics are added. Sautéing vegetables and dried aromatic herbs expands the natural taste of the vegetable base and gets the soup off to a flavorful start. If you want to cook a soup without the fat, you may use water, broth, or one of the nondairy milk beverages, in which case, all the ingredients can be added at once in the beginning.

Some recipes call for caramelized onions, and the sweet intense flavor that comes from heavily browned vegetables. Our French Onion Soup for Everyone (page 80) is a good example of this type of recipe.

Once your soup foundation is formed, the beans, legumes, or other vegetables are added to the simmering liquid. Depending on the variety of soup, a starch—such as pasta or rice or another grain—is also added later in the cooking process.

If you are making a soup such as minestrone with lots of chunky textures, the softer vegetables are added closer to the end of the cooking process to retain the character of the vegetable.

Always season soup with salt and pepper at the end, when the soup is cooked. You may also choose to add certain condiments at this point, such as miso, tamari, lemon juice, ume plum vinegar, rice vinegar, or hot sauce.

Dried vs. Canned Beans

HERE'S a common question: "Should dried or canned beans be used for making soup?" There are clearly merits to cooking a soup from scratch using dried beans. There is a more earthy flavor in dried beans—provided they have not been stored for a very long time. Newly dried beans have a sheen or shiny gloss to the skin, and it remains intact, not peeled and cracked. Old beans look somewhat wrinkled and dusty. Cooking with dry beans or legumes also adds their natural thickening starch to the soup.

Using dried beans is, however, a time-consuming task (but see "Preparing Dried Beans in a Hurry," page 156). Most beans need to be soaked overnight, covered in plenty of water, which shortens the cooking time. If you have the luxury of time on your side, then by all means use dried beans.

Stocks

Vegetable Stock

MAKES 2 QUARTS

1 large onion, chopped

2 large carrots, chopped

3 stalks celery, chopped

1 bunch scallions, chopped, or 1 large
    leek, chopped and washed

1 medium tomato, chopped

1 pint mushrooms, chopped

1 large potato, peeled and chopped

3 cloves garlic

½ bunch parsley

4 sprigs fresh thyme, whole

3 bay leaves

2½ quarts cold water

1 teaspoon white or black
    peppercorns

Salt to taste

THIS is an all-purpose basic vegetable stock that may be used in place of water for all sauces, soups, and stews. The stock must simmer at a gentle and constant 185°F., which will give you a perfectly clear stock that will be light golden. Although this stock may be used in so many ways, it stands firm on its own, and a simple bowl of stock with cooked noodles or rice can be a memorable meal.

Place the onion, carrots, celery, scallions, tomato, mushrooms, potato, garlic, parsley, thyme, and bay leaves in a large stockpot or sauce pot and cover with the cold, clean water. Bring the water to a boil, immediately lower to a simmer, and cook slowly for 45 minutes, uncovered. Add the peppercorns and simmer for 15 minutes longer. Strain the cooked vegetables, and season with salt.

PER 1-CUP SERVING: CALORIES 30; CALORIES FROM FAT 0; CALORIES FROM SATURATED FAT 0; PROTEIN 1 G; CARBOHYDRATE 7 G; TOTAL FAT 0 G; SATURATED FAT 0 G; CHOLESTEROL 0 MG; SODIUM 25 MG; 0% CALORIES FROM FAT

stocks, soups, and chilis

Chicken Stock

MAKES 2 QUARTS

THIS stock is highly nutritious, comforting to the soul, and practical for our health. If you are just making stock, use backs and necks, since they offer good flavor and are inexpensive. Stock can easily be frozen in small containers, heavy-duty plastic bags, or ice cube trays for those times when you need only a small amount.

2 pounds whole chicken, or 2 pounds chicken necks and backs
3 quarts cold water
1 medium onion, chopped
2 large carrots, chopped
2 stalks celery, chopped
1 bunch scallions, chopped, or 1 large leek, chopped and washed
6 sprigs parsley
4 sprigs fresh thyme
3 bay leaves
1 teaspoon white or black peppercorns
Salt to taste

Wash the chicken or bones in a large bowl very well under cold running water for a few minutes, until clean. If using a whole chicken, also clean the inside well under running water. Remove large fat deposits and discard them.

Place the chicken or chicken bones in a large stockpot or sauce pot (5½-quart capacity) with the cold, clean water and bring to a boil. Immediately lower the heat and continue to simmer, uncovered. A foamy layer will form on the surface, which should be skimmed off the surface of the stock after 30 minutes. Add the onion, carrots, celery, and scallions, and simmer for another hour; then add the parsley, thyme, bay leaves, and peppercorns. Simmer slowly for an additional 2 hours.

Cool the stock, and then remove the bones and vegetables. Season with the salt. You may skim the collected fat off the surface after the soup has cooled a bit; however, you might find it easier to first cool the stock at room temperature for 2 hours, then refrigerate for at least 3 hours to remove the hardened fat.

PER 1-CUP SERVING: CALORIES 70; CALORIES FROM FAT 15; CALORIES FROM SATURATED FAT 0; PROTEIN 11 G; CARBOHYDRATE 2 G; TOTAL FAT 1.5 G; SATURATED FAT 0 G; CHOLESTEROL 35 MG; SODIUM 50 MG; 21% CALORIES FROM FAT

Recipe Bonus If you use a whole chicken for this recipe, the cooked meat may be used for a salad (Sonoma Chicken Salad, page 121), a quesadilla (Triple-Pepper, Onion, and Cheese Quesadilla with Chicken, page 148), or a soup (*The* Chicken Soup, page 84).

Stock Variations

Any of these stock variations may be made with either vegetable or chicken stock as the base. You may also juice up and improve any canned or jarred stock bases with these recipes. Water may be used; however, you will have better flavor if you use a stock.

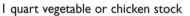

Asian Stock

vegan

MAKES I QUART

1 quart vegetable or chicken stock

1 (3-inch) piece fresh ginger, unpeeled, sliced into ¼-inch-thick rounds

2 cloves garlic, smashed slightly

3 star anise buds

¼ cup tamari or soy sauce

⅛ cup rice vinegar

1 tablespoon toasted sesame oil

2 small dried chili peppers (optional)

THIS Asian-inspired stock may be used for any soup or sauce needing a Chinese or Japanese flavor. It's wonderful served hot with cooked Udon noodles or leftover vegetables, chicken, or seafood. Try it with tiny diced pieces of tofu, minced scallions, and bean sprouts. Highly aromatic, star anise buds are native to a species of evergreen tree that grows in southeastern China.

In a large sauce pot, simmer the stock, ginger, garlic, anise buds, tamari, rice vinegar, sesame oil, and chili peppers, if using, for 35 minutes, uncovered, and strain the stock before using.

PER I-CUP SERVING: CALORIES 130; CALORIES FROM FAT 30; CALORIES FROM SATURATED FAT 0; PROTEIN 2 G; CARBOHYDRATE 18 G; TOTAL FAT 3 G; SATURATED FAT 0 G; CHOLESTEROL 0 MG; SODIUM 750 MG; 23% CALORIES FROM FAT

vegan

Miso Broth

MAKES 1 QUART

MISO is a traditional Japanese seasoning. Remember this important culinary rule when adding miso to a recipe: Always add it last to preserve its flavor and nutrients. The stock should be simmered and miso added *after* you turn off the heat. You should try both sweet white barley miso and hearty red dark miso in your broth and decide which you like best.

1 quart vegetable stock
2 (4-inch) pieces dried kombu (see "Whole Foods Glossary," page 395)
1 (1-inch) piece fresh ginger, unpeeled, sliced into ¼-inch-thick slices
⅛ cup white or red miso

Bring the vegetable stock to a boil with the kombu and ginger in a large sauce pot. Lower to a simmer for 10 minutes, remove the pot from the heat, and add the miso.

PER 1-CUP SERVING: CALORIES 130; CALORIES FROM FAT 5; CALORIES FROM SATURATED FAT 0; PROTEIN 3 G; CARBOHYDRATE 21 G; TOTAL FAT 0.5 G; SATURATED FAT 0 G; CHOLESTEROL 0 MG; SODIUM 320 MG; 4% CALORIES FROM FAT

Roasted Three-Onion Stock

vegan

MAKES 2 QUARTS

1 tablespoon olive oil

2 medium onions, chopped into large pieces

1 large leek, cut into ½-inch-thick slices and washed

4 shallots, peeled and sliced in half

1 head garlic, unpeeled, sliced in half

2 carrots, cut into ½-inch-thick slices

1 large tomato, cut into large chunks

2½ quarts cold water

3 sprigs fresh rosemary

3 sprigs fresh thyme

3 bay leaves

1 teaspoon black peppercorns

¼ cup tamari or soy sauce

THIS is an intensely flavored stock that derives much of its gusto from caramelizing the natural sugar in the vegetables and infusing the stock with sweetness and depth. It is great as a base for hearty dishes like onion or bean soups. Use this stock when you are looking for bold results and a rich mahogany color. For a vegetarian broth, it's rather ... beefy. Try this soup with homemade spaetzle (page 93) and snipped chives.

Preheat the oven to 400°F. In a medium bowl, combine the olive oil with the onions, leek, shallots, garlic, carrots, and tomato and then spread them out on a cookie sheet. Roast the vegetables in the center of the oven for about 1 hour, turning every 15 minutes, until well browned.

Transfer the roasted vegetables to a large sauce pot and cover with the cold water. Bring the water to a boil, lower to a simmer, and cook slowly, uncovered, for 30 minutes. Add the rosemary, thyme, bay leaves, and peppercorns; simmer for an additional 20 minutes. Season with the tamari.

PER 1-CUP SERVING: CALORIES 35; CALORIES FROM FAT 10; CALORIES FROM SATURATED FAT 0; PROTEIN 1 G; CARBOHYDRATE 6 G; TOTAL FAT 1 G; SATURATED FAT 0 G; CHOLESTEROL 0 MG; SODIUM 270 MG; 29% CALORIES FROM FAT

vegan

Terra-Cotta Stock

MAKES 2 QUARTS

WITH intense flavor from cumin, chilies, tomato, and cilantro, this crimson stock enhances Mexican and Latin dishes. We use this stock to add extra flavor power to Tex-Mex cuisine. Dress up this Terra-Cotta Stock with crushed tortilla chips, diced avocado, and minced fresh cilantro for a rich and satisfying meal. It's also exceptional served over cooked quinoa. You may use any strength of dried hot chili; our favorite is the chipotle, which is a smoked dried jalapeño. The unsweetened cocoa adds an underlying resonance that ties the flavors together without being perceived as chocolaty.

2 teaspoons canola oil

I large red onion, chopped

I large red pepper, seeded and chopped

I medium poblano chili, seeded and chopped

3 cloves garlic, peeled and smashed

2 small dried chili peppers

I teaspoon cumin

I tablespoon sweet paprika

2 teaspoons dried oregano

I (14-ounce) can chopped tomatoes

2 quarts cold water

8 sprigs fresh cilantro

Salt to taste

Heat the canola oil over medium heat in a large sauce pot; sauté the onion, red pepper, poblano chili, garlic, chili peppers, cumin, paprika, and oregano for 2 minutes, stirring frequently. Add the tomatoes and cold water. Bring the stock to a boil, lower to a simmer, and cook uncovered for 45 minutes. Add the cilantro and continue to cook for 15 minutes longer. Strain the broth and season with salt to taste.

PER I-CUP SERVING: CALORIES 30; CALORIES FROM FAT 10; CALORIES FROM SATURATED FAT 0; PROTEIN I G; CARBOHYDRATE 5 G; TOTAL FAT I G; SATURATED FAT 0 G; CHOLESTEROL 0 MG; SODIUM 10 MG; 33% CALORIES FROM FAT

Aromatic Broth

1 medium onion, sliced

1 sweet potato, peeled and chopped

1 medium tomato, chopped

4 cloves garlic, minced (2 teaspoons)

⅛ cup minced fresh ginger (2-inch piece)

¼ teaspoon crushed red chili flakes

3 stalks lemongrass, white part only, minced

½ bunch parsley

2½ quarts cold water or vegetable stock

¼ cup tamari or soy sauce

Juice of 1 lemon

WITH the combination of garlic, ginger, lemongrass, red chili flakes, and lemon, this soup is a great thermos companion when you are on the go but not feeling quite right. Most important—it's delicious!

Combine the onion, potato, tomato, garlic, ginger, red chili flakes, lemongrass, and parsley with the cold water and bring to a boil. Lower to a simmer and cook uncovered for 1 hour. Strain the vegetables and season the broth with the tamari and lemon juice.

PER 1-CUP SERVING: CALORIES 25; CALORIES FROM FAT 0; CALORIES FROM SATURATED FAT 0; PROTEIN 1 G; CARBOHYDRATE 6 G; TOTAL FAT 0 G; SATURATED FAT 0 G; CHOLESTEROL 0 MG; SODIUM 280 MG; 0% CALORIES FROM FAT

stocks, soups, and chilis

Soups

vegan

Chilled Strawberry and Rhubarb Soup

SERVES 6 TO 8

THERE is nothing quite like the intense scent of a ripe strawberry. Rhubarb makes a natural tart pairing for this soup. Simmered with cinnamon sticks, the result is intoxicating. If you make this soup during rhubarb season, which is fleeting, surely use fresh. If not, frozen rhubarb is a good alternative. We highly recommend using a cranberry juice that is not oversweetened, to allow the natural fruit flavors to emerge.

1½ quarts cranberry or apple juice
   (or use a mixture of both)
16 ounces strawberries, sliced
8 ounces sliced rhubarb
1 cup lightly packed light brown sugar
2 cinnamon sticks
¼ cup raisins or currants (optional)
⅛ cup arrowroot or cornstarch
   dissolved in ¼ cup water or juice

Place the juice, strawberries, rhubarb, sugar, cinnamon sticks, and raisins, if using, in a large sauce pot, and bring to a boil. Lower to a simmer and cook uncovered for 20 minutes. Add the arrowroot mixture and cook for 2 minutes, until the soup thickens. This soup may be eaten warm if you can't wait; however, when cooled, it becomes dreamy and irresistible.

PER 1-CUP SERVING: CALORIES 160; CALORIES FROM FAT 0; CALORIES FROM SATURATED FAT 0; PROTEIN 1 G; CARBOHYDRATE 39 G; TOTAL FAT 0 G; SATURATED FAT 0 G; CHOLESTEROL 0 MG; SODIUM 15 MG; 0% CALORIES FROM FAT

Gazpacho

1 large onion, roughly chopped

1½ pounds tomatoes, seeded and
    roughly chopped, or 1 (28-ounce)
    can diced tomatoes, undrained

2 large cucumbers, peeled, seeded,
    and roughly chopped (about
    2 cups)

1 medium red pepper, seeded and
    roughly chopped (about 1½ cups)

½ cup roughly chopped fresh cilantro

¼ cup extra-virgin olive oil

1½ cups tomato purée

1 cup tomato juice

1 tablespoon lemon juice

Salt and freshly ground white pepper
    to taste

⅛ cup balsamic vinegar

A timeless and classic chilled soup that marries red juicy tomatoes, cucumbers, garden herbs, and spices. This soup is much better the second day, when the vegetable juices meld. Try drizzling some extra-virgin olive oil over the top and serving with a loaf of olive bread.

Place half the onion, tomatoes, cucumbers, pepper, and cilantro in the bowl of a food processor fitted with a metal blade; pulse to chop coarsely. Remove the chopped vegetables and set aside. Repeat with the second half of these vegetables.

Combine the vegetables with the olive oil, tomato purée, tomato juice, lemon juice, and salt and pepper in a large container. Blend in the balsamic vinegar. Refrigerate for at least 4 hours, but preferably overnight.

PER 1-CUP SERVING: CALORIES 100; CALORIES FROM FAT 50; CALORIES FROM SATURATED FAT 5; PROTEIN 2 G; CARBOHYDRATE 12 G; TOTAL FAT 6 G; SATURATED FAT 1 G; CHOLESTEROL 0 MG; SODIUM 25 MG; 50% CALORIES FROM FAT

stocks, soups, and chilis

Chilled Greek Eggplant Soup

SERVES 6 TO 8

THIS is a refreshing soup that will appeal to you even if you're not crazy about eggplant. Mint and yogurt are great complements to cooked eggplant. For an unusual touch, add a bit of warm basmati rice to the soup as a garnish. The warm rice combined with chilled soup is a welcome treat.

¼ cup olive oil

1 large eggplant, peeled and cut into 1-inch cubes

1 large green pepper, seeded and chopped

2 cloves garlic, minced (1 teaspoon)

¾ cup cold water

6 sprigs fresh mint, minced

1 quart plain yogurt

3 tablespoons minced fresh chives

Heat the olive oil in a pot over medium heat; add the eggplant, pepper, and garlic, and stir to coat the vegetables well with oil. Cover and simmer for 2 minutes. Add the cold water. Cover and simmer for 15 minutes.

Cool the cooked vegetables and add the mint and yogurt. Purée the mixture in a blender. If you prefer a thinner soup, add ½ cup milk or soy milk. Chill the soup for at least 4 hours, but preferably overnight. Sprinkle each serving of cold soup with chives.

PER 1-CUP SERVING: CALORIES 150; CALORIES FROM FAT 70; CALORIES FROM SATURATED FAT 20; PROTEIN 7 G; CARBOHYDRATE 13 G; TOTAL FAT 8 G; SATURATED FAT 2 G; CHOLESTEROL 5 MG; SODIUM 85 MG; 47% CALORIES FROM FAT

Sweet Potato, Corn, and Kale Chowder

vegan

THE velvety consistency of this soup contrasts well with the crinkly texture of chopped kale. Kale is a powerful member of the cruciferous vegetable family (see "Cruciferous Vegetables," page 119). The addition of puréed cashews adds a sultry creaminess and the added benefits of monounsaturated nut oils.

1 tablespoon canola oil

2 medium carrots, chopped

1 medium red onion, chopped

1 stalk celery, chopped

1 large red pepper, seeded and chopped

1 large sweet potato, peeled and chopped

1 sprig fresh thyme, minced

¾ teaspoon turmeric

1 medium tomato, chopped

5 cups cold water or vegetable stock

1 cup fresh or frozen corn kernels

3 cups chopped kale leaves, heavy stems removed and washed

Salt and freshly ground white pepper to taste

Cayenne pepper to taste

1 tablespoon cornstarch

½ cup chopped parsley

½ cup cashew pieces (optional)

In a large pot, heat the canola oil over medium-high heat. Sauté the carrots, onion, celery, pepper, and sweet potato for 3 minutes. Add the thyme and turmeric; combine well with the vegetables. Add the tomato and cold water and simmer for 20 minutes. Add the corn, kale, salt and white pepper, and simmer for 5 minutes. Season with the cayenne pepper.

Combine the cornstarch with 2 teaspoons cold water (but see cashew option below). With the soup simmering, stir in the cornstarch mixture, continue to stir, and simmer for 3 minutes. Remove from the heat and stir in the parsley.

If using cashews, use a blender or food processor to blend the cashews, cornstarch, and ¾ cup of soup broth. Return this mixture to the simmering soup and continue to simmer soup, stirring often for 3 minutes.

PER 1-CUP SERVING: CALORIES 70; CALORIES FROM FAT 15; CALORIES FROM SATURATED FAT 0; PROTEIN 2 G; CARBOHYDRATE 13 G; TOTAL FAT 2 G; SATURATED FAT 0 G; CHOLESTEROL 0 MG; SODIUM 60 MG; 21% CALORIES FROM FAT

stocks, soups, and chilis

67

vegan

Creole Rice and Bean Soup

SERVES 6 TO 8

EVEN in steamy South Florida, this soup is popular year-round. Many people from the Caribbean make their home in Miami, where this soup provides an inexpensive and nutritious meal. The combination of scallions and fresh thyme can be found in many island dishes.

Heat the canola oil in a large pot over medium heat; sauté the carrots, onion, celery, peppers, and dried thyme for 5 minutes, until the vegetables are crisp-tender.

Add the tomato purée, whole tomatoes, cold water, and coconut milk to the pot; simmer for 5 minutes. Break the tomatoes apart with a spoon and add the rice.

Simmer uncovered for 45 to 50 minutes, until the rice is tender. Add the kidney beans, kale, peas, and fresh thyme; simmer for 10 minutes. Add the parsley; season with the salt and pepper.

PER 1-CUP SERVING: CALORIES 110; CALORIES FROM FAT 30; CALORIES FROM SATURATED FAT 20; PROTEIN 5 G; CARBOHYDRATE 16 G; TOTAL FAT 3.5 G; SATURATED FAT 2 G; CHOLESTEROL 0 MG; SODIUM 120 MG; 27% CALORIES FROM FAT

1 tablespoon canola oil
2 large carrots, diced
1 medium onion, diced
2 stalks celery, diced
1 small green pepper, seeded and diced
1 small red pepper, seeded and diced
2 teaspoons dried thyme
1 (28-ounce) can tomato purée
1 (28-ounce) can whole tomatoes with their juice
4 cups cold water or vegetable stock
1 (15-ounce) can coconut milk
¼ cup brown rice
1 (15-ounce) can red kidney beans, drained and rinsed
3 cups chopped and washed kale
1 (10-ounce) package frozen peas
3 to 4 sprigs fresh thyme
½ bunch parsley, chopped
Salt and freshly ground pepper to taste

Panang Green Pea Soup

6 cups cold water

½ cup basmati rice

4 teaspoons green Thai curry paste

6 cloves garlic, minced (1 tablespoon)

⅛ cup minced fresh ginger
(2-inch piece)

1 stalk lemongrass, white part only,
minced

1 tablespoon lime juice

½ cup coconut milk

1 pound frozen peas

⅛ cup chopped fresh basil leaves

⅛ cup tamari

¼ cup chopped fresh cilantro

⅛ cup chopped fresh mint

⅛ cup fish sauce (optional)

THIS green pea soup is an enticing change of pace from the many soup recipes made with dried split peas. Ginger, garlic, lemongrass, and curry paste excite your mouth and perfectly fit the vibrant green color of this soup. It is also great served chilled. Try this over sliced grilled tofu, as well.

Place the cold water, rice, Thai curry paste, garlic, ginger, lemongrass, and lime juice into a soup pot. Bring the liquid to a boil and lower to a simmer. Cook uncovered for 30 minutes. Add the coconut milk and peas; simmer for 5 minutes. Add the basil, tamari, cilantro, mint, and fish sauce, if using; purée the soup in a food processor or with a handheld immersion blender until smooth and creamy.

PER 1-CUP SERVING: CALORIES 100; CALORIES FROM FAT 15; CALORIES FROM SATURATED FAT 10; PROTEIN 4 G; CARBOHYDRATE 18 G; TOTAL FAT 1.5 G; SATURATED FAT 1 G; CHOLESTEROL 0 MG; SODIUM 270 MG; 15% CALORIES FROM FAT

stocks, soups, and chilis

69

White Bean and Swiss Chard Soup

SERVES 6 TO 8

A Tuscan-inspired soup with the buttery texture of cannellini beans—also known as white kidney beans. Swiss chard is part of the cruciferous vegetable family and is a treasure trove of beta-carotene and vitamin C. Chard, sometimes called rhubarb chard, is a relative of the beet—the mystery of why it's called Swiss chard may never be solved.

Heat the olive oil in a soup pot over medium-high heat. Sauté the onion, celery, peppers, and garlic until the onion is translucent. Add the Italian herbs and tomatoes to the aromatics; continue to cook for 1 minute, stirring often. Add the cold water and beans. Bring the soup to a boil; reduce the heat to a simmer. Simmer the soup for about 45 minutes, or until the beans are tender.

Stir in the rice and chard. Continue simmering the soup for about 15 minutes, until the rice is cooked. Season with the salt and pepper.

PER 1-CUP SERVING: CALORIES 45; CALORIES FROM FAT 0; CALORIES FROM SATURATED FAT 0; PROTEIN 2 G; CARBOHYDRATE 8 G; TOTAL FAT 0 G; SATURATED FAT 0 G; CHOLESTEROL 0 MG; SODIUM 130 MG; 0% CALORIES FROM FAT

1 tablespoon olive oil

1 medium red onion, chopped

1 stalk celery, chopped

1 large red pepper, seeded and chopped

½ large green pepper, chopped

2 cloves garlic, minced (1 teaspoon)

⅛ cup dried Italian herbs

1 (14.5-ounce) can diced tomatoes in juice

9 cups cold water or vegetable stock

¾ cup dried white cannellini beans, rinsed

¼ cup basmati rice

3 cups washed and chopped Swiss chard leaves, heavy stems removed

Salt and freshly ground pepper to taste

Spicy Mung Bean Soup

1 cup dried mung beans, washed and
   rinsed

5 cups cold water or vegetable stock

½ teaspoon turmeric

1 teaspoon cumin

½ teaspoon curry powder

1 teaspoon garam masala

4 teaspoons canola oil

1 medium red onion, thinly sliced

3 cloves garlic, minced
   (1½ teaspoons)

2 large tomatoes, chopped

⅛ cup minced fresh ginger
   (2-inch piece)

1 small serrano pepper, very thinly
   sliced

1 cup coconut milk

½ cup minced fresh cilantro

Salt to taste

Juice of 1 lemon

COMMONLY used in Indian cooking, mung beans are small orange-fleshed beans with a green, yellow, or black outer covering. This soup brings out the mellow flavor of the mung bean, which seems to partner well with chilies. Garam masala is a spice mixture—Indian households make their own secret blends. (Our recipe is on page 47.) *Garam* means "hot" and *masala* simply means "spice." The combination is intensely aromatic and spicy.

Place the mung beans in a pot with the cold water. Simmer until the beans are tender, about 40 minutes. Combine the turmeric, cumin, curry powder, and garam masala, and set them aside.

In a large pot, heat the canola oil over medium-high heat. Sauté the onion until it is golden brown. Reduce the heat to medium-low, add the garlic, tomatoes, and ginger, and sauté for 1 minute. Add the combined spices and sliced serrano pepper; sauté for 1 minute. Add the beans and their liquid to the pot with the vegetables and spices. Add the coconut milk. Simmer the soup uncovered for 15 minutes over low heat. Stir in the cilantro.

Season the soup with the salt and lemon juice.

PER 1-CUP SERVING: CALORIES 130; CALORIES FROM FAT 50; CALORIES FROM SATURATED FAT 25; PROTEIN 3 G; CARBOHYDRATE 16 G; TOTAL FAT 6 G; SATURATED FAT 3 G; CHOLESTEROL 0 MG; SODIUM 75 MG; 38% CALORIES FROM FAT

stocks, soups, and chilis

Chipotle Black Bean Soup

SERVES 6 TO 8

THE smoky, spicy almost chocolate-like flavor of this soup comes from chipotle chilies, an ingredient that is very popular in the Southwest. Chipotle chilies, which are smoked jalapeños, can be found dried, pickled, or canned in thick adobo sauce. This recipe calls for unsweetened cocoa, which adds a warmth to the complex flavor of this soup. Enjoy it with corn bread to buffer the chilies.

Heat the olive oil in a large pot over medium-high heat. Add the red onion, peppers, and garlic; sauté until the onion is translucent. Reduce the heat to medium-low, and add the oregano, cumin, chipotle chilies, and adobo sauce; sauté for 1 minute. Add the cold water, bay leaf, and beans. Bring the soup to a boil; then lower to a simmer and cook uncovered for 1 hour, until the beans are tender.

Stir in the cocoa powder, orange juice, cilantro, scallions, and salt; continue to simmer for 5 minutes.

PER 1-CUP SERVING: CALORIES 60; CALORIES FROM FAT 15; CALORIES FROM SATURATED FAT 0; PROTEIN 2 G; CARBOHYDRATE 9 G; TOTAL FAT 2 G; SATURATED FAT 0 G; CHOLESTEROL 0 MG; SODIUM 10 MG; 25% CALORIES FROM FAT

1/8 cup olive oil

2 cups chopped red onion

1 medium red pepper, seeded and chopped

1 medium green pepper, seeded and chopped

2 cloves garlic, minced
(1 teaspoon)

1 tablespoon dried oregano, or 3 tablespoons fresh

1 tablespoon cumin

3 chopped canned chipotle chilies

1/8 cup adobo sauce from canned chipotle peppers

12 cups cold water

1 bay leaf

2 cups dried black beans, rinsed

1 tablespoon unsweetened cocoa powder

3/4 cup orange juice

1/2 cup minced fresh cilantro

6 scallions, thinly sliced

Salt to taste

Roasted Corn Poblano Chowder

2 tablespoons butter

2 cloves garlic, minced (1 teaspoon)

1 stalk celery, chopped

1 medium onion, chopped

¼ cup plus 1 tablespoon unbleached all-purpose flour

6 cups vegetable stock

2 cups milk, or 1 cup milk and 1 cup heavy cream

1½ pounds new potatoes, unpeeled and diced

3 medium poblano chilies, roasted, peeled, seeded, and finely diced (see page 13)

1 (16-ounce) package frozen corn

½ cup chopped jarred roasted red peppers

Salt to taste

Cayenne pepper to taste

IT'S a little bit of "high noon" in a bowl. Corn has been around since 3400 B.C., adding sweetness and flavor to hundreds of dishes throughout our culture, which probably accounts for Americans eating about twenty-five pounds of it per person each year. Poblano chilies are ancho peppers that are still green and have not been dried, and they range from mild to hot. They usually make their appearance as stuffed chiles rellenos; however, we happily add them to this hearty soup.

In a large pot, melt the butter over medium-high heat. Add the garlic, celery, and onion. Cook until the onion is translucent, about 5 minutes. Reduce the heat to low; stir in the flour to make a roux. Cook over low heat, stirring often, for 5 minutes, being careful not to let the flour scorch. Turn the heat to high and slowly whisk in the stock, stirring constantly to prevent lumps.

Add the milk. Bring the soup to a rolling simmer and then simmer for 5 minutes, stirring often. Add the potatoes, poblano chilies, corn, and roasted red peppers. Simmer uncovered for 30 minutes. Add the salt and cayenne pepper.

PER 1-CUP SERVING: CALORIES 130; CALORIES FROM FAT 25; CALORIES FROM SATURATED FAT 15; PROTEIN 5 G; CARBOHYDRATE 22 G; TOTAL FAT 2.5 G; SATURATED FAT 1.5 G; CHOLESTEROL 5 MG; SODIUM 70 MG; 19% CALORIES FROM FAT

stocks, soups, and chilis

73

Butternut Squash Bisque

SERVES 8 TO 10

IT seems butternut squash and carrots make a great couple: sweet soul-satisfying vegetables that compete with one another for beta-carotene content and a sweet, earthy flavor. Appetite-fulfilling without lots of calories, butternut squash makes a creamy soup that is comforting to eat. Try making croutons with cinnamon raisin bread for a unique garnish.

Heat the olive oil or butter over medium heat in a large sauce pot. Sauté the squash, carrots, onion, and ginger for 3 minutes, until they are lightly browned. Add the stock and orange zest, and bring to a boil. Lower to a simmer and cook uncovered for 35 to 40 minutes, until the vegetables are tender. Add the parsley, nutmeg, and salt and pepper. Purée the soup with a handheld immersion blender or in a food processor until smooth and creamy.

1 tablespoon olive oil or butter
2 to 3 pounds butternut squash, peeled and diced into 1-inch chunks
3 large carrots, chopped
1 medium onion, chopped
1 tablespoon minced fresh ginger (1-inch piece)
2 quarts vegetable stock or cold water
$\frac{1}{8}$ cup grated orange zest
1 bunch parsley, chopped
Pinch of ground nutmeg
Salt and freshly ground white pepper to taste

PER 1-CUP SERVING: CALORIES 50; CALORIES FROM FAT 0; CALORIES FROM SATURATED FAT 0; PROTEIN 1 G; CARBOHYDRATE 11 G; TOTAL FAT 0 G; SATURATED FAT 0 G; CHOLESTEROL 0 MG; SODIUM 20 MG; 0% CALORIES FROM FAT

 Recipe Bonus Winter squash is more fibrous and sweet than summer squash and contains an inner cavity with large seeds that can be washed, dried, salted, and then roasted for 10 minutes in a 350°F. oven until golden brown.

THE WHOLE FOODS MARKET COOKBOOK

Triple-Mushroom Bisque

2 tablespoons butter

1 tablespoon olive oil

1 large leek, thinly sliced and washed

1 large shallot, minced

8 ounces button mushrooms, sliced

4 ounces shiitake mushrooms,
   stemmed and sliced

6 ounces portobello mushrooms,
   stemmed and diced (3 small ones)

¼ cup unbleached all-purpose flour

3 cups vegetable or chicken stock

1 cup cream

6 sprigs fresh thyme or tarragon

¼ teaspoon ground nutmeg

¼ cup dry sherry

Juice of 1 lemon

Salt and freshly ground pepper to
   taste

THIS mushroom soup is earthy, dark, and rich with the meaty flavor of portobello mushrooms, softened by the perfume of tarragon and nutty aftertaste of dry sherry. For an extra intense flavor boost, add three or four chopped dried black mushrooms, which add a contrasting texture to this liquid velvet. Try serving with spaetzle (page 93) or croutons.

Heat the butter and olive oil in a large sauce pot over medium heat. Sauté the leek and shallot for 3 minutes, until they are softened. Add the mushrooms, and sauté for another minute. Add the flour and incorporate it into the vegetables; cook for another minute.

Add the stock and stir in well with a spoon. Bring the soup to a boil and continue to stir until the mixture thickens. Lower to a simmer and cook uncovered for 20 minutes. Add the cream, thyme, and nutmeg; simmer for 10 minutes more. Add the sherry and lemon juice, and season with the salt and pepper.

PER 1-CUP SERVING: CALORIES 170; CALORIES FROM FAT 100; CALORIES FROM SATURATED FAT 50; PROTEIN 4 G; CARBOHYDRATE 13 G; TOTAL FAT 12 G; SATURATED FAT 6 G; CHOLESTEROL 30 MG; SODIUM 400 MG; 59% CALORIES FROM FAT

stocks, soups, and chilis

vegetarian

Creamy Spinach Bisque

SERVES 8 TO 10

OUR Boston chefs offer us this potent soup so velvety and rich, it has ardent New Englanders snubbing their taste buds at clam chowder. This soup may also be used as a sauce for vegetables au gratin and casserole dishes. Try serving with spaetzle (page 93).

4 tablespoons butter

2 medium red onions, chopped

2 large leeks, sliced and washed

¼ cup unbleached all-purpose flour

4 cups vegetable or chicken stock (see Note)

1 (16-ounce) package frozen chopped spinach, thawed, squeezed of excess water

3 cups milk

1 pint heavy cream or half and half

Salt and freshly ground white pepper to taste

1 teaspoon ground nutmeg

Melt the butter in a large sauce pot over medium heat. Add the onions and leeks, and sauté them until they're soft, about 2 minutes. Add the flour and cook for 2 minutes to form a roux. Add the stock. Cook and stir constantly until the mixture is smooth and thickened, about 5 minutes. Add the spinach, milk, and cream; bring the soup to a simmer. Cook uncovered for 30 minutes. Add the salt and pepper and nutmeg, and cook for an additional 5 minutes.

NOTE: This soup could be vegetarian if made with vegetable broth.

PER 1-CUP SERVING: CALORIES 220; CALORIES FROM FAT 160; CALORIES FROM SATURATED FAT 100; PROTEIN 5 G; CARBOHYDRATE 11 G; TOTAL FAT 18 G; SATURATED FAT 11 G; CHOLESTEROL 60 MG; SODIUM 370 MG; 73% CALORIES FROM FAT

Carrot Ginger Soup

vegan

SERVES 6 TO 8

1 tablespoon canola oil

4 medium onions, sliced

1 (3-inch) piece fresh ginger

6 cups vegetable stock

8 large carrots, roughly cut in evenly
sized pieces

2 teaspoons salt

¼ teaspoon freshly ground white
pepper

SUCH a stellar taste performance comes as somewhat of a surprise from such a shy and humble root vegetable. The sweet, mellow flavor of carrots pairs well with the peppery bite of ginger in this purée. Serve this simple soup either hot or cold.

Heat the canola oil in a large sauce pot over low heat, and sauté the onions until they are translucent. Cut the peeled ginger into 1-inch slices and then roughly chop. Add the chopped ginger to the onions, and sauté for an additional 2 minutes. Increase heat. Add the stock and carrots. Simmer over medium heat until the carrots are tender. Season with the salt and pepper. Purée.

PER 1-CUP SERVING: CALORIES 90; CALORIES FROM FAT 15; CALORIES FROM SATURATED FAT 0; PROTEIN 2 G; CARBOHYDRATE 16 G; TOTAL FAT 1.5 G; SATURATED FAT 0 G; CHOLESTEROL 0 MG; SODIUM 390 MG; 17% CALORIES FROM FAT

Variation: Reduce the vegetable stock by half and replace the remaining half with orange juice, apple juice, ginger ale, or sparkling cider.

Country Vegetable Soup with Barley and Oats

SERVES 6 TO 8

THIS is like having your breakfast cereal, lunch, and dinner in one dreamy bowl. The comforting consistency of oats pairs well with nutty barley and mild black-eyed peas. A background of vegetable nuggets and smoky dried black mushrooms provides unusual texture. Every tasty spoonful feels like a three-ring vegetable circus. This soup thickens as it sits.

5 dried shiitake mushrooms
1½ cups dried black-eyed peas
½ cup barley
1 tablespoon canola oil
3 medium carrots, diced
1 large onion, diced
2 stalks celery, diced
½ cup chopped green pepper
2 cups broccoli florets
2 cups cauliflower florets
2 cloves garlic, minced (1 teaspoon)
1 tablespoon salt
2½ teaspoons dried thyme (or
   2 tablespoons fresh thyme)
6 cups cold water
5 cups tomato juice
2 bay leaves
1 large yellow squash, diced
1 large zucchini, diced
1 pound button mushrooms, sliced
¼ cup rolled whole oats
½ cup chopped parsley

In a small saucepan, cover the dried shiitakes with 1 cup warm water. Bring to a boil. Immediately remove from the heat and allow to soak for 20 minutes. Remove the stems and chop.

Meanwhile, place the black-eyed peas in a large pot. Add water to cover and bring to a boil. Cook at a rolling boil for 5 minutes. Turn off the heat, and add the barley. Let the mixture sit for 30 minutes.

While the beans are sitting, heat the canola oil over medium heat in a large sauté pan. Add the carrots, onion, celery, pepper, broccoli, cauliflower, and garlic. Season with the salt and thyme.

Sauté for 5 minutes, or until the onion is translucent. Add the cold water to the pot with the beans and barley. Add the tomato juice and bay leaves. Return to a boil. Season with additional salt, if necessary.

Add the squash, zucchini, button and shiitake mushrooms, and oats. Simmer for about 10 minutes, or until the vegetables are firm-tender and the soup is creamy. Stir in the parsley. Remove the bay leaves before serving.

PER 1-CUP SERVING: CALORIES 70; CALORIES FROM FAT 10; CALORIES FROM SATURATED FAT 0; PROTEIN 3 G; CARBOHYDRATE 13 G; TOTAL FAT 1 G; SATURATED FAT 0 G; CHOLESTEROL 0 MG; SODIUM 330 MG; 14% CALORIES FROM FAT

Red Beans and Rice

SERVES 6 TO 8

1 tablespoon olive oil

½ pound cooked andouille sausage, diced

1 medium yellow onion, diced

2 stalks celery, diced

1 large green pepper, seeded and diced

2 cloves garlic, minced (1 teaspoon)

1 teaspoon dried thyme (or 1 tablespoon fresh thyme)

1 teaspoon dried basil

1 teaspoon dried oregano

1 teaspoon sweet paprika

1 bay leaf

8 cups chicken stock or cold water

2 cups tomato juice

1 cup small dried red beans

½ cup basmati rice

2 sprigs fresh thyme

Salt and freshly ground pepper to taste

THIS traditional hearty chowder may be made vegetarian, if you like, by leaving out the andouille sausage. Andouille is a spicy, smoked sausage traditional in Cajun cooking and normally used in jambalaya and gumbo. It is available both cooked and raw—you will need the cooked version for this recipe. This soup is a meal in itself, and many cooks in New Orleans swear it brings good luck when eaten. Try it out on your family and see if it brings you good tidings. The fresh thyme stirred in toward the end adds extra aromatic nuances to the soup.

Heat the olive oil over medium-high heat, add the andouille sausage, and sauté for 1 minute. Stir in the onion, celery, pepper, and garlic, and sauté until the vegetables are tender. Reduce the heat to low, and stir in the dried thyme, basil, oregano, paprika, and bay leaf; cook for 3 minutes, stirring often.

Add the stock, tomato juice, and red beans. Bring the chowder to a boil, lower to a simmer, and cook uncovered for about 45 minutes, until the beans are tender but have not lost their shape. Stir in the rice, add fresh thyme sprigs, and continue to simmer for 15 minutes, until the rice is cooked. Season with the salt and pepper.

PER 1-CUP SERVING: CALORIES 130; CALORIES FROM FAT 50; CALORIES FROM SATURATED FAT 15; PROTEIN 5 G; CARBOHYDRATE 13 G; TOTAL FAT 6 G; SATURATED FAT 2 G; CHOLESTEROL 15 MG; SODIUM 220 MG; 38% CALORIES FROM FAT

stocks, soups, and chilis

French Onion Soup for Everyone

SERVES 6 TO 8

THERE is nothing more fragrant than caramelized onions, especially when they are bubbling away with red wine and herbs. It's kitchen aromatherapy for the whole family. Miso is a pungent soy-based condiment that adds a complex depth of flavor and character to this version of a classic French soup. Miso is a good source of protein and digestive enzymes. Miso is always added last in the cooking process to activate the beneficial enzymes and release their healthy elements. Nutritional yeast has a pleasant smoky flavor and is about 50 percent protein. It also contains all the essential amino acids.

⅛ cup olive oil

3 large onions, thinly sliced

1 large portobello mushroom cap, thinly sliced

3 cloves garlic, minced (1½ teaspoons)

1 teaspoon dried thyme, or 1 tablespoon fresh

¼ cup tomato paste

1 cup dry red wine

4 cups vegetable stock

¼ cup tamari or soy sauce

⅛ cup dark miso dissolved in 1 cup warm water or vegetable stock

1 tablespoon nutritional yeast

Freshly ground pepper to taste

Heat the olive oil in a large sauce pot over medium heat, and sauté the onions for at least 3 minutes before stirring. The onions should start to brown before you move them around with a spoon. Continue to cook the onions, stirring only occasionally in order for the natural sugar to brown. Cook for 20 minutes, until the onions are well browned.

Add the mushroom, garlic, thyme, and tomato paste. Continue to cook for 5 minutes, until the tomato paste turns golden brown.

Add the wine, and scrape the pan bottom, removing all the brown bits that are sticking to it. This is called deglazing. Reduce the wine as you simmer for another 2 minutes. Add the stock, tamari, dissolved miso, and nutritional yeast. Continue to simmer uncovered for 10 minutes longer; season with the pepper.

PER 1-CUP SERVING: CALORIES 140; CALORIES FROM FAT 35; CALORIES FROM SATURATED FAT 5; PROTEIN 4 G; CARBOHYDRATE 16 G; TOTAL FAT 4 G; SATURATED FAT 0.5 G; CHOLESTEROL 0 MG; SODIUM 660 MG; 25% CALORIES FROM FAT

Variation: To make onion soup au gratin, ladle the soup into an ovenproof dish. Drop some toasted bread rounds into the soup. Top with a vegan soy cheese (which contains no casein); sprinkle some over the surface and brown in the oven. For a nonvegan version, sprinkle with mozzarella cheese, Gruyère cheese, or Parmesan cheese and bake the same way until the cheese is melted.

vegetarian

Hungarian Sweet 'n' Sour Cabbage Soup

SERVES 6 TO 8

LITTLE wonder why this soup has been made by thousands of our grandparents before us. The soup was originally a peasant dish (as cabbage was plentiful and inexpensive), providing a filling meal after working in the fields all day. A simple and perfect balance of sweet and sour, the flavors of tart apple cider vinegar and wild blossom honey make an ideal background for the pronounced flavor of cabbage. Caraway seeds add an aromatic zing to each spoonful.

2 teaspoons olive oil

1 medium red onion, diced

3 cloves garlic, minced
   (1½ teaspoons)

1 tablespoon caraway seeds

2 tablespoons sweet paprika

1 (14-ounce) can diced tomatoes
   in juice

1 cup tomato purée

3 cups cold water or vegetable stock

⅛ cup cider vinegar

4 cups shredded green cabbage

2 teaspoons grated lemon zest

1 tablespoon honey

Salt and freshly ground pepper to
   taste

⅛ cup smoked paprika (optional)

Heat the olive oil in a soup pot over medium heat. Add the onion, garlic, and caraway seeds, and sauté, stirring frequently, until the onion is translucent. Stir in the paprika, and cook for 1 minute while stirring continuously.

Add the diced tomatoes (with juice), tomato purée, cold water, and vinegar. Bring the soup to a simmer. Simmer for 5 minutes. Add the cabbage and lemon zest; continue to simmer uncovered for 30 minutes, until the cabbage is tender. Add the honey. Season the soup with the salt and freshly ground pepper and the optional smoked paprika.

PER 1-CUP SERVING: CALORIES 90; CALORIES FROM FAT 10; CALORIES FROM SATURATED FAT 0; PROTEIN 2 G; CARBOHYDRATE 15 G; TOTAL FAT 1 G; SATURATED FAT 0 G; CHOLESTEROL 0 MG; SODIUM 115 MG; 11% CALORIES FROM FAT

Miso Vegetable Chowder

5 cups vegetable stock

4 cloves garlic, minced (2 teaspoons)

¼ cup minced fresh ginger (4-inch piece)

3 stalks lemongrass, white part only, minced

I jalapeño pepper or Thai bird chili, seeded and minced

7 cups total of any combination of the following cut into bite-size pieces: onions, carrots, celery, leeks, cabbage, bok choy, turnips, mushrooms, kale, turnip greens, collard greens, spinach, broccoli, fresh corn, snap peas

¼ cup white miso

Gomasio to garnish

A sparkling example of a delicious, intensely flavored soup that hits the spot when you're feeling under the weather.

Place the stock, garlic, half the ginger, the lemongrass, and chili in a soup pot. Bring the soup to a boil, lower to a simmer, and cook uncovered for 10 minutes. Add the vegetable combination; continue to simmer for 3 minutes, until the vegetables are crisp-tender.

To serve, place 1½ teaspoons of the miso in each bowl with a pinch of the remaining ginger. Stir in a small amount of hot broth into each bowl to dissolve the miso; then ladle hot soup and vegetables into each bowl. Sprinkle some ground gomasio over the bowl as a garnish.

PER 1-CUP SERVING: CALORIES 120; CALORIES FROM FAT 5; CALORIES FROM SATURATED FAT 0; PROTEIN 4 G; CARBOHYDRATE 23 G; TOTAL FAT 1 G; SATURATED FAT 0 G; CHOLESTEROL 0 MG; SODIUM 220 MG; 4% CALORIES FROM FAT

stocks, soups, and chilis

83

The Chicken Soup

SERVES 10 TO 12

HOW many of us associate the smell of simmering chicken soup with home cooking and reminisce about the first time a golden bowl of this restorative broth was placed in front of us? The parsnip and sweet potato in this recipe add subtle sweetness and rich color. Feel free to add cooked noodles of your favorite size and shape.

2 teaspoons canola oil

½ medium onion, chopped

2 large carrots, chopped

2 stalks celery, chopped

½ medium sweet potato, peeled and chopped

2 parsnips, peeled and chopped

2 quarts chicken stock

5 sprigs parsley with stems, minced

3 sprigs fresh dill with stems, minced

Salt and freshly ground white pepper to taste

Heat the canola oil in a large sauce pot over medium heat. Sauté the onion, carrots, celery, sweet potato, and parsnips for 2 minutes to enhance their natural sugars. Add the stock and bring to a boil; lower to a simmer and cook uncovered for 40 minutes, until all the vegetables are tender. Add the parsley and dill; season with salt and pepper.

PER 1-CUP SERVING: CALORIES 70; CALORIES FROM FAT 15; CALORIES FROM SATURATED FAT 5; PROTEIN 3 G; CARBOHYDRATE 12 G; TOTAL FAT 2 G; SATURATED FAT 0.5 G; CHOLESTEROL 5 MG; SODIUM 110 MG; 21% CALORIES FROM FAT

Chicken and Wild Rice Soup

SERVES 4 TO 6

FORE you finish the first spoonful, you will understand
hy it's called *wild* rice. Even though it's not a true rice—but
ong-grain rice grass native to the Great Lakes region—it
early belongs in this soup. It adds a nutty flavor and chewy
xture against the background of mild chicken, shallots,
d mushrooms. Substituting firm tofu for the chicken
akes a very nice version, as well. You may substitute
opped portobello or cremini mushrooms for the button,
you prefer.

2 teaspoons olive oil

3 shallots, finely chopped

1/2 cup sliced button mushrooms

3 to 4 dried shiitake mushrooms
   (optional)

2 cloves garlic, finely minced
   (1 teaspoon)

1 cup wild or brown rice

4 plus 2 cups chicken or vegetable
   stock

8 ounces boneless skinless chicken
   breasts, chopped

1/2 cup cream

1/2 cup chopped parsley or fresh
   chervil

2 teaspoons chopped fresh thyme

Pinch of dry mustard

1 cup dry sherry

Heat the olive oil in large sauce pot over medium
heat. Add the shallots, mushrooms, and garlic;
sauté for 3 minutes.

Add the rice and the 4 cups stock. Cover and cook
the soup over medium heat for about 35 minutes, or
until the rice is almost finished cooking. Add the
remaining 2 cups stock and the chicken. Cook
uncovered for 10 minutes, until the chicken is fully
cooked. Add the cream, parsley, thyme, dry mustard,
and sherry. Simmer for 10 minutes, until the soup is
slightly thickened. Serve hot.

PER 1-CUP SERVING: CALORIES 150; CALORIES FROM FAT 35;
CALORIES FROM SATURATED FAT 15; PROTEIN 8 G;
CARBOHYDRATE 15 G; TOTAL FAT 4 G; SATURATED FAT 1.5 G;
CHOLESTEROL 25 MG; SODIUM 45 MG; 23% CALORIES FROM FAT

Spicy Chicken and Tortilla Sou[

1/8 cup canola oil

1 medium red pepper, seeded and
chopped

1 medium green pepper, seeded and
chopped

1 medium red onion, chopped

2 cloves garlic, minced (1 teaspoon)

2 teaspoons dried oregano, or
1/8 cup fresh

1 teaspoon cumin

3/4 teaspoon chili powder

1 jalapeño pepper, seeded and
chopped

1 cup diced canned tomatoes with
juice

4 cups cold water or chicken stock

2/3 pound boneless skinless chicken
breasts

1 (15-ounce) can cooked black beans,
drained and rinsed

2 cups fresh or frozen corn kernels

1/2 cup minced fresh cilantro

Salt to taste

8 ounces blue corn tortilla chips

The Garnish (Optional)

Diced ripe avocado

A sprinkling of grated Monterey Jack
cheese

THE bold flavors of this soup embody the vi
that we associate with Tex-Mex cuisine. When
tortilla chips soak in the chili-spiked broth, the
the warm broth enhances the subtle corn flavo
tillas. Vegetarians may use vegetable stock a
chicken.

Heat the canola oil in a sauce pot over mediun
heat. Sauté the red and green peppers, onion
garlic, oregano, cumin, and chili powder for 3 min
until the onion is translucent, stirring often. Add th
jalapeño and tomatoes; continue stirring for 1 minu
Add the cold water and the whole chicken breasts.

Bring the soup to a boil, reduce the heat, and sir
uncovered for 20 minutes. Remove the chicken bre
to cool, and cut them into bite-size pieces. Return t
chicken to the soup, add the black beans and corn,
then return the soup to a boil. Remove the soup fro
heat, stir in the cilantro, and season with the salt.

To serve, slightly crunch a small handful of torti
chips in the bottom of each bowl. Ladle the soup o
the chips.

TO PREPARE THE GARNISH After placing tl
chips in the bowl, add the avocado and cheese on t
the chips, then ladle the soup over the top, and serv

PER 1-CUP SERVING: CALORIES 190; CALORIES FROM FAT 40;
CALORIES FROM SATURATED FAT 0; PROTEIN 12 G;
CARBOHYDRATE 27 G; TOTAL FAT 4.5 G; SATURATED FAT 0 G
CHOLESTEROL 20 MG; SODIUM 250 MG; 21% CALORIES FROM

Lentil, Sausage, and Rice Soup

SERVES 6 TO 8

1 tablespoon olive oil

1 medium onion, chopped

4 cloves garlic, minced (2 teaspoons)

2 large carrots, diced

1 teaspoon fennel seeds

½ pound sweet or hot Italian chicken
 or turkey sausage, removed from
 casing

2 bay leaves

12 cups chicken stock

1 cup uncooked lentils, rinsed

½ cup brown rice

10 ounces fresh spinach, washed and
 stemmed, or 5 ounces frozen
 spinach, thawed and excess
 moisture squeezed out

⅛ cup minced fresh basil

SUCH magnificent flavor from such an unassuming tiny orb! Lentils cook quickly and don't need to be soaked. We use brown lentils because they hold their shape in this blend of basmati rice, root vegetables, and smoky sausage. You may make a vegetarian version of this soup by leaving out the sausage and substituting vegetable broth for the chicken broth.

Heat the olive oil in a large sauce pot over medium heat; add the onion, garlic, carrots, and fennel; cook until soft and golden, about 5 minutes.

Add the raw sausage and cook over medium heat for 3 minutes, stirring often to break up the sausage. Add the bay leaves and stock. Bring the soup to a boil; reduce the heat to a simmer. Add the lentils and rice. Simmer uncovered for about 45 minutes, or until the lentils and rice soften.

Add the fresh spinach during the last 5 minutes of cooking. (Add the frozen spinach during the last 15 minutes of cooking.) Add the fresh basil when the soup has finished cooking.

PER 1-CUP SERVING: CALORIES 110; CALORIES FROM FAT 25; CALORIES FROM SATURATED FAT 10; PROTEIN 7 G; CARBOHYDRATE 14 G; TOTAL FAT 2.5 G; SATURATED FAT 1 G; CHOLESTEROL 5 MG; SODIUM 125 MG; 23% CALORIES FROM FAT

Bahamian Conch Chowder

SERVES 6 TO 8

CONCHS are strange and curious mollusks that are quite popular in South Florida. Most of the conchs used there come from the Bahamas, where they are plentiful. If you can't get frozen conchs, chopped clams make a great substitute. If you use chopped clams, add them at the last moment to keep them tender. This soup is delicious with toasted bread rounds. This chowder is chunky, spicy, and packed with textures, colors, and robust flavor. Bahamian spices such as allspice and thyme, combined with the pungent last-minute addition of green onions, give this soup an unusual twist.

1 tablespoon olive or canola oil

1 medium onion, chopped

2 stalks celery, chopped

2 large carrots, chopped

1 red pepper, seeded and chopped

1 medium potato, sweet potato, or yucca, peeled and chopped

1 teaspoon dried thyme, or 6 sprigs fresh

¼ teaspoon crushed red chili flakes

¼ teaspoon ground allspice

3 bay leaves

1 (16-ounce) can chopped tomatoes

1 (16-ounce) can clam juice

2 cups cold water

1 pound chopped frozen conch, defrosted, or 16 ounces chopped clams with liquid

1 tablespoon malt or red wine vinegar

6 sprigs parsley, chopped

4 scallions, minced

Salt to taste

Cayenne pepper to taste

Heat the olive or canola oil in a large sauce pot over medium heat. Sauté the onion, celery, carrots, red pepper, potato, thyme, red chili flakes, allspice, and bay leaves for 5 minutes, until they begin to soften. Add the tomatoes, clam juice, and cold water. Bring to a boil and immediately lower to a simmer.

If using defrosted conch meat, add now and cook for 35 minutes, uncovered. Then add the malt, parsley, scallions, salt, and cayenne pepper, and simmer for 5 minutes.

If using chopped clams, add now along with the malt or red wine vinegar, parsley, scallions, salt, and cayenne pepper, and simmer for 5 minutes longer.

PER 1-CUP SERVING: CALORIES 80; CALORIES FROM FAT 10; CALORIES FROM SATURATED FAT 0; PROTEIN 7 G; CARBOHYDRATE 10 G; TOTAL FAT 1.5 G; SATURATED FAT 0 G; CHOLESTEROL 15 MG; SODIUM 170 MG; 13% CALORIES FROM FAT

Chili

Such a controversial food really needs its own section, if not its own book. Folks from all over the Southwest are sure there is only one kind of chili—theirs. Of course, we couldn't get anyone to agree on the best, so we offer you a few options from our creative cooks all across the country. After tasting the chilies, we think you will agree that there is no one best—just don't tell them that in Texas.

Sweet Potato Chili

SERVES 6 TO 8

1 tablespoon olive oil

1 medium onion, chopped

1 large red pepper, seeded and chopped

1 large clove garlic, minced (¾ teaspoon)

1 pound boneless skinless chicken breast, chopped

1 (15-ounce) can cannellini beans, drained and rinsed

1 cup chicken stock

2½ cups cold water

2 pounds sweet potatoes, peeled and diced (about 6 cups)

2 teaspoons crushed red chili flakes

1 teaspoon cumin

2 teaspoons chili powder

½ teaspoon cayenne pepper

2 ounces canned diced chilies or 1 fresh jalapeño pepper, minced

1 bunch scallions, minced

THE natural creamy sweet flesh makes the perfect flavor foil for spicy chilies, pungent cilantro, and fragrant cracked cumin seeds. The sweet potato chunks tend to soak up the wonderful flavors and concentrate the spices. This chili is great the second day—if there's any left.

For a vegetarian version of this chili, use vegetable stock and omit the chicken.

In a large pot, heat the olive oil over medium heat, and sauté the onion, red pepper, and garlic until firm-tender.

Add the chicken breast and sauté for 2 minutes, until opaque. Add the beans, stock, water, potatoes, red chili flakes, cumin, chili powder, cayenne pepper, and chilies. Bring to a boil, reduce the heat, and simmer uncovered for about 30 minutes, or until the potatoes are tender. Garnish with the chopped scallions. Top the chili with a dollop of sour cream, if desired.

PER 1-CUP SERVING: CALORIES 170; CALORIES FROM FAT 25; CALORIES FROM SATURATED FAT 5; PROTEIN 13 G; CARBOHYDRATE 24 G; TOTAL FAT 2.5 G; SATURATED FAT 0.5 G; CHOLESTEROL 25 MG; SODIUM 110 MG; 15% CALORIES FROM FAT

Variation: Use chipotle chilies for a spicier version.

vegan

Chunky Garden Vegetable Chili

SERVES 6 TO 8

THIS garden chili gets its great texture from dense cracked wheat. Even meat-eating chili traditionalists crave a bowl of this chili topped with sharp cheddar, sour cream, and chopped scallions. It looks like a lot of ingredients, but it's worth the effort and cooks quickly because everything just gets put in one pot and simmered.

Heat the olive or canola oil in a large sauce pot over medium heat, and sauté the onion, carrots, celery, peppers, garlic, jalapeño, oregano, cumin, and chili powder for 2 minutes to combine well.

Add the tomato purée, tomatoes, cold water, cracked wheat, red or white beans, and black beans; simmer uncovered for 50 minutes, until blended. You may add additional vegetable stock, water, or tomato juice to adjust the consistency, if needed.

Add the lime juice, tamari, and cilantro. Serve with plain yogurt or sour cream, grated cheddar, and minced scallions.

PER 1-CUP SERVING: CALORIES 110; CALORIES FROM FAT 10; CALORIES FROM SATURATED FAT 0; PROTEIN 5 G; CARBOHYDRATE 20 G; TOTAL FAT 1.5 G; SATURATED FAT 0 G; CHOLESTEROL 0 MG; SODIUM 570 MG; 9% CALORIES FROM FAT

1 tablespoon olive or canola oil
1 medium onion, chopped
2 large carrots, chopped
2 stalks large celery, chopped
1 medium green pepper, seeded and chopped
1 medium red pepper, seeded and chopped
3 cloves garlic, minced (1½ teaspoons)
1 jalapeño pepper, seeded and minced
1 tablespoon dried oregano
2 teaspoons cumin
1 tablespoon chili powder
1 cup tomato purée
1 (28-ounce) can chopped tomatoes
2 quarts cold water or vegetable stock
1 cup cracked wheat
1 (16-ounce) can red or white beans, rinsed and drained
1 cup cooked black beans
Juice of 2 limes
½ cup tamari or soy sauce
1 bunch fresh cilantro, minced

Chili Blanco with Chicken

1 pound boneless skinless chicken breast, diced into ½-inch cubes

The Marinade

1 tablespoon extra-virgin olive oil

1 teaspoon cumin

1 tablespoon dried oregano

1 teaspoon chili powder

1 medium jalapeño pepper, seeded and minced

2 cloves garlic, minced (1 teaspoon)

1 tablespoon olive oil

1 medium onion, chopped

2 stalks celery, chopped

1 large leek, sliced and washed

1 large green pepper, seeded and chopped

1 teaspoon cumin

1 tablespoon dried oregano

1 tablespoon chopped chipotle chilies in adobo

1 bottle beer (light Pilsner style)

2 cups chicken stock

1 (16-ounce) can white cannellini beans, drained and rinsed

6 sprigs fresh cilantro, minced

Juice of 1 lime

Salt to taste

THIS chili packs all the punch of a classic chili, but without the red color. Creamy white beans absorb and intensify the flavor of jalapeños, oregano, chipotle chili, and cilantro. If you prefer to use all stock without the beer, feel free. Give the seafood chili a try, too, which can be made using the same white base.

TO PREPARE THE MARINADE Marinate the chopped chicken in the olive oil, with the cumin, oregano, chili powder, minced jalapeño, and garlic for a few minutes.

Heat a large sauce pot over medium heat, and add the chicken. Sauté for 2 minutes, until the chicken turns opaque. Add additional olive oil, and sauté the onion, celery, leek, green pepper, cumin, oregano, and chilies. Sauté for 2 minutes, until well combined.

Add the beer, stock, and beans. Bring the chili to a boil, lower to a simmer, and cook for 30 minutes. Add the cilantro, lime juice, and salt. This dish is great with a dollop of plain yogurt or sour cream and diced avocado.

PER 1-CUP SERVING: CALORIES 170; CALORIES FROM FAT 45; CALORIES FROM SATURATED FAT 10; PROTEIN 17 G; CARBOHYDRATE 13 G; TOTAL FAT 5 G; SATURATED FAT 1 G; CHOLESTEROL 35 MG; SODIUM 170 MG; 26% CALORIES FROM FAT

Variation: For 20,000 Leagues Under the Seafood Chili, substitute shrimp, scallops, chopped clams, and diced firm-fleshed meat fish (like cod, halibut, grouper, wahoo, salmon, or tuna). You may use a combination of any or all of these denizens of the deep. Marinate and sauté them just like the chicken; then remove the seafood from the pan and continue the recipe, putting the sautéed seafood back into the simmering vegetables during the last 10 minutes of cooking.

Soup Garnishes

A great bowl of soup may well turn into a memorable meal if you add a special garnish. There are many garnish varieties from which to select. These flavor- and texture-enhancing ingredients can be as simple as a crouton. You may also make little dumplings called spaetzle, which truly transform a soup into a hearty lunch or dinner. Most soups and broths make perfect backgrounds for chopped vegetables, grains, pasta shapes, or other protein sources, such as tofu, poultry, or beef. Here are some suggestions.

Croutons

Croutons are the ultimate soup garnish. It's "clash of the titans" in a bowl pitting the pleasant texture of warm comforting soup against the crunch and crackle of toasted bread spiked with aromatic herbs. Most people have never tried homemade croutons, which are unlike the dry deep-fried bread chunks stored in plastic bags on a restaurant shelf for days before they land in your soup. Homemade croutons are more flavorful and far less salty than many packaged varieties. Croutons also give you a creative outlet for stale bread, muffins, or focaccia. Here's a good basic recipe, but experiment—there are as many types of croutons as there are versions of cream of broccoli soup.

Preheat the oven to 375°F. Combine the bread, olive oil, Italian herbs, salt and pepper, and optional cheese. Spread them out on a cookie sheet. Bake for 10 minutes, turning the croutons a few times, until they are a light golden brown. Remove and cool slightly before serving. Croutons may be kept in a sealed container at room temperature for 3 days.

PER ¼ RECIPE SERVING: CALORIES 60; CALORIES FROM FAT 35; CALORIES FROM SATURATED FAT 0.5; PROTEIN 1 G; CARBOHYDRATE 5 G; TOTAL FAT 3.5 G; SATURATED FAT 0.5 G; CHOLESTEROL 0 MG; SODIUM 60 MG; 58% CALORIES FROM FAT

2 cups diced bread (Use any bread, except sweet bread like raisin, if you are going to drop it into a savory soup. The bread should be cut in ½-inch squares.)

⅛ cup extra-virgin olive oil

1 tablespoon dried Italian herbs

Salt and freshly ground pepper to taste

1 tablespoon grated Parmesan or Romano cheese (optional)

Bread Rounds

Slices of French bread, rolls, or baguettes lightly toasted with one of our spread recipes, such as Warm Herbed Goat Cheese Dip (page 319) or Red Pepper Hummus (page 323), and dropped into soup add a unique component to your meal. Bread rounds may be prepared earlier in the day and kept in the refrigerator until ready to toast and serve.

Spaetzle or Spatzle

Thankfully, there are some brilliant foods that have been around for centuries. Imagine taking four or five ingredients that have never met each other before and introducing them—only to have them form a culinary bond that withstands decades of eating pleasure. Spaetzle is one of those foods. These little irregular pasta shapes are a cross between dumplings and noodles. They may be eaten alone, sautéed in butter or olive oil with salt and pepper. When you put them in soup, they soak up moisture and intensify the broth flavor tenfold. Here's a basic spaetzle. You may add chopped herbs, poppy seeds, spinach, smoked salmon, or any favorite food. They can be made up to 3 days before you want them for dinner.

1 1/2 cups unbleached all-purpose flour

1/2 cup whole wheat flour

3 large eggs, beaten

1/2 cup milk or water or oat milk

1 tablespoon canola oil

Salt and freshly ground white pepper to taste

Ground nutmeg to taste

In a large bowl, combine the flours. In another bowl, mix the eggs, liquid, canola oil, salt, pepper, and nutmeg together, and slowly add to the flour. Mix well with a wooden spoon until just combined; then place your entire hand into the thick batter and mix with your fingers for 2 minutes, until smooth. The mixture should resemble very thick pancake batter.

Bring 6 cups of salted water to a boil. Using a colander or spaetzle maker, drizzle the batter a little at a time through the colander or spaetzle maker into the boiling water. The dumplings will form. You will have to lightly press the batter through the holes with a spatula or spoon. Simmer for 3 minutes, and the spaetzle will plump up and form irregular-shaped noodles that float when they are cooked. Immediately plunge them in cold water to set. After cooling, they can be heated through and eaten immediately or lightly tossed with oil and stored in the refrigerator.

PER 1/4 RECIPE SERVING: CALORIES 170; CALORIES FROM FAT 40; CALORIES FROM SATURATED FAT 1; PROTEIN 7 G; CARBOHYDRATE 25 G; TOTAL FAT 4.5 G; SATURATED FAT 1 G; CHOLESTEROL 80 MG; SODIUM 35 MG; 24% CALORIES FROM FAT

Protein Garnishes

Tiny cubes of firm tofu may be dropped into soup. You may also marinate tofu with one of our marinade recipes (see "Sauces, Dressings, Dips, and Salsas," page 303) and bake for 15 minutes in a 375°F. oven for a more concentrated flavor. Silken tofu is very custardlike and may be scooped into a bowl of steaming hot broth for a meal soup—especially with the addition of sliced raw vegetables. Precooked protein, such as shredded chicken, pork, shrimp, scallops, or firm flaked fish are also welcome soup additions.

Freshly Grated Parmesan or Romano Cheese

Simple yet scrumptious, grated hard cheese is a perfect garnish.

Au Gratin

Remember, any soup may earn the au gratin title if you sprinkle it with your favorite cheese or nondairy cheese. Make sure you ladle soup into an ovenproof dish and place under a broiler or in a 425°F. oven to melt the cheese until golden and bubbly.

Starches and Grains

Whimsical small cooked pasta shapes, such as orzo, stellini (little stars), alphabet noodles (not just for kids!), or ditalini (baby shells), may be added once the soup has cooked and cooled. If you combine pasta into a pot of hot soup, the pasta will swell and soak up much of the liquid broth—making the soup too thick. Cooked long pasta such as Udon or soba noodles as well as cellophane rice noodles lend themselves to Asian-inspired soups. Cooked grains add a contrasting texture and earthy taste to many soups. Barley, oats, kamut, spelt, quinoa, couscous, and cracked wheat all work well. Stir into the hot soup just before serving.

Vegetables

Crisp shredded vegetables, such as kale, Napa cabbage, green cabbage, carrots, sugar snap peas, nasturtium flowers, or raw corn kernels, add contrast to soups. Root vegetables like carrots, parsnips, turnips, or beets may be diced, lightly steamed (or cooked momentarily in a microwave), and then dropped into the soup bowls before serving. For an exotic texture and flavor, try shredded, plumped strands of sea vegetables, such as arame, wakame, and kombu. Plants from the sea offer a briny, pleasantly salty taste that cannot be found in any other ingredient grown on land.

Herbs

Fresh snipped herbs, such as dill, tarragon, chives, basil, parsley, and cilantro, add perfume and an intense burst of flavor to a cooked soup. Always use an herb that is already an ingredient of the soup. For example, our Spicy Chicken and Tortilla Soup (page 85) is great with fresh cilantro.

 Tip from the Team: An easy way to remove cilantro leaves from their stems: Hold the whole bunch in one hand by the stems. In the other hand, use a fork to roughly "comb" through the cilantro. The leaves come off *whole* and in a pile on your cutting board.

Flavor Drizzles

Some of the ingredients in our pantry are perfect drizzled or sprinkled into a steaming bowl of soup just before serving. Try toasted sesame oil, miso, or gomasio in Asian-inspired soups, or a flavored olive oil, with citrus or fresh herbs, on the Mediterranean-type recipes. A dollop of pesto is also nice.

Big and Small Salads

BISTRO BOW TIE SALAD ♠ MOROCCAN TOASTED COUSCOUS WITH SPICED HONEY CITRUS DRESSING ♠ LEMON CAPELLINI SALAD ♠ SMOKED MOZZARELLA AND PENNE SALAD ♠ CHILLED LINGUINE WITH GORGONZOLA AND BASIL ♠ BARLEY PRIMAVERA ♠ WILD RICE WITH PECANS AND DRIED CRANBERRIES ♠ WHEAT BERRIES WITH GREEN CHILIES AND ROASTED PUMPKIN SEEDS ♠ THAI BLACK RICE SALAD ♠ QUINOA TABBOULEH ♠ SPINACH, BEET, AND WALNUT SALAD ♠ FATTOUSH ♠ ESSENTIAL SEA VEGETABLE SALAD ♠ "IT'S ALIVE" SALAD ♠ THAI CUCUMBER SALAD ♠ ALGERIAN EGGPLANT SALAD ♠ CHIPOTLE POTATO SALAD ♠ JAPANESE KALE SALAD WITH SHIITAKE MUSHROOMS ♠ SOUTHERN-STYLE POWER SLAW ♠ SZECHWAN SLAW ♠ SONOMA CHICKEN SALAD ♠ BLACKENED CHICKEN SALAD ♠ ENLIGHTENED CAESAR CHICKEN SALAD ♠ MEDITERRANEAN TUNA SALAD ♠ SOUTHWESTERN CALAMARI SALAD

Back in the late 1950s and throughout the 1960s, salad was a thick wedge of iceberg lettuce, some shredded carrot, and a few tomato slices that had no chance of ever ripening before being sacrificed. Many of us can still remember pouring on the Thousand Island, creamy Russian, or brightly colored French dressing, which blanketed the family salad plate.

In the late 1960s we sensed the need for lighter fare, perhaps realizing we are mortal, after all. Or perhaps it was the influx of women into the workforce that created the phenomenon of salad bars sprouting up everywhere. Whatever the reason, our obsession with salad started to grow—we added sunflower seeds, sprouts, lentils and beans, cooked pasta salads, spinach, raw cauliflower, and broccoli to our salad plates. Some of these ingredients were healthful, some not so, but our tastes were changing, and we craved variety.

More than twenty years ago, salad began to achieve a more upscale status with the availability of mesclun, also known as field greens. Seemingly overnight other interesting vegetables, mostly from California—like baby vegetables, fennel, radicchio, and jicama—began to show up in salads with fresh herbs such as basil and cilantro. Other greens like watercress, arugula, and kale made their way into salad bowls, as well. Cooked grains like brown rice and cracked wheat, along with pasta, took on starring roles, adding individuality and flavor.

Today, salad can be a light appetizer or a meal in itself, a simple combination of greens or an exotic assortment of ethnic ingredients. Making a great salad is like assembling an orchestra of flavors and textures. Most of the ingredients that make up a salad are raw, depending solely on absolute freshness and peak flavor to harmonize with one another. Salad ingredients are a window into each season's best offerings, and, for the creative cook, an inspiring medium for an endless variety of wonderful dishes.

Bistro Bow Tie Salad

 vegetarian

SERVES 6

½ pound bow tie pasta

I small zucchini, sliced into thin rounds

¼ red onion, thinly sliced

I cup pitted Kalamata olives

I cup crumbled feta cheese

I large tomato, cut into thin wedges

½ cup sun-dried tomatoes, plumped and thinly sliced (see page 12 and Note)

2 cups packed baby spinach, washed and stemmed

1¼ cups favorite bottled Italian herb vinaigrette, or see our recipe on page 329

THIS lighthearted salad has lots of personality. Whimsical butterfly-shaped pasta holds the vinaigrette well within its creases. If you prefer, use sliced plum or eggplant tomatoes instead of vine tomatoes. This is a great salad base to which you can add sliced grilled chicken, cooked shrimp, cooked flaked salmon, or diced baked tofu.

I n a large pot of salted boiling water, cook the pasta until it is al dente. Drain into a colander, and run cold water over the pasta until chilled through. Combine the zucchini, red onion, olives, feta cheese, tomato, sun-dried tomatoes, spinach, and vinaigrette. Mix all the ingredients together well, and serve.

NOTE: Many of our stores and some specialty stores carry oven-roasted tomatoes that may be used, as well.

PER SERVING: CALORIES 390; CALORIES FROM FAT 170; CALORIES FROM SATURATED FAT 45; PROTEIN 12 G; CARBOHYDRATE 49 G; TOTAL FAT 18 G; SATURATED FAT 5 G; CHOLESTEROL 20 MG; SODIUM 1,310 MG; 43% CALORIES FROM FAT

 Recipe Bonus If you want to make this salad up to 2 days before serving, combine all ingredients except the spinach and dressing. Store in a covered container in the refrigerator. Toss in the spinach and vinaigrette just before serving.

Moroccan Toasted Couscous with Spiced Honey Citrus Dressing

SERVES 8

DON'T be put off by the lengthy ingredient list. The combination of diverse ingredients—sweet dried fruit, crispy roasted pistachios, and comforting large grains of couscous—delivers tremendous flavor. Toasting couscous gives it an aromatic nuance. We use larger grains of Israeli couscous, which is similar in flavor to its traditional tiny counterpart. Israeli couscous is about half the size of a pea. It's available in many Whole Foods Market stores and Middle Eastern markets, but you may substitute regular couscous if that's what is available.

The spiced honey citrus dressing makes a flavorful addition to salad greens and sliced seasonal vegetables. You may also use it as a marinade for poultry, pork, seafood, or tofu.

TO PREPARE THE DRESSING In a large bowl, combine the cumin, cardamom, cinnamon, citrus juices, ginger, honey, lemon oil, and salt and pepper. Blend well, using a wire whisk or a handheld immersion blender. The dressing may be made a few days ahead and kept refrigerated.

TO PREPARE THE SALAD Preheat the oven to 375°F. Place the couscous on a baking pan. Roast the couscous for 10 minutes, until golden brown; cool and place the couscous in a bowl.

Combine the water with the turmeric, and bring to a boil. Pour the turmeric water over the couscous and cover. Simmer the couscous loosely covered for 10 to 15 minutes. Set aside, covered, for an additional

The Dressing

½ teaspoon cumin
¼ teaspoon cardamom
¼ teaspoon cinnamon
¼ cup lemon juice
¼ cup orange juice
1 tablespoon minced fresh ginger (1-inch piece)
1 tablespoon honey
¼ cup lemon oil (see page 9)
Salt and freshly ground pepper to taste

The Salad

1½ cups Israeli couscous
1½ cups water
¼ teaspoon turmeric
1 small red pepper, seeded and chopped
1 small yellow pepper, seeded and chopped
½ small red onion, minced
10 dried figs, sliced
10 dried apricots, sliced
½ cup raisins
1 cup shelled pistachios, toasted
½ cup minced fresh cilantro
1½ tablespoons grated orange zest

10 minutes, until all the water is absorbed and the couscous becomes tender. Use a fork to fluff the couscous, breaking up any lumps. Combine the plumped couscous with the peppers, onion, figs, apricots, raisins, pistachios, cilantro, and orange zest.

Pour the dressing over the salad, and mix together well.

PER SERVING: CALORIES 400; CALORIES FROM FAT 140; CALORIES FROM SATURATED FAT 20; PROTEIN 9 G; CARBOHYDRATE 61 G; TOTAL FAT 15 G; SATURATED FAT 2 G; CHOLESTEROL 0 MG; SODIUM 20 MG; 35% CALORIES FROM FAT

big and small salads

vegan

Lemon Capellini Salad

SERVES 8

SIMPLICITY is a powerful concept often overlooked in the kitchen. This salad, made with tender capellini pasta, has a bright citrus taste, complemented by the perfume of fresh basil and earthiness of roasted garlic. You may substitute additional extra-virgin olive oil in place of the lemon oil, if you prefer. Try to find the juiciest ripe tomatoes for this dish.

½ pound capellini

Grated zest of 1 lemon

¼ cup chopped fresh basil

¼ cup plus 2 tablespoons lemon juice

6 cloves roasted garlic, chopped
(see page 10)

⅛ cup extra-virgin olive oil

⅛ cup lemon oil (see page 9)

Salt and freshly ground pepper
to taste

1 pound plum tomatoes, diced

In a large pot of boiling salted water, cook the capellini until it is al dente, drain, and chill completely in an ice-water bath. When the pasta is completely chilled, drain it well and transfer it to a large bowl. Combine the lemon zest, basil, lemon juice, garlic, olive oil, lemon oil, and salt and pepper. Toss the capellini with the dressing. Add the tomatoes to the pasta, and gently toss.

PER SERVING: CALORIES 120; CALORIES FROM FAT 60; CALORIES FROM SATURATED FAT 10; PROTEIN 2 G; CARBOHYDRATE 14 G; TOTAL FAT 7 G; SATURATED FAT 1 G; CHOLESTEROL 0 MG; SODIUM 180 MG; 50% CALORIES FROM FAT

Smoked Mozzarella and Penne Salad

SERVES 8

The Parmesan Dressing

¼ cup grated Parmesan cheese

½ cup chopped parsley

½ cup mayonnaise

¼ cup white wine vinegar

3 cloves garlic, minced
(1½ teaspoons)

Pinch of cayenne pepper

Salt and freshly ground pepper to
taste

The Salad

½ pound penne pasta

2 cups packed baby spinach, washed
and stemmed

2 small jarred roasted red peppers,
diced

½ pound smoked mozzarella cheese,
diced

GREAT for parties, buffets, and simple dinners. Remember to fold in the fresh spinach just before serving to keep it crisp. This salad blows away the ubiquitous coleslaw or potato salads that turn up at every gathering. If you prefer, make this salad with regular mozzarella.

TO PREPARE THE PARMESAN DRESSING

Combine the Parmesan cheese, parsley, mayonnaise, vinegar, garlic, cayenne pepper, and salt and pepper with a hand mixer or in a the bowl of food processor or in a blender until the dressing is smooth.

TO PREPARE THE SALAD
In a large pot of boiling salted water, cook the pasta until it is al dente. Drain the pasta into a colander, run cold water over it or submerge it in ice water until chilled through, and drain well. In a large mixing bowl, combine the cooked pasta, spinach, roasted red peppers, and smoked mozzarella.

Toss the salad with the dressing. Serve immediately.

PER SERVING: CALORIES 190; CALORIES FROM FAT 100; CALORIES FROM SATURATED FAT 45; PROTEIN 11 G; CARBOHYDRATE 12 G; TOTAL FAT 11 G; SATURATED FAT 4.5 G; CHOLESTEROL 20 MG; SODIUM 380 MG; 53% CALORIES FROM FAT

 Recipe Bonus You may make this salad up to 2 days ahead of time; just add the spinach and dressing before serving. The pasta base keeps perfectly well for up to 3 days in the refrigerator.

vegetarian

Chilled Linguine with Gorgonzola and Basil

SERVES 8

THIS wonderful and extremely pungent ripe Italian blue cheese is buffered with cooked linguine and the sweetness of balsamic vinegar. Make sure you add the spinach just prior to serving so it just wilts nicely. For a nice addition, try this sliced with a ripe pear or an apple.

½ pound linguine (regular, spinach, or a mixture of both)

¼ cup balsamic vinegar

¼ cup extra-virgin olive oil

2 small cloves garlic, minced (1 teaspoon)

¼ cup chopped fresh basil

¼ teaspoon salt

½ tablespoon freshly ground pepper

3 cups baby spinach leaves, loosely packed, washed and cut into slices

4 ounces Gorgonzola or other blue cheese, crumbled

1 cup walnuts, toasted

3 scallions, sliced thinly and diagonally

In a large pot of boiling salted water, cook the linguine until it is al dente; drain and chill the pasta in an ice bath until chilled through.

To prepare the dressing, combine the balsamic vinegar, olive oil, garlic, basil, salt, and pepper with a hand mixer or in the bowl of a food processor or in a blender.

Mix the cooked pasta, spinach, cheese, walnuts, scallions, and vinaigrette together well.

PER SERVING: CALORIES 260; CALORIES FROM FAT 180; CALORIES FROM SATURATED FAT 40; PROTEIN 9 G; CARBOHYDRATE 12 G; TOTAL FAT 20 G; SATURATED FAT 4.5 G; CHOLESTEROL 15 MG; SODIUM 270 MG; 69% CALORIES FROM FAT

Tip from the Team: To get a high-quality, refined, aged balsamic flavor from your average vinegar, simmer over medium heat until reduced by half. Cool and store as usual.

Recipe Bonus Don't rinse the pasta, and serve this salad warm as a side dish; it takes on a different personality as the cheese flavor intensifies and the spinach softens against the crunchy walnuts.

Barley Primavera

1¼ cups pearled barley

6 cups water

¼ cup canola oil

4 cloves garlic, minced (2 teaspoons)

1 large red pepper, seeded and
chopped

1 small green pepper, seeded and
chopped

1 small yellow pepper, seeded and
chopped

¼ cup minced parsley

1 small zucchini, chopped

1 small yellow squash, chopped

1 medium carrot, grated

3 scallions, sliced thinly and diagonally

½ cup raspberry vinegar

1 teaspoon salt

½ teaspoon freshly ground pepper

BARLEY has been around since the Stone Age and has been used in countless ways since then for both medicinal and culinary purposes. Pearled barley has had the outer husk and bran layers removed through a polishing process. Primavera refers to springtime vegetables, and you may add any fresh colorful seasonal vegetables to this salad. Soft, comforting barley absorbs the raspberry vinegar, which adds a welcome tart flavor. Try this salad with sherry vinegar as well.

Place the barley and water into a saucepan. Bring the water to a boil, cover the pan with a lid, and simmer the barley for 20 minutes, until tender. When the barley is cooked, drain it well and chill completely.

Heat the canola oil and garlic in a small sauté pan over low heat. Slowly cook the garlic for 2 minutes, until golden brown, and transfer to a large mixing bowl. In the same bowl, combine the peppers, parsley, zucchini, yellow squash, carrot, and scallions with the cooked barley. Add the vinegar and season with the salt and pepper.

PER SERVING: CALORIES 190; CALORIES FROM FAT 70; CALORIES FROM SATURATED FAT 5; PROTEIN 4 G; CARBOHYDRATE 30 G; TOTAL FAT 7 G; SATURATED FAT 0.5 G; CHOLESTEROL 0 MG; SODIUM 250 MG; 37% CALORIES FROM FAT

big and small salads

vegan

Wild Rice with Pecans and Dried Cranberries

SERVES 6

SOME ingredients are destined to end up in the same dish. Nutty, chewy wild rice belongs with toasted pecans and sweet sun-dried cranberries in this entrée salad. These perfectly suited food mates are bound together by a light and tart raspberry vinaigrette. You'll notice that wild rice needs to be cooked in much more liquid than does any other rice.

The Balsamic-Raspberry Dressing

3 tablespoons balsamic vinegar

3 tablespoons raspberry vinegar

¼ cup extra-virgin olive oil

Salt and freshly ground pepper to taste

TO PREPARE THE BALSAMIC-RASPBERRY DRESSING Combine the vinegars, olive oil, and salt and pepper with a hand mixer or in the bowl of a food processor or in a blender until smooth.

TO PREPARE THE SALAD Place the wild rice and water in a saucepan, and bring to a boil. Cover the rice, reduce the heat to a simmer, and cook for about 45 minutes, or until the rice is tender. Drain the rice, and chill it completely in the refrigerator for at least 1 hour.

Place the cooked rice in a large mixing bowl. Add the pecan halves, pepper, cranberries, parsley, and scallions. Combine the dressing with the salad ingredients, and mix well.

The Salad

1 cup wild rice

4 cups water

1 cup pecan halves, toasted

1 yellow pepper, seeded and diced

½ cup dried cranberries

½ cup minced parsley

4 scallions, sliced thinly and diagonally

PER SERVING: CALORIES 380; CALORIES FROM FAT 210; CALORIES FROM SATURATED FAT 20; PROTEIN 6 G; CARBOHYDRATE 43 G; TOTAL FAT 23 G; SATURATED FAT 2.5 G; CHOLESTEROL 0 MG; SODIUM 330 MG; 55% CALORIES FROM FAT

 Recipe Bonus The rice may be cooked up to 2 days before you make the salad.

Wheat Berries with Green Chilies and Roasted Pumpkin Seeds

SERVES 8

1 ½ cups wheat berries

¾ cup brown rice

1 ½ cups pumpkin seeds

2 whole jalapeño peppers

1 (16-ounce) can red kidney beans, drained and rinsed

¼ cup plus 1 tablespoon lime juice

½ cup minced fresh cilantro

¼ cup plus 2 tablespoons extra-virgin olive oil

1 ¼ teaspoons salt

ALTHOUGH most of us are familiar with many products made from wheat, few people know the pleasures of flavorful whole wheat berries. They are also called groats and are the unprocessed whole wheat kernel. These tiny round berries take an hour to cook unless you soak them overnight. The rewards are a hearty-flavored and chewy-textured food that works well in many recipes, from soups and stews to salad toppings. In this versatile salad spicy jalapeños and nutty roasted pumpkin seeds are enhanced by fresh lime juice and cilantro. It is best served at room temperature. This salad may easily be made into enchiladas by rolling the wheat berry salad in a flour tortilla, or into quesadillas by sandwiching it between two flour tortillas along with a handful of grated cheese. It also makes a great base for the addition of cooked chopped chicken, shrimp, or tofu.

Cover the wheat berries with water and soak at room temperature overnight. After soaking, place the wheat berries in a large saucepan with 8 cups of water. Bring to a boil, reduce the heat, and simmer uncovered for 40 minutes, until tender. Drain and chill in the refrigerator completely.

Place the rice into a small saucepan with 1¾ cups of water. Bring to a boil, cover, reduce the heat, and simmer for 35 to 40 minutes, until the rice is cooked and all the liquid has been absorbed. Chill in the refrigerator completely.

Place the pumpkin seeds and jalapeños on a sheet pan in a 400°F. oven for 10 minutes, until the pumpkin seeds are brown and crisp and the jalapeños are browned. Cool at room temperature. Remove the seeds from the chilies, and chop the peppers.

In a large bowl, mix the wheat berries, rice, pumpkin seeds, roasted peppers, beans, lime juice, cilantro, olive oil, and salt. Combine well and serve.

PER SERVING: CALORIES 420; CALORIES FROM FAT 210; CALORIES FROM SATURATED FAT 35; PROTEIN 15 G; CARBOHYDRATE 45 G; TOTAL FAT 23 G; SATURATED FAT 3.5 G; CHOLESTEROL 0 MG; SODIUM 420 MG; 50% CALORIES FROM FAT

big and small salads

Thai Black Rice Salad

SERVES 8

SWEET and aromatic black Japonica rice is a unique blend of both medium-grain mahogany-colored rice and black rice, both originating in Japan. Japonica rice has striking visual appeal in addition to its unique earthy taste, making it a great dish for entertaining. Sweet bell peppers and roasted cashews blend well in this dish. Japonica also makes great new-wave rice pudding.

TO PREPARE THE SESAME-GINGER DRESSING
Purée the toasted sesame oil, tamari, brown rice syrup, red chili flakes, minced garlic, and ginger with a hand mixer or in the bowl of a food processor or in a blender.

TO PREPARE THE SALAD Place the Japonica rice and water into a covered saucepan and bring to a boil. Reduce the heat to a simmer, cover the rice, and cook it over low heat for about 35 minutes, or until the rice is tender. The rice will remain chewy. Transfer the cooked rice to a large mixing bowl, and while it's still warm add the peppers, carrot, cashews, and scallions. Add the dressing, and combine well. Although this dish may be served chilled, it is best when served at room temperature.

The Sesame-Ginger Dressing
1/4 cup plus 1 tablespoon toasted sesame oil
1/4 cup plus 2 tablespoons tamari
1/8 cup brown rice syrup
1/4 teaspoon crushed red chili flakes
2 cloves garlic, minced (1 teaspoon)
1 tablespoon grated fresh ginger (1-inch piece)

The Salad
2 cups black Japonica rice
2 1/2 cups water
1 medium green pepper, seeded and chopped
1 medium red pepper, seeded and chopped
1 small carrot, grated
1 cup cashews, toasted
5 scallions, sliced thinly and diagonally

PER SERVING: CALORIES 410; CALORIES FROM FAT 160; CALORIES FROM SATURATED FAT 25; PROTEIN 8 G; CARBOHYDRATE 57 G; TOTAL FAT 18 G; SATURATED FAT 3 G; CHOLESTEROL 0 MG; SODIUM 830 MG; 39% CALORIES FROM FAT

Quinoa Tabbouleh

SERVES 6

2 cups quinoa, rinsed well

3½ cups water

2 cups chopped parsley

1 pound plum tomatoes, seeded, diced small

¼ cup plus 2 tablespoons lemon juice

¼ cup plus 2 tablespoons extra-virgin olive oil

3 small cloves garlic, minced (1½ teaspoons)

1½ tablespoons minced fresh mint

½ teaspoon salt

½ teaspoon freshly ground pepper

GROWN high in the Andes, quinoa is an ancient grain rich with history and flavor. This tiny protein-packed seed has a buttery taste and flavor similar to popcorn and is as simple to cook as rice. Here we take a classic Middle Eastern salad and replace the cracked wheat with quinoa. The golden color of quinoa looks appealing next to ripe tomatoes and emerald green mint.

Place the quinoa into a fine-mesh colander. Rinse the quinoa under cold running water; drain well. Place the quinoa and water in a saucepan and cover. Bring to a boil, reduce the heat to a simmer, and cook the quinoa over low heat for 20 minutes, until it is tender and the liquid is absorbed. Fluff the quinoa grains with a fork, and spread them out evenly on a plate to chill completely before mixing with the remaining ingredients.

Combine the cooked quinoa, parsley, tomatoes, lemon juice, olive oil, garlic, and mint. Season with the salt and pepper.

PER SERVING: CALORIES 260; CALORIES FROM FAT 45; CALORIES FROM SATURATED FAT 5; PROTEIN 9 G; CARBOHYDRATE 46 G; TOTAL FAT 5 G; SATURATED FAT 0.5 G; CHOLESTEROL 0 MG; SODIUM 190 MG; 17% CALORIES FROM FAT

Variation: Quinoa Tabbouleh may be served as a light entrée by stuffing it into a tomato or roasted pepper. For an impressive, more substantial vegetarian entrée, hollow out a 1-pound block of firm tofu; marinate it with a bit of soy sauce or Roasted Sesame–Honey Dressing (page 334); bake it on a baking pan in a 375°F. oven for 20 minutes, until golden brown; and fill it with the tabbouleh. This stuffed tofu boat will serve two.

big and small salads

109

Spinach, Beet, and Walnut Salad

SERVES 4

THIS salad is so . . . California, even though it hails from our New England stores. It is just plain elegant and bursting with vibrant sweet beet taste. The combination of bitter endive, sweet beets, earthy walnut oil, and tart sherry vinegar make this salad memorable. The mild goat cheese combines with the other unusual ingredients to elevate this salad to a dish worthy of the most food-savvy guests.

The Walnut Dressing

⅛ cup walnut oil

3 tablespoons sherry vinegar

3 tablespoons minced shallot

The Salad

4 small beets, unpeeled and washed well

6 ounces baby spinach leaves, washed and stemmed

2 Belgian endives, thinly sliced

¾ plus ½ cup walnuts, toasted

Salt and freshly ground pepper to taste

4 ounces mild goat cheese such as Montrachet, crumbled

TO PREPARE THE WALNUT DRESSING Whisk the walnut oil, sherry wine vinegar, and shallot together in a small bowl.

TO PREPARE THE SALAD Scrub the beets; remove the stems and root ends. Steam or boil the beets for approximately 20 minutes, until tender when pierced with a sharp knife; chill completely. When the beets are chilled, gently remove the outer peel and cut the beets into thin wedges. Dress the beet wedges with a small amount of the dressing.

In a medium bowl, combine the spinach, Belgian endives, the ¾ cup walnuts, and the remaining dressing. Mix well. Season the greens with the salt and pepper. Divide the salad mixture onto 4 salad plates. Arrange the beets on the salad plates. Sprinkle the top of each salad with the crumbled Montrachet, and top with the remaining ½ cup toasted walnuts.

PER SERVING: CALORIES 360; CALORIES FROM FAT 280; CALORIES FROM SATURATED FAT 70; PROTEIN 12 G; CARBOHYDRATES 13 G; TOTAL FAT 31 G; SATURATED FAT 8 G; CHOLESTEROL 20 MG; SODIUM 230 MG; 78% CALORIES FROM FAT

 Recipe Bonus This is a great salad for entertaining, because the beets may be cooked up to 2 days prior to assembling the salad, and the dressing may also be made a few days ahead. Just toss it all together when it's time for dinner.

Fattoush

SERVES 4

The Lemony Dressing

1/8 cup lemon juice

3 tablespoons red wine vinegar

1/4 cup extra-virgin olive oil

3 cloves garlic, minced
(1 1/2 teaspoons)

2 teaspoons sumac

Salt and freshly ground pepper to
taste

The Salad

6 cups romaine lettuce, cut in bite-
size pieces

1 large cucumber, peeled, seeded, and
chopped

1/2 small red onion, minced

2 large tomatoes, chopped

3/4 cup parsley, chopped

1/2 cup chopped fresh mint

2 pieces of pita bread, stale (leave out
unwrapped for several hours or
toast), torn into bite-size pieces

TOASTED pita bread makes this traditional Lebanese salad unusual. The dry pita soaks up the tart vinaigrette and blends well with the crisp vegetables. Ground sumac is a ruddy burgundy-colored spice made from the berries of a bush that grows wild in the Middle East and in parts of Italy. It has a lemony, fruity flavor and can be found in most Middle Eastern grocery stores. Once you have it in the house, you will find yourself sprinkling it on everything. This colorful salad is great for entertaining; it's always the center of conversation.

TO PREPARE THE LEMONY DRESSING In a small bowl, combine the lemon juice, red wine vinegar, olive oil, garlic, sumac, and salt and pepper.

TO PREPARE THE SALAD Combine the romaine, cucumber, red onion, tomatoes, parsley, mint, and torn pita in a large bowl.

Just before serving the salad, gently toss with the dressing.

PER SERVING: CALORIES 260; CALORIES FROM FAT 130; CALORIES FROM SATURATED FAT 20; PROTEIN 6 G; CARBOHYDRATE 29 G; TOTAL FAT 14 G; SATURATED FAT 2 G; CHOLESTEROL 0 MG; SODIUM 190 MG; 50% CALORIES FROM FAT

vegan

Essential Sea Vegetable Salad

SERVES 8

SEAWEED is a good source of concentrated minerals, with an appealing briny, naturally salty flavor (see "Whole Foods Glossary," page 395). (We like to call them sea vegetables as opposed to seaweed; it sounds much more appetizing.) They provide a crunchy texture that no other raw ingredient offers. Most sea vegetables, with the exception of mild, purple-hued dulse, need to be reconstituted in water before use. Dulse is also available smoked, which adds a nice underlying flavor.

Try this with the Spicy Asian Flank Steak (page 142) or Teriyaki Turkey Burgers with Green Onion and Ginger (page 217), or add it to sandwiches to provide a nice crunch.

- 1 ounce arame
- 1 ounce hijiki
- 1 ounce dulse, cut into strips
- 1 cup grated carrots
- ¼ pound baby spinach leaves, washed and stemmed
- ⅛ cup tamari or soy sauce
- 1 tablespoon minced fresh ginger (1-inch piece)
- ½ cup sunflower seeds, toasted
- 3 tablespoons extra-virgin olive oil
- ⅛ cup brown rice vinegar

Place the arame and hijiki in a large bowl. Bring 2 cups of water to a boil and pour it over the arame and hijiki. Allow the sea vegetables to soak for 30 minutes before draining them into a colander and rinsing with cold water.

Place the plumped sea vegetables in a mixing bowl; add the dulse, carrots, spinach, tamari, ginger, sunflower seeds, olive oil, and rice vinegar, and mix well.

NOTE: Sea vegetable slaw makes a delicious sandwich topping. Drain the excess moisture before adding to your favorite sandwich. Also makes a great partner for grilled fish or shellfish.

PER SERVING: CALORIES 140; CALORIES FROM FAT 90; CALORIES FROM SATURATED FAT 10; PROTEIN 9 G; CARBOHYDRATE 15 G; TOTAL FAT 10 G; SATURATED FAT 1 G; CHOLESTEROL 0 MG; SODIUM 180 MG; 64% CALORIES FROM FAT

"It's Alive" Salad

vegan

SERVES 8

½ pound firm tofu, cut into ½-inch
dice

1½ tablespoons tamari

The Sesame-Tamari Dressing

3 tablespoons toasted sesame oil

⅛ cup Szechwan sauce

3 tablespoons tamari

3 tablespoons brown rice vinegar

1 tablespoon sugar

The Salad

¼ pound pea green sprouts

¼ pound sunflower sprouts

1 cup mung bean sprouts

6 large button mushrooms, sliced

4 scallions, sliced diagonally

1 cup grated carrots

ALTHOUGH sprouts were once looked upon as typical hard-core health food, they have now become a common sight in many stores and salad bars. Their fresh, delicate flavor has been appreciated for centuries by Asian cultures. This living salad is vibrant and refreshing. It must be tossed in the dressing just before you serve it so that the sprouts stay crisp. You may use any combination of sprouts; each has its own taste, texture, and shape. (Premixed sprout combinations that include sprouted lentils, chickpeas, daikon, or adzuki beans are often available.)

Preheat the oven to 400°F. Gently toss the diced tofu with the 1½ tablespoons tamari. Lay the tofu in a single layer on a foil-lined baking sheet. Bake the tofu for about 20 minutes, or until lightly golden. Transfer to a bowl and chill completely.

TO PREPARE THE SESAME-TAMARI DRESSING
In a mixing bowl, with a wire whisk, combine the sesame oil, Szechwan sauce, 3 tablespoons tamari, brown rice vinegar, and sugar.

TO PREPARE THE SALAD Gently mix the sprouts, mushrooms, scallions, carrots, and tofu.

Toss the salad with the dressing just before serving. Serve immediately.

PER SERVING: CALORIES 130; CALORIES FROM FAT 50; CALORIES FROM SATURATED FAT 10; PROTEIN 7 G; CARBOHYDRATE 14 G; TOTAL FAT 6 G; SATURATED FAT 1 G; CHOLESTEROL 0 MG; SODIUM 630 MG; 38% CALORIES FROM FAT

big and small salads

Thai Cucumber Salad

SERVES 8

THIS Thai-inspired salad is a good example of multi-ethnic global cuisine. If you have access to Thai bird chilies, they make an authentic alternative to jalapeños, although they are somewhat spicier. The tart lemon flavor and intense citrus aroma of lemongrass is commonly found in many Thai dishes. The delicate, clean-tasting cucumbers make a nice foil to the pungent lemongrass and chilies in this salad.

TO PREPARE THE CURRY-LEMONGRASS DRESSING In a bowl, combine the brown rice vinegar, sugar, curry powder, garlic, lemongrass, and salt.

TO PREPARE THE SALAD In a large bowl, combine the cucumbers, jalapeño, scallions, and cilantro and marinate with the dressing 15 to 20 minutes before serving. Roughly chop the peanuts and sprinkle over the top of the salad just before serving.

PER SERVING: CALORIES 100; CALORIES FROM FAT 60; CALORIES FROM SATURATED FAT 10; PROTEIN 4 G; CARBOHYDRATE 8 G; TOTAL FAT 7 G; SATURATED FAT 1 G; CHOLESTEROL 0 MG; SODIUM 120 MG; 60% CALORIES FROM FAT

The Curry-Lemongrass Dressing

1/2 cup brown rice vinegar

2 teaspoons sugar

1 teaspoon curry powder

1 large clove garlic, minced (1/4 teaspoon)

2 stalks lemongrass, white part only, minced

1/2 teaspoon salt

The Salad

2 pounds cucumbers (about 6 medium ones), peeled in stripes, seeded, and thinly sliced

1 jalapeño pepper, seeded and minced

3 scallions, sliced thinly and diagonally

1/4 cup minced fresh cilantro

3/4 cup dry roasted peanuts

 Recipe Bonus Serve this salad over uncooked, washed kale or Swiss chard leaves for a beautiful presentation. Try adding some sliced apple or chunks of orange to this salad.

Algerian Eggplant Salad

SERVES 8

¼ cup plus 2 tablespoons extra-virgin
   olive oil

I teaspoon turmeric

I teaspoon cumin

½ teaspoon crushed red chili flakes

½ cup lime juice

8 cloves garlic, minced (4 teaspoons)

I cup minced fresh cilantro

3 pounds eggplant, peeled and cut
   lengthwise into 1-inch-thick slices

I pound plum tomatoes, cut in half
   lengthwise

4 medium green peppers, halved and
   seeded

2 small jalapeño peppers, halved and
   seeded

Salt to taste

THE grilled vegetables appearing in this salad have a sweet, smoky flavor that complements the lime juice. The exotic spices that flavor this salad are commonly used in the North African spice mixture called dersa, which is the Algerian equivalent of curry powder. This makes a great entrée salad and may also be used as a sandwich filling. Try slightly hollowing out a baguette, filling it with the vegetable mixture, adding some hummus or sharp cheese, and pressing the baguette between two plates for about an hour.

To make the marinade, in a bowl, combine the olive oil, turmeric, cumin, red chili flakes, lime juice, garlic, and half the cilantro. Gently toss and marinate the eggplant, tomatoes, green peppers, and jalapeño peppers in the marinade at room temperature for at least 30 minutes.

Preheat the grill so that you can hold your hand 4 inches above the surface for a count of 4 seconds. Grill all the vegetables for 4 to 5 minutes on each side, until cooked but not mushy.

Chill the vegetables completely. Cut the tomatoes into wedges, cut the eggplant and green peppers into bite-size pieces, and mince the jalapeño peppers. Gently toss all the vegetables together with the remaining cilantro. Season with the salt.

PER SERVING: CALORIES 180; CALORIES FROM FAT 100; CALORIES FROM SATURATED FAT 15; PROTEIN 3 G; CARBOHYDRATE 21 G; TOTAL FAT 11 G; SATURATED FAT 1.5 G; CHOLESTEROL 0 MG; SODIUM 20 MG; 55% CALORIES FROM FAT

big and small salads

Chipotle Potato Salad

SERVES 8

CHIPOTLES are actually smoked dried jalapeños. They are available in several forms: dried, pickled, and (our preference) canned in adobo sauce. Chipotles in adobo sauce are slightly sweet, smoky, and have an almost chocolate-like flavor. Here they add a warm touch to the boiled potatoes. Kernels of corn and the red peppers add a sweet crunch while sharp cilantro rounds out this salad. Serve at room temperature for best flavor or warm for a nice change of pace.

TO PREPARE THE CHIPOTLE DRESSING Combine the chipotle pepper and adobo sauce, garlic, olive oil, vinegar, pepper, and salt in a blender until puréed, or combine all the ingredients in a mixing bowl with a wire whisk.

TO PREPARE THE SALAD Steam or boil the potatoes for about 20 minutes, or until cooked through but still firm. Chill the potatoes completely. Transfer the potatoes to a large mixing bowl, and add the diced peppers, onion, corn, and cilantro.

Toss the salad with the dressing, and serve.

PER SERVING: CALORIES 180; CALORIES FROM FAT 80; CALORIES FROM SATURATED FAT 10; PROTEIN 4 G; CARBOHYDRATE 23 G; TOTAL FAT 9 G; SATURATED FAT 1 G; CHOLESTEROL 0 MG; SODIUM 10 MG; 44% CALORIES FROM FAT

The Chipotle Dressing

1 canned chipotle pepper in
   1/8 cup adobo sauce
3 small cloves garlic, minced
   (1 1/2 teaspoons)
1/4 cup plus 1 tablespoon extra-virgin
   olive oil
1/4 cup white wine vinegar
1/4 teaspoon freshly ground pepper
Salt to taste

The Salad

2 pounds small red potatoes,
   unpeeled and quartered
1/2 medium red pepper, diced
1/2 medium green pepper, diced
1/2 small red onion, diced
1 1/2 cups corn kernels, fresh or
   frozen
1/4 cup minced fresh cilantro

 Recipe Bonus Try this potato salad warm served underneath a grilled chicken breast or lean grilled sausage. Just add a warm loaf of sourdough or rosemary bread for a rustic dinner.

Chipotle Chilies

CHIPOTLE chilies add a robust, smoky flavor to sauces, soups, marinades, and stews. They are not a variety of chili pepper but are actually smoked, dried jalapeño peppers.

Chipotles are strong in flavor and a little goes a long way. They can be found dried or canned in adobo sauce, which is a tomato-based thick purée that can be incorporated into recipes along with the chilies.

vegan

Japanese Kale Salad with Shiitake Mushrooms

SERVES 8

KALE used to be the stuff that supermarkets garnished their seafood cases with. It's now one of the darlings of the cruciferous plant kingdom. While others have been decorating with it, we have been serving kale for years. Shredded kale is paired with shiitake mushrooms, the meaty full-flavored Asian mushroom that is linked to many potential health benefits. This combination of ingredients offers the perfect balance of sweet, sour, bitter, and salty. If you like a bit of spice, add a sprinkling of crushed red chili flakes.

The Tamari Dressing

¼ cup tamari

⅛ cup brown rice vinegar

⅛ cup canola oil

The Salad

1 cup packed dry arame

2 cups boiling water

2 teaspoons canola oil

⅛ cup sesame oil

½ pound shiitake mushrooms, sliced (2 cups)

2 bunches kale, chopped (6 to 8 cups)

1 cup grated carrots

½ cup grated daikon radish

3 tablespoons sesame seeds, toasted

TO PREPARE THE TAMARI DRESSING In a bowl, combine the tamari, brown rice vinegar, and canola oil. Blend well and reserve.

TO PREPARE THE SALAD Cover the arame with the boiling water, and allow it to soak for 30 minutes. Drain and rinse the arame under cold water. While the arame is soaking, heat the oils over high heat in a small sauté pan. When the oil is very hot, sauté the shiitake mushrooms until golden brown; cool.

Steam or microwave the kale in ¼ cup water for 3 minutes until bright green; immediately remove the kale and plunge into an ice-water bath to stop the cooking process. Gently squeeze the water out of the kale and fluff it up in a bowl.

Combine the cooked kale, plumped arame, carrots, daikon, sautéed mushrooms, and sesame seeds in a large bowl. Just before serving, gently toss the salad with the dressing.

PER SERVING: CALORIES 140; CALORIES FROM FAT 90; CALORIES FROM SATURATED FAT 10; PROTEIN 4 G; CARBOHYDRATE 9 G; TOTAL FAT 10 G; SATURATED FAT 1 G; CHOLESTEROL 0 MG; SODIUM 540 MG; 64% CALORIES FROM FAT

Southern-Style Power Slaw

vegetarian

SERVES 8

The Cajun Dressing

1 cup mayonnaise

⅛ cup Dijon mustard

3 tablespoons sugar

3 tablespoons cider vinegar

1½ teaspoons Cajun spices

1 teaspoon salt

The Salad

6 cups thinly sliced green cabbage

4 cups thinly sliced red cabbage

4 large collard green leaves, thinly
sliced

6 scallions, thinly sliced

UNCOOKED collard greens, a member of the leafy cruciferous vegetable family, add a unique crunchy texture and fresh herblike taste to this beautiful pale green salad. Dijon mustard and Cajun spice add some heat to the dressing for this slaw, which can be served as a side dish or used as a sandwich topping. Try some over a grilled chicken breast sandwich.

TO PREPARE THE CAJUN DRESSING Combine the mayonnaise, mustard, sugar, vinegar, Cajun spice, and salt in a mixing bowl large enough to hold the salad ingredients. Mix well with a wire whisk until combined.

TO PREPARE THE SALAD Combine the cabbages, collard greens, and scallions in the bowl with the dressing, and mix until combined well. Allow to marinate for 1 hour before serving.

PER SERVING: CALORIES 130; CALORIES FROM FAT 100; CALORIES FROM SATURATED FAT 20; PROTEIN 1 G; CARBOHYDRATE 6 G; TOTAL FAT 11 G; SATURATED FAT 2 G; CHOLESTEROL 10 MG; SODIUM 290 MG; 77% CALORIES FROM FAT

Cruciferous Vegetables

REMEMBER when your mother told you to eat your broccoli? She knew what she was talking about. Cruciferous vegetables are the family that includes broccoli, artichokes, brussels sprouts, turnips, rutabagas, and leafy greens such as kale, collard greens, chard, and bok choy. These vegetables contain compounds that appear to be effective in protecting against some forms of cancer. Cruciferous vegetables also contain sizable quantities of fiber as well as the antioxidant nutrients beta-carotene and vitamin C.

big and small salads

119

Szechwan Slaw

SERVES 8

THIS is not your traditional slaw—it has a crisp, clean flavor balanced by rice vinegar and sugar. Grated fresh ginger adds a pungent kick. Crunchy and refreshing, this slaw works well on a sandwich or wrapped in lettuce leaves. You may also mix it with diced tofu or shredded chicken.

TO PREPARE THE SZECHWAN DRESSING In a bowl, combine the vinegar, canola oil, sugar, ginger, red chili flakes, cilantro, and salt. Set aside.

TO PREPARE THE SALAD Combine the red and green cabbages, red pepper, scallions, carrot, snow peas, and sesame seeds. Fifteen minutes before serving time, toss the cabbage mixture with the dressing, as this allows the flavors to meld while keeping the crisp vegetables intact.

PER SERVING: CALORIES 130; CALORIES FROM FAT 70; CALORIES FROM SATURATED FAT 5; PROTEIN 2 G; CARBOHYDRATE 13 G; TOTAL FAT 8 G; SATURATED FAT 0.5 G; CHOLESTEROL 0 MG; SODIUM 20 MG; 54% CALORIES FROM FAT

 Tip from the Team: Try placing a piece of plastic wrap across your grater next time you need to grate ginger—it will all stick to the plastic, and once you peel the plastic off after you're finished grating, you'll be able to use every single spicy drop.

The Szechwan Dressing

¼ cup rice wine vinegar

¼ cup canola oil

¼ cup sugar

2 teaspoons grated fresh ginger

¼ teaspoon crushed red chili flakes

¼ cup minced fresh cilantro

Salt to taste

The Salad

3 cups thinly sliced red cabbage

3 cups thinly sliced green cabbage

1 large red pepper, seeded and thinly sliced

4 scallions, sliced thinly and diagonally

1 large carrot, grated

¼ pound snow peas, sliced thinly and diagonally

⅛ cup black sesame seeds

Sonoma Chicken Salad

The Dressing

1 cup mayonnaise

4 teaspoons cider vinegar

5 teaspoons honey

2 teaspoons poppy seeds

Salt and freshly ground white pepper
to taste

The Salad

2 pounds boneless and skinless
chicken breasts

¾ cup pecan pieces, toasted

2 cups red seedless grapes

3 stalks celery, thinly sliced

SONOMA Chicken Salad is one of our classic Whole Foods Market dishes. The origin is shrouded in mystery because no one remembers who created this gem. However, the taste of this salad is known throughout our stores. The tender chicken breast, crunchy pecans, and the juicy bursting of sweet grapes with each bite are hard to top. Poppy seeds help orchestrate flavors and textures into one of the best chicken salads you will ever find.

TO PREPARE THE DRESSING In a bowl, combine the mayonnaise, vinegar, honey, poppy seeds, and salt and pepper. Reserve the dressing in the refrigerator. This step may be done 2 days prior to mixing the salad.

TO PREPARE THE SALAD Preheat the oven to 375°F. Place the chicken breasts in one layer in a baking dish with ½ cup water. Cover the dish with foil, and bake the chicken breasts for 25 minutes, until cooked completely through. Remove the chicken breasts from the pan, cool slightly at room temperature, and then completely chill, lightly covered with plastic wrap, in the refrigerator. When the breasts are cold, dice them into bite-size pieces, and transfer the pieces to a large bowl.

Combine the chicken with the pecans, grapes, celery, and dressing.

PER SERVING: CALORIES 520; CALORIES FROM FAT 260; CALORIES FROM SATURATED FAT 45; PROTEIN 46 G; CARBOHYDRATE 21 G; TOTAL FAT 29 G; SATURATED FAT 5 G; CHOLESTEROL 115 MG; SODIUM 490 MG; 50% CALORIES FROM FAT

Variation: Sonoma Chicken Salad makes a great sandwich and is also comfortable atop a bed of field greens. This entrée salad is also delicious when stuffed inside a melon half for brunch or dinner.

big and small salads

Blackened Chicken Salad

SERVES 6

CAJUN seasoning, or blackening spices, is very popular in New Orleans. Made with a blend of up to twenty herbs and spices, it can be used to liven up many foods. This entrée salad is good for simple sandwiches or beautifully arranged salad plates with greens and sliced seasonal vegetables. A heavy-bottom cast-iron skillet works best for blackening (if you don't own one, you may want to remedy that—they are inexpensive and may be used for many dishes), but you can use a regular skillet, as well.

The Mustard Dressing

1 cup mayonnaise
¼ cup Dijon mustard
¼ cup cider vinegar

The Salad

2½ pounds boneless skinless chicken breasts
⅛ cup canola oil
⅓ cup Cajun seasoning (see Note)
1 large carrot, grated
½ red onion, minced
3 scallions, sliced thinly and diagonally

TO PREPARE THE MUSTARD DRESSING
Combine the mayonnaise, mustard, and vinegar in a large mixing bowl. Set aside.

TO PREPARE THE SALAD Brush one side of the chicken breasts with half the canola oil, sprinkle with half the Cajun seasoning, and press the seasoning onto the chicken breasts, using your hand or the back of a spoon. Turn the chicken breasts over and repeat the seasoning process.

Heat a cast-iron skillet until it is very hot. Carefully place the chicken breasts into the pan. Cook the breasts without moving them for 5 minutes on each side. Transfer the iron pan to the oven or transfer the breasts to a baking sheet and finish cooking in a 375°F. oven for 10 minutes, until cooked through and well browned. Chill the chicken breasts completely. Cut the chicken into bite-size pieces.

Transfer the chicken to a large bowl and add the carrot, onion, and scallions. Add the dressing, and mix well.

NOTE: If you wish to make your own Cajun seasoning, try the following recipe for Cajun Spice, which will last for 4 to 6 months, then lose some of its punch.

PER SERVING: CALORIES 500; CALORIES FROM FAT 220; CALORIES FROM SATURATED FAT 40; PROTEIN 56 G; CARBOHYDRATE 9 G; TOTAL FAT 25 G; SATURATED FAT 4.5 G; CHOLESTEROL 145 MG; SODIUM 1,980 MG; 44% CALORIES FROM FAT

Cajun Spice

1/4 cup plus 1 tablespoon paprika

1/8 cup dried thyme

1/8 cup dried oregano

1 tablespoon cumin powder

1 tablespoon onion powder

1/8 cup garlic powder

1/8 cup dried sweet basil

1 tablespoon freshly ground black pepper

1 tablespoon freshly ground white pepper

1 tablespoon cayenne pepper

1/8 cup salt

Combine all the ingredients in the bowl of a food processor and pulse until well blended or mix thoroughly in a large bowl with a spoon or wire whisk. Keep stored in a covered jar in a cool dark place for up to 6 months.

big and small salads

Enlightened Caesar Chicken Salad

SERVES 6

YOU ask, "Why enlightened?" Because traditionally Caesar salad is made with lots of egg yolks and oil, and this one isn't.

This is actually a simple way to make a very unusual chicken salad. When baked, the Parmesan cheese browns onto the surface of the chicken. This caramelized cheese crust imparts a sharp flavor to the dressing after the salad has been put together. We recommend making this salad a few hours before serving it so the flavors marry. You may marinate the chicken overnight with the olive oil mixture for added flavor. Serve this entrée salad stuffed into a pineapple or melon for a great luncheon. Also, try it on a bed of leaf spinach garnished with roasted piquillo peppers.

1 tablespoon extra-virgin olive oil
⅛ cup lemon juice
2 cloves garlic, minced (1 teaspoon)
¼ teaspoon freshly ground pepper

2 pounds boneless skinless chicken breasts
½ cup grated Parmesan cheese

½ cup chopped parsley
2 stalks celery, chopped
¼ cup mayonnaise
1 tablespoon plain yogurt
Salt and freshly ground pepper to taste

Preheat the oven to 375°F. In a large bowl, mix the olive oil, lemon juice, garlic, and ¼ teaspoon pepper together. Toss the chicken breasts in this marinade, and then place them in a single layer on a baking pan. Sprinkle the chicken with half the Parmesan cheese.

Bake the chicken for 20 minutes and then chill completely. Cut the chicken into bite-size pieces. Combine the chicken with the remaining Parmesan cheese and the parsley, celery, mayonnaise, and yogurt, and season with the salt and pepper.

PER SERVING: CALORIES 330; CALORIES FROM FAT 110; CALORIES FROM SATURATED FAT 35; PROTEIN 48 G; CARBOHYDRATE 3 G; TOTAL FAT 13 G; SATURATED FAT 4 G; CHOLESTEROL 125 MG; SODIUM 350 MG; 38% CALORIES FROM FAT

Mediterranean Tuna Salad

SERVES 6

4 (6-ounce) cans albacore tuna,
   drained well

1 (14-ounce) can quartered artichoke
   hearts, drained well

½ cup chopped red pepper

¾ cup sliced Greek olives

½ small red onion, minced

¼ cup minced Italian parsley

¼ cup minced fresh basil

2 cloves garlic, minced (1 teaspoon)

1 teaspoon dried oregano, or
   1 tablespoon fresh

1 cup mayonnaise

3 tablespoons lemon juice

Freshly ground pepper to taste

THIS colorful combination of tuna and artichokes has universal appeal—great for entertaining or for kids' lunch box meals. Try it over a bed of field greens or in large lettuce leaf cups. Use a good-quality Greek olive such as a Kalamata for this salad. For a smoky flavor, try roasted red peppers or piquillo peppers; they add lots of character. A great way to try this salad is to slice a 9-inch round focaccia bread in half lengthwise, fill it with the tuna, and press a plate down on top of the round bread. Place a heavy can or weight on top for an hour, and the dressing will seep into the bread. Slice and serve.

In a large bowl, combine the tuna, artichoke hearts, red pepper, olives, onion, parsley, basil, garlic, oregano, mayonnaise, lemon juice, and pepper. Mix all the ingredients together well.

PER SERVING: CALORIES 360; CALORIES FROM FAT 200; CALORIES FROM SATURATED FAT 30; PROTEIN 22 G; CARBOHYDRATE 13 G; TOTAL FAT 22 G; SATURATED FAT 3.5 G; CHOLESTEROL 35 MG; SODIUM 1,190 MG; 55% CALORIES FROM FAT

Kalamata Olives

KALAMATA olives grow only in Greece and are considered one of the world's finest olives. Authentic Kalamatas are recognizable by their almond-shaped point, deep purple color, and firm texture. The hills around Sparta, Greece, are commonly regarded as one of the best growing areas for this varietal. Kalamata olives have a rich, firm texture and a smoky, wine-infused snap that bring life to salads, pizzas, and pastas. A traditional way to enjoy Kalamatas is to simply serve the whole, unpitted olives with a chunk of real sheep's milk feta, good extra-virgin olive oil, and a loaf of pita bread. To pit a Kalamata, gently push down on the olive with the flat side of your knife blade to loosen the pit from the flesh. The meat of the olive should cut away easily.

Southwestern Calamari Salad

SERVES 8

CALAMARI sounds a lot friendlier than *squid*. This delicious member of the mollusk family ranges from one inch long to the ninety-foot giant squid of legends that sailors once dreaded. They might not have been so afraid if they had tried this salad first. Always look for small fresh squid tubes or shells instead of the frozen rings. They have a much better flavor and texture. Be sure to cook squid quickly, as it tends to become very rubbery if cooked too long. This is a beautiful salad—full of color and shapes.

I n a saucepan, bring 3 quarts of water to a boil. Add the calamari slices to the boiling water, and stir. Allow the calamari to cook for 1 minute over high heat. Remove immediately, drain, and chill in an ice-water bath.

TO PREPARE THE SOUTHWESTERN DRESSING Heat the olive oil and minced garlic over a low flame in a large sauté pan. Cook the garlic slowly for 3 minutes, until it is golden brown; then cool the garlic. Add the jalapeño, sherry vinegar, lime juice, cumin, chili powder, paprika, hot pepper sauce, and salt and pepper.

TO PREPARE THE SALAD When the calamari is chilled, drain it well and transfer to a large salad bowl. Combine the calamari, red pepper, onion, black beans, cilantro, and dressing.

PER SERVING: CALORIES 240; CALORIES FROM FAT 70; CALORIES FROM SATURATED FAT 5; PROTEIN 33 G; CARBOHYDRATE 10 G; TOTAL FAT 8 G; SATURATED FAT 0.5 G; CHOLESTEROL 0 MG; SODIUM 180 MG; 29% CALORIES FROM FAT

3 pounds calamari, cleaned, cut into 1/2-inch rings

The Southwestern Dressing

3 tablespoons extra-virgin olive oil

2 cloves garlic, minced (1 teaspoon)

1 jalapeño pepper, seeded and minced

2 ounces sherry vinegar

1/4 cup lime juice

1/2 teaspoon cumin

1/2 teaspoon chili powder

1/2 teaspoon paprika

8 to 12 dashes of hot pepper sauce, or to taste

Salt and freshly ground pepper to taste

The Salad

1 large red pepper, seeded and chopped

1/2 red onion, minced

1 (15-ounce) can black beans, drained and rinsed

1/4 cup plus 2 tablespoons chopped fresh cilantro

Between the Bread

PORTOBELLO MUSHROOM CLUB ♠ FIRE-ROASTED VEGETABLE AND HUMMUS CLUB ♠ THAI VEGETABLE WRAP ♠ MEDITERRANEAN VEGETABLE WRAP ♠ SANTA FE VEGETABLE WRAP ♠ GREEN CHILI PISTACHIO MOLE ENCHILADAS ♠ TOFU REUBEN ♠ CAPE COD WRAP ♠ CALIFORNIA HIGH ROLLER ♠ JAMAICAN JERK CHICKEN WRAP ♠ SMOKED TURKEY COBB WRAP ♠ SPINACH AND PINE NUT QUICHE ♠ SPICY ASIAN FLANK STEAK SUBMARINE WITH SZECHWAN SLAW AND PEANUT SAUCE ♠ EIGHT-LAYER TORTILLA PIE ♠ JERK CHICKEN ♠ TRIPLE-MUSHROOM AND LEEK STRUDEL **QUESADILLAS** ♠ TRIPLE-PEPPER, ONION, AND CHEESE QUESADILLAS ♠ WOODLAND MUSHROOM QUESADILLAS ♠ MUSHROOM GOAT-CHEESE QUESADILLAS ♠ SWEET POTATO QUESADILLAS

Bread is one of the most vital elements of global sustenance. Every culture depends on some form of bread for scooping, wrapping, and enjoying its nation's indigenous cuisine. From hearth-baked Mediterranean pita breads, Italy's bruschetta, and Mexico's tacos and quesadillas to Asian rice paper wrappers and California's genuine sourdough bread, it's easy to see why bread is called the staff of life. In England during the late 1700s, the first sandwich was created, and since then countless ingredients have found their way in between two pieces of sliced bread.

A well-made sandwich can be extremely gratifying. A wrap sandwich is welcome handheld fuel for a busy day. It can just as easily be a comforting meal served with a bowl of steaming soup. We've expanded this chapter to include other interpretations of the sandwich—something rolled or wrapped, a tortilla-stacked meal, even a savory pastry baked in a flour shell.

In choosing recipes for this chapter we had to define some Between the Bread criteria: innovative fillings, contrasting textures, and bold-flavored spreads to daub across the bread. Convenience was also a consideration, and most of these dishes can be picked up in one hand and eaten. This chapter covers a lot of ground.

In this group you will find a variety of stacked tortillas filled with sharp cheeses, fresh salsas, and everything from grilled chicken to giant mushroom caps. We included a fabulous Spinach and Pine Nut Quiche (page 141) with an alluring sage-infused custard encased in a crispy outer shell. You'll never look at strudel the same way after you slice the flaky end off our Triple-Mushroom and Leek Strudel (page 146), exposing a filling of caramelized leeks and three kinds of meaty mushrooms. Crack open the corn tortilla shell of our Green Chili Pistachio Mole Enchiladas (page 134) to smell the roasted pistachios, cilantro, serrano peppers, and cinnamon of the rich mole sauce.

All these recipes are appropriate for any meal, and the wrap sandwiches, if cut into 1-inch-thick slices, become stunning party food. Don't hesitate to fill your children's lunch boxes with any of our suggestions; they may never eat white bread and bologna again.

Portobello Mushroom Club

SERVES 2

2 large portobello mushrooms, wiped
   clean, stems removed

¼ cup Italian Herb Vinaigrette
   (page 329), or your favorite herb
   dressing, plus more for serving,
   if desired

3 slices provolone cheese

1 (6 x 6-inch) piece focaccia bread
   or 1 kaiser roll

3 jarred roasted red peppers,
   drained well

Handful of arugula leaves, washed

THE king of mushrooms really makes his presence known in this royal club. The oregano- and garlic-infused mushroom cap has a beefy texture that is complemented by sweet pepper and sharp provolone cheese. The crown of arugula adds a nutty aftertaste. Feel free to substitute fresh spinach for the arugula.

Marinate the portobello mushrooms at room temperature in the vinaigrette for 20 minutes. Grill the mushrooms over coals or on a gas grill over medium heat for 5 minutes per side, until nicely browned. This may be done 1 day prior to making the sandwiches. You may also broil the mushrooms 3 inches from the broiling element of your oven for 6 to 7 minutes per side, until lightly browned.

Half the focaccia or roll horizontally, and place the cheese on one piece of the bread. Cut the grilled mushrooms into 1-inch-thick slices diagonally, and arrange them over the cheese. Place the peppers over the mushrooms, and top with the arugula. If you like, sprinkle a little vinaigrette over the arugula, and close up the sandwich.

PER SERVING: CALORIES 460; CALORIES FROM FAT 230; CALORIES FROM SATURATED FAT 45; PROTEIN 13 G; CARBOHYDRATE 45 G; TOTAL FAT 26 G; SATURATED FAT 5 G; CHOLESTEROL 10 MG; SODIUM 840 MG; 50% CALORIES FROM FAT

between the bread

Vegan

Fire-Roasted Vegetable and Hummus Club

SERVES 6

THE natural sugar from the roasted vegetables melts into the balsamic vinegar to produce a sweet-tart flavor. The crisp fire-roasted vegetables provide great contrast when piled over a layer of creamy hummus. Serve these fire-roasted vegetables over salad greens, or tossed into an omelette, as well. They are equally good at room temperature or slightly warm.

I medium red pepper, halved and seeded, cut into 1-inch-wide strips

I medium green pepper, halved and seeded, cut into 1-inch-wide strips

½ medium red onion, cut into 1-inch-thick slices

I medium zucchini, cut into ½-inch-thick slices

I medium yellow squash, cut into ½-inch-thick slices

I tablespoon extra-virgin olive oil

2 teaspoons balsamic vinegar

I teaspoon lemon juice

2 teaspoons dried Italian herbs

Salt and freshly ground pepper to taste

6 kaiser or onion rolls, or 6-inch squares of focaccia bread

2 cups hummus (pages 322 or 323, or ready made)

If you are roasting the vegetables in the oven, preheat it to 500°F.

Combine the peppers, onion, zucchini, and yellow squash with the olive oil, vinegar, lemon juice, dried Italian herbs, and salt and pepper. Spread the vegetables out on a baking pan and roast for 20 minutes, until they begin to caramelize and become tender but not mushy.

If you're grilling, grill the vegetables over coals or in a gas grill for 10 minutes, turning them occasionally, until browned and tender. You may use a grill screen for cooking the vegetables. This inexpensive piece of barbecue equipment makes this task easier.

To assemble each sandwich, slice the rolls or focaccia in half horizontally. Spread the hummus evenly over the bottom of the roll or focaccia bread. Arrange the vegetables evenly over the hummus, and place the other half of the roll over the vegetables.

PER SERVING: CALORIES 100; CALORIES FROM FAT 20; CALORIES FROM SATURATED FAT 0; PROTEIN 3 G; CARBOHYDRATE 16 G; TOTAL FAT 2.5 G; SATURATED FAT 0 G; CHOLESTEROL 0 MG; SODIUM 170 MG; 20% CALORIES FROM FAT

Thai Vegetable Wrap

SERVES 2

¼ pound firm tofu, sliced ½ inch
  thick lengthwise, grilled or broiled
2 ounces Creamy Peanut Sauce
  (page 312)
½ cup snow peas
½ cup thinly sliced red onion
¾ cup thinly sliced red pepper
½ cup bean sprouts
½ cup grated carrots
1 (12-inch) flour tortilla
1 tablespoon hoisin sauce
2 leaves leaf lettuce

ALTHOUGH any combination of vegetables may be used for this wrap, sweet peppers and crisp snow peas and sprouts create a crunchy complement to the tender tofu filling. There are a few tofu options: You may use tofu out of the package (use pregrilled, seasoned tofu) or cook the tofu yourself first by grilling or broiling. The vegetables are tossed with just enough Creamy Peanut Sauce.

Also try Thai Dipping Sauce (page 316) instead of the Creamy Peanut Sauce, but note that the dish will no longer be vegan or vegetarian.

Gently brush the tofu with some Creamy Peanut Sauce.

Blanch the snow peas for 1 minute in boiling water. You can use a small basket or colander. Drain and rinse the peas in cold water. Toss the onion, pepper, bean sprouts, snow peas, and carrots in the remaining Creamy Peanut Sauce.

Spread the tortilla with the hoisin sauce and top with one of the lettuce leaves. Place the sliced tofu over the lettuce, arrange the vegetable mixture over the tofu, top with the remaining lettuce leaf, and roll tightly. Cut in half diagonally.

PER SERVING: CALORIES 370; CALORIES FROM FAT 110; CALORIES FROM SATURATED FAT 20; PROTEIN 13 G; CARBOHYDRATE 54 G; TOTAL FAT 12 G; SATURATED FAT 2 G; CHOLESTEROL 0 MG; SODIUM 590 MG; 30% CALORIES FROM FAT

Fire-Roasted Vegetable and Hummus Club

zucchini &
squash slices

red & green
bell peppers

focaccia bread

onion

creamy hummus

Mediterranean Vegetable Wrap

SERVES 2

CRISP and crunchy Greek salad surrounded with creamy hummus makes this wrap refreshing and light. Make sure you find ripe tomatoes with lots of juice to moisten the flour tortilla just a bit. If you like, drizzle with a little extra-virgin olive oil and a squeeze of lemon before rolling. The Greek word *opa* roughly translates to "joyous life," which perfectly describes the feeling when eating this sandwich.

S pread the tortilla with the hummus. Scatter the spinach over the hummus. Place the sliced cucumber, sliced tomato, artichoke quarters, sliced onions, and olives over the spinach. Sprinkle with the feta cheese, roll tightly, and slice diagonally in half.

PER SERVING: CALORIES 490; CALORIES FROM FAT 180; CALORIES FROM SATURATED FAT 80; PROTEIN 18 G; CARBOHYDRATE 59 G; TOTAL FAT 20 G; SATURATED FAT 8 G; CHOLESTEROL 40 MG; SODIUM 1,310 MG; 37% CALORIES FROM FAT

1 (12-inch) flour tortilla

⅓ cup hummus (pages 322 or 323, or ready made)

2 cups stemmed spinach leaves, washed

½ cucumber, peeled and sliced lengthwise

1 medium tomato, thinly sliced

8 canned artichoke quarters, drained well

3 very thin red onion slices

¼ cup olive halves, preferably Kalamata olives

⅓ cup crumbled feta cheese

Santa Fe Vegetable Wrap

SERVES 2

1 (12-inch) flour tortilla, flavor of
   your choice (try cilantro)

1½ tablespoons cream cheese, at
   room temperature

3 leaves leaf lettuce

4 slices pepper Monterey Jack cheese

4 thin slices tomato

½ avocado, thinly sliced

4 thin slices red onion

½ cup jicama thinly sliced into
   matchsticks

¼ cup sweet corn kernels, fresh or
   frozen and defrosted

¼ cup cooked black beans, drained
   and rinsed

AN explosion of traditional Southwest flavors and textures describes the first bite; the rest is pure joy. If you want to add some heat, try mixing a teaspoon of chipotle chili in adobo sauce to the cream cheese before spreading it on the tortilla. When the wraps are made, the filling looks like an edible mosaic of black beans, yellow sweet corn, white jicama, pale green avocado, and red tomatoes. Serve these wraps for parties by slicing into 1-inch-thick slices—they have tremendous eye appeal. Serve these with a bit of tomato salsa and sour cream or plain yogurt on the side for dipping.

Spread the tortilla thinly with the cream cheese. Place 2 lettuce leaves over the cream cheese. Layer the pepper Monterey Jack cheese over the cream cheese. Layer the tomato, avocado, onion, and jicama over the cheese. Spoon on the corn and black beans evenly. Top with the remaining lettuce leaf, and roll tightly. Slice in half diagonally.

PER SERVING: CALORIES 490; CALORIES FROM FAT 190; CALORIES FROM SATURATED FAT 70; PROTEIN 19 G; CARBOHYDRATE 58 G; TOTAL FAT 21 G; SATURATED FAT 8 G; CHOLESTEROL 25 MG; SODIUM 610 MG; 39% CALORIES FROM FAT

Jicama

THIS large, round, thin-skinned vegetable, also called a Mexican potato, has a wonderfully sweet flavor and crunchy texture. It was once only available in Hispanic markets, but you can now find it in markets everywhere. Like a giant water chestnut, jicama can be eaten raw or cooked. After peeling the outer skin, try grating or thinly slicing jicama. Then simply dress it with a sprinkling of lime juice and salt. Jicama will keep for about a week in the refrigerator.

Green Chili Pistachio Mole Enchiladas

SERVES 8

THIS green sauce is unlike any other because of the pistachio oil, which adds a vivid bright green color when combined with cilantro and chilies. A background of cinnamon and clove adds an underlying warm nuance that rounds out the rich flavor. Corn tortillas are preferable, although you may make these enchiladas with flour or whole wheat tortillas, as well. Serve with Cilantro Lime Rice (page 172).

TO PREPARE THE GREEN CHILI PISTACHIO MOLE SAUCE Toast the pistachios in a large, dry, deep skillet over medium heat for 5 minutes, stirring frequently, until the nuts are lightly browned. Remove from the pan and reserve. Add the olive oil to the pan and sauté the tomatillos, chilies, onion, garlic, cinnamon, cumin, and cloves over medium heat for 3 minutes, until they begin to brown. Place the sautéed tomatillo mixture, cilantro, and browned pistachios in a food processor or blender with the 3 cups water or stock, and purée until smooth. Place the puréed mixture back into the skillet, and bring it to a boil. Lower to a simmer, and cook slowly for 30 minutes, gradually adding more water or stock until a medium-thick sauce is formed (it will coat a spoon). Season with the salt and lime juice.

TO PREPARE THE ENCHILADAS Steam the tortillas one at a time for 1 to 2 minutes in a steamer lined with a damp towel. You may also wrap 3 tortillas at a time in a damp paper towel and heat for about 1 minute in a microwave oven. This makes the tortillas malleable and easy to stuff. Flour tortillas take only 45 seconds to soften.

The Green Chili Pistachio Mole Sauce

1 cup shelled pistachios
2 teaspoons olive oil
8 tomatillos, husked, washed, and roughly chopped, or 1 1/2 cups canned tomatillos, drained
2 serrano chilies or 1 jalapeño pepper, halved, seeded, and roughly chopped
1/2 red onion, chopped
2 cloves garlic, chopped (1 teaspoon)
1 (1-inch) cinnamon stick
1 teaspoon whole cumin seeds
2 whole cloves
1 cup loosely packed fresh cilantro leaves
3 cups plus 1 cup water or chicken stock
Salt to taste
Juice of 1 lime

The Enchiladas

8 (9-inch) corn tortillas
1 1/2 pounds cooked, shredded, boneless skinless chicken breasts
1 cup grated Monterey Jack cheese
Cilantro sprigs to garnish (optional)
Sour cream or plain yogurt to serve (optional)

Fill each tortilla with 2 to 3 tablespoons of the shredded chicken, dividing the mixture evenly between the 6 to 8 tortillas. Roll the tortilla around the chicken tightly, and place seam side down in a 13 × 9-inch baking dish. When all the tortillas are placed in the dish, cover with the mole sauce, and shake the pan to distribute the sauce evenly. Sprinkle the cheese over the top, and bake for 20 minutes, until the cheese is melted and the enchiladas are heated through. Garnish with cilantro sprigs, and serve with sour cream or plain yogurt, if desired.

PER SERVING: CALORIES 330; CALORIES FROM FAT 130; CALORIES FROM SATURATED FAT 30; PROTEIN 34 G; CARBOHYDRATE 16 G; TOTAL FAT 15 G; SATURATED FAT 3.5 G; CHOLESTEROL 75 MG; SODIUM 190 MG; 39% CALORIES FROM FAT

Tofu Reuben

SERVES 2

THIS Reuben is a far cry from the original mile-high structure made with corned beef, Russian dressing, and lots of melted cheese. This sandwich makes your mouth happy, as the layers of sauerkraut, tofu, and cheese work so well nestled between the griddled crispy rye bread. You may make a vegan version of this sandwich by substituting a soy-based mayonnaise and using a soy-based cheese.

The Russian Dressing

1 tablespoon mayonnaise
1 teaspoon ketchup
1 teaspoon pickle relish (sweet or dill)

2 slices rye bread with seeds
¼ pound firm tofu, sliced lengthwise, ¼ inch thick
⅓ cup sauerkraut, well drained
2 ounces Swiss cheese, thinly sliced, or soy cheese of your choice
Vegetable or olive oil for oiling pan

TO PREPARE THE RUSSIAN DRESSING In a small bowl, combine the mayonnaise, ketchup, and pickle relish.

Spread the Russian dressing over the inside of both slices of rye bread. Arrange the tofu slices over the dressing. Spread the sauerkraut evenly over the tofu. Top with the cheese and then with the remaining bread slice.

Heat a nonstick pan over medium heat. Lightly oil or spray the pan with the oil. Place the sandwich in the pan, and put a plate on top of the sandwich. Weigh the plate down with a can or a heavy sauce pot, and press gently. Lower the heat, and cook the sandwich for 4 minutes, until golden brown. Flip the sandwich over, and repeat the process until the sandwich is golden on both sides and heated through. Cut in half, and serve immediately.

PER SERVING: CALORIES 260; CALORIES FROM FAT 120; CALORIES FROM SATURATED FAT 50; PROTEIN 15 G; CARBOHYDRATE 20 G; TOTAL FAT 13 G; SATURATED FAT 6 G; CHOLESTEROL 25 MG; SODIUM 580 MG; 46% CALORIES FROM FAT

Cape Cod Wrap

SERVES 2

1 medium red onion, sliced ½ inch
thick

Olive oil for brushing the onion

Salt and freshly ground pepper to
taste

1 teaspoon sugar (optional)

1 teaspoon grated orange zest

1 tablespoon cream cheese

1 (12-inch) flour tortilla (whole wheat
or your favorite flavor)

2 cups fresh baby spinach leaves

6 ounces sliced smoked turkey

2 ounces whole berry cranberry
relish

THIS recipe isn't originally from Cape Cod, but it is well known in our mid-Atlantic stores. We think Cape Codders would embrace this sandwich as their own. There is something about the combination of cranberry relish, smoked turkey, and grilled red onions that speaks to all of us, and the addition of the citrus cream cheese makes this a winner. This sandwich relies on simple contrast of flavors and textures. You should also try this with apple or pear chutney or preserves instead of cranberries.

Preheat the oven to 375°F. Brush the onion slices lightly with the olive oil, and sprinkle with the salt and pepper. Spread them out on a sheet pan and bake for 30 minutes, stirring occasionally until golden brown. You may sprinkle 1 teaspoon of sugar over the onion for a little extra sweetness and browning. You may also grill the onion on a gas grill or barbecue for 4 minutes per side, until browned. This will give it a smoky flavor.

In a small bowl, combine the orange zest and cream cheese.

Spread the citrus cream cheese on the tortilla. Place the spinach leaves over the cream cheese. Scatter the onion over the spinach. Arrange the smoked turkey over the onion, covering the entire surface of the tortilla. Place the berry relish over the turkey in a 1-inch-thick line along the bottom edge of the tortilla. Roll up tightly, and slice diagonally in half.

PER SERVING: CALORIES 370; CALORIES FROM FAT 120; CALORIES FROM SATURATED FAT 30; PROTEIN 20 G; CARBOHYDRATE 43 G; TOTAL FAT 14 G; SATURATED FAT 3 G; CHOLESTEROL 40 MG; SODIUM 1,030 MG; 32% CALORIES FROM FAT

 Recipe Bonus For extra kick, add a spoonful of orange marmalade to the cream cheese.

California High Roller

SERVES 4

THIS wrap may be made with fresh roast turkey breast (our recommendation) or your favorite sliced deli meat. Make sure the avocado is very ripe for this sandwich. Look for a California Hass variety, which is ambrosial and creamy. To make things easier, you may mash an avocado with a touch of lemon or lime juice and salt at least an hour before making sandwiches, and reserve it in the refrigerator.

Use a thick tomato salsa with some body. Also be sure that the lettuce leaves are dry. Any excess moisture will make a sandwich soggy. Try Monterey Jack with jalapeños for a bit of heat. You may use your favorite tortillas; there are many available in various flavors. Our favorites are cilantro or spinach flavored.

2 (9-inch) flour tortillas
1 small ripe avocado, sliced or mashed
4 large leaves leaf lettuce, green or red
10 to 12 ounces thinly sliced turkey breast
1 cup grated Monterey Jack cheese
1/3 cup favorite salsa, plus extra to serve

Arrange the tortillas in front of you on the kitchen counter or for easier rolling on a piece of parchment paper. Spread the avocado thinly over the tortillas. Overlap two dry lettuce leaves over the avocado with the frilly part to the left and right outside of the tortilla. Arrange the turkey over the lettuce leaves. Sprinkle the cheese over the turkey. Sprinkle the salsa over the length of the wrap, forming a 1-inch strip across the center.

Wrap the sandwich firmly by rolling the edge closest to you over itself and the filling until a pinwheel is formed. Cut each sandwich in half diagonally. Secure with a toothpick if you like. Serve with extra salsa for dipping.

PER SERVING: CALORIES 360; CALORIES FROM FAT 150; CALORIES FROM SATURATED FAT 5; PROTEIN 26 G; CARBOHYDRATE 29 G; TOTAL FAT 17 G; SATURATED FAT 5 G; CHOLESTEROL 45 MG; SODIUM 1,300 MG; 42% CALORIES FROM FAT

 Recipe Bonus For extra color, fiber, and texture, mash cooked black beans and blend them into the avocado.

Jamaican Jerk Chicken Wrap

SERVES 2

1 tablespoon cream cheese

1 (12-inch) flour tortilla

3 leaves leaf lettuce, red or green

8 ounces grilled Jerk Chicken (see page 145), chopped

8 very thin slices red onion

½ cup prepared fruit chutney

SPICY, sweet, and crunchy with a tropical flavor, this sandwich may be made using Grilled Jerk Chicken from our recipe or with any cooked chicken. If you are short on time, chop up some leftover cooked chicken and marinate with your favorite jerk sauce or seasoning mix. There are many fruit chutneys available for the sauce: Try a mango, peach, or tropical fruit variety. The cream cheese seals the wrap and keeps it from opening, once rolled.

Spread the cream cheese thinly over the tortilla. Place 2 leaves of lettuce on the bottom half of the tortilla. Spread the jerk chicken over the lettuce. Scatter the red onion over the chicken. Spoon the fruit chutney over the onions. Top with the remaining lettuce leaf. Roll up the tortilla tightly, and cut it diagonally in half.

PER SERVING: CALORIES 590; CALORIES FROM FAT 150; CALORIES FROM SATURATED FAT 45; PROTEIN 41 G; CARBOHYDRATE 67 G; TOTAL FAT 17 G; SATURATED FAT 5 G; CHOLESTEROL 105 MG; SODIUM 420 MG; 25% CALORIES FROM FAT

between the bread

Smoked Turkey Cobb Wrap

SERVES 2

HOW ingenious—a classic Cobb salad wrapped up in a flour tortilla that may be eaten on the run. The flavors and textures of this sandwich are brilliant and surprising. A mild blue cheese shows off the smoky turkey and rich avocado while the slightly sweet bacon provides a nice background note. Use roasted unsmoked turkey breast if you prefer; either way, it's a picnic favorite. Cream cheese mixed with blue cheese holds this wrap together well.

1 tablespoon crumbled blue cheese

1 tablespoon cream cheese

1 (12-inch) flour tortilla

2 leaves leaf lettuce

6 ounces thinly sliced smoked turkey

4 thin slices tomato

1 large egg, hard-boiled and sliced

4 thin slices red onion

½ ripe avocado, thinly sliced

3 strips cooked bacon

In a small bowl, lightly blend the cheeses with the back of a fork until combined. Spread the cheese blend evenly over the tortilla. Top with the lettuce; then arrange the turkey over the surface of the lettuce. Layer the tomato, egg, onion, and avocado over the turkey, and top with the bacon. Roll tightly and cut in half diagonally.

PER SERVING: CALORIES 510; CALORIES FROM FAT 210; CALORIES FROM SATURATED FAT 60; PROTEIN 30 G; CARBOHYDRATE 47 G; TOTAL FAT 24 G; SATURATED FAT 7 G; CHOLESTEROL 160 MG; SODIUM 1,400 MG; 41% CALORIES FROM FAT

 Tip from the Team: When you want to serve avocado slices, the best way to remove the seed is by chopping into the seed with a knife (just one chop, hard enough to stick the knife in the seed—do not stab) and twisting. The seed will pop right out.

Spinach and Pine Nut Quiche

1 (9-inch) frozen ready-made
  piecrust

1½ tablespoons olive oil

2 large cloves garlic, sliced

6 cups fresh spinach leaves, washed
  and dried

1 teaspoon salt

¼ teaspoon freshly ground pepper

1 teaspoon dried sage, or
  1 tablespoon chopped fresh

½ cup pine nuts, toasted

1 cup grated mozzarella cheese

¼ cup grated Parmesan cheese

1 cup milk

2 large eggs

1 large red bliss potato, steamed until
  firm-tender, sliced ¼ inch thick

IT'S phenomenal how much taste and appeal can be captured in a delicate pastry shell. As you prepare this quiche, aromas of roasting garlic, heady sage, and the unmistakable smell of golden pine nuts will fill your kitchen. Red bliss potatoes provide a surprising twist. This quiche may be made up to three days before serving. Serve it at room temperature, or reheat it slowly in a 325°F. oven for 30 minutes, until heated through.

Preheat the oven to 350°F. Remove the piecrust from the freezer, and let it thaw for 10 minutes. Prick the bottom with a fork and bake for 7 to 10 minutes, until lightly browned. Remove the crust from the oven to cool.

Heat the olive oil in a medium sauté pan. Add the garlic, spinach, salt, pepper, and sage. Cook, stirring constantly, for about 1 minute, or until the spinach is just wilted. Stir in the pine nuts.

In a small bowl, mix the mozzarella and Parmesan cheeses. In another bowl, whisk the milk and eggs together.

Sprinkle ¼ cup of the cheese mixture on the piecrust. Top with half the spinach mixture. Place the potato slices on top of the spinach. Add half the remaining cheese mixture and then the remaining spinach mixture. Top with the rest of the cheese. Place the pie pan on a sheet pan. Carefully pour in the milk mixture. Bake for 45 to 50 minutes, until a knife inserted into the center comes out clean. Cool slightly before cutting.

PER SERVING: CALORIES 260; CALORIES FROM FAT 160; CALORIES FROM SATURATED FAT 40; PROTEIN 12 G; CARBOHYDRATE 16 G; TOTAL FAT 17 G; SATURATED FAT 4.5 G; CHOLESTEROL 65 MG; SODIUM 520 MG; 61% CALORIES FROM FAT

Spicy Asian Flank Steak Submarine with Szechwan Slaw and Peanut Sauce

SERVES 6

IN order to obtain the best flavor, marinate this flank steak for at least twenty-four hours in Roasted Sesame–Honey Dressing. We've also added a few ingredients such as five-spice powder, star anise buds, and a bit of molasses, which help the flank steak form a rich, dark caramelized glaze. This sandwich is great with the beef served hot, at room temperature, or even chilled. If you like, use a favorite bottled Asian-inspired dressing and just add the extra flavor boosters. Five-spice powder (a combination of cinnamon, cloves, peppercorns, star anise, and fennel, and occasionally nutmeg or ginger) and star anise buds are available in most Whole Foods Market stores, as well as in Asian markets.

The Asian Flank Steak

1 cup Roasted Sesame–Honey Dressing (page 334)
2 teaspoons grated orange zest
½ teaspoon five-spice powder
6 scallions, sliced diagonally
1 tablespoon molasses
⅓ cup star anise buds
2 pounds flank or skirt steak, well trimmed

The Submarines

6 submarine rolls, 6 inches long, or lengths of baguettes
¼ cup plus 2 tablespoons Creamy Peanut Sauce (page 312) or favorite bottled variety
¼ cup Szechwan Slaw, well drained (page 120)
Lettuce and sliced tomatoes (optional)

TO PREPARE THE ASIAN FLANK STEAK

Combine the Roasted Sesame–Honey Dressing with the orange zest, five-spice powder, scallions, molasses, and star anise buds, and pour it over the beef in a container just large enough to hold the steak. Marinate in the refrigerator for at least 24 hours (longer if you have the time). You may leave the beef in this marinade for up to 4 days. The pineapple juice helps to tenderize it.

Grill the beef over coals or on a gas grill for 6 to 8 minutes per side for medium doneness. You may also broil the beef in your oven broiler about 3 inches from the heating element for 8 to 10 minutes per side, until medium doneness. Allow the meat to sit for at least 5 minutes before slicing. Thinly slice the beef diagonally, against the grain.

TO PREPARE THE SUBMARINES Slice the rolls horizontally. Drizzle 1 tablespoon of the sauce on the bottom of each sub roll. Arrange the sliced beef over the sauce, and top with the drained Szechwan Slaw. Top with the bread cover. Add lettuce and tomato, if desired.

PER SERVING: CALORIES 890; CALORIES FROM FAT 300; CALORIES FROM SATURATED FAT 80; PROTEIN 57 G; CARBOHYDRATE 91 G; TOTAL FAT 33 G; SATURATED FAT 9 G; CHOLESTEROL 100 MG; SODIUM 1,040 MG; 34% CALORIES FROM FAT

Slicing Against the Grain

CERTAIN cuts of meat, like flank steak or brisket of beef, should be sliced against the grain in order to be tender. When looking at the meat, you will see the muscle structure that appears to run in long straight lines from end to end. These lines are what is meant by the "grain" of the beef. When cutting, make sure to slice perpendicular to, or against, these long lines to make the slices easy to chew and enjoy. This technique is also sometimes referred to as "slicing on the bias."

Eight-Layer Tortilla Pie

SERVES 6 (AS AN APPETIZER)

THIS savory layered pie is the ultimate dish for gatherings. It may be assembled and then stored in the refrigerator, ready to be popped in the oven. Cut this into small wedges for a crowd-pleaser of an appetizer.

The Mexican Spice Mixture

I tablespoon chili powder

2 teaspoons cumin

I teaspoon dried oregano

2 teaspoons unsweetened cocoa powder

2 cups grated cheddar cheese

1½ cups grated Monterey Jack cheese

Vegetable oil for spraying pan

4 (9-inch) flour tortillas (flavor of your choice)

I (15-ounce) can black beans, drained and rinsed

I (15-ounce) can white beans (cannellini), drained and rinsed

I (15-ounce) can kidney or pinto beans, drained and rinsed

I (16-ounce) bottle tomato salsa

Preheat the oven to 375°F.

TO PREPARE THE MEXICAN SPICE MIXTURE Combine the chili powder, cumin, oregano, and cocoa powder in a small bowl and reserve.

Combine the cheeses in a large mixing bowl.

Spray a 10-inch springform pan lightly with the vegetable oil. Place a flour tortilla on the bottom of the pan.

Place each bean variety in a separate bowl. Divide the Mexican spice mixture into thirds, and combine well with each of the beans.

Place half the black beans on the tortilla in the springform pan, spreading evenly. Spoon ¼ cup of the salsa over the beans, and spread evenly. Sprinkle with ½ cup of the cheese mixture.

Top with another tortilla. Repeat layers using half the white beans and half the kidney beans, and then do another layer of each until all are used. You will end up with two layers of each bean variety. When you are done, there will be ½ cup of cheese left and ¼ cup of salsa. Place the last tortilla on top of the pie, and spread the remaining salsa over the top. Sprinkle with the remaining cheese, and cover loosely with foil. Bake for 30 minutes, until the pie is heated through and the cheese is melted. Remove the foil, and bake for 10 minutes longer, until the cheese turns a golden brown. Allow the pie to cool for at least 15 minutes; slice into wedges.

PER SERVING: CALORIES 420; CALORIES FROM FAT 80; CALORIES FROM SATURATED FAT 30; PROTEIN 22 G; CARBOHYDRATE 64 G; TOTAL FAT 9 G; SATURATED FAT 3 G; CHOLESTEROL 10 MG; SODIUM 1,360 MG; 19% CALORIES FROM FAT

Jerk Chicken

2½ pounds bone-in chicken, cut into eight pieces

1½ cups plus ½ cup Jamaican Jerk Sauce, separated (page 307)

JERKING is a process of marinating that imparts an intense, fiery, hot, and smoky taste to poultry, pork, or red meat. Traditional Jamaican jerk meats are grilled slowly over wood in a covered metal drum. We've combined an authentic marinade recipe with modern cooking techniques so you can enjoy this dish in your home kitchen. While this recipe calls for bone-in chicken pieces, you may substitute an equal amount of boneless, skinless chicken breast, lamb, beef, or pork.

To marinate, place the chicken pieces in a bowl and cover with 1½ cups of the marinade. Securely cover the bowl and leave in the refrigerator overnight or for up to three days. Turn the chicken a few times during this process to make sure the marinade is distributed evenly.

To cook over coals or on a gas grill, bring the coals to a medium heat. Remove the chicken from the marinade and place directly on the grill. If your grill has a cover, cook with it closed. If you do not have a cover, loosely cover the chicken with foil or the lid of a large pot while cooking. This will ensure a more authentic flavor. Cook over medium heat, turning occasionally, for 40 minutes until cooked through and crispy on the outside.

To cook in the oven, preheat the oven to 375°F. Remove the chicken from the marinade and place on a baking pan. Bake, turning occasionally, for 45 to 50 minutes until golden outside and cooked through.

Serve with the additional ½ cup of marinade as a dipping sauce.

PER SERVING: CALORIES 350; CALORIES FROM FAT 180; CALORIES FROM SATURATED FAT 50; PROTEIN 36 G; CARBOHYDRATE 6 G; TOTAL FAT 20 G; SATURATED FAT 6 G; CHOLESTEROL 110 MG; SODIUM 230 MG; 51% CALORIES FROM FAT

Recipe Bonus Try this Jerk Chicken with Havana Black Beans (page 166) and Cilantro Lime Rice (page 172) for a wonderful taste combination. The mahogany colored chicken, green rice, and jet black beans also make an attractive plate presentation.

Triple-Mushroom and Leek Strudel

SERVES 8 (AS AN APPETIZER)

WHEN sliced, this flaky puff pastry–encrusted strudel offers an aromatic filling of three kinds of sautéed mushrooms and golden brown leeks. Not unlike uncorking a fine bottle of wine and whiffing the grape essence, be ready to inhale deeply as soon as the first cut is made. A word of advice: When you serve this strudel at a party, remove a slice for yourself before placing on the dinner table. It may be the only chance you get. The puff pastry wrapper makes this strudel unusual. We feel the pastry dough absorbs the piquant mushroom flavor better than the traditional phyllo dough. Premade puff pastry may be found in many markets in the frozen food section.

3 tablespoons olive oil

4 large leeks, sliced and washed

5 medium portobello mushrooms, stemmed and chopped

4 cups sliced button mushrooms

1 cup sliced shiitake mushrooms

4 cloves garlic, minced (2 teaspoons)

1 teaspoon dried thyme, or
    2 teaspoons minced fresh

1/2 cup dry white wine

1/2 cup vegetable stock

1/2 cup dried bread crumbs

1 tablespoon lemon juice

Salt and freshly ground pepper to
    taste

1 (6 x 10-inch) sheet frozen puff
    pastry, defrosted

Flour for dusting work area

1 large egg, lightly beaten

Vegetable oil for spraying

Preheat the oven to 400°F.

Heat the olive oil in a large sauté pan over medium heat. Add the leeks, and sauté for 3 minutes, until they begin to color. Add the mushrooms, along with the garlic and thyme; continue to sauté for 3 minutes, until the mushrooms soften.

Add the wine and stock, and continue to sauté for a few minutes longer, until all the vegetables are tender. The liquid will reduce by half, and there will be about 1/2 cup left in the pan. Drain the mushrooms, and reserve the remaining liquid.

Add the bread crumbs and lemon juice to the mushrooms and season with the salt and pepper. Cool the stuffing at room temperature for 15 minutes, and then refrigerate it for at least 20 minutes. (By storing it in the refrigerator, you may make the filling up to 2 days prior to rolling the strudel.)

Lay the rectangle of puff pastry on a lightly floured work surface with the long side closest to you. Roll out lightly until it measures about 8 × 12 inches.

Arrange the mushroom stuffing in a log about 2 inches wide for the entire length of the dough. Leave an inch of dough exposed from the long side closest to you. Leave $\frac{1}{2}$ inch of dough on each short side exposed.

Brush a little of the beaten egg around the border of the dough. Fold the dough over the mushroom filling, pressing the dough together all along the seam, and press down gently with the back of a fork.

Make 3 slits on the top of the strudel, and brush the entire strudel with the rest of the egg. Place the strudel on a baking pan sprayed lightly with the vegetable oil, and bake the strudel for 30 minutes, until the crust is golden brown and the filling is heated through.

PER SERVING: CALORIES 330; CALORIES FROM FAT 160; CALORIES FROM SATURATED FAT 25; PROTEIN 8 G; CARBOHYDRATE 33 G; TOTAL FAT 18 G; SATURATED FAT 2.5 G; CHOLESTEROL 25 MG; SODIUM 170 MG; 48% CALORIES FROM FAT

Variation: Try adding $\frac{1}{2}$ cup of oven-toasted walnuts to the filling before wrapping the strudel.

Quesadillas

Quesadillas are sandwiches made with two corn or flour tortillas that hold a savory stuffing of some sort. There are hundreds of possible fillings, ranging from traditional cheese and beans to chorizo, potatoes, or simply green chilies. Then there are the more inventive quesadillas that may be made from roast duck, tempeh, and even wild mushrooms. Although they originate in Mexico, modern versions have no particular ethnic allegiance.

Triple-Pepper, Onion, and Cheese Quesadillas

SERVES 5

HERE is an all-purpose filling with aromatic Southwestern spices, sweet peppers, onions, and chilies. It keeps for up to five days in the refrigerator and may also be heated and used as a topping for grilled or baked tofu, chicken, beef, or pork. It's the essential filling with which to build great quesadillas.

TO PREPARE THE TRIPLE-PEPPER AND ONION FILLING Heat the canola oil to medium high in a large sauté pan. Add the peppers, chilies, onions, and garlic. Sauté, stirring often, for 2 minutes. Blend in the cumin, oregano, chili powder, and salt and pepper. Cook for 2 minutes. The peppers and onions should still be firm, not mushy. Place the mixture in a bowl to cool.

Preheat the oven to 350°F. Place 1 flour tortilla on the work surface. Spread with $1/2$ cup of the pepper-onion mixture, leaving a $1/2$-inch border with no filling at the edge of the tortilla. Sprinkle with 3 tablespoons of the cheese. Top with a plain tortilla. Repeat until all the filling, cheese, and tortillas are used.

The Triple-Pepper and Onion Filling

$1/8$ cup canola oil

5 cups seeded and thinly sliced assorted medium peppers (red, yellow, green)

2 large poblano chilies, seeded and sliced

3 medium onions, sliced

3 cloves garlic, minced ($1 1/2$ teaspoons)

1 tablespoon cumin

1 tablespoon dried oregano

2 teaspoons chili powder

Salt and freshly ground pepper to taste

10 (8-inch) flour tortillas

$1 1/2$ cups grated Monterey Jack cheese

To Serve (Optional)
Sour cream or plain yogurt
Chopped fresh cilantro
Salsa
Tomatillo Sauce (page 306)

Line a baking sheet with parchment paper, or spray it with vegetable oil. Place the filled tortillas on the sheet pan; make sure the sides do not touch. Bake the tortillas in the oven for about 5 minutes, or until the cheese has just melted. Remove the quesadillas with a wide spatula, cut into wedges, like pizza, and serve immediately with sour cream or plain yogurt, chopped cilantro, salsa, and/or Tomatillo Sauce, if desired.

PER SERVING: CALORIES 480; CALORIES FROM FAT 150; CALORIES FROM SATURATED FAT 50; PROTEIN 20 G; CARBOHYDRATE 64 G; TOTAL FAT 16 G; SATURATED FAT 6 G; CHOLESTEROL 20 MG; SODIUM 720 MG; 31% CALORIES FROM FAT

Variation: You may replace 1 cup of the pepper-onion filling with 1 to 1½ cups of shredded cooked chicken. Try cheddar instead of the Monterey Jack for a sharper flavor.

Woodland Mushroom Quesadillas

SERVES 8

CONCENTRATED juices of mushrooms and shallots give this filling its rich flavor.

Preheat the oven to 350°F. Heat the olive oil in a large sauté pan. Add the shallots and garlic, and sauté for 1 minute, stirring often. Add the mushrooms along with the salt and pepper, and cook over medium heat, stirring often. Continue cooking until the mushrooms are tender but not mushy, about 5 minutes. Stir in the marinara or adobo sauce, if desired.

Place 1 flour tortilla on the work surface. Spread with ½ cup of the mushroom mixture, leaving a ½-inch border with no filling at the edge of the tortilla. Sprinkle with 3 tablespoons of the cheese. Top with a plain tortilla. Repeat until all the filling, cheese, and tortillas are used.

Line a baking sheet with parchment paper, or spray it with vegetable oil. Place the filled tortillas on the sheet pan; do not allow the sides to touch. Gently press the tortillas down to make the filling a uniform thickness.

Bake in the oven for about 5 minutes, or until the cheese has just melted. Remove with a wide spatula. Cut into wedges, like pizza, and serve immediately.

3 tablespoons olive oil

¼ cup chopped shallots

3 cloves garlic, minced (1½ teaspoons)

¾ pound button mushrooms, thinly sliced (about 5 cups)

2 large portobello mushroom caps, chopped (about 2 cups)

1 cup stemmed and chopped shiitake mushrooms

2 teaspoons salt

½ teaspoon freshly ground pepper

¾ cup marinara or adobo sauce (optional)

16 (8-inch) flour tortillas

1½ cups grated Monterey Jack cheese

PER SERVING: CALORIES 470; CALORIES FROM FAT 150; CALORIES FROM SATURATED FAT 45; PROTEIN 18 G; CARBOHYDRATE 65 G; TOTAL FAT 16 G; SATURATED FAT 5 G; CHOLESTEROL 10 MG; SODIUM 1,150 MG; 32% CALORIES FROM FAT

Mushroom Goat-Cheese Quesadillas

SERVES 8

¼ cup balsamic vinegar

½ cup olive oil

2 cloves garlic, minced (1 teaspoon)

1 teaspoon salt

½ teaspoon freshly ground pepper

4 large portobello mushroom caps, stems removed

6 ounces cream cheese

4 ounces mild goat cheese

16 (8-inch) flour tortillas

1½ cups Onion Chutney (page 338)

1½ cups grated mozzarella cheese

THESE quesadillas have a deep, earthy, winelike flavor and elegant aftertaste. The sweet caramelized onion and woodsy portobello mushroom blend perfectly with the mild goat cheese. Make sure you wipe the large mushroom caps clean with a damp towel before marinating. These are wonderful for company or for a special dinner party. Serve with a field green salad and a glass of pinot noir or merlot wine for a complete epicurean experience.

Place the balsamic vinegar, olive oil, garlic, salt, and pepper in a large bowl. Mix well, and add the portobello mushroom caps. Marinate for 20 to 30 minutes, turning the portobellos once or twice.

Preheat the oven to 350°F. While the mushrooms are marinating, blend the cream cheese and goat cheese in a medium bowl with a fork or by hand.

Grill the mushrooms until tender-crisp, about 4 minutes per side. You may also broil the mushrooms in the oven about 3 inches from the broiler element, 4 to 5 minutes per side. Cut the mushroom caps into slices about ¼ inch thick.

Place 1 flour tortilla on the work surface. Top with about 2 tablespoons of the cheese mixture, spread to within ½ inch of the edge of the tortilla. Top with 2 to 3 tablespoons of the Onion Chutney, spreading it evenly. Top with 3 to 4 slices of the mushrooms. Sprinkle with 3 tablespoons of the mozzarella cheese. Top with a tortilla. Repeat until all the cheese filling, chutney, mushrooms, mozzarella, and tortillas are used.

Line a baking sheet with parchment paper, or spray it with vegetable oil. Place the filled tortillas on the sheet pan; don't allow the sides to touch. Bake in the oven for about 5 minutes, or until the cheese has just melted. Remove the quesadillas with a wide spatula, cut into wedges, like pizza, and serve immediately.

PER SERVING: CALORIES 540; CALORIES FROM FAT 200; CALORIES FROM SATURATED FAT 90; PROTEIN 22 G; CARBOHYDRATE 62 G; TOTAL FAT 22 G; SATURATED FAT 10 G; CHOLESTEROL 35 MG; SODIUM 770 MG; 37% CALORIES FROM FAT

Sweet Potato Quesadillas

SERVES 6

THE most common comment heard after customers eat a wedge of these nontraditional quesadillas is "Incredible!" It must be the unexpected sweet taste and interesting combination of blue cheese and chilies. Try these dipped in a simple sauce made by combining bitter orange marmalade with orange juice. If you're entertaining company, slice these quesadillas into smaller wedges. If you enjoy corn tortillas instead of flour, give them a shot in this recipe.

1 tablespoon canola oil

1 cup seeded and chopped red pepper

1 cup chopped yellow onion

2 cloves garlic, minced (1 teaspoon)

1 large poblano chili, roasted and chopped (see page 13)

2 large sweet potatoes or yams (about 1½ pounds), cooked, peeled, and mashed (you should have 4 cups of mashed sweet potatoes)

⅛ cup chopped fresh cilantro

¼ cup crumbled blue cheese

1½ teaspoons salt

12 (8-inch) flour tortillas

1½ cups grated Monterey Jack cheese

Preheat the oven to 350°F. Heat the canola oil in a large sauté pan. Add the pepper, onion, and garlic, and sauté until the onion is translucent, 2 to 3 minutes. Add in the chopped poblano chili.

Mix the sweet potatoes with the sautéed pepper mixture. Add the cilantro, blue cheese, and salt, blending well.

Place ½ cup of the sweet-potato mixture in the center of 1 flour tortilla, and spread the mixture out evenly to within ½ inch of the outer edge of the tortilla. Sprinkle with 3 tablespoons of the Monterey Jack. Place another flour tortilla over the filling to form a sandwich. Repeat with the remaining tortillas until all the filling is used.

Line a baking sheet with parchment, or spray it with vegetable oil. Place the filled tortillas on the sheet pan; don't allow the sides to touch. Bake in the oven for about 5 minutes, or until the cheese has just melted. Remove the quesadillas with a wide spatula, cut into wedges, like pizza, and serve immediately.

PER SERVING: CALORIES 530; CALORIES FROM FAT 130; CALORIES FROM SATURATED FAT 45; PROTEIN 18 G; CARBOHYDRATE 83 G; TOTAL FAT 14 G; SATURATED FAT 5 G; CHOLESTEROL 15 MG; SODIUM 1,040 MG; 24% CALORIES FROM FAT

THE WHOLE FOODS MARKET COOKBOOK

Beans, Legumes, and Whole Grains

Few ingredients are capable of completely regenerating

themselves when placed into the soil. This says a lot about the powerful nutritional qualities of grains, beans, and legumes. But nutrition is only the beginning. These little colorful gems lend immense diversity of flavor and character to our dinner tables.

Grains, dried beans, and legumes feed the world, and in some cases are the main form of nutritional sustenance. Many civilizations have enjoyed them for ages. Lentils, dried peas, and beans are some of the oldest recorded agricultural crops. Legumes have been found in Egyptian tombs and ancient Greek pottery dating back more than ten thousand years.

Grains supply more than 50 percent of the world's calories. They are perhaps more popular in other countries because in the United States we see grains as difficult and time-consuming to cook, as well as potentially fattening. In fact, most grains are as simple to prepare as rice, each offering a different flavor. Most grain or grain-based dishes become calorie-laden because of ingredient add-ons such as butter, cream sauce, or cheese. Most of the grain dishes in this chapter are made with olive oil, not butter.

Every country offers a national dish made with grains or beans, including staples such as North African couscous; rice dishes from Asia, South America, or Mexico; Italian pasta; and Indian lentil dal. Each kind has its own unique flavor, but few foods are as adaptable, combining so well with so many different seasonings.

Scientifically speaking, legumes are edible seeds enclosed in pods. Although they are part of a single plant family, legumes come in many forms. There is such a wide variety of shapes and colors from which to choose, each with its individual identity. Legumes are extremely varied and include peanuts, carob, dried peas, lentils, and dozens of dried beans. Beans contain good amounts of protein and fiber, in addition to complex carbohydrates.

Although grains, beans, and legumes can richly enhance everyone's diet nutritionally, and are a vegetarian's best friend, it's their taste and satisfying texture that keep us coming back for second helpings.

Cooking Grains

Most grains may be cooked up to 2 days in advance. Some whole grains, such as wheat berries, spelt, and kamut, must be soaked for at least 6 hours before cooking. They may then be simmered in boiling water, to which you may add a little salt. The amount of time grains must be cooked in water depends on the structure of the individual grain. Each kind absorbs a different amount of water or liquid. Consult your grain package for directions, or see "Grain Cooking Times" on page 158. For variety, when appropriate you may cook grains in liquids other than water. Try broth, for example, or a mixture of fruit or vegetable juice and water, or add a splash of wine to a dish like a risotto.

After cooking grains, you can cool them by spreading them out on a baking pan or cookie sheet before storing in a covered container in the refrigerator. Cooked grains may be made into pilafs, salads, stuffings, or side dishes. Remember that some grain varieties are softer and contain more starch, lending themselves toward risotto dishes, desserts, and salads. When you cook smart, preparing your grains ahead, you'll find so many recipes can be made in minutes by adding the appropriate garnish, vegetable, or protein. Obviously, some dishes, like risotto, are best made just before serving, but most grains are sturdy and can be a flexible part of lots of interesting dishes.

Quinoa

QUINOA must always be washed in a strainer before cooking because it's covered with a layer of saponin. This is a natural coating that has a slightly bitter flavor, to keep pests and birds away from the grain while it grows. When you rinse quinoa, it looks a bit frothy in the water. This is the saponin washing away. The water no longer looks soapy when all the saponin is rinsed away. Quinoa is versatile in the kitchen. It's cooked just like rice. After washing, place 1 cup of quinoa and 2 cups of water or vegetable stock in a saucepan, and bring it to a boil. Cover the pan, and lower to a simmer. It takes about 20 minutes to cook until tender. When cooked, the seeds almost have a caviar consistency—they pleasantly pop in your mouth and have a rich, nutty flavor.

Preparing Dried Beans in a Hurry

HERE'S a quick-cook method for beans:

Place the beans in a medium pot and cover with cold water by at least 2 to 3 inches. Bring to a boil and immediately turn off the heat; cover the pot and allow the beans to rest at room temperature for at least 1 hour.

Drain off all the cooking liquid, rinse with cold water, and then cook beans according to your recipe. This will also lessen the stomach-irritability qualities associated with beans. Many cooks insist that cooking dried beans with a small piece of wakame, a sea vegetable, makes the bean more digestible, as well.

Cooking Beans and Legumes

Canned and jarred beans and legumes have really come a long way and are perfectly suited to today's modern kitchen. Always read the label when shopping for canned beans and legumes. Be aware of the salt content and added ingredients or fat. We think that jarred beans normally have better flavor and texture than canned beans.

The bean and legume recipes in this chapter specify canned or jarred beans to save time. You may make any of the recipes by cooking the beans yourself from scratch.

Most canned beans were at one time extremely mushy and full of salt. The quality of cooked beans and legumes has improved in the past few years. You can now find almost every variety of canned legume cooked with care retaining much of its texture and character. Many are low in sodium or are sodium free. Jarred beans and legumes are handled with even more mastery and are often as good as those fresh cooked. Beans may be cooked in advance and refrigerated, ready for action, or frozen as a finished recipe, to simply be reheated for a warming dinner in little time.

If you prefer to use dried beans, then there are some bean facts you should know:

- Larger beans may be soaked overnight covered in water and then simmered until tender for later use.
- Never salt water for cooking beans; it toughens the outer skin.
- If the water evaporates too quickly, add more so that the beans don't dry out or scorch.
- After cooking the beans, rinse, drain, and then store them in covered containers in your refrigerator. Cooked beans may be stored in a covered container for up to

BEAN COOKING TIMES

BEAN VARIETY 1 CUP DRIED	SOAK TIME	SIMMER	
		Cups Water	Time
Adzuki	Optional	4	1½ hours
Black, Turtle	At least 4 hours	4	1½ hours
Black-eyed Peas	Optional	4	1 hour
Chickpea	At least 4 hours	4	3 to 4 hours
Great Northern	At least 4 hours	4	2 hours
Kidney	At least 4 hours	4	1½ to 2 hours
Lentil Red/Green	Not required	3	25 to 40 minutes
Lima	6 to 8 hours	3	1½ to 2 hours
Mung	6 to 8 hours	3	1½ to 2 hours
Navy	6 to 8 hours	3	1½ hours
Soybean	6 to 8 hours	4	3½ to 4 hours
Green or Yellow Split Pea	Not required	3	45 minutes

4 days in your refrigerator. Having cooked beans on hand allows you to quickly make stir-fries, stews, salads, burgers, and quick pan-sautéed items.

- Lentils may be prepared by simmering them until tender and then draining and storing them the same way as beans. Lentils do not need to be soaked, as they cook rather quickly. Many salads, stews, and quick sautés can be made using your cooked legumes.

GRAIN COOKING TIMES

GRAIN VARIETY 1 CUP DRIED	STOVETOP COOKING	
	Cups Water	Time (Min.)
Amaranth	2	25
Barley, pearled	2½	40
Barley, whole	3	60
Buckwheat (raw kasha—toasted)	3	30
Bulgur	2	15
Corn, grits	3	20
Corn, meal	4	30
Kamut	3	60
Millet	3	30
Oats, rolled	2½	30
Oats, steel cut	3	40
Quinoa	2	20
Rice, Basmati, brown	2	40
Rice, Basmati, white	1¾	35
Rice, brown, long-grain	2	50
Rice, brown, medium-grain	2	50
Rice, brown, short-grain	2	60
Rice, sweet	1½	30
Rice, white	1½	30
Rye	2½	60
Rye flakes	3	30
Spelt	3	25
Teff	3	60
Wheat berries	4	60
Wheat, cracked	3	25
Wild rice	2½	50

Barbecue Lentils with Eggplant

SERVES 4

⅛ cup olive oil

1 large eggplant, peeled and diced into
    1-inch cubes (2 cups)

1 cup thinly sliced red onion

1 cup finely chopped diced tomatoes

1½ tablespoons fresh oregano

3 cloves garlic, minced
    (1½ teaspoons)

¼ teaspoon freshly ground pepper

1 tablespoon tamari

½ cup favorite barbecue sauce

1 tablespoon lemon juice

1 tablespoon honey

1 (15-ounce) can cooked lentils with
    liquid

¼ cup finely chopped parsley

1 scallion, finely diced

Salt to taste

MEATY chunks of eggplant are simmered in a smoky tomato sauce with the sweet-and-sour overtones of lemon and honey (not barbecued on the grill in the literal sense). You may easily cook your own lentils for this dish. Lentils need no presoaking and they cook quickly. Substitute 1 cup of dried lentils (brown or green) for the canned. Cook them in 3 cups water or Vegetable Stock (see page 57), and then add them as you would the canned. If you like spicy, add a minced serrano or jalapeño to the onions when you sauté. Try serving this over polenta, steamed basmati or short-grain brown rice, or couscous. This makes a great Sunday night dinner served with a field green salad and a loaf of bread.

In a heavy-bottom sauce pot, heat the olive oil over medium heat and sauté the eggplant for 10 minutes, sprinkling with a bit of water if needed to prevent sticking. Add the onion, tomatoes, oregano, garlic, and pepper to the eggplant, and continue to sauté for 5 minutes.

Add the tamari, and stir thoroughly. Add the barbecue sauce, lemon juice, and honey, stirring thoroughly to evenly coat all the vegetables. This will form a sauce around the eggplant. Add the lentils with their liquid to the pot, and simmer for about 15 minutes, adding a bit of water if the sauce looks thick. Add the parsley and scallion. Season with the salt.

PER SERVING: CALORIES 370; CALORIES FROM FAT 130; CALORIES FROM SATURATED FAT 20; PROTEIN 14 G; CARBOHYDRATE 50 G; TOTAL FAT 15 G; SATURATED FAT 2.5 G; CHOLESTEROL 0 MG; SODIUM 580 MG; 35% CALORIES FROM FAT

 Recipe Bonus You may also place the eggplant mixture in an ovenproof casserole dish and top it with provolone cheese; then bake it.

beans, legumes, and whole grains

159

Adzuki Bean Loaf

SERVES 4

ADZUKI (or aduki) beans have been cherished in Japan and Asia for centuries and are usually served at festive occasions. Chinese cultures believe they bring good luck when eaten. This sweet ruddy-colored bean with a white crack running down the center is relatively small, about half the size of a black bean. Adzuki beans are frequently cooked along with rice, imparting to the grain an attractive pink hue. They are also sweetened for desserts, confections, and chilled beverages. Adzuki beans are normally available canned in most natural foods markets and Asian grocery stores. The natural sweet taste of adzuki beans goes well with the sautéed root vegetables in this unique recipe for "meatless" meat loaf. It's comfort food your mother never dreamed of.

2 (15-ounce) cans cooked adzuki beans, rinsed and drained well

1 large Idaho potato, peeled and cut into large pieces

1 tablespoon olive oil

½ medium onion, finely diced

1 stalk celery, finely chopped

1 large carrot, finely chopped

1 large pita bread, torn into small pieces and soaked in 1 cup water

1 tablespoon tamari

½ cup finely chopped parsley

1 teaspoon salt

2 teaspoons freshly ground pepper

¼ cup finely chopped fresh oregano

¼ cup finely chopped fresh basil

1 teaspoon lime juice

Vegetable oil for spraying loaf pan

Preheat the oven to 350°F.

Place the drained beans in a large mixing bowl. Bring a saucepan of water to a boil, add the potato, and cook until tender, about 10 minutes. Drain and set it aside in the bowl with the beans.

In a large sauté pan, heat the olive oil over medium heat, and sauté the onion, celery, and carrot for 3 minutes, until all the vegetables are tender; add this to the beans.

Squeeze excess moisture from the pita bread, and add the bread to the beans. Add the tamari, parsley, salt, pepper, oregano, basil, and lime juice.

Mash the beans and vegetables with a vegetable masher until all the ingredients are coarsely blended.

Spray a standard-size rectangular loaf pan with the vegetable oil, and evenly spread the adzuki bean mixture into the pan with a rubber spatula. Tap the loaf pan on a cutting board to make sure the mixture settles to the bottom well. Score the surface of the bean crust with a butter knife in a crisscross fashion. Bake the loaf in the oven for about 45 minutes, or until golden brown on the surface.

NOTE: You may bake the loaf up to 3 days before serving. This makes it easy to slice. Try a few slices with some melted cheese, sliced onion, lettuce, and tomato on a sub roll or serve warm, sliced over a field green salad.

PER SERVING: CALORIES 310; CALORIES FROM FAT 40; CALORIES FROM SATURATED FAT 0.5; PROTEIN 15 G; CARBOHYDRATE 54 G; TOTAL FAT 4.5 G; SATURATED FAT 0.5 G; CHOLESTEROL 0 MG; SODIUM 1,270 MG; 13% CALORIES FROM FAT

vegan

Chickpeas Florentine with Roasted Peppers

SERVES 6

PAN-SAUTÉED onions, golden-tinged garlic, and smoky roasted peppers add Mediterranean flavor to chickpeas, also called garbanzo beans. Baby spinach goes into this dish at the last minute. Warmth from the simmering beans barely wilts the tender leaves. Jarred piquillo peppers lend pleasant spiciness to this dish. You may use canned chickpeas; however, the jarred ones are so much better. If you have the time, home-cooked beans are also delicious. Try this bean stew over polenta or as a base for Broiled Tuna Stuffed with Spinach and Sun-Dried Tomatoes (page 247). This recipe may be enjoyed warm from the pan, at room temperature, or chilled.

⅛ cup olive oil

1 cup thinly sliced red onion

4 cloves garlic, minced (2 teaspoons)

½ cup drained and finely chopped jarred roasted piquillo peppers

¼ cup finely chopped fresh oregano

½ teaspoon crushed red chili flakes

5 cups cooked chickpeas, well drained (1¾ cups dried)

½ cup water or vegetable stock

2 cups coarsely chopped washed baby spinach leaves

1 tablespoon lemon juice

Salt to taste

In a large sauté pan, heat the olive oil over medium heat. Sauté the onion and garlic for 5 minutes. Add the roasted piquillo peppers, oregano, and red chili flakes, and continue to sauté for 1 minute. Add the chickpeas to the sauté pan with the water, and simmer for 5 minutes. Add the spinach leaves, fold them into the chickpeas, and cook them for 1 minute, until the spinach leaves just wilt. Add the lemon juice, and season with the salt.

PER SERVING: CALORIES 240; CALORIES FROM FAT 80; CALORIES FROM SATURATED FAT 5; PROTEIN 9 G; CARBOHYDRATE 35 G; TOTAL FAT 8 G; SATURATED FAT 0.5 G; CHOLESTEROL 0 MG; SODIUM 500 MG; 33% CALORIES FROM FAT

Yellow Split Peas with Fresh Dill and Crispy Garlic

SERVES 6

2 cups yellow split peas

5 cups water

½ teaspoon turmeric

Salt to taste

⅛ cup olive oil

12 whole cloves garlic, peeled and thinly sliced

1 cup finely chopped fresh dill

RESIDENTS of Scandinavia and Northern Europeans prefer yellow split peas. They are creamier than the American green split peas and have a nuttier, buttery flavor. Although neither require soaking, this process alleviates some of the stomach distress associated with eating legumes. Discard the soaking water, and begin cooking with fresh water. Lightly browning the paper-thin garlic slices is an important step in this dish. Be sure to remove them from the heat just as they begin to turn an amber color—they will continue to cook in the hot oil, and will taste bitter if allowed to become too brown.

Serve this dish piping hot with white basmati rice or with Cilantro Lime Rice (page 172).

Rinse the yellow split peas, and soak them, covered in water, for about 30 minutes. Drain the water, rinse the peas well, and transfer them to a medium pot. Add the quart of water, turmeric, and salt to the pot. Bring the water to a boil, and simmer the yellow split peas uncovered until they are slightly pulpy and cooked through, about 45 minutes. Add more water if it is needed. The peas should appear somewhat moist. Drain the peas when cooked, and set them aside in a large mixing bowl.

In a skillet, heat the olive oil over medium heat. Sauté the garlic slivers to a light golden brown, taking care not to burn them. Stir the garlic slivers with the oil into the yellow split peas. Stir in the dill.

PER SERVING: CALORIES 280; CALORIES FROM FAT 40; CALORIES FROM SATURATED FAT 5; PROTEIN 18 G; CARBOHYDRATE 45 G; TOTAL FAT 4.5 G; SATURATED FAT 0.5 G; CHOLESTEROL 0 MG; SODIUM 10 MG; 14% CALORIES FROM FAT

 Recipe Bonus Serve chilled with small cubes of firm tofu or tempeh mixed in.

beans, legumes, and whole grains

White Bean and Kale Gratin with English Farmhouse Cheddar

SERVES 4

THINK of this as a very sophisticated bean dip with sharp taste and lots of personality inherited from the creamy white beans and crisp, crinkly kale leaves. The almonds roast onto the surface of the cheddar cheese, forming a crispy, aromatic mantle, which is easily cracked open to expose the bubbling beans. This dish may be completely made in an ovenproof casserole or baking dish up to three days before serving and popped in the oven when ready.

Serve hot with crusty French bread.

6 whole kale leaves
3 cloves garlic, thinly sliced
1 tablespoon olive oil

2 (15-ounce) cans cooked white beans, rinsed and drained well
6 ounces sharp cheddar cheese, grated (1 1/2 cups)
1 tablespoon tamari
1/4 teaspoon white pepper
Salt to taste
Vegetable oil for spraying the casserole dish
1/4 cup chopped almonds

Preheat the oven to 350°F. Wash the kale, and remove all the heavy stems. Fill a 3-quart saucepan with water, and bring it to a boil. Blanch the kale in the water for 1 to 2 minutes, until it turns bright green. Immediately remove it from the water, rinse in ice-cold water, drain, and let it cool a little. Coarsely chop the kale, and set it aside. In a large sauté pan over medium heat, sauté the garlic in the olive oil for 1 to 2 minutes, until it is golden brown. Be careful not to burn the garlic.

In a large mixing bowl, combine the white beans, cooked kale, garlic with the oil, cheddar cheese, tamari, white pepper, and salt, and mix thoroughly. Spray a 1-quart ovenproof casserole dish with the vegetable oil. Transfer the bean mixture to it.

Sprinkle with the chopped almonds and bake for 20 minutes.

PER SERVING: CALORIES 410; CALORIES FROM FAT 170; CALORIES FROM SATURATED FAT 50; PROTEIN 24 G; CARBOHYDRATE 28 G; TOTAL FAT 19 G; SATURATED FAT 6 G; CHOLESTEROL 25 MG; SODIUM 990 MG; 41% CALORIES FROM FAT

Borracho Beans

SERVES 4

1 tablespoon olive oil

½ medium onion, chopped

1 stalk celery, chopped

½ green pepper, chopped

½ jalapeño pepper, finely chopped

2 cloves garlic, minced (1 teaspoon)

1 teaspoon chili powder

1 teaspoon cumin

1 tomato, chopped

1 tablespoon smoked soy "bacon bits," plus extra to garnish

2 (15-ounce) cans pinto beans, rinsed and drained well

1 cup amber ale or water

Salt to taste

½ cup finely chopped fresh cilantro

BORRACHO means "drunken," and this recipe's title refers back to when border towns cooked beans in beer, usually with bacon or lard. Our version is lighter, although it's still looped with ale. We use soy-based "bacon bits," but you may use regular bacon if you prefer. These beans make a great soul mate for Cilantro Lime Rice (page 172), or try serving them with Carne Asada with Jalapeño Cilantro Pesto (page 255).

Heat the olive oil over medium heat in a large sauce pot, and sauté the onion, celery, green pepper, jalapeño, and garlic for about 5 minutes. Add the chili powder, cumin, tomato, and soy "bacon bits" to the pan, and continue to sauté for 5 more minutes.

Add the beans with the ale to the pan. Combine the ingredients well with a spoon to prevent the beans and vegetables from sticking. Simmer the beans for 20 minutes, until they appear saucy but not runny. Season with the salt. Garnish the beans with the cilantro and extra soy "bacon bits," and serve.

PER SERVING: CALORIES 270; CALORIES FROM FAT 50; CALORIES FROM SATURATED FAT 5; PROTEIN 14 G; CARBOHYDRATE 38 G; TOTAL FAT 5 G; SATURATED FAT 0.5 G; CHOLESTEROL 0 MG; SODIUM 480 MG; 19% CALORIES FROM FAT

beans, legumes, and whole grains

Havana Black Beans

SERVES 4

GLOSSY black turtle beans are popular in the southeastern United States, Mexico, and the Caribbean. They have a creamy white flesh that easily absorbs bold flavors like cumin, garlic, and chipotle chilies. This dish may be made without coconut milk by substituting water or vegetable stock. This becomes a nutritious complete cross-cultural meal coupled with rice in many areas of the world. The lime juice, cilantro, and scallions add character when added after the beans are cooked. Try adding a shot of dry sherry for the Bahamian version.

Heat the olive oil in a medium saucepan, and sauté the onion for 3 minutes, until it is golden brown. Add the peppers and garlic; continue to sauté for 2 minutes. Add the cumin, dried thyme, bay leaves, and chipotle chilies; combine well.

Add the black beans, water, and coconut milk to the pot, and stir well. Simmer the beans for 10 to 15 minutes. Stir in the lime juice and salt.

Ladle the beans into serving bowls, and top each bowl with the chopped scallions and cilantro.

PER SERVING: CALORIES 280; CALORIES FROM FAT 100; CALORIES FROM SATURATED FAT 50; PROTEIN 13 G; CARBOHYDRATE 34 G; TOTAL FAT 11 G; SATURATED FAT 6 G; CHOLESTEROL 0 MG; SODIUM 780 MG; 36% CALORIES FROM FAT

1 tablespoon olive oil

½ medium onion, finely chopped

½ medium red pepper, finely chopped

½ medium green pepper, finely chopped

1 clove garlic, minced (½ teaspoon)

1 teaspoon cumin

1 teaspoon dried thyme, or 1 tablespoon fresh

2 bay leaves

1 teaspoon canned chipotle chilies, minced with sauce

2 (15-ounce) cans cooked black beans, rinsed and drained well

1 cup water

1 cup coconut milk

1 teaspoon lime juice

Salt to taste

2 scallions, finely chopped

½ cup finely chopped fresh cilantro

 Recipe Bonus For a special serving option, bake or steam whole seeded acorn squash with the top inch removed. The squash acts as a soup bowl, and, with a scoop of basmati rice in the bottom topped with the beans, it makes a beautiful and satisfying meal.

Warm Quinoa Salad with Shrimp and Asparagus

SERVES 4

1 tablespoon olive oil

2 cloves garlic, minced (1 teaspoon)

½ medium red onion, finely diced

½ cup sun-dried tomatoes, unreconstituted, julienned

½ cup vegetable stock or water

½ cup white wine

⅛ cup lemon juice

1 tablespoon grated lemon zest

½ teaspoon freshly ground pepper

Salt to taste

½ cup quinoa

½ pound medium shrimp, peeled and deveined

½ pound asparagus, cut into 1-inch pieces, woody bottoms discarded

¼ cup green peas, fresh or frozen

½ cup roasted cashew pieces

6 scallions, minced

¼ cup finely chopped parsley

Salt and freshly ground pepper to taste

AN unfried "fried" rice of sorts, made with golden quinoa and tender asparagus. The shrimp provide bounce to your bite. Try adding ½ pound of diced firm tofu for even more protein and texture. The chopped roasted cashews and herbs add color and flavor. The warm cooked grains lightly soften the scallions and parsley, releasing a fresh herbal fragrance and lively flavor. This is a fabulous spring dish.

In a saucepan, heat the olive oil over medium heat, and sauté the garlic and onion for 3 minutes. Add the sun-dried tomatoes, and continue to sauté for 1 more minute. Add the vegetable stock, white wine, lemon juice, lemon zest, pepper, and salt, and bring it to a boil. Stir in the quinoa, and simmer on a low heat with the saucepan covered for about 20 minutes, or until the quinoa is almost tender to the bite.

Add the shrimp to the saucepan on top of the quinoa, and simmer for 3 more minutes. Add the asparagus and peas on top of the shrimp, and simmer for 3 more minutes. Top the dish with the roasted cashew pieces, scallions, and chopped parsley. Season to taste with the salt and pepper.

PER SERVING: CALORIES 330; CALORIES FROM FAT 120; CALORIES FROM SATURATED FAT 20; PROTEIN 20 G; CARBOHYDRATE 30 G; TOTAL FAT 14 G; SATURATED FAT 2.5 G; CHOLESTEROL 110 MG; SODIUM 270 MG; 36% CALORIES FROM FAT

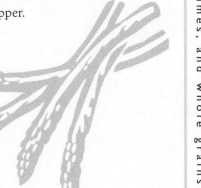

beans, legumes, and whole grains

167

Quinoa Stuffed Peppers

SERVES 6

THIS delicate supergrain seems to have found a natural home inside roasted sweet peppers, complemented by onions, herbs, and garlic. This dish tastes even better when topped with cheese such as mozzarella or Monterey Jack sprinkled over before baking. You may also bake the stuffed peppers in two cups of your favorite marinara sauce.

2 cups water or vegetable stock

I cup quinoa, well rinsed and drained

2 large red peppers, halved and seeded

2 large green peppers, halved and seeded

Vegetable or olive oil for spraying peppers and casserole dish

Salt to taste

$1/2$ teaspoon cayenne pepper

In a saucepan, bring the 2 cups water to a boil, add the quinoa to it, and simmer on low heat with the saucepan covered. Cook the quinoa until the liquid has evaporated and the quinoa is very tender, about 30 minutes. Set the quinoa aside. (The quinoa may be cooked up to 2 days before the peppers are stuffed.)

Preheat the oven to 400°F.

Spray the pepper halves with the oil and season with the salt and cayenne pepper. Place the peppers on a baking pan, and bake for 15 minutes, until softened a little.

TO PREPARE THE STUFFING Heat the olive oil in a pan, and sauté the onion, carrot, celery, pumpkin seeds, garlic, cumin, and chili powder for 3 to 4 minutes, until the vegetables begin to soften and become lightly browned. Add the cooked quinoa, oregano, and basil to the vegetables, and continue to sauté for 1 more minute, until all the ingredients are blended well. Salt to taste.

The Stuffing

$2^{1}/_{2}$ tablespoons olive oil

$1/2$ medium onion, finely diced

I carrot, finely diced

2 stalks celery, finely diced

$1/2$ cup shelled pumpkin seeds

2 cloves garlic, minced (I teaspoon)

$1/2$ teaspoon cumin

I teaspoon chili powder

$1/8$ cup finely chopped fresh oregano

$1/8$ cup finely chopped fresh basil

Salt to taste

Vegetable oil for spraying the casserole dish

$1/2$ cup water or vegetable stock

Fill each pepper half with even amounts of the quinoa filling, and place them in a lightly oiled ovenproof casserole dish. Add the ½ cup water to the pan. Cover the dish with foil, and bake the stuffed peppers for 20 to 25 minutes, until the peppers are tender.

PER SERVING: CALORIES 220; CALORIES FROM FAT 80; CALORIES FROM SATURATED FAT 10; PROTEIN 6 G; CARBOHYDRATE 33 G; TOTAL FAT 9 G; SATURATED FAT 1 G; CHOLESTEROL 0 MG; SODIUM 35 MG; 36% CALORIES FROM FAT

Quinoa Stuffed Pepper

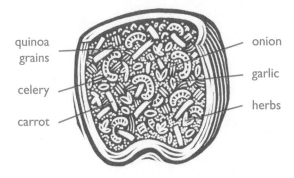

quinoa grains

celery

carrot

onion

garlic

herbs

Ancient Grain Pilaf

SERVES 6

THE grains in this dish need to be cooked separately. You may cook all the grains up to three days ahead to make this a bit easier to manage. The couscous is merely reconstituted—not actually cooked. If you want to sample the pure taste of whole grains, this dish is worth it. Each grain has a distinctive character, flavor, and texture that is not masked by the lightly sautéed root vegetables. You may use any combination of grains, so this is a good recipe to think of if you have some grain leftovers in your refrigerator. Mix in chopped sautéed chicken, tofu, tempeh, or other favorite protein source, which makes this rice dish a complete entrée.

2 cups water
½ cup brown rice
Pinch of salt

1½ cups water
¼ cup bulgur
Pinch of salt

1½ cups boiling water
⅛ cup olive oil
1 cup couscous

1 cup water
¼ cup whole spelt grain

⅛ cup olive oil
1 medium onion, finely chopped
2 stalks celery, finely diced
2 large carrots, finely diced
6 cloves garlic, minced (1 tablespoon)
¼ cup tamari or soy sauce
3 scallions, finely chopped
½ cup finely chopped parsley
Salt and freshly ground pepper to taste

In a large saucepan, bring the 2 cups water to a boil, and add the brown rice and a pinch of salt. Reduce the heat, and cover the saucepan. Simmer the rice for 45 to 50 minutes, until the rice is completely cooked. Let the rice cool.

In another saucepan, boil the 1½ cups water. Add the bulgur and a pinch of salt to the water. Reduce the heat to low, and cover the saucepan. Simmer the bulgur for 10 to 15 minutes, until it is cooked through. Remove the bulgur from the heat, and set it aside for 15 minutes. Drain the remaining water, and let the bulgur cool.

Plump the couscous by pouring the 1½ cups boiling water and ⅛ cup olive oil over the couscous in a sauce pot with a tight-fitting lid. Stir the couscous with a fork to prevent it from sticking and getting lumpy. Cover the pot, and set it aside to cool for at least 20 minutes.

To cook the whole spelt grain, combine the 1 cup water and the spelt in a saucepan, and bring it to a boil, uncovered. Lower the heat, and simmer for 45 minutes, stirring occasionally, until the spelt is cooked through (see Note).

(Spelt retains a firm texture even after cooking. It is this quality that helps make the overall character of this dish work so well.) Drain the excess water, and set the spelt aside to cool.

Heat the ⅛ cup olive oil in a large sauté pan over medium heat. Sauté the onion, celery, carrots, and garlic for 5 minutes, until they begin to turn golden brown. Add the cooked rice, bulgur, couscous, and spelt. Add the tamari, scallions, and parsley, and stir for 1 more minute, mixing thoroughly. Season with the salt and pepper.

NOTE: Spelt can be plumped in water overnight, which softens the whole grain and shortens cooking time by a third. Cover the spelt with a couple of inches of water.

PER SERVING: CALORIES 290; CALORIES FROM FAT 90; CALORIES FROM SATURATED FAT 10; PROTEIN 23 G; CARBOHYDRATE 51 G; TOTAL FAT 10 G; SATURATED FAT 1.5 G; CHOLESTEROL 0 MG; SODIUM 470 MG; 31% CALORIES FROM FAT

beans, legumes, and whole grains

Cilantro Lime Rice

SERVES 4

SIMPLICITY is the beauty of this rice dish: steamed basmati rice scented with the aroma of roasting almonds. When the warm rice combines with raw spinach and cilantro, the delicate flavors are released. The lemony rice takes on a pale green color, adding great plate appeal. Try this as a side dish under grilled seafood or poultry or with Havana Black Beans (page 166) or Borracho Beans (page 165). It may also be used as a stuffing for poultry dishes, tofu, or hollowed vegetables such as eggplant, tomatoes, or zucchini.

2 cups water
1 cup basmati rice
3 tablespoons olive oil
2 cloves garlic, minced (1 teaspoon)
1 teaspoon grated lemon zest
1 tablespoon lime juice
Salt to taste
2 cups finely chopped fresh cilantro
2 cups washed finely chopped baby spinach
3 scallions, finely chopped
Salt to taste

In a large saucepan, bring the water to a boil. Add the rice, olive oil, garlic, lemon zest, lime juice, and salt, and reduce to medium heat. Stir gently, cover, and simmer slowly for about 25 minutes, or until the rice is tender. Leave the rice covered so the steam stays in, making the rice fluffy.

Transfer the rice to a large mixing bowl. Add the cilantro, spinach, scallions, and salt. Combine thoroughly.

PER SERVING: CALORIES 290; CALORIES FROM FAT 100; CALORIES FROM SATURATED FAT 15; PROTEIN 5 G; CARBOHYDRATE 44 G; TOTAL FAT 11 G; SATURATED FAT 1.5 G; CHOLESTEROL 0 MG; SODIUM 35 MG; 34% CALORIES FROM FAT

Wild Rice with Pecans and Cranberries

SERVES 6

8 cups water

12 ounces wild rice

1 teaspoon salt

⅓ cup sun-dried cranberries

1 cup chopped parsley

⅓ cup pecans

6 scallions, finely chopped

1 cup diced yellow tomatoes

1 cup Raspberry Vinaigrette
(see page 324)

Salt and freshly ground pepper to
taste

WILD rice is actually a long-grain marsh grass, not a rice species at all. Sporting formal black color and roasted nutty flavor, it adds elegance to any meal. Make sure you wash the rice well before cooking; small pieces of debris, by-products of the harvesting process, are commonly found in many wild rice brands. Just rinse the rice in a colander under cold water. In this recipe, sweet sun-dried cranberries, tart tomato, and crunchy pecans highlight the coffee-flavored wild rice and the chewy texture. You may use Raspberry Vinaigrette or your favorite bottled brand of vinaigrette to dress this salad.

In a large saucepan, bring the water to a boil and add the wild rice and salt. Reduce the heat, and cover the saucepan. Cook the rice for 50 to 60 minutes, until the rice is completely tender. Drain the excess water, and let the rice cool.

Once the rice is cooled, transfer it to a large mixing bowl, and add the cranberries, parsley, pecans, scallions, yellow tomatoes, and Raspberry Vinaigrette. Add the salt and pepper, and mix the rice salad thoroughly.

PER SERVING: CALORIES 470; CALORIES FROM FAT 210; CALORIES FROM SATURATED FAT 30; PROTEIN 9 G; CARBOHYDRATE 56 G; TOTAL FAT 24 G; SATURATED FAT 3 G; CHOLESTEROL 0 MG; SODIUM 330 MG; 45% CALORIES FROM FAT

beans, legumes, and whole grains

Orange Cashew Rice

SERVES 4

SOME dishes are just naturally uplifting and sunny, and this is one of those dishes. Everyone enjoys seeing a plate in front of them mounded with this colorful rice. The rice takes on a slightly sweet citrus flavor, roasted cashews add crunch, and bell peppers supply a juicy bite. This looks spectacular next to bright Emerald Sesame Kale (page 283).

I cup water

I cup orange juice

2 teaspoons grated orange zest

I tablespoon olive oil

Salt to taste

I cup basmati rice

½ cup roasted cashew pieces

¼ cup chopped yellow peppers

¼ cup chopped red peppers

3 scallions, minced

I teaspoon salt

Freshly ground white pepper to taste

I (8-ounce) can mandarin orange segments, drained well

In a 2-quart sauce pot, bring the water, orange juice, orange zest, olive oil, and salt to a boil, and stir in the rice. Cover the sauce pot, and simmer the rice for 25 to 30 minutes, until the rice is cooked through and the liquid has totally evaporated.

Empty the orange rice into a large mixing bowl, and add the cashew pieces, peppers, and scallions. Just before serving, season the rice with the salt and white pepper, and add the drained mandarin orange segments to the rice, folding them in gently to prevent the oranges from breaking.

PER SERVING: CALORIES 370; CALORIES FROM FAT 110; CALORIES FROM SATURATED FAT 20; PROTEIN 7 G; CARBOHYDRATE 61 G; TOTAL FAT 12 G; SATURATED FAT 2.5 G; CHOLESTEROL 0 MG; SODIUM 490 MG; 30% CALORIES FROM FAT

Wheat Berry Waldorf Salad

2 cups wheat berries

7 cups water

1 cup chopped walnuts

2 medium apples, unpeeled, cored and
  chopped

1 cup raisins

1 cup finely chopped parsley

¼ cup apple cider vinegar

¼ cup apple juice

1 tablespoon salt

½ teaspoon freshly ground pepper

½ teaspoon ground nutmeg

½ teaspoon cinnamon

½ cup extra-virgin olive oil

⅛ cup lemon juice

WHEAT berries are the mother grain from which pasta, bread, and flour are derived. Most of us have never tasted the true flavor of wheat. Little wheat berries pack a nutlike flavor and are pleasantly chewy. Use a crunchy, firm, sweet-tart apple (such as a Granny Smith or Gala) for this salad. Lemon juice and vinegar keep chopped apples from darkening so you may make this salad the day before serving. Try substituting dried apples for fresh for another flavor variation.

Soak the wheat berries at least 6 to 8 hours or overnight in water to cover by a couple of inches. Drain the water, and set aside the wheat berries.

In a saucepan, bring the water to a boil. Add the wheat berries to the boiling water and simmer them uncovered for about 50 minutes, or until they are totally cooked through. Wheat berries retain a firm, chewy texture when cooked. Drain the water, and set aside the wheat berries to cool. Then transfer the wheat berries to a large mixing bowl, and add the walnuts, apples, raisins, parsley, apple cider vinegar, apple juice, salt, pepper, nutmeg, cinnamon, olive oil, and lemon juice. Mix everything thoroughly. Add more salt if necessary, and serve.

PER SERVING: CALORIES 420; CALORIES FROM FAT 210; CALORIES FROM SATURATED FAT 35; PROTEIN 15 G; CARBOHYDRATE 45 G; TOTAL FAT 23 G; SATURATED FAT 3.5 G; CHOLESTEROL 0 MG; SODIUM 420 MG; 50% CALORIES FROM FAT

beans, legumes, and whole grains

Pasta and Other Warming Starches

COOKING PASTA ◆ BOW TIE PASTA WITH KASHA, CARAMELIZED ONIONS, AND WATERCRESS ◆ SPELT PENNE WITH PEAS AND WALNUTS ◆ FETTUCCINE WITH GARLIC, PARSLEY, AND PARMESAN ◆ ORECCHIETTE PASTA WITH SHIITAKE MUSHROOMS AND SUGAR SNAP PEAS ◆ ORZO AND FETA WITH LEMON-CAPER DRESSING AND KALAMATA OLIVES ◆ ROASTED BUTTERNUT SQUASH WITH PENNE PASTA ◆ PAN-SAUTÉED PORTOBELLO PASTA WITH ROASTED GARLIC AND SUN-DRIED TOMATOES ◆ WHOLE WHEAT LINGUINE WITH BROCCOLI ◆ POTATO CORN SEMI-SOUFFLÉ ◆ PUMPKIN POBLANO CORN PUDDING ◆ SPRING COUSCOUS WITH ASPARAGUS AND ORANGE ◆ SURF AND TURF PASTA ◆ SEITAN LASAGNA ◆ GARLIC SPINACH STELLINI PASTA ◆ SPINACH MUSHROOM LASAGNA ◆ SAVORY TOMATO PESTO POLENTA ◆ CAUSA LIMENA WITH TUNA ◆ BOW TIES WITH SMOKED SALMON, ASPARAGUS, AND SPICY PISTACHIOS ◆ SOUTHWEST KING RANCH CASSEROLE ◆ PAD THAI

A steaming bowl of pasta is comforting to the soul. Pasta, as well as other nourishing starches such as polenta or mashed potatoes, provides immense pleasure —from the inside out. Although the true origins of pasta are unclear, references have been traced back to the late 1200s to several cultures, including Etruscan, Roman, Arabian, and Chinese. Imagine the alchemy resulting from the mere combination of flour and water. Boundless culinary horizons were created as the first hands mixed a bit of water, a sprinkling of salt, and some freshly milled wheat. Our dinner tables would never be the same.

Pasta is merely one group within the universe of starch dishes; however, it is a galaxy full of shapes, sizes, flavors, and textures. Many of us are familiar with the whimsical shapes and forms traditional durum wheat or more coarsely ground semolina pasta comes in. However, there are dozens of other whole-grain pastas on our shelves, each with its own character. Alternative whole-grain pastas, many of them made from organic grains such as quinoa, corn, and rice (see "Whole Foods Glossary," page 395), have an earthy taste that semolina doesn't offer. Though they are cooked a bit differently from durum wheat varieties, the rewards are great. Imagine the flavor of corn pasta, sizzled in the pan with sweet corn, jalapeños, red onion, and cilantro. Penne or little pasta quills made from ancient spelt (also called farro) has intense flavor when tossed with peas, roasted walnuts, and naturally cured bacon. It's our modern-day fortune that ages ago someone decided pasta needed to take on playful shapes. For example, concave, rounded little pasta called orecchiette, Italian for "little ears," is able to capture every last drizzle of flavorful sauce and transport it into our mouths, not losing a drop. The bow tie or farfalle is a dressy pasta, ready for any dining occasion.

Pasta is but one main character in this chapter. We also feature creamy cornmeal-based polenta, one of the most versatile foods to grace our palates. Polenta began as a simple cornmeal mush or cereal made from ground maize. It's matured into a modern dish full of panache. Polenta is a universal carrier for all sorts of additions, such as pesto, sun-dried tomatoes, roasted garlic, and ricotta cheese. Not only can it be eaten warm and soft right from the pan, polenta may also be brushed with flavored oil and char-grilled, broiled, or sautéed until crispy.

Classic lasagna and stacked pasta casseroles appear in this chapter, with the twist of sautéed mushrooms and spinach or spicy Mexican chicken in our Southwest King Ranch Casserole (page 203). We also felt it was important to offer a lasagna recipe that may be made without dairy cheese (see Seitan Lasagna, page 194). While pasta dishes lend themselves toward casual meals for family and company, they may also be served in smaller portions as appetizers.

Cooking Pasta

Cooking pasta eventually becomes intuitive; however, there are some basics. Many fine brands of both organic and conventionally produced durum wheat pastas are available. Experiment with a few brands before settling on the one that you can't live without. There are also many alternative grain pastas, each with its own distinctive personality.

Pasta may be cooked a day or two before you incorporate it into your dishes. In a restaurant kitchen, that's normally how the cooks are able to serve large numbers of dinners in a short period of time. This does not take away from the quality or character of the dish. Using this method allows you to prepare some items over the weekend and save yourself time during the week when the pressure of the workday bears down on you.

Durum wheat dried pasta needs to be cooked in plenty of boiling water. Normally speaking, 1 pound of dried pasta should be cooked in 4 to 6 quarts of boiling water to which a tablespoon or two of salt has been added. Make sure the water is at a solid rolling boil before adding the pasta—you want the pasta to cook as quickly as possible. Stir it often to prevent sticking. When the pasta is cooked, drain it in a large colander. Do not rinse if you are using right away; just finish the recipe and serve. If you want to reserve the pasta for later use, rinse it in ice water to stop the cooking process. You may lightly oil the cooked rinsed pasta and store it, well covered, in your refrigerator for up to 3 days.

REHEATING PASTA

You have two choices. If you just want to make the pasta hot and serve it with a sauce, dip it in a colander into boiling salted water for 1 minute, until it is heated through. Drain very well.

If you are going to prepare a pasta dish with vegetables or another garnish like chicken, shrimp, or red meat, here's how to reheat. In a large sauté pan over high heat, sauté the cooked pasta in olive oil for 2 minutes. You may add any herbs or other garnish that your recipe calls for. If you are making a simple dish of pasta with Parmesan and peas, for example, just sauté the peas; then add the cooked pasta to your pan. Dinner can be ready in less than 10 minutes.

How Do You Know Al Dente?

TO see if pasta is done, a few minutes before the anticipated end of cooking time, test a small piece of pasta and repeat this process until the pasta still remains firm but slightly tender to the bite (al dente). The pasta will taste raw if it's not cooked through, and it will have an opaque white center streak.

Cooking Couscous

Cooking couscous is very different from cooking any other form of pasta, since the grain is actually precooked. Once only the traditional tiny grains of couscous were available, which had to be steamed. Now there are several sizes of couscous, such as larger Israeli and Lebanese, to name a few. Here's how to cook them:

Traditional Couscous

Tiny semolina grains are actually plumped, not boiled like pasta. Liquid such as water, stock, or fruit juice is boiled with a few teaspoons of oil and a sprinkle of salt. The oil makes the couscous tender and prevents it from clumping. This hot liquid is poured over the couscous and quickly covered so the couscous can reconstitute or plump for about 10 minutes. Normally 1¾ cups of hot liquid combined with 1 tablespoon of olive oil and a pinch of salt is needed for 1 cup of dry couscous.

Israeli Couscous

Larger in size than traditional couscous, Israeli couscous needs to be cooked almost the same way a rice pilaf is made. The best way to cook Israeli couscous is to heat 2 teaspoons of olive oil and add whatever spices and vegetables you enjoy (such as curry powder or a few cloves of garlic and maybe a small minced onion). After sautéing these spices and vegetables, add 1 cup of Israeli couscous and stir well. Add 2 cups of liquid, either water or stock, and bring to a boil. Cover the pan and simmer for 10 to 15 minutes while stirring occasionally, until all the liquid is absorbed and the couscous is tender. Turn off the heat and allow the couscous to sit, covered, for an additional 5 to 10 minutes before serving to make the it fluffier.

Cooking Wheat-Free Pastas

Our stores carry a wide range of pastas that contain no wheat or gluten for folks who are sensitive to these ingredients. Although they are great tasting, they are a bit more challenging to cook because gluten is the ingredient that holds the form and shape of a wheat pasta. These nonwheat pasta varieties must be cooked in plenty of boiling water and must never be overcooked. If they are cooked just a few minutes too long, they have a tendency to fall apart. Wheat-free pasta should be cooked al dente and eaten immediately. We don't recommend cooking ahead and storing these pasta varieties. Try a bit of global cuisine harmonizing by preparing corn pasta with some Tex-Mex seasoning or rice pasta with Asian ingredients.

For many people with wheat allergies and sensitivities to semolina wheat flour, these pastas offer a welcome alternative source of flavor and recipe possibilities. Pasta made from rice, potato, quinoa, brown rice, spelt, corn, and kamut is available in a variety of shapes and lengths. Here are a few whole-grain pasta cooking tips to keep in mind when using nonwheat-based pastas.

- Some of the pastas also contain some amount of semolina wheat. Always check the ingredients label in case you are allergic.
- Alternative grain pastas always cook quicker than traditional durum semolina pastas.
- Besides salting the water, add a tablespoon of oil—these nonwheat pastas need a little bit more help to prevent sticking together.
- Always cook the pasta using 4 to 6 quarts of boiling water to 1 pound of dried pasta. Many whole-grain pastas come in smaller boxes than 1 pound, so figure accordingly.

WHOLE-GRAIN PASTA COOKING CHART

Here are some general cooking times for 1 pound of whole-grain pastas. The times vary a little, depending on the shape and length of the pasta, so check the box first. Begin to check doneness a minute before you think it may be ready.

Brown rice pasta	5 to 8 minutes	chewy, dense, earthy
Corn pasta	4 to 8 minutes	delicate, very soft, light
Kamut pasta	4 to 10 minutes	strong, nutty, dense
Potato pasta	5 to 8 minutes	starchy, soft, comforting
Quinoa pasta	4 to 6 minutes	buttery, soft, nutty
Rice pasta	8 to 12 minutes	mild, chewy, comforting
Semolina pasta	12 to 14 minutes	chewy, neutral-flavored
Spelt pasta	5 to 7 minutes	nutty, chewy, strong flavor
Whole wheat pasta	7 to 9 minutes	dense, nutty, chewy

vegetarian

Bow Tie Pasta with Kasha, Caramelized Onions, and Watercress

SERVES 4

BUTTERFLY-SHAPED pasta is used in this modern rendition of an ancient Russian dish called Kasha and Varnishkes (which means "bow ties"). The combination of tender pasta and earthy-tasting kasha (also called buckwheat groats) is great together. The sweet onion acts like a flavor chaperone, balancing the two tastes appropriately. The crispy watercress offers a pleasant refreshing texture to this dish.

1 tablespoon canola oil
1 cup kasha (whole buckwheat groats)
1 large egg, lightly beaten
2 cups Vegetable Stock (page 57) or water

1 pound farfalle (bow tie) pasta
¼ cup extra-virgin olive oil
2 cups diced yellow onion
¾ cup watercress, roughly torn into large pieces
Salt and freshly ground pepper to taste

Heat the canola oil in a medium saucepan. In the meantime, with a fork, mix the kasha with the beaten egg. Add the kasha to the hot oil, and sauté for 1 minute to coat the kasha kernels. Add the stock, and bring to a boil. Reduce the heat to low; cover the pan tightly; simmer for 15 to 20 minutes, until the kasha is tender and the liquid is absorbed.

While the kasha is cooking, bring a large pot of salted water to a boil. Add the pasta, and cook for 10 to 12 minutes, until it reaches the desired doneness. Drain, rinse with cold water, and reserve the pasta. This step may be done up to 2 days before making this dish. The pasta may be kept in a covered container in the refrigerator.

In a large sauté pan, heat the olive oil, and add the onions, stirring occasionally for 5 to 7 minutes, until the onions are well browned and crispy. You may add a sprinkling of water to prevent sticking.

Fluff the cooked kasha with a fork until the grains are separated. Combine the kasha with the cooked pasta, caramelized onions, and watercress. Season with the salt and pepper. Serve immediately

PER SERVING: CALORIES 500; CALORIES FROM FAT 180; CALORIES FROM SATURATED FAT 20; PROTEIN 13 G; CARBOHYDRATE 71 G; TOTAL FAT 20 G; SATURATED FAT 2.5 G; CHOLESTEROL 55 MG; SODIUM 40 MG; 36% CALORIES FROM FAT

Spelt Penne with Peas and Walnuts

SERVES 6

3 cups water

1½ teaspoons salt

1 cup spelt

1 pound spelt penne pasta

¼ cup olive oil

1½ cups diced onions

1 cup walnut pieces, toasted

¾ cup frozen peas, thawed

¼ cup chopped parsley

Salt and freshly ground pepper
to taste

FOR centuries, spelt has been a mainstay of Tuscany in the northeastern area of Italy, where it is called farro. Not only is spelt more hearty than wheat, but it also contains significantly more protein and is high in fiber. If you prefer, substitute semolina penne.

In a medium sauce pot, bring the water and ½ teaspoon of the salt to a boil. Stir in the spelt, reduce the heat, cover, and simmer for 25 to 35 minutes, until tender. Remove from the heat. Set aside (see Note). Meanwhile, bring a large pot of salted water to a boil. Add the pasta, and cook for 7 to 8 minutes, until it reaches the desired doneness. Drain the pasta and reserve.

Place the olive oil in a large sauté pan, and heat over medium-high heat. Add the onions, reduce the heat to medium, and cook until golden brown, about 8 minutes. In the same sauté pan, combine the caramelized onions, cooked pasta, spelt, walnuts, peas, and parsley. Season with salt and pepper. Combine all the ingredients well, and serve immediately.

NOTE: To shorten the spelt cooking time by a third, soak overnight in plenty of cold water to cover.

PER SERVING: CALORIES 590; CALORIES FROM FAT 200; CALORIES FROM SATURATED FAT 20; PROTEIN 18 G; CARBOHYDRATE 88 G; TOTAL FAT 22 G; SATURATED FAT 2.5 G; CHOLESTEROL 0 MG; SODIUM 810 MG; 34% CALORIES FROM FAT

pasta and other warming starches

183

Fettuccine with Garlic, Parsley, and Parmesan

SERVES 4

THERE is nothing more rewarding than the taste of perfectly cooked pasta with a fruity olive oil enhanced by sharp Parmesan cheese. Of course, the mellow flavor of golden brown garlic cloves is a welcome addition. This pasta is excellent served at room temperature or directly from the pan.

1 pound fettuccine
¼ cup olive oil
12 cloves garlic
¾ cup grated Parmesan cheese
1 cup minced fresh parsley
1 teaspoon lemon pepper

Bring a large pot of salted water to a boil. Add the fettuccine, and cook until the pasta is al dente, 6 to 8 minutes. When the pasta is cooked, rinse it in cold water, drain well, and reserve.

While the pasta is cooking, heat the olive oil over medium heat in a large nonstick sauté pan. Add the garlic cloves and sauté them very gently, turning often for 4 minutes, until light golden brown and softened. Remove the garlic cloves from the pan, and reserve. Add the drained pasta to the pan, and sauté over medium heat for 2 minutes, until warmed through. Add the browned garlic cloves, Parmesan cheese, parsley, and lemon pepper, and toss the pasta well to combine.

PER SERVING: CALORIES 410; CALORIES FROM FAT 180; CALORIES FROM SATURATED FAT 50; PROTEIN 19 G; CARBOHYDRATE 40 G; TOTAL FAT 20 G; SATURATED FAT 5 G; CHOLESTEROL 15 MG; SODIUM 840 MG; 44% CALORIES FROM FAT

Variation: For extra flavor and protein, try adding grilled or sautéed shrimp or bite-size pieces of grilled or sautéed chicken breast, tofu, or small chunks of smoked mozzarella to the final pasta toss.

Oil in the Water?

MANY cooks feel that adding a bit of oil to the cooking water prevents the pasta from sticking. It's really not necessary. If you cook your pasta in plenty of vigorously boiling water and give it a stir from time to time, it will be the best method of making sure that there's no sticky business taking place in your pasta pot.

Orecchiette Pasta with Shiitake Mushrooms and Sugar Snap Peas

SERVES 4

12 ounces orecchiette pasta

1 tablespoon olive oil

1 cup minced red onion

1 cup stemmed and sliced shiitake
    mushrooms

1 large portobello cap, diced
    (about 1½ cups)

1 cup sugar snap or snow peas,
    strings removed

1 cup minced scallions

½ cup grated Parmesan cheese

Salt and freshly ground pepper to
    taste

WHO doesn't love this whimsical concave shape of orecchiette ("little ears") pasta that comes from Puglia, Italy? The pasta holds the natural sauce created by the concentrated juices produced by the mushrooms as they cook down. If there is any leftover pasta, it is delicious served at room temperature the next day. Try adding some toasted pine nuts for a garnish—they add a pleasing crunch.

Bring a large pot of salted water to a boil. Add the pasta and cook for 8 to 9 minutes, until it is al dente. Drain the pasta, reserving about ½ cup of the cooking liquid. Place the cooked pasta in a bowl large enough for easy mixing.

Heat the olive oil in a 10- or 12-inch nonstick sauté pan over medium heat. Add the onion, and sauté for 1 minute to wilt the onion; add the shiitake and portobello mushrooms, and sauté for 4 to 5 minutes. Add the sugar snap peas, and sauté 2 additional minutes.

Add the sautéed vegetables to the bowl with the cooked pasta. Toss well, adding a tablespoon or so of the reserved pasta water, if needed, for moisture. Add the scallions, Parmesan cheese, and salt and pepper, and toss lightly to blend.

PER SERVING: CALORIES 270; CALORIES FROM
FAT 70; CALORIES FROM SATURATED FAT 25;
PROTEIN 13 G; CARBOHYDRATE 39 G; TOTAL FAT
8 G; SATURATED FAT 3 G; CHOLESTEROL 10 MG;
SODIUM 1,200 MG; 26% CALORIES FROM FAT

pasta and other warming starches

vegetarian

Orzo and Feta with Lemon-Caper Dressing and Kalamata Olives

SERVES 6

ORZO are little rice-shaped pasta that appear in many authentic Greek dishes. In this recipe they absorb the citrus juice and olive oil just enough to balance the flavor of tart capers and strong Greek Kalamata olives. The Mediterranean taste of this salad is bright and lively. Orzo is cooked with turmeric in the water, which imparts a golden-yellow color to the small pasta. For an extra colorful dish, use Whole Foods Markets tricolor orzo. This is a great buffet dish because it tastes wonderful served at room temperature. Serve as a salad or warmed through for a side dish.

I teaspoon turmeric
I pound orzo

½ cup extra-virgin olive oil
¼ teaspoon freshly ground white pepper
I teaspoon salt
½ cup finely minced fresh parsley
⅛ cup lemon juice
I tablespoon capers, drained
½ teaspoon sugar
I cup julienned sun-dried tomatoes
½ cup pitted, roughly chopped Kalamata olives
I cup crumbled feta cheese

Bring a large pot of salted water to a boil. Add the turmeric, and then add the orzo; cook for 10 to 15 minutes, until it is al dente. Drain the orzo, and rinse it in cold water. Set aside.

In a bowl large enough to hold the orzo, make a dressing by blending the olive oil, white pepper, salt, parsley, lemon juice, capers, and sugar. Add the cooked orzo to the dressing, and combine. Stir in the sun-dried tomatoes and olives. Carefully toss in the feta cheese, mixing lightly, so the feta stays in nice uniform pieces.

PER SERVING: CALORIES 530; CALORIES FROM FAT 230; CALORIES FROM SATURATED FAT 60; PROTEIN 14 G; CARBOHYDRATE 61 G; TOTAL FAT 26 G; SATURATED FAT 6 G; CHOLESTEROL 20 MG; SODIUM 1,100 MG; 43% CALORIES FROM FAT

Feta

KNOWN for its Greek origins, feta cheese is now produced around the world. The crumbly white cheese, originally from goat's or ewe's milk, is now commonly made in the United States with pasteurized cow's milk. If desired, feta's strong salty flavor can be mellowed by soaking for a few minutes in fresh, cold water or milk.

Roasted Butternut Squash with Penne Pasta

SERVES 4

1 medium butternut squash

1½ cups diced onion

3 cloves garlic, minced
   (1½ teaspoons)

½ teaspoon crushed red chili flakes

3 tablespoons olive oil

1 tablespoon lemon juice

2 teaspoons salt

1 pound penne pasta

½ cup minced parsley

½ cup grated Parmesan cheese

Salt and freshly ground pepper to
   taste

WHEN creamy orange-colored roasted butternut squash is mixed into penne pasta, the combination forms a complete and hearty meal. Chunks of this hard winter squash are loaded with natural sugar, which browns easily and forms a light coating over the penne. Room temperature is the best way to enjoy this rustic dish. Try topping with some toasted pumpkin seeds (see Note, page 318)—the crunchy texture pairs well with the sweet squash.

Preheat the oven to 375°F.

Peel the butternut squash (a vegetable peeler works best). Using a heavy knife, cut the squash in half lengthwise. Scoop out the seeds, and discard them. Dice the squash into 1-inch cubes (you should have about 4 cups). Place the squash cubes in a large mixing bowl, and add the onion, garlic, red chili flakes, olive oil, lemon juice, and the 2 teaspoons salt. Toss the ingredients to mix well.

Place the mixture in a large roasting pan, and roast for about 45 minutes, or until golden brown, stirring occasionally. The squash should be firm-tender, not mushy.

Bring a large pot of salted water to a boil. Add the pasta, and cook for 10 to 12 minutes, until it is al dente. Drain the pasta, and place it in a large serving bowl. Mix in the cooked squash mixture, parsley, Parmesan cheese, and salt and pepper.

PER SERVING: CALORIES 400; CALORIES FROM FAT 130; CALORIES FROM SATURATED FAT 35; PROTEIN 13 G; CARBOHYDRATE 56 G; TOTAL FAT 15 G; SATURATED FAT 4 G; CHOLESTEROL 10 MG; SODIUM 1,660 MG; 33% CALORIES FROM FAT

pasta and other warming starches

vegan

Pan-Sautéed Portobello Pasta with Roasted Garlic and Sun-Dried Tomatoes

SERVES 4

JUICY portobello mushroom caps add a wild, complex flavor to penne pasta. The penne, or little quill-shaped pasta, conveniently captures the marinade inside the hollow tunnel running through it. Feel free to substitute domestic button mushrooms for a milder flavor. If you want a smoky flavor, grill the mushroom caps instead of pan sautéing.

1 pound penne pasta

¼ cup julienned sun-dried tomatoes
1 cup boiling water

⅛ cup olive oil
2 large portobello mushrooms, stemmed and wiped clean, diced
¼ cup minced parsley
¼ teaspoon salt
Freshly ground pepper to taste
¾ cup sliced scallions
1 cup roughly chopped roasted garlic (see Note)
¾ cup Italian Herb Vinaigrette (page 329), or your favorite bottled dressing

B ring a large pot of salted water to a boil. Add the penne; cook for 8 to 10 minutes, until it reaches the desired doneness.

While the pasta is cooking, reconstitute the sun-dried tomatoes in the boiling water for about 20 minutes. Drain and rinse the pasta in ice-cold water, and reserve. Drain the tomatoes, and set them aside.

In a large sauté pan, heat the olive oil over high heat, and sauté the mushrooms until tender, 3 to 5 minutes. In a large bowl, combine the cooked pasta with the sun-dried tomatoes, sautéed mushrooms, parsley, salt, pepper, scallions, and roasted garlic. Pour the vinaigrette over the pasta, and toss lightly to blend.

NOTE: To save time, you may use a good-quality prepared roasted garlic.

PER SERVING: CALORIES 460; CALORIES FROM FAT 200; CALORIES FROM SATURATED FAT 25; PROTEIN 12 G; CARBOHYDRATE 58 G; TOTAL FAT 22 G; SATURATED FAT 2.5 G; CHOLESTEROL 0 MG; SODIUM 1,040 MG; 43% CALORIES FROM FAT

Variation: Add 1 pound sliced or chopped grilled boneless skinless chicken breast. You may also add diced, baked, or grilled tofu cut into 1-inch cubes.

Whole Wheat Linguine with Broccoli

SERVES 4

1 pound whole wheat linguine or
  spaghetti

⅛ cup olive oil

1 head of broccoli, trimmed and cut
  into small florets

3 cloves garlic, minced
  (1½ teaspoons)

¼ teaspoon crushed red chili flakes

1 tablespoon tamari

¼ cup grated Parmesan cheese

⅛ cup pine nuts, toasted

Juice of 1 lemon

Salt and freshly ground pepper to
  taste

THIS uncomplicated pasta dish may soon become a family favorite. Crisp florets of broccoli and whole wheat pasta combine well with bits of golden brown garlic and sharp Parmesan cheese. The pronounced robust flavor of wheat sings in this dish. Try this dish at room temperature or warm from the pan.

Bring a large pot of salted water to a boil. Cook the pasta for 7 to 9 minutes, until it is al dente. Drain and rinse the pasta in cold water. This step may be done up to 2 days prior to finishing the dish. If cooking ahead, lightly oil the cooked pasta, and store it in a covered dish in the refrigerator.

Heat the olive oil in a large sauté pan over medium heat, and sauté the broccoli florets, stirring often, for 5 minutes. You may sprinkle a little water over the florets to prevent sticking, using caution—the oil may splatter a bit. Add the garlic and the red chili flakes. Sauté for 1 minute longer. Add the cooked pasta to the broccoli, and combine well. Add the tamari, Parmesan cheese, and pine nuts. Add the lemon juice and season with the salt and pepper.

PER SERVING: CALORIES 400; CALORIES FROM FAT 90; CALORIES FROM SATURATED FAT 15; PROTEIN 15 G; CARBOHYDRATE 67 G; TOTAL FAT 10 G; SATURATED FAT 1.5 G; CHOLESTEROL 0 MG; SODIUM 530 MG; 22% CALORIES FROM FAT

pasta and other warming starches

Potato Corn Semi-Soufflé

SERVES 6

ALTHOUGH this is not a classic soufflé, the results are similar, and the process is much easier. Air trapped in the egg whites expands between the potato layers and rises during baking, which lifts the layers, producing a fluffy duet of potato and sweet corn. Try adding a sprinkling of Monterey Jack or crumbled mild feta cheese to the top. If you like heat, add a bit of minced serrano chili to lift this soufflé even more.

2 large russet potatoes (about 1/2 pound)
1 1/2 cups (15-ounce can) creamed corn
1/2 teaspoon salt
Freshly ground white pepper to taste
Pinch of cinnamon
1/8 cup flour
2 large egg whites, stiffly beaten
Vegetable or canola oil for spraying pan

Preheat the oven to 375°F. Peel the potatoes, and slice them very thinly; reserve them in a bowl of cold water. Combine the corn, salt, pepper, cinnamon, and flour. Gently fold the egg whites into the corn mixture.

Drain the potatoes, and pat them dry with paper towels. Place the potatoes on a sheet pan sprayed or lightly oiled with the vegetable or canola oil. Roast them in a 375°F. oven for about 15 minutes, or until firm-tender. Cool the potatoes. Leave the oven on.

Spray an 8- or 9-inch square baking pan with the vegetable or canola oil.

Place a layer of cooked potatoes on the bottom of the baking pan. Measure out 1/2 cup of the corn mixture and carefully spread over the potatoes. Add another single layer of potatoes and then 1 cup of the corn mixture. Add a final layer of the remaining potatoes and the remaining corn mixture.

Bake for 35 to 45 minutes, until the potatoes test tender when a sharp knife is inserted into them and the surface is golden brown.

PER SERVING: CALORIES 90; CALORIES FROM FAT 0; CALORIES FROM SATURATED FAT 0; PROTEIN 3 G; CARBOHYDRATE 21 G; TOTAL FAT 0 G; SATURATED FAT 0 G; CHOLESTEROL 0 MG; SODIUM 360 MG; 0% CALORIES FROM FAT

Pumpkin Poblano Corn Pudding

2¹/₂ cups cornmeal

2 teaspoons baking powder

1¹/₂ teaspoons salt

3 large eggs, beaten

¹/₄ cup canola oil

1 (15-ounce) can creamed corn

1¹/₄ cups canned pumpkin

1 cup ricotta cheese

1 cup diced red onion

³/₄ cup seeded and diced poblano
  chilies

1 tablespoon minced fresh ginger
  (1-inch piece)

1 clove garlic, minced (¹/₂ teaspoon)

Canola oil for oiling pan

THIS pudding is a tremendous holiday dish with complex rich flavors of sweet pumpkin and corn punched up by sharp poblano chilies. The chili-laden aroma that will float from your oven is intoxicating. You may use either white or yellow cornmeal. If you like a juicier bite, add an ear of fresh-shucked corn kernels to the batter. Serve this pudding as an appetizer or side dish with grilled vegetables, poultry, or Carne Asada (page 255).

Preheat the oven to 350°F. Combine the cornmeal, baking powder, and salt in a bowl. Make an indentation in the center of the mixture. Place the beaten eggs, the ¹/₄ cup canola oil, and the creamed corn into the indentation. Using a whisk, combine the ingredients. Stir in the pumpkin and ricotta cheese. Blend well. Stir in the red onion, poblano chilies, ginger, and garlic.

Oil a 13 × 9-inch glass baking dish with the canola oil. Pour the batter into the dish. Smooth out the top. Bake for about 45 minutes, or until the mixture is set like soft pudding. Serve warm.

PER SERVING: CALORIES 270; CALORIES FROM FAT 100; CALORIES FROM SATURATED FAT 35; PROTEIN 9 G; CARBOHYDRATE 35 G; TOTAL FAT 12 G; SATURATED FAT 4 G; CHOLESTEROL 75 MG; SODIUM 1000 MG; 37% CALORIES FROM FAT

pasta and other warming starches

Vegan

Spring Couscous with Asparagus and Orange

SERVES 4

TINY mild grains of semolina pasta combine well with the asparagus and tart citrus flavor of fresh orange sections. Asparagus, from the family of leeks, onions, and lilies, has been revered as a treasured vegetable since ancient times. Asparagus is full of nutrients just as it is rich in flavor. It's important to shock asparagus in ice water right after cooking if you are not going to eat it right away. This stops the cooking process and preserves the bright green color. The chilled spears may be stored up to two days in the refrigerator. For a sweeter flavor, use tiny mandarin oranges.

1 cup dried couscous
1 cup orange juice
1 cup water
2 teaspoons olive oil
1 teaspoon salt
2 teaspoons grated fresh ginger

1 teaspoon olive oil
8 stalks asparagus, trimmed and cut
   into 1-inch lengths (about 2 cups)
1 cup seeded and diced red pepper
1/2 cup fresh or thawed frozen peas
1 navel orange, peeled and sliced
   into wedges
4 scallions, trimmed and minced
1 teaspoon salt
Cayenne pepper to taste

Place the couscous in a large bowl. In a sauce pot, bring the orange juice, water, the 2 teaspoons olive oil, the 1 teaspoon salt, and ginger to a boil. Stir well. Remove from the heat and immediately pour over the couscous. Stir in the hot liquid to distribute evenly. Quickly cover and allow the couscous to reconstitute for 15 to 20 minutes.

In the meantime, heat the remaining 1 teaspoon olive oil in a nonstick pan, and sauté the asparagus for about 2 minutes, or until crisp-tender. Add the red pepper and peas, and cook for 1 minute longer. Add the sautéed vegetables, orange wedges, scallions, the remaining 1 teaspoon salt, and the cayenne pepper to the reconstituted couscous. Fluff with a fork to blend. Serve warm or at room temperature.

PER SERVING: CALORIES 280; CALORIES FROM FAT 35; CALORIES FROM SATURATED FAT 5; PROTEIN 10 G; CARBOHYDRATE 52 G; TOTAL FAT 4 G; SATURATED FAT 0.5 G; CHOLESTEROL 0 MG; SODIUM 970 MG; 12% CALORIES FROM FAT

Variation: Add 1 pound of diced tofu, cooked shrimp, or chicken to the couscous. Or try this with whole wheat couscous.

Surf and Turf Pasta

SERVES 4

1 pound penne pasta

12 ounces chicken sausage

1/8 cup olive oil

1 cup diced red pepper

1 1/2 cups cooked small shrimp

3 scallions, trimmed and minced

1/2 cup roughly chopped fresh basil
  leaves

3/4 cup Italian Herb Vinaigrette
  (page 329), or your favorite
  bottled dressing

15 small cherry or grape tomatoes,
  halved

1 cup diced fresh mozzarella cheese

PASTA is a backdrop for the unusual combination of pan-seared sausage and shrimp. This simple but unconventional salad exudes elegance and is very easy to prepare. You may serve this pasta at room temperature or, by heating it quickly in a sauté pan, warm. If you want to splurge, try chunks of cooked lobster meat instead of shrimp. As an alternative pasta shape, try orecchiette ("little ears") pasta; it cradles the shrimp and sausage well.

Bring a large pot of salted water to a boil. Add the pasta, and cook for 10 to 12 minutes, until it is al dente. Drain and rinse the pasta under cold water.

Slice the sausage into 1/2-inch-thick slices. Heat the olive oil in a medium skillet, add the sausage, and cook for 3 to 4 minutes, turning the slices, until just golden. Stir in the red pepper, and immediately remove the pan from the heat.

In a large bowl, toss the drained pasta with the sausage mixture, shrimp, scallions, and basil. Blend well. Add the vinaigrette, and toss lightly. Gently stir in the tomatoes and mozzarella.

PER SERVING: CALORIES 760; CALORIES FROM FAT 400; CALORIES FROM SATURATED FAT 90; PROTEIN 47 G; CARBOHYDRATE 44 G; TOTAL FAT 44 G; SATURATED FAT 11 G; CHOLESTEROL 250 MG; SODIUM 1,680 MG; 53% CALORIES FROM FAT

Variation: For a smokier flavor, use an outdoor grill to cook the sausage and red pepper before adding them to the pasta. (Dice the pepper after grilling it whole for 1 minute on each side.) For variety, try different flavors of chicken sausage such as roasted garlic, smoked apple, or andouille.

pasta and other warming starches

Seitan Lasagna

SERVES 12

SEITAN, although it has an odd-sounding name, is one of the most flavorful and versatile sources of nonmeat protein. Also called wheat gluten or wheat meat, seitan was originally created by Buddhist monks as a rich protein source (see "Whole Foods Glossary," page 395). In this lasagna it takes on the taste and feel of a complex Bolognese sauce. Our recipe calls for soy cheese, but you may use dairy cheese if you prefer. To save time, we've called for ready-to-bake lasagna sheets. You may cook dried lasagna pasta, and use it instead.

The Seitan Sauce

I tablespoon olive oil

½ onion, chopped

2 cloves garlic, minced (I teaspoon)

I pound seitan, chopped coarsely

⅛ cup dried oregano (or ¼ cup fresh oregano)

I sprig fresh rosemary, whole on the stem

I (26-ounce) jar marinara sauce; plus more to serve if desired

½ cup chopped fresh basil

12 oven-ready sheets dried lasagna pasta

4 cups grated soy mozzarella cheese

½ cup grated soy Parmesan cheese, plus more to serve if desired

TO PREPARE THE SEITAN SAUCE Heat the olive oil in a large nonstick saucepan over medium heat. Add the onion and garlic; sauté for 2 minutes. Add the chopped seitan, and continue to sauté for 3 to 4 minutes, until the seitan begins to brown. Add the oregano and rosemary stem, and sauté for 1 minute longer. Add the marinara sauce, and simmer the sauce slowly for 30 minutes. Add the chopped basil, and stir well. Remove the rosemary sprig. The sauce may be made up to 3 days prior to assembling the lasagna.

To assemble the lasagna, in a 13 × 9 × 2-inch lasagna pan, spread about 1 cup of the sauce on the bottom. Lay 4 sheets of the lasagna pasta across the sauce—don't overlap them, as they expand quite a bit when cooking. (Overlap slightly if substituting cooked noodles.) Spread about ¾ cup of the seitan sauce evenly over the pasta. Sprinkle 1 cup of soy mozzarella cheese over the sauce.

Repeat this process 2 more times until all the pasta sauce and cheese is used. Make sure the top layer is spread evenly with sauce and cheese.

Sprinkle the soy Parmesan cheese evenly over the surface of the lasagna. Cover the pan well with foil. Bake for 35 minutes, until the lasagna is cooked and the pasta is tender. Remove the foil, and continue to bake for an additional 10 to 15 minutes, until the cheese is melted and the surface is lightly browned. Allow the lasagna to stand for 15 minutes before cutting it into squares. You may serve this dish with additional sauce and grated soy Parmesan cheese, if desired.

PER SERVING: CALORIES 190; CALORIES FROM FAT 30; CALORIES FROM SATURATED FAT 0; PROTEIN 15 G; CARBOHYDRATE 28 G; TOTAL FAT 3.5 G; SATURATED FAT 0 G; CHOLESTEROL 0 MG; SODIUM 250 MG; 16% CALORIES FROM FAT

Variation: If you prefer a lasagna with chunky garden vegetables, add 2 cups of chopped seasonal vegetables—like peppers, zucchini, yellow squash, mushrooms, and broccoli—along with the seitan when making the sauce.

Garlic Spinach Stellini Pasta

SERVES 4

1 pound dried stellini pasta

⅛ cup olive oil

4 large cloves garlic, minced
(2 teaspoons)

12 cups washed and dried spinach

1 tablespoon lemon juice

1 teaspoon lemon pepper, or more to
taste

Salt to taste

STELLINI pasta is star shaped. It works wonderfully with the barely wilted spinach in this dish, which may be served as a warm salad or side dish. Kids love this dish, which may also be made with alphabet letters providing more entertainment around the dinner table.

B ring a large pot of salted water to a boil. Add the pasta; cook until it is al dente, 8 to 10 minutes. Drain the pasta, and set it aside.

Heat the olive oil in a very large sauté pan over low heat. Add the garlic, cook slowly, and stir often, until the garlic is golden brown and nicely caramelized, 10 to 15 minutes. Raise the heat to medium, and add the spinach. Cook, stirring constantly, until the spinach is lightly wilted, 30 to 60 seconds. Add the lemon juice and the cooked pasta. Cook until just heated through. Toss with the lemon pepper and season with the salt and additional lemon pepper as desired.

PER SERVING: CALORIES 490; CALORIES FROM FAT 90; CALORIES FROM SATURATED FAT 15; PROTEIN 18 G; CARBOHYDRATE 87 G; TOTAL FAT 10 G; SATURATED FAT 1.5 G; CHOLESTEROL 0 MG; SODIUM 1,250 MG; 18% CALORIES FROM FAT

Spinach Mushroom Lasagna

SERVES 10

A classic lasagna takes a new turn, layered with sautéed spinach and mushrooms. This recipe mostly involves building, not cooking. To make this even easier, use no-cook lasagna noodles that are readily available.

TO PREPARE THE SPINACH MIXTURE Heat the canola oil in a large sauté pan. Add the onion and garlic, and cook over medium heat until golden brown, about 5 minutes. Add the mushrooms; sauté for 2 minutes. Stir in the tamari, salt, and pepper, blending well. Mix in the spinach.

Preheat the oven to 375°F. Bring a large pot of salted water to a boil. Add the lasagna noodles, and cook until they are al dente, 6 to 8 minutes, or follow the directions on the package. Drain and run cold water over the noodles to separate. (Skip this step if using no-cook lasagna noodles.)

To assemble, spread about ½ cup of the marinara sauce in a 9 × 13-inch dish that's at least 3 inches deep. Top with a layer of the lasagna noodles, about ¾ cup of the ricotta cheese, about 1½ cups of the mozzarella cheese, ½ cup of the Parmesan cheese, and one third of the spinach mixture. Repeat with another ½ cup of the marinara sauce, a layer of lasagna noodles placed in the opposite direction of the first layer, ¾ cup of the ricotta, 1½ cups of the mozzarella, ½ cup of the Parmesan, and half of the remaining spinach mushroom mixture. Repeat with a third layer, using

The Spinach Mixture

3 tablespoons canola oil

1½ cups chopped onion

3 garlic cloves, minced
    (1½ teaspoons)

2 cups sliced white button
    mushrooms

1½ tablespoons tamari

½ teaspoon salt

¼ teaspoon freshly ground pepper

1 pound chopped frozen spinach,
    defrosted and moisture squeezed
    out

1 pound dried lasagna noodles
    (semolina, spinach, or whole wheat)

1½ to 2 cups prepared marinara
    sauce

2¼ cups ricotta cheese

6 cups grated mozzarella cheese,
    divided in four parts

1½ cups grated Parmesan cheese

1½ cups of the mozzarella and the other remaining ingredients, ending with the marinara sauce on top.

Bake in the oven for 30 minutes. Top with the remaining 1½ cups mozzarella, and bake for 5 to 8 minutes, until hot and bubbly. Allow the lasagna to set for 15 to 20 minutes before cutting into squares.

PER SERVING: CALORIES 550; CALORIES FROM FAT 240; CALORIES FROM SATURATED FAT 150; PROTEIN 38 G; CARBOHYDRATE 40 G; TOTAL FAT 27 G; SATURATED FAT 17 G; CHOLESTEROL 75 MG; SODIUM 1,400 MG; 44% CALORIES FROM FAT

Spinach Mushroom Lasagna

mozzarella & ricotta cheese

chopped spinach

pasta

sauce

mushrooms

vegetarian

Savory Tomato Pesto Polenta

SERVES 8

THIS rainbow-hued recipe consists of three layers of polenta that look like the colors in the Italian flag when combined. Each flavored layer of polenta—pesto, sun-dried tomato, and corn—has a distinctive taste that complements the others well. Although this looks like a lot of work, it's mostly assembling. After preparing the polenta, layering is simple. This dish is extremely attractive and makes an impressive entrée for family gatherings. Preparing the polenta in a springform pan makes it easy to remove. Serve a slice of the tricolor polenta with a vegetable- or meat-based stew, a marinara sauce, or a grilled poultry dish.

TO PREPARE THE BASIC POLENTA Bring the water to a boil in a large saucepan. Adding just a small amount at a time, gradually whisk in the cornmeal. Continue cooking and whisking over medium-low heat until the polenta is smooth and very thick, 8 to 10 minutes. If using the mascarpone, add it at this time. Pour the mixture into a 12 × 12-inch pan sprayed with vegetable oil. Allow the polenta to cool for 15 minutes. While the mixture is cooling, prepare the pestos.

   TO PREPARE THE SUN-DRIED TOMATO PESTO Place the reconstituted sun-dried tomatoes, parsley, salt, pepper, garlic, and olive oil in the bowl of a food processor fitted with a metal blade. Blend until smooth, 2 to 3 minutes, scraping down the sides of the bowl as necessary. Transfer the tomato mixture to a bowl, and stir in the Parmesan cheese. (This pesto may be kept refrigerated in a tightly covered jar for 2 to 3 weeks.)

The Basic Polenta

2½ cups water, vegetable stock, or milk

¾ cup cornmeal (yellow or white)

¼ cup mascarpone or cream cheese (optional)

Vegetable oil for spraying pan

The Sun-Dried Tomato Pesto

1 cup sun-dried tomatoes, reconstituted in warm water for 10 to 15 minutes and gently squeezed dry

½ cup chopped parsley

1 teaspoon salt

½ teaspoon freshly ground pepper

2 large cloves garlic, chopped

½ cup olive oil

½ cup grated Parmesan or Romano cheese

The Basil Pesto

2 cups fresh basil leaves

½ cup chopped parsley

1 teaspoon salt

½ teaspoon freshly ground pepper

2 large cloves garlic, chopped

½ cup olive oil

¼ cup pine nuts or chopped walnuts

½ cup grated Parmesan or Romano cheese

TO PREPARE THE BASIL PESTO Place the basil, parsley, salt, pepper, garlic, olive oil, and pine nuts in the bowl of a food processor fitted with a metal blade. Blend until smooth, 2 to 3 minutes, scraping down the sides of the bowl when necessary. Transfer the basil mixture to a bowl, and stir in the cheese. (This pesto may be kept refrigerated in a tightly covered jar for 2 to 3 weeks.)

When the basic polenta has cooled, divide it into thirds, placing it in 3 separate bowls. Spray a 9-inch springform pan with vegetable oil, and spread one third of the basic polenta into the pan. Place the pan in the freezer for 10 minutes.

Add the sun-dried tomato pesto to the second bowl of basic polenta, stirring to blend well. Remove the springform pan from the freezer, and carefully spread the sun-dried tomato pesto polenta mixture on top. Place the pan in the freezer for 10 minutes.

Add the basil pesto to the third bowl of basic polenta, stirring to blend well. Remove the springform pan from the freezer, and carefully spread the basil pesto polenta mixture on top. Refrigerate until firm (overnight is best).

To serve, remove the outside of the springform pan and cut the polenta into wedges. The polenta wedges may be served at room temperature or baked with marinara and a sprinkling of Parmesan or mozzarella cheese over the top. You may also brush olive oil onto chilled wedges of polenta and grill them over coals or in a gas barbecue until golden brown.

PER SERVING: CALORIES 400; CALORIES FROM FAT 320; CALORIES FROM SATURATED FAT 70; PROTEIN 9 G; CARBOHYDRATE 13 G; TOTAL FAT 35 G; SATURATED FAT 7 G; CHOLESTEROL 15 MG; SODIUM 950 MG; 80% CALORIES FROM FAT

Causa Limena with Tuna

SERVES 6

THIS traditional Peruvian potato torte, with its layer of tuna salad, is eaten predominantly in the summer months. It's easy to see why. Outside of cooking the potatoes, which may be done up to two days prior to serving, the remainder of preparation is merely assembling. This dish is normally made with a simple tuna salad—mashed tuna mixed with mayonnaise—but you may also make it with a salmon or crabmeat salad.

Canola or vegetable oil for spraying pan

The Tuna Salad

2 (6-ounce) cans water-packed tuna, drained well and flaked

¼ cup mayonnaise

1 tablespoon lemon juice

Salt and freshly ground pepper to taste

The Mashed Potatoes

4 large Idaho potatoes, peeled, boiled, and mashed (4 cups)

¼ cup plus 2 tablespoons extra-virgin olive oil

⅛ cup lemon juice

1½ teaspoons salt

½ teaspoon freshly ground pepper

1 to 2 tablespoons jalapeño pepper, minced

Spray a 6-inch-wide, 3-inch-deep tart pan, spring-form pan, or other appropriate mold with canola or vegetable oil.

TO PREPARE THE TUNA SALAD Combine the tuna, mayonnaise, lemon juice, and salt and pepper in a bowl, and mix well.

TO PREPARE THE MASHED POTATOES Place the mashed potatoes in a medium bowl, and add the olive oil, lemon juice, salt, pepper, and jalapeño.

TO ASSEMBLE In another medium bowl, mix the eggs with the mayonnaise, red onion, salt, and pepper. Take the tart pan, and measure 1½ cups of the potato mixture into it, filling the bottom of the mold evenly. Top with 1½ cups of the tuna salad, patting it down gently. Sprinkle with ⅛ cup of the olives. Add a layer of half of the egg mixture, smoothly and evenly. Add another 1½ cups of the potatoes, and pat down. Add the remainder of the tuna, and then the olives. Top with the rest of the egg mixture and the remainder of the potato mixture. Tamp down with the back of a large spoon until the mixture is firmly placed within the mold and smooth on top. Sprinkle with the peppers. Cover and refrigerate until firm, about 3 hours. To serve, cut into wedges to show the colorful layers inside.

To Assemble

4 large eggs, hard-boiled and minced

1 tablespoon mayonnaise

2 tablespoons minced red onion,

½ teaspoon salt

¼ teaspoon freshly ground pepper

½ cup pitted and finely chopped
    Kalamata olives

¼ cup finely minced red pepper

¼ cup finely minced green pepper

PER SERVING: CALORIES 470; CALORIES FROM FAT
260; CALORIES FROM SATURATED FAT 45; PROTEIN
22 G; CARBOHYDRATE 31 G; TOTAL FAT 29 G;
SATURATED FAT 5 G; CHOLESTEROL 155 MG;
SODIUM 1,210 MG; 55% CALORIES FROM FAT

 Recipe Bonus This
attractive dish is perfect on a
brunch or dinner buffet—try serving it on a
cake pedestal for a knockout presentation.

Bow Ties with Smoked Salmon, Asparagus, and Spicy Pistachios

SERVES 4

SMOKED salmon and pistachios sound like an unlikely couple, but they bond very well in this unusual pasta dish. The lightly smoked flavor of the salmon is offset by the mild sweetness of pistachios. This dish seems to jump off the plate because of the soft pink color of the salmon and vivid green of the pistachios. The spicy pistachios are an excellent snack served on their own.

The Spicy Pistachios

¾ cup shelled pistachios

1 teaspoon canola oil

Salt to taste

Pinch of cayenne pepper

½ pound farfalle (bow tie) pasta

6 to 8 stalks fresh asparagus, trimmed and cut into 2-inch lengths

4 ounces smoked salmon, cut into bite-size pieces

Freshly ground pepper to taste

½ cup chopped fresh cilantro

1½ tablespoons extra-virgin olive oil

TO PREPARE THE SPICY PISTACHIOS Place the pistachios and canola oil in a sauté pan over medium heat. Sauté, stirring constantly for about 1 minute. Drain the nuts on paper towels to remove excess oil. Place the pistachios in a small bowl and sprinkle them lightly with the salt and a pinch of cayenne pepper (or to taste). This can be done up to 2 days before making the pasta.

Bring a large pot of salted water to a boil. Add the pasta, and cook for 2 minutes before adding the asparagus. Cook the pasta until it is al dente, 5 to 6 minutes; at this point, the asparagus will be done, too. Drain the pasta and asparagus well and place in a large bowl. Add the salmon, pepper, cilantro, spicy pistachios, and olive oil. Toss lightly, and serve warm.

PER SERVING: CALORIES 440; CALORIES FROM FAT 180; CALORIES FROM SATURATED FAT 25; PROTEIN 20 G; CARBOHYDRATE 51 G; TOTAL FAT 20 G; SATURATED FAT 2.5 G; CHOLESTEROL 5 MG; SODIUM 820 MG; 41% CALORIES FROM FAT

Southwest King Ranch Casserole

The Mexican Chicken Filling

3 tablespoons canola oil

1½ cups diced yellow onions

2 cloves garlic, minced (1 teaspoon)

2 teaspoons paprika

1 teaspoon cumin

½ teaspoon coarsely ground black
  pepper

1 teaspoon salt

3 cups shredded cooked boneless
  chicken

½ cup chopped fresh cilantro

The Casserole

2 cups grated Monterey Jack cheese

1 cup grated cheddar cheese

2 cups bottled tomatillo sauce

8 corn tortillas

1½ cups sour cream

½ cup chopped green chilies, drained

THEY don't call this the king for nothing. It's like a lasagna gone completely Tex-Mex. Corn tortillas act like pasta sheets layered between mild green chilies and spicy shredded chicken. It's preferable to make this casserole at least one and up to three days before serving so the flavors may mingle. It also allows the dish to set up and makes slicing easy. Garnish servings with a small dollop of sour cream and a sprig of fresh cilantro.

TO PREPARE THE MEXICAN CHICKEN FILLING
Preheat the oven to 350°F.

Heat the canola oil over medium-high heat in a large sauté pan. Add the onions, and cook them until they are translucent, 2 to 3 minutes. Blend in the garlic, paprika, cumin, black pepper, and salt. Add the chicken, and heat through. Remove the pan from the heat; stir in the cilantro.

TO PREPARE THE CASSEROLE In a small bowl, combine the cheeses.

On the bottom of an 8 × 8½-inch pan at least 2 inches deep, spread 1 cup of the tomatillo sauce. Top with 4 tortillas, overlapping as necessary. Spread half the sour cream evenly over the tortillas. Add ½ cup of the remaining tomatillo sauce, 1½ cups of the chicken filling, 1 cup of the cheese mixture, and one half of the green chilies.

Top with 4 more tortillas, the remainder of the sour cream, tomatillo sauce, and chicken filling, 1 cup of the cheese mixture, and the remaining green chilies. End with 1 cup of the cheese mixture sprinkled on top. Bake for about 25 minutes, or until hot and bubbly on the surface.

PER SERVING: CALORIES 410; CALORIES FROM FAT 230; CALORIES FROM SATURATED FAT 110; PROTEIN 28 G; CARBOHYDRATE 16 G; TOTAL FAT 26 G; SATURATED FAT 12 G; CHOLESTEROL 85 MG; SODIUM 550 MG; 56% CALORIES FROM FAT

 Recipe Bonus For the simplest preparation, use leftover ready-made rotisserie chicken.

pasta and other warming starches

Pad Thai

SERVES 6

RICE noodle pasta has a texture that's entirely different from its traditional wheat-based counterpart. The mild noodles provide a perfect background for pungent Asian fish sauce, fiery chili paste, and crisp juicy vegetables. Be sure not to overcook the noodles; they'll get mushy and lose their silken texture. Peanuts are a traditional garnish.

½ pound flat rice noodles or mung bean noodles

½ cup canola oil

3 cloves garlic, minced (1½ teaspoons)

2 teaspoons red chili paste

1 teaspoon sugar

3 tablespoons Thai fish sauce

½ cup water

2 large eggs, beaten

¼ cup thinly sliced scallions

½ cup snow peas, strings removed and finely julienned

1½ cups fresh bean sprouts

¼ teaspoon crushed red chili flakes

1 tablespoon lime juice

3 tablespoons chopped fresh cilantro

¼ cup finely chopped dry roasted peanuts

Bring a large pot of water to a boil, add the noddles, and cook just until the water returns to a boil. Remove the noodles immediately, and drain them. Rinse in ice-cold water to stop the noodles from cooking further.

Heat the canola oil in a wok or large sauté pan. Add the garlic, chili paste, sugar, fish sauce, and water. Cook for 1 to 2 minutes, until slightly thickened. Add the beaten eggs, stirring constantly, until the eggs are soft set.

Add the noodles to the pan with the chili paste mixture, toss, and sauté for 3 to 4 minutes over medium-high heat. Add the scallions, snow peas, bean sprouts, red chili flakes, and lime juice. Toss to mix well and heat through, about 1 minute. Place on a serving platter, and sprinkle with the cilantro and peanuts.

PER SERVING: CALORIES 280; CALORIES FROM FAT 210; CALORIES FROM SATURATED FAT 20; PROTEIN 7 G; CARBOHYDRATE 13 G; TOTAL FAT 23 G; SATURATED FAT 2.5 G; CHOLESTEROL 75 MG; SODIUM 710 MG; 75% CALORIES FROM FAT

Burgers, Patties, and Griddlecakes

BURGER BASICS ♠ SPINACH, GARLIC, AND ROSEMARY GRIDDLECAKES ♠ "FEEL YOUR OATS" BURGERS ♠ COUSCOUS CAKES WITH MINT AND RED PEPPER ♠ PORTOBELLO BURGERS ♠ NOT YOUR GRANDMOTHER'S VEGETABLE LATKES ♠ RISOTTO CAKES ♠ MILLET AND YAM BURGERS ♠ QUINOA VEGETABLE CAKES ♠ SPICY SMASHED POTATO PATTIES ♠ TERIYAKI TURKEY BURGERS WITH GREEN ONION AND GINGER ♠ THAI FISH CAKES ♠ CAJUN SEAFOOD CAKES ♠ GREEK BEEF MEATBALLS

A juicy burger, with all the trimmings, topping a freshly baked

bun is perhaps as close to a national dish as America has. For those of us giving up or cutting back on meat, the hamburger presents a major stumbling block. Many of us crave a burger made with poultry, seafood, grains, or legumes, but we don't want to sacrifice taste and texture, the main criteria for a great burger-eating experience. Burgers, patties, and griddlecakes must hold together, which is easy when making beef or poultry burgers, but it becomes more elusive when working with grains, seafood, vegetables, or legumes that tend to be mushy or soft to the bite. The natural fat content in red meat or poultry also helps contain the shape of a traditional burger, and the lack of it must be compensated for when working with alternative ingredients.

The terminology of burgers, patties, and griddlecakes is somewhat interchangeable. Griddlecakes are usually the flattest of the three, with the most surface area to brown—our Spinach, Garlic, and Rosemary Griddlecakes (opposite) are a good example. Patties are usually a bit thicker, like the Cajun Seafood Cakes (page 218), and have a moist center. Burgers are what most of us grew up with on our dinner tables and in our backyards.

These recipes sizzle with innovative flavors, making them perfect for today's dinner table. All the burgers may be eaten on a bun or be served as entrées, set alongside a grain dish or mashed potatoes or perched on a bed of braised greens.

Burger Basics

- Scoop burger mixtures with an ice cream scoop to make sure each burger is a uniform size.
- Wet your hands with cool water. This will prevent the burger mixture from sticking to your hands.
- When cooking the formed burgers, make sure the oil is hot and turn the burgers only once to keep their shape, using a wide spatula.

Spinach, Garlic, and Rosemary Griddlecakes

MAKES 10 (8-OUNCE) CAKES

1 pound Idaho or Yukon Gold potatoes, peeled and cut into large pieces

⅛ cup olive oil

1 medium onion, minced

2 cloves garlic, minced (1 teaspoon)

1 tablespoon minced fresh rosemary

1 pound frozen chopped spinach, thawed, drained, and squeezed dry

1 cup crumbled feta cheese

½ cup grated Parmesan cheese

1 large egg

2 teaspoons dried oregano

2 teaspoons salt, or to taste

1 teaspoon freshly ground pepper

1 cup dried bread crumbs

Marinara sauce (or other favorite sauce) to serve

WITH a mild background of spinach, the aromatic fresh rosemary shines in this recipe. Mashed potatoes impart a comforting texture to these griddlecakes and the sharp feta cheese adds a pleasing bite. You may make these cakes without the feta and Parmesan for a nondairy version. Use an equivalent amount of natural egg substitute as the binding ingredient instead of eggs.

Preheat the oven to 375°F.

Cover the potatoes with cold water and bring to a boil. Simmer uncovered for 12 to 15 minutes, until tender. Drain and mash lightly with a fork or potato masher. Heat 1 tablespoon of the olive oil in a large nonstick pan, and sauté the onion, garlic, and rosemary for 2 minutes, until the onion is softened. Add the spinach to the vegetables. Combine the sautéed vegetables, cooked potatoes, feta cheese, Parmesan cheese, egg, oregano, salt, pepper, and bread crumbs in a large bowl and mix well.

Using an 8-ounce scoop as a measure, form the mixture into 10 griddlecakes. Heat the remaining 1 tablespoon olive oil in a large sauté pan. Sauté the griddlecakes until golden brown on both sides, about 2 minutes per side. Place the griddlecakes on a baking pan in the oven for 10 minutes to cook through. Serve with marinara or your favorite sauce.

PER SERVING: CALORIES 200; CALORIES FROM FAT 80; CALORIES FROM SATURATED FAT 35; PROTEIN 9 G; CARBOHYDRATE 22 G; TOTAL FAT 9 G; SATURATED FAT 4 G; CHOLESTEROL 40 MG; SODIUM 780 MG; 40% CALORIES FROM FAT

 Tip from the Team: When you're frying foods without a thermometer to check the temperature of the oil, drizzle a pinch of flour into it—the oil is ready for frying if the flour "sizzles"!

burgers, patties, and griddlecakes

"Feel Your Oats" Burgers

MAKES 8 (8-OUNCE) BURGERS

THESE are probably the most unusual grain-based burgers due to the soft texture and earthy flavor of rolled oats. As the oat mixture cools down, it hardens and forms a soft shell for the chopped, sautéed vegetables. It's pleasant running into a tidbit of sweet pepper or onion as you devour these. You can add any chopped seasonal vegetables to the oat mixture. Feel creative? Stuff the burger mixture into a porto-bello mushroom cap or shiitake mushroom. Try a warm oat burger over a field green salad, or smother it with sautéed mushrooms and onions.

4½ cups water

½ cup tamari

4½ cups rolled oats, plus extra for sprinkling

¼ cup olive oil

1 teaspoon canola oil

2 cloves garlic, minced (1 teaspoon)

1 medium red pepper, seeded and diced

2 large onions, diced

2 large carrots, grated

1 teaspoon dried basil (or 1 tablespoon fresh basil)

1 teaspoon dried oregano (or 1 tablespoon fresh oregano)

Vegetable oil for spraying burgers

Preheat the oven to 400°F. In a large sauce pot, bring the water, tamari, oats, and olive oil to a boil; simmer for 12 minutes over low heat while stirring frequently, until a very thick mixture forms. Remove from the heat. Heat the canola oil in a nonstick sauté pan over medium heat, and cook the garlic, pepper, onions, carrots, basil, and oregano for about 2 minutes, or until soft—fold this into the oat mixture and allow it to cool. Using an 8-ounce scoop as a measure, form into 8 burgers 1 inch thick, and place on a baking pan lined with parchment paper. Flatten the tops of each burger slightly with a spatula, and sprinkle each with about 1 teaspoon raw oats. Spray the burgers lightly with the vegetable oil, and bake for 20 minutes, until golden brown.

PER SERVING: CALORIES 290; CALORIES FROM FAT 90; CALORIES FROM SATURATED FAT 15; PROTEIN 10 G; CARBOHYDRATE 41 G; TOTAL FAT 10 G; SATURATED FAT 1.5 G; CHOLESTEROL 0 MG; SODIUM 1,020 MG; 31% CALORIES FROM FAT

Couscous Cakes with Mint and Red Pepper

MAKES 10 (8-OUNCE) CAKES

1½ cups dried couscous

⅛ cup plus 1 tablespoon olive oil

2 cups water

½ cup minced red pepper

½ cup minced green pepper

1 medium onion, minced

3 cloves garlic, minced
   (1½ teaspoons)

1 teaspoon lemon pepper

1 teaspoon dried Italian herbs

¼ cup minced fresh mint leaves

¼ cup unbleached all-purpose flour

2 large eggs

1 cup crumbled feta cheese
   (4 ounces)

½ cup frozen peas, thawed

1 teaspoon salt, or to taste

1 cup yellow cornmeal

Vegetable or olive oil for spraying pan

COUSCOUS, a staple of North African cuisine, is actually a tiny grain of semolina, which helps this cake hold together. Plumped couscous forms a crunchy golden crust on the surface with a moist center underneath.

Place the couscous, 1 tablespoon of the olive oil, and water in a large sauce pot, bring to a boil, stir well, and remove the pot from the heat. Cover the couscous tightly and allow it to reconstitute for at least 15 to 20 minutes.

Heat the rest of the olive oil in a large sauté pan, add the peppers, onion, garlic, lemon pepper, and Italian herbs, and sauté for 4 to 5 minutes, until tender and lightly browned. Place the mixture in a large bowl. Add the plumped couscous, mint, flour, and eggs; mix well. The mixture should stick together when pressed with the back of a spoon. Stir in the feta cheese and peas. Season with the salt.

Refrigerate the mixture for at least 30 minutes before forming into cakes. Preheat the oven to 325°F. Using an 8-ounce scoop as a measure, form the mixture into 10 (½-inch-thick) slightly flattened cakes. When ready to cook, lightly dust the cakes with the cornmeal. Spray the oil in a large nonstick sauté pan. Lightly brown the cakes, about 2 minutes per side, and then transfer them to a large baking pan. Bake in the oven for 5 to 8 minutes.

PER SERVING: CALORIES 290; CALORIES FROM FAT 150; CALORIES FROM SATURATED FAT 40; PROTEIN 8 G; CARBOHYDRATE 27 G; TOTAL FAT 17 G; SATURATED FAT 4 G; CHOLESTEROL 55 MG; SODIUM 380 MG; 52% CALORIES FROM FAT

Variation: Use ¾ cup grated mozzarella cheese and ¼ cup grated Parmesan cheese in place of the feta cheese.

burgers, patties, and griddlecakes

209

vegan

Portobello Burgers

MAKES 8 (4-OUNCE) BURGERS

PORTOBELLO mushrooms, mellow white miso, and puréed nuts give this star-status burger a rich, earthy flavor. Portobello burgers rely on the starch from short-grain brown rice to keep their shape, which pairs well with the raw nuts. Try this burger on sourdough bread with sautéed onions to spoon on top—it's worth the effort. Add a slice of goat cheese to place this in the burger hall of fame.

2 large portobello mushroom caps, cut into chunks
2 cups button mushrooms, trimmed
1 tablespoon olive oil
1 large onion, chopped
1 small carrot, grated
2 cloves garlic

1 cup raw cashews
$\frac{1}{3}$ cup sunflower seeds
$\frac{1}{8}$ cup white miso
2 teaspoons lemon juice
1 tablespoon sherry
$\frac{1}{2}$ teaspoon freshly ground pepper
1 cup cooked short-grain brown rice
1 cup dried bread crumbs
Vegetable or olive oil for greasing pan

Pulse the portobello and button mushrooms in the bowl of a food processor fitted with a metal blade until coarsely chopped. Heat the olive oil, and sauté the mushrooms, onion, carrot, and garlic until the vegetables are wilted, 2 to 3 minutes. Place the mushroom mixture in a large bowl. In the bowl of the same processor fitted with a metal blade, combine the cashews, sunflower seeds, miso, lemon juice, sherry, and pepper to make a light paste. Add this to the mushrooms in the bowl. Add the rice and bread crumbs; blend all the ingredients together.

Although you may make the burgers now, it's best to allow the mixture to stand for at least 6 hours in the refrigerator—they will hold their shape better. When ready to cook, preheat the oven to 375°F. Use an ice cream scoop or other 4-ounce scoop to place 8 rounded balls of the mixture onto a lightly greased baking pan, at least 4 inches apart. Lightly press the scooped mixture and flatten it to form a 1-inch-thick burger. Bake on the middle rack in the oven for 25 to 30 minutes, until golden brown. Or you may lightly sauté the burgers in 2 teaspoons of olive oil in a nonstick sauté pan on medium heat for 3 to 5 minutes per side, until golden brown.

PER SERVING: CALORIES 420; CALORIES FROM FAT 200; CALORIES FROM SATURATED FAT 35; PROTEIN 13 G; CARBOHYDRATE 46 G; TOTAL FAT 22 G; SATURATED FAT 4 G; CHOLESTEROL 0 MG; SODIUM 460 MG; 48% CALORIES FROM FAT

THE WHOLE FOODS MARKET COOKBOOK

210

Not Your Grandmother's Vegetable Latkes

MAKES 8 EXTRA-LARGE LATKES

2 large russet potatoes, peeled

I large onion

I large carrot

I medium yellow squash

I medium zucchini

I cup unbleached all-purpose flour

I teaspoon salt

2¹/₂ teaspoons baking powder

I teaspoon freshly ground pepper

2 large eggs

Canola oil for brushing tops of latkes

GRANDMOTHERS might think our vegetable griddlecakes aren't traditional latkes. They're right. The confetti of shredded carrot, yellow squash, and zucchini contributes lots of eye appeal as well as enhances the flavor of the traditional grated-potatoes version. Our latkes are also baked in a hot oven until crispy, not pan-fried in oil. Serve these with plain yogurt, raita, marinara sauce, or cinnamon-spiked applesauce.

Preheat the oven to 425°F.

Grate the potatoes into a large bowl. Cover the potatoes with cold water so they won't brown. Into another bowl, grate the onion, carrot, yellow squash, and zucchini. Drain the potatoes well, and press out the excess moisture in a colander. Combine the potatoes and the grated onion, carrot, yellow squash, and zucchini. Add the flour, salt, baking powder, pepper, and eggs, and mix well. Using an 8-ounce scoop as a measure (see Note), form the mixture into 8 (¹/₂-inch-thick) round pancakes about 4 inches across the top. Place on a baking pan lined with parchment paper. Brush or spray the tops lightly with the canola oil. Bake in the oven for 20 minutes, until golden brown and crispy.

NOTE: You may use the lid of a large jar to form the pancakes. Line the lid with plastic wrap and press the vegetable mixture in until a pancake is formed. Unmold on the baking pan.

PER SERVING: CALORIES 150; CALORIES FROM FAT 30; CALORIES FROM SATURATED FAT 5; PROTEIN 5 G; CARBOHYDRATE 26 G; TOTAL FAT 3 G; SATURATED FAT 0.5 G; CHOLESTEROL 55 MG; SODIUM 410 MG; 20% CALORIES FROM FAT

 Tip from the Team: When you're frying Vegetable Latkes (or anything else in oil), fill a pie plate with white vinegar, set it on a counter undisturbed for 8 to 10 hours, and any unpleasant odors will vanish!

Risotto Cakes

MAKES 14 (4-INCH) CAKES

ALTHOUGH these cakes contain a long list of ingredients, this is a simple recipe to make. Arborio rice, a short-grain variety grown in Italy and used to make classic risotto, is deliciously creamy because of its high starch content. These cakes offer comforting texture with contrasting small nuggets of sweet peas, corn, and squash. Italian cheeses round out the flavor. Little silver-dollar versions of the risotto cakes make great appetizers for parties.

1 tablespoon butter or olive oil

1 small onion, minced

1 small carrot, minced

2 cloves garlic, minced (1 teaspoon)

1 teaspoon dried thyme, or
   1 tablespoon fresh

1 cup arborio rice

1/2 cup dry white wine

2 cups vegetable stock or water, plus
   more as needed

1 teaspoon salt

1/2 teaspoon freshly ground pepper

1/4 cup chopped zucchini

1/4 cup frozen peas, thawed

1/2 cup frozen corn, thawed

1/2 cup grated mozzarella cheese

1/2 cup grated provolone cheese

1/2 plus 1/4 cup grated Parmesan
   cheese

1/8 cup chopped parsley

1 tablespoon chopped fresh basil

2 scallions, chopped

Melt the butter in a large skillet. Add the onion, carrot, garlic, and thyme, and sauté for 3 minutes. Add the arborio rice, and sauté for 3 minutes to coat the rice, stirring occasionally. Add the wine; stir until the wine is absorbed. Add the vegetable stock, salt, and pepper. Turn the temperature down; cover the skillet and simmer for 25 minutes, stirring frequently. Check the tenderness of the grain—it should be al dente. If necessary, add more stock and continue to cook until the liquid is absorbed and the rice is tender.

Preheat the oven to 375°F.

Add the zucchini, peas, corn, mozzarella cheese, provolone cheese, and the 1/4 cup Parmesan cheese; stir well. Remove the pan from the heat. Add the parsley,

basil, and scallions. Using a 4-ounce scoop to measure, form the mixture into 14 (1-inch-thick) patties, and place on a parchment-lined baking pan. Dust the surface of each cake evenly with the remaining ½ cup Parmesan cheese. Bake in the oven for about 25 minutes, or until golden brown.

PER SERVING: CALORIES 150; CALORIES FROM FAT 50; CALORIES FROM SATURATED FAT 25; PROTEIN 7 G; CARBOHYDRATE 15 G; TOTAL FAT 6 G; SATURATED FAT 3 G; CHOLESTEROL 10 MG; SODIUM 350 MG; 33% CALORIES FROM FAT

Risotto Cakes

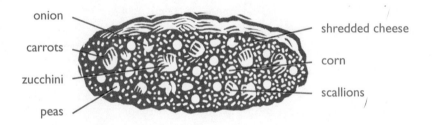

onion
carrots
zucchini
peas

shredded cheese
corn
scallions

Quinoa Vegetable Cakes

MAKES 6 (8-OUNCE) BURGERS

THE delicate, buttery flavor of quinoa pairs well with sweet nuggets of tender vegetables. Oven-roasting these cakes enhances quinoa's nutty qualities and forms a golden crust. You'll love the way the small kernels pop pleasantly in your mouth.

1 cup dried quinoa

2 cups water

1 tablespoon corn or olive oil

1 small onion, finely chopped

2 small carrots, grated

1 small zucchini, grated

1 (10-ounce) package frozen chopped spinach, thawed and squeezed dry

⅛ cup unbleached all-purpose flour

½ teaspoon baking powder

1 tablespoon plain yogurt

⅛ cup tahini

2 teaspoons salt

1 teaspoon freshly ground pepper

⅛ cup chopped fresh dill

2 teaspoons lemon juice

2 teaspoons dried Italian herbs

Canola or olive oil for spraying or brushing parchment paper

Place the quinoa, water, and corn oil in a large sauce pot, and bring it to a boil. Lower to a simmer, and cook the quinoa, covered, stirring occasionally for 20 minutes, until tender and all the liquid is absorbed. Cool the quinoa.

Preheat the oven to 400°F. Place the cooked quinoa into a large bowl with the onion, carrots, zucchini, spinach, flour, baking powder, yogurt, tahini, salt, pepper, dill, lemon juice, and Italian herbs, and mix well.

Line a baking pan with parchment paper. Lightly oil the paper. Using an 8-ounce scoop to measure, place the scooped grain mixture on the paper and press down lightly to form 6 (1-inch-thick) patties. Bake for about 20 minutes, or until lightly browned.

PER SERVING: CALORIES 230; CALORIES FROM FAT 60; CALORIES FROM SATURATED FAT 10; PROTEIN 8 G; CARBOHYDRATE 33 G; TOTAL FAT 7 G; SATURATED FAT 1 G; CHOLESTEROL 0 MG; SODIUM 790 MG; 26% CALORIES FROM FAT

Spicy Smashed Potato Patties

3 pounds russet potatoes

⅛ cup canola oil

1 medium red onion, minced

3 cloves garlic, minced
   (1½ teaspoons)

3 tablespoons minced fresh ginger

1 jalapeño pepper, seeded and minced

1½ teaspoons garam masala

1½ teaspoons curry powder

1½ teaspoons cumin

½ teaspoon turmeric

3 tablespoons minced fresh cilantro

¼ cup lemon juice

1½ teaspoons salt

Freshly ground pepper to taste

SMASHED potatoes may be quiet and unassuming, but not in this recipe. Cooked potatoes are a perfect medium for the thundering flavors of garlic, ginger, jalapeño, and Indian garam masala spices. The potatoes absorb the flavors and distribute these bold tastes in a harmonious way. Turmeric has been used in cooking since 600 B.C., and in biblical times it was used as a perfume base and dyeing agent for clothing. It's what gives American mustard its bright yellow hue. Here it gives our patties a vibrant color and adds aromatic qualities to this exotic offering.

Peel and dice the potatoes. Simmer them in water to cover until fully cooked, about 15 minutes. In a small skillet, heat 1 tablespoon of the canola oil, and sauté the onion, garlic, ginger, and jalapeño pepper until the onion is translucent. Add the garam masala, curry powder, cumin, and turmeric; sauté for half a minute, and remove the spices from the heat. Add the potatoes, and mash together well. Add the cilantro, lemon juice, salt, and pepper; combine well.

Shape the potato mixture into 12 (2-inch-thick) patties; refrigerate the patties for at least 1 hour. Heat the remaining 1 tablespoon canola oil in a large skillet over high heat. The oil should be hot enough that a bead of water sizzles loudly when dropped into it. Place the patties into the oil and cook over high heat until a deep golden brown crust forms, about 3 minutes. Turn the patties over and cook for another 3 minutes, until you have a deep golden brown crust on both sides.

PER SERVING: CALORIES 130; CALORIES FROM FAT 25; CALORIES FROM SATURATED FAT 0; PROTEIN 2 G; CARBOHYDRATE 25 G; TOTAL FAT 2.5 G; SATURATED FAT 0 G; CHOLESTEROL 0 MG; SODIUM 240 MG; 19% CALORIES FROM FAT

burgers, patties, and griddlecakes

Millet and Yam Burgers

MAKES 6 (8-OUNCE) PATTIES

ALTHOUGH millet is grown primarily as bird feed in our country, this protein-rich cereal grass has been a staple food in Asia and Africa for centuries, where it's traditionally used to make puddings, pilafs, and breads. Millet, with its very mild flavor and pleasant buttery aftertaste, combines well with yams. Cook millet the same way you cook rice. When the yams begin to caramelize, they enhance the elegant flavor of the millet. This natural combination belongs together in a burger.

I cup dried millet
I large yam, peeled and chopped
3 cups water
I cup cooked chickpeas
⅛ cup shoyu or tamari
I teaspoon olive oil
I medium carrot, grated
½ cup sunflower seeds
I teaspoon cumin
I teaspoon coriander
I teaspoon ground fennel seeds
½ teaspoon freshly ground pepper
¼ teaspoon cayenne pepper
I tablespoon potato starch or cornstarch
⅛ cup parsley
Vegetable or olive oil to spray on burgers

Preheat the oven to 400°F. Rinse the millet in a fine sieve. Place in a sauce pot over medium heat with the yam and water. Simmer covered for about 30 minutes, or until both the millet and the yam are soft and the liquid has cooked out. Place in a large bowl and add the chickpeas; mash together with the back of a large spoon. Add the shoyu or tamari, olive oil, carrot, sunflower seeds, cumin, coriander, fennel, pepper, cayenne, potato starch, and parsley; blend well.

Using an 8-ounce scoop, form the mixture into 6 patties and place on a baking pan lined with parchment paper. Spray lightly with vegetable or olive oil. Bake in the oven for 20 minutes, until golden brown.

PER SERVING: CALORIES 230; CALORIES FROM FAT 80; CALORIES FROM SATURATED FAT 10; PROTEIN 7 G; CARBOHYDRATE 34 G; TOTAL FAT 9 G; SATURATED FAT 1 G; CHOLESTEROL 0 MG; SODIUM 440 MG; 35% CALORIES FROM FAT

Teriyaki Turkey Burgers with Green Onion and Ginger

MAKES 6 (8-OUNCE) BURGERS

1 pound ground turkey

6 scallions, thinly sliced

1 large carrot, grated

1 (8-ounce) can water chestnuts, drained and finely chopped

2 cloves garlic, minced (1 teaspoon)

2 teaspoons toasted sesame oil

⅛ cup tamari

½ tablespoon bottled Szechwan sauce

2 quarter-size slices fresh ginger, grated

1 cup dried bread crumbs

¼ cup white sesame seeds

¼ cup black sesame seeds

THESE burgers are lighter and leaner than ones made with beef, and they possess a lively Asian flavor rich with green onion (scallions), ginger, soy, and sesame. The water chestnuts add textural contrast and moisture to the turkey, which can sometimes be dry. Try these burgers on a bun with Japanese Kale Salad with Shiitake Mushrooms (page 118) and Creamy Peanut Sauce (page 312).

Preheat the oven to 375°F. In a large bowl, combine the turkey, scallions, carrot, water chestnuts, garlic, sesame oil, tamari, Szechwan sauce, ginger, and bread crumbs until well blended. Using an 8-ounce scoop, form into 6 (1-inch-thick) patties, and place on a parchment-paper-lined sheet pan. Flatten the tops of the patties by pressing lightly with a cookie sheet. In a shallow bowl, combine the white and black sesame seeds and coat each burger with a mixture of the mixed seeds.

Bake in the oven for 20 minutes, until golden brown on the outside and cooked through.

NOTE: To form the burgers easily, use a screw top from a large jar 3 to 4 inches in diameter. Line the top with plastic wrap and press the burger mixture into it, forming a perfect burger.

PER SERVING: CALORIES 300; CALORIES FROM FAT 130; CALORIES FROM SATURATED FAT 20; PROTEIN 20 G; CARBOHYDRATE 23 G; TOTAL FAT 14 G; SATURATED FAT 2 G; CHOLESTEROL 60 MG; SODIUM 600 MG; 43% CALORIES FROM FAT

Variation: Brush with our Triple Citrus Teriyaki Marinade (page 44) or your favorite bottled teriyaki sauce, and broil for 5 minutes, until glazed and golden brown. You may also cook these burgers on a grill with excellent results, or sear them in a cast-iron skillet, and finish cooking them in the oven.

burgers, patties, and griddlecakes

Cajun Seafood Cakes

MAKES 10 (8-OUNCE) PATTIES

ANY fish variety works well in this recipe. The fish, shrimp, and scallops may be steamed, broiled, or placed in a saucepan with a bit of water and white wine, covered, and cooked slowly for about 10 minutes, until opaque and cooked through. You may also substitute canned tuna or splurge with fresh crab in this recipe. If you prefer, make these cakes without shellfish. Try one on a bun with Creole Remoulade Sauce or resting against a bed of pasta with marinara sauce.

1 pound Idaho potatoes, peeled and
    cut into 2-inch dice
½ cup plus 1 tablespoon canola oil
1 large onion, minced
3 cloves garlic, minced
    (1½ teaspoons)
¼ cup thinly sliced celery
2 teaspoons Cajun spices
1 tablespoon dried Italian herbs
1 pound assorted fish fillets, cooked
    and flaked
¼ pound small shrimp, cooked
¼ pound bay or sea scallops, cooked
2 cups chopped fresh parsley, divided
4 cups dried bread crumbs, divided
2 teaspoons salt, or to taste
1 teaspoon freshly ground pepper
⅛ cup Szechwan sauce
2 teaspoons lemon juice
Creole Remoulade Sauce (page 314)
    to serve

Cover the potatoes with cold water and bring to a boil. Simmer uncovered for 12 to 15 minutes, until tender. Drain and mash lightly with a fork or potato masher.

Preheat the oven to 375°F. In a nonstick pan, heat the 1 tablespoon canola oil over medium heat. Sauté the onion, garlic, celery, Cajun spices, and Italian herbs for 2 minutes, until lightly browned. Cool the onion mixture slightly. Place the fish along with the shrimp and scallops in a large bowl, and add the onion mixture, cooked potatoes, 1 cup of the parsley, 1 cup of the bread crumbs, salt, pepper, Szechwan sauce, and lemon juice. Mix the remaining 3 cups bread crumbs and the remaining 1 cup parsley together in a shallow bowl.

Using an 8-ounce scoop as a measure, form the mixture into 10 (½-inch-thick) slightly flattened cakes. Dredge each in the bread crumb mixture, gently pressing the crumbs onto the outside of the cakes. Heat some of the remaining ½ cup canola oil in a large sauté pan. Sauté the cakes in the oil for 2 minutes on each side, until the cakes are golden brown. Be sure to change the oil in the pan if it gets too dark.

Place the browned seafood cakes on a sheet pan in the oven for 15 minutes, until the cakes are cooked through. Serve with the Creole Remoulade Sauce.

PER SERVING: CALORIES 400; CALORIES FROM FAT 130; CALORIES FROM SATURATED FAT 15; PROTEIN 23 G; CARBOHYDRATE 45 G; TOTAL FAT 14 G; SATURATED FAT 1.5 G; CHOLESTEROL 50 MG; SODIUM 970 MG; 32% CALORIES FROM FAT

Thai Fish Cakes

MAKES 8 (4-OUNCE) CAKES

1 pound cod or other mild firm
  whitefish fillets, such as tilapia

2 teaspoons Thai red curry paste

2 teaspoons Thai fish sauce

⅛ cup cornstarch

1 large egg

4 teaspoons lime juice

½ jalapeño pepper, seeded

2 scallions, minced

¼ pound green beans, thinly sliced on
  an angle

⅓ cup chopped fresh cilantro

½ cup canola oil

THIS is our interpretation of a classic Thai appetizer. Try using a fleshy, white-meat fish like cod or tilapia. These cakes are a bit soft when raw, and so need extra care when handling, but develop a silky smooth texture that allows the intense Thai chili paste, tart lime juice, and cilantro to ring through. Fish sauce (called *nam pla*), made with salted fermented fish, is a widely used pungent condiment in many Southeast Asian cultures. Serve with Creamy Peanut Sauce (page 312) or Tikka Salad Dressing (page 327).

Preheat the oven to 375°F. Place the fish, curry paste, fish sauce, cornstarch, egg, lime juice, and jalapeño in the bowl of a food processor fitted with a metal blade. Process until well combined. Place the mixture in a bowl. Mix in the scallions, green beans, and cilantro, and combine well until a smooth mixture is formed.

Heat the canola oil in a large nonstick skillet. Using a 4-ounce scoop to measure, shape the paste into 8 (½-inch-thick) cakes. Pan-sauté each cake for about 2 minutes on each side, or until golden brown. Transfer the cakes to a sheet pan, and place in the center of the oven. Bake for 10 minutes, until the cakes are cooked through.

PER SERVING: CALORIES 210; CALORIES FROM FAT 130; CALORIES FROM SATURATED FAT 10; PROTEIN 14 G; CARBOHYDRATE 4 G; TOTAL FAT 15 G; SATURATED FAT 1.5 G; CHOLESTEROL 60 MG; SODIUM 170 MG; 62% CALORIES FROM FAT

burgers, patties, and griddlecakes

219

Greek Beef Meatballs

MAKES 16 (2-OUNCE) MEATBALLS

THESE aren't actually burgers, but rather well-rounded distant cousins. Based upon the hallmarks of Greek cooking—roasted red pepper, fresh mint, oregano, and feta cheese—these meatballs are so resonant in flavor that you may serve them in their own juices or with your choice of marinara sauce, mushroom pan gravy, or even Cucumber Raita (page 340). Try serving these on a nest of warm orzo pasta with extra-virgin olive oil and a squeeze of lemon.

1 pound lean ground beef

⅛ cup chopped fresh oregano, leaves only

⅛ cup chopped fresh mint, leaves only

½ cup finely minced parsley

3 cloves garlic, minced (1½ teaspoons)

1 (12-ounce) jar roasted red peppers, drained, patted dry, and chopped

2 teaspoons lemon pepper

2 teaspoons salt

1 cup crumbled feta cheese

2 teaspoons lemon juice

P reheat the oven to 350°F. Mix the ground beef, oregano, mint, parsley, garlic, red peppers, lemon pepper, salt, feta cheese, and lemon juice together in a large bowl, blending in the cheese until no large crumbles remain. Using a 2-ounce scoop (⅛ cup) to measure, roll into 16 balls and place on a large baking pan. Bake for about 25 minutes, or until the outside of the meatballs brown and the center is cooked through.

PER SERVING: CALORIES 80; CALORIES FROM FAT 40; CALORIES FROM SATURATED FAT 20; PROTEIN 8 G; CARBOHYDRATE 2 G; TOTAL FAT 4.5 G; SATURATED FAT 2.5 G; CHOLESTEROL 20 MG; SODIUM 440 MG; 50% CALORIES FROM FAT

Main Attractions

KUNG PAO TOFU • JAVANESE ROASTED TOFU WITH PEPPER RAINBOW •
IMPERIAL ORANGE TOFU • GRIDDLED SESAME AND GARLIC TOFU WITH
WILTED BOK CHOY • BRAISED FIVE-SPICE TOFU • CHICKEN TOSCANA
WITH WHITE BEANS • WOK-SAUTÉED MIZUNA WITH MINCED CHICKEN •
CHICKEN BREAST PICCATA FLORENTINE • LIGURIAN CHICKEN BREASTS
• ATHENIAN CHICKEN ROLL-UPS • CHICKEN BREASTS STUFFED WITH
GOAT CHEESE AND ROASTED RED PEPPER TAPENADE • POMEGRANATE
GLAZED CHICKEN • CARAMELIZED ONION TURKEY ROULADE •
FIRECRACKER SHRIMP • BAY SCALLOPS DIJON • LIME SEARED SCALLOPS
OVER BABY SPINACH • RED-CHILI-RUBBED SALMON • BROILED TUNA
STUFFED WITH SPINACH AND SUN-DRIED TOMATOES • PECAN
CORNMEAL DUSTED CATFISH • HAZELNUT CRUSTED PORK LOIN •
CUBANO-STYLE PORK LOIN • GRILLED LEMON PEPPER RIB-EYE STEAKS •
PASTEL DE CHOCLO • CARNE ASADA WITH JALAPEÑO CILANTRO PESTO
• PERSIAN LAMB ROAST À LA GRAND-MÈRE

A large platter set on the center of the table symbolized an era of family dining and still evokes a communal feeling.

However, the traditional concept of family has evolved and so has the definition of *dinner*. Today many of us graze, eating small meals during the day. Yet, the thought of a centerpiece of a garlic- and oregano-scented lasagna or an herb-encrusted roast still say dinner like nothing else.

Our main attractions include some traditional items but also reflect a unique blend of ethnic backgrounds and diverse flavors. From kale- and potato-stuffed Ligurian chicken braised in olive oil, lemon, and tomatoes (page 232) to crimson-colored spicy Red-Chili-Rubbed Salmon with New Mexican dried red chili peppers (page 246), we offer you entrées that are suitable for weekday dinners or entertaining.

We've chosen extremely versatile entrées. Our tofu dishes are excellent served hot or cold. Whole roasted sides of salmon are incredible served at room temperature. They can be made the day before dinner and just placed on your table when you are ready to dine. They also make very impressive party food menu items for brunch or dinner. Leftovers may be made into seafood cakes or salad. Leftover grilled and roasted meat items like our Carne Asada with Jalapeño Cilantro Pesto (page 255), Hazelnut Crusted Pork Loin (page 250), or Persian Lamb Roast à la Grand-Mère (page 256) may be sliced for sandwiches or stuffed into quesadillas and wraps. We think these recipes will give you a great reason to get back to the dinner table. Tradition has never tasted so good.

Kung Pao Tofu

SERVES 4

The Kung Pao Sauce Base

1/2 cup brown rice syrup

1/4 cup rice wine vinegar

2 1/2 teaspoons cornstarch

2 teaspoons tamari

1/4 teaspoon cayenne pepper

1 1/2 cups prepared teriyaki marinade

1 pound extra-firm tofu, cut into
  1/2-inch cubes

1 tablespoon toasted sesame oil

1/2 tablespoon canola oil

1 1/4 teaspoons crushed red chili flakes

2 teaspoons minced fresh ginger

2 cloves garlic, minced (1 teaspoon)

1 cup chopped peanuts

3 scallions, sliced thinly and diagonally

3/4 cup diced green pepper

3/4 cup diced red pepper

OUR Kung Pao is similar in taste to the Kung Pao dishes we are familiar with in Chinese restaurants, except the use of mild brown rice syrup lends a very delicate sweetness and body that is not overpowering. Minced fresh ginger, garlic, red chili flakes, and peanuts liven up the flavor. Serve the tofu over cooked rice noodles or steamed brown rice.

Preheat the oven to 350°F.

TO PREPARE THE KUNG PAO SAUCE BASE Combine the brown rice syrup, rice wine vinegar, cornstarch, tamari, and cayenne pepper in a small bowl, and mix until well blended. Set aside.

In a medium bowl, place the teriyaki marinade. Add the tofu cubes, and gently toss to coat well. Remove the tofu from the marinade with a slotted spoon, draining off the excess liquid, and place it on a baking pan in a single layer. Bake the tofu in the oven for 15 to 20 minutes, until it is lightly browned.

Heat the oils in a large sauté pan until almost smoking. Add the red chili flakes, ginger, garlic, and peanuts. Sauté for 3 minutes. Add the cooked tofu and scallions, and sauté for 1 minute. Add half the reserved Kung Pao sauce base, stirring constantly until the sauce thickens.

Add the remaining half of the sauce base, and stir until glossy. Stir in the peppers; cook for 1 to 2 minutes, until the peppers are firm-tender.

PER SERVING: CALORIES 430; CALORIES FROM FAT 220; CALORIES FROM SATURATED FAT 30; PROTEIN 19 G; CARBOHYDRATE 38 G; TOTAL FAT 25 G; SATURATED FAT 3.5 G; CHOLESTEROL 0 MG; SODIUM 730 MG; 51% CALORIES FROM FAT

 Recipe Bonus Try this rolled into a whole wheat tortilla with raw spinach and bean sprouts.

main attractions

223

Javanese Roasted Tofu with Pepper Rainbow

SERVES 3

ALTHOUGH this dish originates from our stores in the midwestern United States, it certainly had a Javanese spirit during creation. It is full of spice and lively flavors reminiscent of Indonesian cooking, and the mild-flavored tofu acts as a perfect common denominator for the creamy peanut butter. The salt from tamari and the sweet-sour tastes of honey and lemon effectively temper the spicy cayenne pepper. This tofu dish is excellent served chilled as well. Try the tofu in a pita sandwich or sliced on top of a field green salad with Roasted Sesame–Honey Dressing (page 334).

I pound extra-firm tofu

½ cup peanut butter
¼ cup tamari or shoyu
3 tablespoons honey
½ cup water
I teaspoon lemon juice
2 cloves garlic, minced (I teaspoon)
¼ teaspoon cayenne pepper
I teaspoon salt

⅛ cup canola oil
I cup thinly sliced red pepper
I cup thinly sliced green pepper
I cup thinly sliced yellow pepper

Preheat the oven to 350°F. Cut the tofu into 1-inch-thick slices across the short side of the tofu block. You will have 6 slices. Place the slices on a baking sheet, and bake them in the oven for 25 minutes. The tofu should not be crispy—you want it to simply dry out and firm up.

While the tofu is baking, in a medium bowl blend the peanut butter, tamari, honey, water, lemon juice, garlic, cayenne pepper, and salt.

Pour the peanut butter sauce over the cooked tofu, cover the pan with aluminum foil, and continue to bake at 350°F. for 25 minutes, stirring occasionally. Remove the tofu from the oven, and place on a serving dish.

Just before the tofu is done, heat the canola oil in a large sauté pan, and sauté the red, green, and yellow peppers for 2 minutes, until softened. Top the tofu with the peppers.

PER SERVING: CALORIES 480; CALORIES FROM FAT 250; CALORIES FROM SATURATED FAT 35; PROTEIN 24 G; CARBOHYDRATE 42 G; TOTAL FAT 27 G; SATURATED FAT 3.5 G; CHOLESTEROL 0 MG; SODIUM 1,440 MG; 52% CALORIES FROM FAT

Imperial Orange Tofu

1 pound extra-firm tofu

½ cup cornstarch or arrowroot

2 large egg whites

½ cup dry sherry

¼ cup plus 2 tablespoons canola oil

Imperial Orange Sauce (page 309)

2 scallions, chopped

THIS crusty tofu dish is fried to achieve a crisp result. If you prefer a dish using less oil, pan-sear it instead, following the same procedure as for Griddled Sesame and Garlic Tofu (page 226), and serve it with the intensely flavored orange sauce. This dish offers lots of culinary features. Imperial Orange Tofu has a sweet, piquant flavor with just enough heat to get noticed. Bite into a crispy surface, and you'll find a moist center within. Try sautéing some snow pea pods, peppers, scallions, and carrots to place on top of the tofu. Udon noodles or steamed basmati rice make a great serving partner. There's no need to press the excess moisture from the tofu, as the cornstarch crust dries the surface out well.

Cut the tofu into 6 slices about 1 inch thick. Place the slices on paper towels to release excess moisture.

In a small bowl, combine the cornstarch, egg whites, and sherry, mixing well to blend into a smooth batter.

Pour the canola oil into a 10-inch frying pan, and heat to medium-high. Place the tofu slices in the batter, turning once or twice to nicely coat each slice with batter. Carefully place the battered tofu into the hot oil, and cook until golden brown, for 4 to 5 minutes, turning once. Drain on paper towels.

Place the tofu on a serving dish, and spoon on the Imperial Orange Sauce. Sprinkle with the scallions.

PER SERVING: CALORIES 560; CALORIES FROM FAT 310; CALORIES FROM SATURATED FAT 25; PROTEIN 16 G; CARBOHYDRATE 43 G; TOTAL FAT 34 G; SATURATED FAT 3 G; CHOLESTEROL 0 MG; SODIUM 850 MG; 55% CALORIES FROM FAT

main attractions

vegan

Griddled Sesame and Garlic Tofu with Wilted Bok Choy

SERVES 4

THE flavors of ginger, garlic, and golden brown sesame seeds are locked inside tender tofu steaks that are seared over high heat until crispy. If you prefer a stronger miso flavor, use a dark brown or red miso. It's preferable to leave the tofu to marinate overnight in the refrigerator.

Bok choy is also called Chinese mustard cabbage, resembling a cross between celery and Swiss chard. While the stem is rather sweet, the leaves have a pleasant bitter flavor. If you can find baby bok choy, use it for this recipe; the cooking time will be reduced almost by half. You may quarter the whole heads of baby bok choy lengthwise and wilt them. Wilted bok choy is delicious served chilled the following day. Bok choy pairs well with any Asian-inspired dish.

C ut the tofu lengthwise into 4 (½-inch-thick) rectangular "steaks," about 4 ounces each.

TO PREPARE THE SESAME-MISO MARINADE
Combine the garlic, ginger, sesame oil, tamari, rice vinegar, brown sugar, sesame seeds, red chili flakes, water, and miso in the bowl of a food processor fitted with a metal blade. Process until smooth. Place the marinade in a shallow dish, and add the tofu, turning to coat well. Marinate the tofu for at least 2 hours, preferably overnight, in the refrigerator.

Preheat the oven to the lowest setting, about 185°F., to keep the tofu warm while you wilt the bok choy. Spray a large nonstick sauté pan with vegetable oil. Heat over high heat. Remove the tofu from the marinade, allowing the excess liquid to drain. Reserve

1 pound firm tofu

The Sesame-Miso Marinade
3 cloves garlic
2 teaspoons minced fresh ginger
2 teaspoons toasted sesame oil
¼ cup tamari or soy sauce
1 tablespoon rice vinegar or cider vinegar
1 tablespoon light brown sugar
1 tablespoon sesame seeds, or a mixture of black and regular sesame seeds
1 teaspoon crushed red chili flakes
¾ cup water or apple or pineapple juice
¼ cup white miso
Vegetable oil for spraying pan

The Wilted Bok Choy
1 teaspoon peanut or canola oil
1 teaspoon sesame oil
1 medium head bok choy, washed and sliced diagonally, or 4 heads baby bok choy, quartered lengthwise
2 cloves garlic, minced (1 teaspoon)
1 teaspoon minced fresh ginger
1 tablespoon tamari or soy sauce
6 to 8 scallions, sliced diagonally
Sesame seeds for sprinkling

the marinade. Place the tofu in the hot sauté pan and sear for 2 minutes on each side, or until well browned, turning once. Place the tofu in the warm oven, and prepare the bok choy.

TO PREPARE THE WILTED BOK CHOY Heat the peanut and sesame oils over moderate heat in a nonstick sauté pan. Add the bok choy, garlic, and ginger, and sauté, stirring frequently for 4 minutes, until almost tender. Add the tamari and scallions, and remove from the heat.

To assemble, place a bed of bok choy on each plate. Arrange a tofu steak over the bok choy, and drizzle with some of the reserved marinade. Sprinkle with sesame seeds.

TOFU PER SERVING: CALORIES 80; CALORIES FROM FAT 35; CALORIES FROM SATURATED FAT 0; PROTEIN 9 G; CARBOHYDRATE 3 G; TOTAL FAT 3.5 G; SATURATED FAT 0 G; CHOLESTEROL 0 MG; SODIUM 240 MG; 44% CALORIES FROM FAT

BOK CHOY PER SERVING: CALORIES 50; CALORIES FROM FAT 25; CALORIES FROM SATURATED FAT 0; PROTEIN 4 G; CARBOHYDRATE 6 G; TOTAL FAT 2.5 G; SATURATED FAT 0 G; CHOLESTEROL 0 MG; SODIUM 390 MG; 50% CALORIES FROM FAT

 Tip from the Team: If you do a lot of Asian cooking or cooking with garlic and ginger, peel and purée them together in the bowl of a food processor, spoon the paste into a small jar, and keep it in the fridge. This way, you're always ready to turn out a delicious meal, fast!

vegan

Braised Five-Spice Tofu

SERVES 4

FIVE-SPICE powder is highly aromatic and flavorful. It normally contains star anise, a dried star-shaped flower bud that tastes like licorice. Also included in the background is cinnamon, clove, Szechwan peppercorns, and fennel seed. In this recipe we use whole star anise buds, as well. Orange peel and hoisin sauce add great depth of flavor to this dish. Hoisin sauce is a common Asian soy-based table condiment. It can be found in many Whole Foods Market stores and in Chinese grocery stores. You may make the sauce ahead and keep it for a week in the refrigerator. It can be used to cook chicken, shrimp, eggplant, or tempeh with equally flavorful results.

TO PREPARE THE FIVE-SPICE SAUCE Combine the tomato juice, ketchup, molasses, rice vinegar, tamari, ginger, garlic, five-spice powder, star anise buds, orange zest, red chili flakes, and hoisin sauce in a mixing bowl.

In a large sauté pan, heat the oils over medium heat. Add the tofu cubes, and brown them without stirring. Turn the tofu when it's browned on one side, and repeat until the tofu is nicely browned on all sides, about 2 minutes per side. Add the scallions, carrots, peppers, tomato, and onion to the tofu. Stir in the five-spice sauce. Cover the pan, lower the heat to simmer, and cook for 15 minutes, until the vegetables are crisp-tender.

The Five-Spice Sauce

1 cup tomato juice

½ cup ketchup

⅛ cup molasses

1 tablespoon rice vinegar or cider vinegar

¼ cup tamari or soy sauce

1 tablespoon grated fresh ginger

3 cloves garlic, minced (1 teaspoon)

2 teaspoons five-spice powder

3 star anise flower buds

1 tablespoon grated orange zest

½ teaspoon crushed red chili flakes

⅛ cup hoisin sauce

2 teaspoons canola oil

1 teaspoon toasted sesame oil

1 pound firm or extra-firm tofu, cut into 1-inch cubes

6 to 8 scallions, cut diagonally into 1-inch lengths

1 cup sliced carrots, cut diagonally

1 cup chopped green peppers

1 cup chopped tomato

1 cup chopped onion

PER SERVING: CALORIES 250; CALORIES FROM FAT 60; CALORIES FROM SATURATED FAT 5; PROTEIN 13 G; CARBOHYDRATE 40 G; TOTAL FAT 7 G; SATURATED FAT 1 G; CHOLESTEROL 0 MG; SODIUM 1,130 MG; 24% CALORIES FROM FAT

 Recipe Bonus For a thicker sauce, bring the tofu and vegetable mixture to a boil, stir in 2 teaspoons of cornstarch dissolved in ¼ cup water, and continue cooking until the mixture thickens.

Chicken Toscana
with White Beans

SERVES 6

The Toscana Marinade

¹⁄₃ cup extra-virgin olive oil

3 cloves garlic, minced
    (1¹⁄₂ teaspoons)

¹⁄₈ cup lemon juice

4 sprigs fresh oregano leaves

4 sprigs fresh tarragon leaves

4 sprigs fresh basil leaves

4 sprigs parsley

2 sprigs fresh rosemary

Freshly ground pepper to taste

2 pounds boneless skinless chicken
    breasts, cut into 1-inch cubes

¹⁄₈ cup olive or canola oil

¹⁄₂ medium red onion, thinly sliced

1¹⁄₂ cups cooked white cannellini
    beans

Salt and freshly ground pepper to
    taste

DELICATE chicken soaks in the flavor of fresh puréed aromatic herbs, which release intense flavor and aroma when sautéed. Pull the tender herb leaves from the oregano, tarragon, basil, and rosemary stalks before puréeing. The natural starch of the white beans will lightly thicken the sauce. This dish can be enjoyed hot from the pan, at room temperature, or chilled the day after cooking. It also makes a flavorful sandwich filling stuffed into a loaf of semolina bread and drizzled with extra-virgin olive oil.

TO PREPARE THE TOSCANA MARINADE In the bowl of a food processor or in a blender, place the olive oil, garlic, lemon juice, leaves of oregano, tarragon, basil, parsley, rosemary, and the pepper. Blend all ingredients well until a smooth bright green paste is formed. You may add a few spoonfuls of water to help this process if the mixture looks too thick. You may also make the marinade using an immersion blender.

Marinate the cubed chicken in the refrigerator with the Toscana Marinade for at least 2 hours, or overnight if possible.

Heat the olive oil in a large pan over moderate heat until hot, about 2 minutes. Add the cubed chicken, and allow it to brown lightly without stirring initially. Begin turning the chicken after 3 minutes, and add the onion. Sauté for 2 minutes, until the onion begins to soften. Add the white cannellini beans, and continue to cook for 2 minutes longer, until the chicken is cooked through and a light sauce forms around the chicken pieces. Season with the salt and pepper.

PER SERVING: CALORIES 340; CALORIES FROM FAT 90; CALORIES FROM SATURATED FAT 20; PROTEIN 50 G; CARBOHYDRATE 10 G; TOTAL FAT 10 G; SATURATED FAT 2 G; CHOLESTEROL 130 MG; SODIUM 250 MG; 26% CALORIES FROM FAT

main attractions

Wok-Sautéed Mizuna with Minced Chicken

SERVES 6

MIZUNA is a small, feathery, pointed green leaf in the mustard green family. It has a slightly bitter flavor and is often included in field green salad mixes. You may substitute watercress, baby spinach leaves, or mustard greens. Mizuna leaves are added last and barely cooked to preserve their character. If substituting kale, add it a bit earlier in the recipe, with the carrot and onion, so it will be tender.

This dish takes on a smoky flavor when cooked in a wok because of the high heat used and the increased surface area of the pan. Any way you decide to prepare it, serve with basmati rice or short-grain brown rice.

1 large egg white, lightly beaten
½ teaspoon tamari or soy sauce
2 cloves garlic, minced (1 teaspoon)
1 pound boneless skinless chicken breasts, minced

2 teaspoons canola or peanut oil
⅓ cup minced carrot
⅓ cup minced onion
¼ cup minced water chestnuts
1 teaspoon tamari or soy sauce
½ teaspoon chili paste with garlic (Thai chile paste is a good substitute)
1 tablespoon lime juice
1 pound mizuna, ends trimmed
¼ cup minced scallions to garnish

In a medium bowl, mix the egg white with the tamari, garlic, and minced chicken. Mix well to coat the chicken evenly. Marinate, refrigerated, for 1 hour.

When you are ready to cook, heat 1 teaspoon of the canola oil in a wok or sauté pan over high heat. Sauté the minced chicken for 4 to 6 minutes, stirring constantly until the chicken is cooked through and appears opaque. Remove the chicken from the pan. Add the remaining 1 teaspoon oil to the pan, and sauté the carrot, onion, and water chestnuts for 1 minute, stirring constantly. Add the tamari, chili paste, lime juice, and mizuna leaves. Cook until the mizuna has wilted slightly, stirring often.

Return the cooked chicken to the pan, and mix well. Garnish with the scallions.

NOTE
- Leftover chicken filling can be served over a salad or stuffed into a pita bread.
- If you happen to have pizza dough or puff pastry in your freezer, minced chicken is an excellent filling.

PER SERVING: CALORIES 120; CALORIES FROM FAT 30; CALORIES FROM SATURATED FAT 5; PROTEIN 19 G; CARBOHYDRATE 3 G; TOTAL FAT 3.5 G; SATURATED FAT 0.5 G; CHOLESTEROL 50 MG; SODIUM 160 MG; 25% CALORIES FROM FAT

Chicken Breast Piccata Florentine

½ cup unbleached all-purpose flour

2 large eggs, beaten

¾ cup grated Parmesan cheese

2 cups fresh chopped spinach leaves, washed, or 1 cup frozen chopped leaf spinach, thawed

2 teaspoons dried Italian herbs

2 garlic cloves, minced (1 teaspoon)

2 teaspoons salt

1 teaspoon freshly ground pepper

3 tablespoons olive oil

2 whole boneless skinless chicken breasts, cut in half and pounded lightly, or 4 (3-ounce) boneless turkey breast medallions, pounded lightly

THIS piccata batter flecked with bits of spinach and garlic may be used for chicken breast, turkey, or even tofu and vegetable steaks. Make sure that the oil is hot when the breast is placed in the pan so the coating will immediately seal the chicken—this completely locks in all the natural juices. Use a good-quality Parmesan cheese like Reggiano or Grana Padano. You may also use a mixture of Parmesan and Romano cheeses. Always freshly grate cheese yourself, if you have the time—the flavor is much better.

Preheat the oven to 375°F. Place the flour in a bowl large enough to dredge the chicken breasts in.

Combine the eggs, Parmesan cheese, spinach, Italian herbs, garlic, salt, and pepper in a large bowl, blending well. The mixture should be the consistency of pancake batter.

Place the olive oil in a large nonstick sauté pan over medium-high heat. Dredge the chicken breasts first in the flour, dusting off any excess, and then in the batter, and carefully place in the hot oil. Sauté, turning once, until just golden brown on both sides, about 3 minutes per side.

Place the breasts on a baking dish, and transfer to the oven to finish cooking, for 10 to 15 minutes.

PER SERVING: CALORIES 440; CALORIES FROM FAT 200; CALORIES FROM SATURATED FAT 60; PROTEIN 42 G; CARBOHYDRATE 15 G; TOTAL FAT 23 G; SATURATED FAT 7 G; CHOLESTEROL 200 MG; SODIUM 1,400 MG; 45% CALORIES FROM FAT

Variation: Try a variation on this recipe by topping each chicken breast with a slice of prosciutto and a slice of smoked mozzarella about 3 minutes before the baking time is up. Serve with roasted red pepper polenta made by adding ½ cup jarred roasted red pepper strips to instant polenta. You may also top the breasts with some marinara and mozzarella during the last 5 minutes of baking, for a chicken-Parmesan-like dish.

main attractions

Ligurian Chicken Breasts

SERVES 4

LIGURIA, Italy, is the birthplace of Columbus and of many culinary treasures, including San Remo basil, considered the most fragrant in the world. This Ligurian Chicken Breast—an authentic family recipe—was passed on to one of our chefs while visiting this area. It has since become one of our favorites.

This makes an impressive dinner when baked in a ceramic dish, which may be placed on the table after baking. The tomato, onion, and lemon bake directly into the surface of the chicken, which imparts a sweet citrus taste. The light pan juices are fragrant with basil, mint, and Kalamata olives and should be spooned over the crispy potato-stuffed breasts when served.

The potato-kale stuffing may be served alone as a side dish with seafood, game, poultry, or beef. Leftover chilled breasts may be sliced into ¾-inch-thick medallions and served as hors d'oeuvres or snacks.

TO PREPARE THE POTATO-KALE STUFFING

Place the potatoes in a medium bowl, and mash lightly with a fork (you should have about 1½ cups). Heat the olive oil in a large sauté pan over medium heat, and sauté the garlic and kale for 4 to 5 minutes, tossing often, until the greens are wilted. Add the kale to the potatoes, along with the scallions, basil, and salt and pepper. Cool the potato mixture completely in the refrigerator.

Preheat the oven to 375°F. Place about ½ cup of the potato-kale filling in the center of each pounded chicken breast. Fold the top of the breast over the filling to form a package, tucking in the breast wherever

The Potato-Kale Stuffing

2 large Yukon Gold potatoes, peeled and boiled

⅛ cup olive oil

2 cloves garlic, minced (1 teaspoon)

4 cups chopped kale

2 scallions, chopped

6 fresh basil leaves, chopped

Salt and freshly ground pepper to taste

2 large boneless skinless whole chicken breasts, cut in half and pounded lightly

1 medium tomato, cored and cut into 4 slices

4 slices red onion, about ¼ inch thick

½ lemon, cut into 4 thin slices

1 cup Sauternes or other sweet white wine

¼ cup olive oil

Juice of 1 lemon

3 sprigs fresh mint, leaves torn or chopped

6 fresh basil leaves, torn or chopped

1 tablespoon capers, drained

¼ cup Kalamata olives, pitted and chopped

needed. Place the chicken on an ungreased baking pan, leaving a small space in between each breast. Top the breasts with a slice of tomato, a slice of onion, and a slice of lemon. Secure the stuffed breast with a toothpick if necessary.

Mix the Sauternes, olive oil, and lemon juice together. Pour the wine mixture around the chicken, and then sprinkle with the mint, basil leaves, capers, and olives. Cover with aluminum foil, and bake for 35 minutes. Uncover, brush the vegetables and chicken breasts with some of the pan drippings, and cook an additional 10 minutes, uncovered, until golden.

PER SERVING: CALORIES 490; CALORIES FROM FAT 230; CALORIES FROM SATURATED FAT 35; PROTEIN 32 G; CARBOHYDRATE 28 G; TOTAL FAT 26 G; SATURATED FAT 4 G; CHOLESTEROL 75 MG; SODIUM 760 MG; 47% CALORIES FROM FAT

 Tip from the Team: When cooking Italian food, we find it more fun to put on a recording of an Italian opera, such as Mozart's *Don Giovanni* or *The Marriage of Figaro*. Also, drink a glass of Italian wine, such as a good Sangiovese or Chianti.

Ligurian Chicken Breast

capers
tomatoes
onion
scallions
kale

olives
mint sprigs
lemon slices
potatoes

Athenian Chicken Roll-Ups

SERVES 6

THIS Greek-inspired spinach stuffing is bright green, flecked with sharp feta cheese, and fragrant with dill. We always make extra stuffed breasts, some to serve hot for an entrée and the remainder to chill for roll-up slices. They take on a totally different flavor when chilled. They also make a delicious sandwich when stuffed into pita bread.

2½ pounds boneless skinless chicken breasts (6 halves)

¼ cup Italian Herb Vinaigrette (page 329)

The Stuffing

1 tablespoon olive oil

½ medium onion, chopped

2 cloves garlic, minced (1 teaspoon)

2 teaspoons dried oregano, or ⅛ cup fresh

1 (16-ounce) bag frozen chopped leaf spinach, thawed

½ cup feta cheese, crumbled

½ cup dried bread crumbs plus ¼ cup for topping

Juice of 1 lemon

½ cup minced fresh dill, or 2 tablespoons plus 2 teaspoons dried

Lemon pepper to taste

½ cup dry white wine (optional)

½ cup water

1 tablespoon extra-virgin olive oil

Remove any excess fat from the chicken breasts. If using whole breasts, cut them into 2 separate pieces. Pound the breasts lightly. Marinate the breasts in the vinaigrette for 1 hour or overnight for best flavor.

TO PREPARE THE STUFFING In a large pan, heat the olive oil over medium heat. Sauté the onion, garlic, and oregano for 2 minutes, until the onion is softened. Add the spinach and continue cooking for 5 minutes. Remove the pan from the heat, and add the feta cheese, the ½ cup bread crumbs, lemon, dill, and lemon pepper to taste. Cool the stuffing in the refrigerator completely before stuffing the chicken breasts. The stuffing may be made up to 2 days before using.

When chilled, divide the stuffing among the 6 breasts and fill the center of each breast with a generous handful of spinach stuffing. Gently wrap the breast around the stuffing and join the breast meat around the bottom so the stuffing is held inside. Place the chicken seam side down into a baking dish large enough to hold all the breasts. Leave a small space in between the breasts.

Preheat the oven to 375°F.

Add the ½ cup wine, if using, and ½ cup water to the pan. (You may substitute all water if you prefer.) Drizzle the breasts with the extra-virgin olive oil and sprinkle the remaining ¼ cup bread crumbs over the breasts. Loosely cover the baking dish with foil.

Bake the roll-ups for 45 minutes. Remove the foil and continue to bake for another 10 minutes, until lightly browned and cooked through. Serve immediately as an entrée. Or cool, cover, and refrigerate overnight. For medallions, slice the cooked breasts into ½-inch-thick slices with a sharp knife and serve with either Creole Remoulade Sauce (page 314) or your favorite dipping sauce, or on thinly sliced baguettes.

PER SERVING: CALORIES 450; CALORIES FROM FAT 140; CALORIES FROM SATURATED FAT 40; PROTEIN 60 G; CARBOHYDRATE 14 G; TOTAL FAT 16 G; SATURATED FAT 4.5 G; CHOLESTEROL 155 MG; SODIUM 480 MG; 31% CALORIES FROM FAT

Chicken Breasts Stuffed with Goat Cheese and Roasted Red Pepper Tapenade

SERVES 4

A brightly colored center of green leaf spinach, red roasted pepper, and mild white goat cheese fills these breasts of chicken and makes an attractive presentation. This filling melts in your mouth. Serve this chicken hot, at room temperature, or chilled. Offer these to your guests over a nest of Fettuccine with Garlic, Parsley, and Parmesan (page 184) or a small whimsical pasta, such as star-shaped stellini pasta. Try using piquillo peppers for the roasted peppers in this dish—they are wonderful in this recipe. You may stuff the breasts and freeze them for future use, as well. Chilled, sliced breasts become a beautiful tricolor roulade or roll-up, which may be served as an appetizer.

1 tablespoon olive oil

2 cloves garlic, minced (1 teaspoon)

1 shallot, minced

1 teaspoon minced fresh thyme leaves

6 cups fresh washed spinach leaves

Salt and freshly ground pepper to taste

½ cup drained, chopped jarred roasted red peppers

3 tablespoons pitted and chopped Kalamata olives

1 tablespoon chopped capers

1 teaspoon balsamic vinegar

2 boneless skinless whole chicken breasts, cut in half and pounded lightly

4 ounces mild goat cheese, at room temperature

1 tablespoon olive oil for brushing chicken

¼ cup chopped parsley

Heat the olive oil in a large skillet over medium-high heat. Sauté the garlic, shallot, and thyme for 2 minutes, until softened. Add the spinach, and sauté for 1 minute longer, until just wilted. Season with the salt and pepper. Remove the skillet from the heat, and let the aromatics cool.

Preheat the oven to 375°F. In a small bowl, mix the roasted red peppers with the olives, capers, and balsamic vinegar.

Place about ¼ cup of the spinach mixture in the center of each pounded chicken breast. Evenly divide the goat cheese among the chicken breasts, placing a small piece over the spinach; then top with 1 tablespoon of the roasted red peppers.

Fold the top of the breast over the filling to form a package, sealing the bottom of the chicken packages wherever needed. Place the chicken on a baking pan. Cover with aluminum foil, and bake in the oven for 25 minutes. Uncover, brush the chicken with a little olive oil, and cook an additional 10 minutes, until the chicken is brown.

Place the chicken on a serving platter and sprinkle it with the parsley.

PER SERVING: CALORIES 340; CALORIES FROM FAT 180; CALORIES FROM SATURATED FAT 70; PROTEIN 35 G; CARBOHYDRATE 6 G; TOTAL FAT 20 G; SATURATED FAT 8 G; CHOLESTEROL 95 MG; SODIUM 730 MG; 53% CALORIES FROM FAT

 Tip from the Team: Use the skin on whole chickens or skin-on parts to baste and seal in added flavor by nicking at the membrane under the skin with the tip of a sharp knife until the skin lifts to make a pocket/flap. Before roasting, place fresh herbs and chopped garlic under the skin and fold the skin over. Discard the skin after cooking, if desired.

Pomegranate Glazed Chicken

SERVES 4

THIS uncommon dish uses a unique ingredient that is becoming more and more popular. Pomegranate molasses is the deep red, tart, concentrated juice of ripe pomegranates. It's almost like balsamic vinegar in color and flavor, just a bit fruitier. Pomegranate molasses lends tremendous color and flavor to this chicken dish. Although it is normally used in Middle Eastern dishes, it works particularly well here, paired with aromatic fennel bulb and crunchy walnuts. You can find it in many ethnic grocery stores and in Middle Eastern markets. You may substitute the molasses with the pomegranate syrup recipe (see Note) with equally good results.

The Pomegranate Marinade

3 tablespoons pomegranate molasses (see Note)

1/2 cup plus 2 tablespoons port wine

1/4 cup water

4 bone-in chicken breasts (8 to 10 ounces each)

The Pomegranate Glaze

1/8 cup pomegranate molasses (see Note)

1 tablespoon cider vinegar or 1 tablespoon lemon juice

1 tablespoon sugar

3/4 cup port wine

3 tablespoons cornstarch

1 1/2 tablespoons water

1 large fennel bulb, chopped

2 large shallots, chopped

1/8 cup olive oil

Salt to taste

1/2 cup walnuts, toasted and chopped

1/4 cup pomegranate seeds, removed from half a large pomegranate

1/4 cup chopped parsley

TO PREPARE THE POMEGRANATE MARINADE
In a shallow dish large enough to hold the chicken, combine the pomegranate molasses with the port wine and water. Add the chicken, and marinate at least 1 hour or overnight, turning occasionally. Remember, the longer you allow the chicken to marinate, the more flavor it will absorb.

Preheat the oven to 375°F.

TO PREPARE THE POMEGRANATE GLAZE
Combine the pomegranate molasses with the cider vinegar, sugar, and port wine in a small saucepan. Bring the glaze to a boil over medium-high heat. In a small bowl, blend the cornstarch and water until smooth. Add the cornstarch mixture to the glaze, stirring constantly, until the glaze becomes slightly thickened.

Place the chicken in a large baking dish. Bake in the oven for 30 to 40 minutes, until the chicken is cooked through.

While the chicken is baking, in a medium bowl toss the fennel with the shallots, olive oil, and salt. Place the fennel mixture in a medium baking dish, and roast for

12 to 15 minutes, until the fennel is tender yet still firm. Remove the dish from the oven, add the walnuts, and toss with 1 tablespoon of the glaze. Remove the chicken from the oven, and spoon on the remaining glaze.

Place the fennel mixture on a serving platter. Top with the chicken. Sprinkle the chicken with the pomegranate seeds and parsley.

NOTE: If you can't find pomegranate molasses, substitute 4 cups bottled pomegranate juice and 2 cups sugar.

Combine the pomegranate juice and sugar in a medium saucepan. Bring to a boil over medium-high heat. Cook until the mixture looks like thick syrup, 25 to 30 minutes.

It takes 8 to 12 fresh pomegranates to make 1 cup of juice. If you wish to use the fresh fruit, squeeze pomegranate halves on a juicer.

PER SERVING: CALORIES 580; CALORIES FROM FAT 200; CALORIES FROM SATURATED FAT 30; PROTEIN 58 G; CARBOHYDRATE 23 G; TOTAL FAT 22 G; SATURATED FAT 3 G; CHOLESTEROL 145 MG; SODIUM 180 MG; 34% CALORIES FROM FAT

 Tip from the Team: To easily remove the seeds from a pomegranate, fill a bowl with cold water, cut the fruit in half, and scoop the seeds and pulp into the bowl of water. The seeds will sink to the bottom and the pith will float. Skim the pith off the top and gather the seeds by straining the liquid.

Pomegranates

A native of Persia, the pomegranate is still popular after four hundred years of cultivation. The Latin name *granatum* means "fruit of many seeds" with good reason. This three-inch round ruby-colored bulb with thick leathery skin houses hundreds of seeds, each surrounded with juicy, red, tart flesh. Some people eat the seeds and some discard them; that's up to you. Look for brightly colored fruits; avoid washed-out or wrinkled-looking fruits. They keep for about 3 weeks in your refrigerator. Pomegranate seeds make an excellent garnish for many dishes, including our Pomegranate Glazed Chicken.

Caramelized Onion Turkey Roulade

SERVES 6

THIS pinwheel made with lean ground turkey is rolled around sweet caramelized onions. This very attractive entrée may be made several days before serving and is excellent hot or chilled on a sandwich. You can make this roulade even more creative and colorful by adding chopped spinach or roasted red peppers to the stuffing.

2½ pounds ground turkey
1 cup fresh bread crumbs
2 large eggs
1 tablespoon Dijon mustard
1 tablespoon dried Italian herbs
Salt and freshly ground pepper to taste

⅛ cup olive oil
2 medium onions, thinly sliced
½ cup red wine or water
¼ cup tomato ketchup, or favorite barbecue sauce, for glazing

Combine the turkey, bread crumbs, eggs, mustard, Italian herbs, and salt and pepper in a large mixing bowl. Mix well until all the ingredients are combined; cover and place in the refrigerator while making the onions.

Heat the olive oil in a large sauté pan over moderate heat. Sauté the onions; do not stir initially, to help the browning process. After 3 minutes, begin to stir occasionally, and cook the onions for 6 to 8 minutes, until browned. Deglaze the pan with the wine and continue to cook for another 2 minutes, until all the liquid is evaporated and the onions are well browned.

Transfer the onions to a plate, and cool them completely; you can put them in the freezer for 10 minutes to speed up the process.

Preheat the oven to 375°F.

Lay a piece of parchment or waxed paper on the kitchen counter, and spread the turkey mixture evenly over the paper, about 1½ inches thick. You will have a 10 × 14-inch rectangle.

Spread the onions evenly over the turkey, leaving a 1-inch border all around. Lift the paper closest to you and roll up the turkey over itself, until a large log is formed. Remove the paper, and discard it. Seal the turkey loaf ends, and transfer the loaf to a baking pan large enough to hold it.

Bake the loaf for 40 to 45 minutes, until cooked through and golden brown. Brush the surface with the ketchup or barbecue sauce, and continue to cook for 5 minutes longer, until glazed and shiny. Cool for 10 minutes before slicing.

PER SERVING: CALORIES 390; CALORIES FROM FAT 180; CALORIES FROM SATURATED FAT 45; PROTEIN 32 G; CARBOHYDRATE 20 G; TOTAL FAT 20 G; SATURATED FAT 5 G; CHOLESTEROL 190 MG; SODIUM 510 MG; 46% CALORIES FROM FAT

Firecracker Shrimp

SERVES 6

THIS shrimp is spicy and vibrantly flavored with a fiery almond pesto made from cilantro, jalapeños, and scallions. It's a quick flash in the pan before you're ready to enjoy this delicious dish. Try serving it with steamed basmati rice or Orange Cashew Rice (page 174).

TO PREPARE THE FIRECRACKER SPICE MASH
Place the almonds, jalapeño peppers, cilantro, scallions, garlic, cumin, olive oil, and water in the bowl of a food processor or in a blender, and blend for 1 minute, until a smooth paste is formed.

Marinate the shrimp in the refrigerator in a covered container for at least 1 hour in the paste.

Heat the olive oil over moderate heat in a large sauté pan. Sauté the shrimp, stirring continuously for 4 minutes, until pink and opaque. Deglaze the pan with the lemon juice, and season with the salt.

TO PREPARE THE GARNISH Garnish the shrimp with the sliced avocado, cilantro sprigs, and cherry tomato halves.

PER SERVING: CALORIES 320; CALORIES FROM FAT 160; CALORIES FROM SATURATED FAT 25; PROTEIN 33 G; CARBOHYDRATE 8 G; TOTAL FAT 18 G; SATURATED FAT 2.5 G; CHOLESTEROL 230 MG; SODIUM 240 MG; 50% CALORIES FROM FAT

The Firecracker Spice Mash

$1/3$ cup sliced or whole almonds

2 jalapeño peppers, seeded and halved

1 bunch cilantro, stems removed

6 scallions, cut into 2-inch lengths

3 cloves garlic

2 teaspoons cumin

$1/8$ cup olive oil

$1/4$ cup water

2 pounds medium to large shrimp, peeled and deveined

1 tablespoon olive oil

$1/8$ cup lemon juice

Salt to taste

The Garnish

1 small avocado, thinly sliced

6 sprigs fresh cilantro

6 cherry or grape tomatoes, halved

Bay Scallops Dijon

SERVES 4

1 pound linguine

2 teaspoons olive oil

1 cup thinly sliced red pepper

1 cup thinly slivered red onion

1 clove garlic, minced (½ teaspoon)

¾ pound bay scallops

½ cup white or rosé wine, or ⅓ cup sweet vermouth

3 tablespoons Dijon mustard

¼ cup chopped parsley

USE either bay or larger sea scallops for this simple pan sauté. Bay scallops are very small, only ½ inch in diameter. They are sweet and succulent, and they offset the spice of Dijon mustard and dry wine. Just cook the scallops until they're barely opaque to keep them tender. If you prefer to use large sea scallops, cook them for an additional minute. Serve the scallops over linguine or couscous. The pan juices make a delicate sauce flavored with the reduced wine essence and sharp mustard taste.

Bring a large pot of salted water to a boil. Add the linguine.

While the linguine is cooking, heat the olive oil in a medium sauté pan over medium-high heat. Add the red pepper, red onion, and garlic. Sauté, stirring often, until the vegetables are soft, for about 2 minutes. Add the scallops and cook for 30 seconds. Add the wine, and simmer for 1 to 2 minutes to reduce the liquid in the pan and concentrate the flavor. Stir in the mustard and parsley, and heat through. Be careful not to overcook the scallops. Serve over the drained linguine.

PER SERVING: CALORIES 360; CALORIES FROM FAT 45; CALORIES FROM SATURATED FAT 0; PROTEIN 29 G; CARBOHYDRATE 42 G; TOTAL FAT 5 G; SATURATED FAT 0 G; CHOLESTEROL 55 MG; SODIUM 550 MG; 12% CALORIES FROM FAT

Variation: Want more of a French touch? Add 1½ teaspoons fresh thyme leaves and 1 medium ripe tomato, seeded and chopped, at the same time as you stir in the mustard and parsley. For a stellar presentation, serve the scallops over molded rice or orzo, speared with a thyme sprig. To mold rice or orzo, press hot rice or orzo into a small lightly oiled cup or soufflé dish. Allow the rice or orzo to rest for 15 seconds; then unmold it onto a serving plate.

main attractions

Lime Seared Scallops over Baby Spinach

SERVES 6

THESE plump white scallops are presented in a nest of bright green barely cooked spinach leaves. Crispy sweet caramelized walnuts create sharp contrast to the tender mollusks, which have been marinated in tart lime zest and tarragon. You may substitute peeled fresh shrimp for the sea scallops if you prefer. Marinate the scallops for only 30 to 45 minutes to flavor; otherwise, the acid in the lime will "cook" the scallops much like ceviche.

The Lime-Tarragon Marinade
2 teaspoons extra-virgin olive oil
2 cloves garlic, minced (1 teaspoon)
1 small shallot, minced
2 sprigs fresh tarragon, minced, or
    ½ teaspoon dried tarragon leaves
1 teaspoon grated lime zest
Juice of 2 limes

2 pounds sea scallops

The Caramelized Walnuts
¼ cup walnut pieces
1 teaspoon sugar

2 teaspoons olive oil

The Spinach
2 teaspoons olive oil
1 clove garlic, minced (½ teaspoon)
1½ pounds baby spinach leaves
Salt and freshly ground pepper to
    taste

TO PREPARE THE LIME-TARRAGON MARINADE Combine the olive oil, garlic, shallot, tarragon, lime zest, and half the lime juice.

Toss the scallops with the marinade, and set it aside in the refrigerator to marinate for no longer than 30 to 45 minutes.

TO PREPARE THE CARAMELIZED WALNUTS Meanwhile, place the walnuts in a dry nonstick pan on medium heat. Sprinkle them with the sugar, and cook until they are shiny and brown, 4 to 5 minutes, shaking the pan continuously. Reserve these for the garnish.

Heat a heavy-bottom pan over moderate heat for about 2 minutes. Add the olive oil to the pan, and heat. Drain the scallops from the marinade, and rest them on a paper towel for a moment to dry. Gently add them to the pan; try not to crowd them together. Do not move them, as that makes the searing process more difficult. Cook them on one side for 2 to 3 minutes, until the scallops are browned. Turn them over, and repeat the process.

When the scallops are cooked through and opaque, deglaze the pan by adding the rest of the lime juice over the scallops. Remove the scallops and the accumulated pan juices, and place them on a covered plate to keep warm until the spinach is sautéed.

TO PREPARE THE SPINACH Heat the olive oil in a hot pan, add the garlic, and lightly brown it. Immediately add the spinach, and cook briefly until the leaves are wilted. Season with the salt and pepper.

Form a nest with the sautéed spinach on each plate. Place a portion of the cooked scallops over the spinach, add a little of the pan juices, and top with the caramelized walnuts.

PER SERVING: CALORIES 240; CALORIES FROM FAT 60; CALORIES FROM SATURATED FAT 5; PROTEIN 34 G; CARBOHYDRATE 9 G; TOTAL FAT 7 G; SATURATED FAT 0.5 G; CHOLESTEROL 75 MG; SODIUM 450 MG; 25% CALORIES FROM FAT

Red-Chili-Rubbed Salmon

SERVES 6

RED chili rub may be made with any favorite dried red chili peppers. This rub is extremely easy to make in a blender and may be kept in the refrigerator for weeks. Red chili paste is burgundy in color and has a chocolate-like, spicy aftertaste. It may be used on seafood, red meat, and poultry. You may also brush it on tofu or tempeh steaks before broiling them. Try roasting a whole unsliced side of salmon fillet, especially for gatherings. Place a line of thinly sliced limes down the center of the salmon before baking for an impressive presentation. Try a slice of chilled salmon on top of Caesar salad or field greens.

3 large dried red chili peppers

1½ cups lightly packed light brown sugar

1 tablespoon lime juice

2 garlic cloves, minced (1 teaspoon)

1 teaspoon dried oregano, or 1 tablespoon fresh

1 tablespoon salt

3 pounds salmon fillet, cut into 6 pieces

2 limes, thinly sliced

1 tablespoon canola oil

Fresh cilantro sprigs for garnish

Soak the chili peppers in enough warm water to cover them for 30 minutes, until soft. When the peppers are soft, remove the stems and seeds. Place the chilies, brown sugar, lime juice, garlic, oregano, and salt in a blender, and purée until you have a pastelike consistency. If the mixture isn't pastelike, add a little of the soaking liquid, 1 teaspoon at a time, until the desired consistency is reached.

Preheat the oven to 350°F. Line a large baking sheet with parchment paper. Place the salmon fillets side by side, touching, so it looks like one whole side of salmon. Spread the purée evenly over the tops of the salmon to completely cover the fillets. Lay 2 overlapping slices of the lime on each portion of the salmon, lining up the lime slices so they make a strip down the center of the "whole" fillet. Lightly brush the lime slices with the canola oil. Bake the salmon uncovered for 25 to 30 minutes, until the salmon is golden brown and fully cooked through.

Carefully remove the salmon fillets to a serving platter, re-creating the "whole" shape. Serve hot from the oven, at room temperature, or chilled.

When ready to serve, garnish the "whole" fillet with fresh cilantro sprigs.

PER SERVING: CALORIES 680; CALORIES FROM FAT 160; CALORIES FROM SATURATED FAT 35; PROTEIN 85 G; CARBOHYDRATE 40 G; TOTAL FAT 18 G; SATURATED FAT 4 G; CHOLESTEROL 195 MG; SODIUM 1170 MG; 23% CALORIES FROM FAT

Broiled Tuna Stuffed with Spinach and Sun-Dried Tomatoes

SERVES 4

The Mediterranean Marinade

⅛ cup extra-virgin olive oil

¼ cup dry white wine

2 cloves garlic, minced (1 teaspoon)

1 teaspoon Dijon mustard

Freshly ground pepper to taste

2 pounds fresh tuna, cut into 4 steaks
1½ to 2 inches thick

The Spinach–Sun-Dried-Tomato Filling

½ cup chopped sun-dried tomatoes
packed in olive oil, including the oil

⅛ cup capers

2 cloves garlic, minced (1 teaspoon)

2 cups chopped fresh and washed
spinach

1½ tablespoons pine nuts

¼ cup chopped parsley

Salt and freshly ground pepper to
taste

THIS Mediterranean-touched dish offers a surprise gift of sun-dried tomatoes, spinach, and capers discreetly tucked inside the tuna steak. A small pocket in the tuna is easily made with a paring knife. Broiling allows the flavors stuffed inside to permeate the entire tuna steak. If you prefer grilling the stuffed tuna steak, soak a toothpick in water for thirty minutes prior to grilling, and use it to seal the pocket. This will hold in the stuffing without burning the toothpick. Try this recipe with other firm fish steaks, such as halibut, swordfish, and salmon.

TO PREPARE THE MEDITERRANEAN MARINADE
Mix the olive oil, white wine, garlic, Dijon mustard, and pepper in a medium bowl.

Add the tuna steaks, and marinate in the refrigerator for at least 1 hour, turning occasionally.

TO PREPARE THE SPINACH–SUN-DRIED-TOMATO FILLING Mix the sun-dried tomatoes, capers, garlic, spinach, pine nuts, parsley, and salt and pepper in a small bowl.

Preheat the broiler.

Remove the tuna from the marinade, and place it on a broiling pan. Carefully cut a horizontal slit in the center of each piece of tuna, without going through to the other side. You should now have a small pocket for the filling. Stuff each pocket with the sun-dried-tomato mixture.

Place the tuna under the broiler for 4 to 5 minutes on each side, until lightly browned and cooked to medium doneness inside. Be careful not to overcook the tuna.

PER SERVING: CALORIES 350; CALORIES FROM FAT 80; CALORIES FROM SATURATED FAT 15; PROTEIN 60 G; CARBOHYDRATE 7 G; TOTAL FAT 9 G; SATURATED FAT 1.5 G; CHOLESTEROL 110 MG; SODIUM 390 MG; 23% CALORIES FROM FAT

main attractions

Pecan Cornmeal Dusted Catfish

SERVES 4

A crunchy cornmeal and pecan crust with underlying cilantro-pepper flavor works perfectly on any mild delicate white fish fillet, such as tilapia, orange roughy, flounder, or sole. Here we use catfish, which is traditionally fried in a similar corn- and flour-based crust. The buttermilk marinade adds a pleasant sharp twang without taking away from the natural seafood taste. For a delicious combination, try topping a fillet of catfish over a mound of sweet and crunchy Mardi Gras Jicama Slaw (page 287).

Preheat the oven to 375°F.

In a dish, combine the flour, salt, pepper, and Cajun spices.

In a shallow dish or bowl, blend the eggs with the buttermilk until well incorporated.

TO PREPARE THE PECAN CRUST In a third bowl, combine the bread crumbs, cornmeal, pecans, parsley, cilantro, salt, and pepper. Line up the three dishes from left to right—dredging flour, egg mixture, and pecan-crust mixture.

Have a large clean sheet of waxed paper laid out on your work counter (about 12 × 12 inches, or large enough to lay the breaded fillets on). Dredge each catfish fillet in the seasoned dredging flour, then in the egg mixture, and then in the pecan-crust mixture, pressing the crumbs and nuts into the fillets if necessary.

Heat the canola oil in a large nonstick sauté pan over medium-high heat. The oil is hot enough when you can see faint ripples in the oil and a light smoke appears over the surface of the pan. Carefully add the breaded catfish fillets, and brown them quickly on each side for 2 minutes, turning just once.

½ cup unbleached all-purpose flour

1½ teaspoons salt

½ teaspoon freshly ground pepper

1 teaspoon Cajun spices

2 large eggs

¾ cup buttermilk

The Pecan Crust

1¾ cups fresh bread crumbs

¼ cup cornmeal

1 cup pecans, toasted and finely chopped

⅛ cup chopped parsley

⅛ cup chopped fresh cilantro

½ teaspoon salt

¼ teaspoon freshly ground pepper

1½ pounds catfish fillets (4 fillets)

¼ cup canola oil

Remove the fillets from the sauté pan, and place them on a large baking sheet. Place the fillets in the oven, and cook until the fish feels firm when pushed with your fingers, 3 to 5 minutes.

PER SERVING: CALORIES 820; CALORIES FROM FAT 440; CALORIES FROM SATURATED FAT 60; PROTEIN 37 G; CARBOHYDRATE 60 G; TOTAL FAT 49 G; SATURATED FAT 7 G; CHOLESTEROL 175 MG; SODIUM 1,720 MG; 54% CALORIES FROM FAT

main attractions

Hazelnut Crusted Pork Loin

SERVES 8

A perfect autumn dish. A hazelnut crust seals in the juices and adds a sharp contrast to the sage-infused stuffing. The pork is easy to open up or butterfly and stuff, especially by placing a piece of plastic wrap over the pork while pounding. This produces an even flattened surface for stuffing. Use crisp apples for the stuffing and chutney, such as Granny Smith, Fuji, or Gala varieties. The tart flavor of Cran-Apple Raspberry Chutney goes well with pork. Cranberries are acidic, which aids in the digestion of succulent pork. If you don't own a rack to place the roast on, place a few large carrots underneath—they work just as well, and they add flavor.

2 tablespoons butter

1 small onion, chopped

2 stalks celery, chopped

2 tart apples, such as Granny Smith, peeled and chopped

¼ cup white or rosé wine, or apple juice

2 teaspoons chopped fresh thyme leaves, or ½ teaspoon dried

2 teaspoons chopped fresh sage, or 1 teaspoon dried

2 teaspoons chopped parsley

1 teaspoon salt

½ teaspoon freshly ground pepper

2 cups cubed French baguette or sourdough bread, lightly toasted

½ to ¾ cup chicken or vegetable stock

4 pounds boneless pork loin

Salt and freshly ground pepper to taste

1 tablespoon olive oil

1 cup finely chopped hazelnuts

1 cup dried bread crumbs

Cran-Apple Raspberry Chutney (page 338)

Preheat the oven to 350°F. Melt the butter in a large sauté pan. When the butter is sizzling, add the onion, celery, and apples. Cook over medium heat for 30 seconds, stirring often. Add the wine, and continue cooking until the vegetables and apples are soft but still firm, for 2 to 3 minutes. Mix in the thyme, sage, parsley, salt, and pepper. Stir in the bread, drizzle the stock to moisten the stuffing, and mix well.

Trim the pork loin of excess fat, and cut a long slit from one horizontal end to the other in butterfly fashion, but without cutting through. The pork should look like an open book.

Place a piece of plastic wrap over the pork. Pound the pork slightly to flatten a little; then season the inside with the salt and pepper.

Spoon the stuffing onto the center of the pork loin. Bring the top of the pork loin over the bottom portion to close the open book. Tie with butcher's twine, pushing any stuffing that falls out back into the pork. Rub the pork with the olive oil, and season with additional salt and pepper. Mix the chopped hazelnuts and bread crumbs together in a shallow pan, and roll the pork loin in the mixture, pressing the hazelnuts into the pork so they adhere well. Place on a rack centered on a baking pan, and roast in the oven for 1½ to 2 hours, until the pork reaches an internal temperature of 185°F.

Remove the pork from the oven, and transfer it to a carving board. Allow the pork loins to cool for 15 to 30 minutes before slicing. Serve with the Cran-Apple Raspberry Chutney.

PER SERVING: CALORIES 780; CALORIES FROM FAT 410; CALORIES FROM SATURATED FAT 100; PROTEIN 68 G; CARBOHYDRATE 25 G; TOTAL FAT 45 G; SATURATED FAT 11 G; CHOLESTEROL 185 MG; SODIUM 580 MG; 52% CALORIES FROM FAT

main attractions

Cubano-Style Pork Loin

SERVES 8

MILD pork will captivate your appetite in this Cuban-inspired dish with aromas of citrus, coffee, and vibrant cumin. Mojo is a traditional Cuban marinade made with sour oranges, spices, and garlic. Sour oranges are used in many Hispanic dishes, and they are available in ethnic grocery stores. If you can find some sour oranges, try them—the juice is similar in acidity to lemon juice, with an orange flavor. Mojo is used as a marinade for pork, chicken, and seafood before cooking. It acts to tenderize any cut of meat and can be used to make ceviche, as well.

This family recipe is made with black coffee, which adds a roasted nutty flavor and dark color to the roast. Coffee is traditionally used in Cuban family recipes to marinate fresh hams and large cuts of meat.

½ cup orange juice or sour orange juice
⅛ cup lime juice
½ cup strong black coffee
⅛ cup extra-virgin olive oil
4 cloves garlic, minced (2 teaspoons)
1 teaspoon crushed red chili flakes
1 teaspoon cumin

4 pounds boneless pork loin
2 teaspoons salt
½ teaspoon freshly ground pepper
Raisin-Orange Sauce (page 311)
Sprigs of fresh cilantro to garnish (optional)

Mix the orange juice, lime juice, coffee, olive oil, garlic, red chili flakes, and cumin in a shallow baking pan large enough to hold the pork loin. Place the pork loin in the marinade, cover, and refrigerate overnight, or for at least 2 hours, turning several times.

Heat the oven to 325°F. Place the pork in a roasting pan, and pour the marinade over it. Season the pork with the salt and pepper. Bake for 1½ to 2 hours, until a meat thermometer registers 185°F., basting every 30 minutes.

Remove the pork from the baking dish and transfer to a carving board. Allow to cool for 15 to 30 minutes before slicing and dressing with the sauce. Garnish with fresh cilantro.

PER SERVING: CALORIES 350; CALORIES FROM FAT 150; CALORIES FROM SATURATED FAT 50; PROTEIN 47 G; CARBOHYDRATE 1 G; TOTAL FAT 16 G; SATURATED FAT 6 G; CHOLESTEROL 135 MG; SODIUM 580 MG; 43% CALORIES FROM FAT

 Recipe Bonus Here are some ways to use Cubano-Style Pork Loin.
- Slice and serve with fresh fruit salsa.
- Serve in soft tacos or sandwiches.

Grilled Lemon Pepper Rib-Eye Steaks

SERVES 6

2 pounds rib-eye steaks, well trimmed
(2 large steaks)

The Lemon Pepper Marinade

2 teaspoons coarsely ground black
peppercorns

¼ cup honey

1 tablespoon extra-virgin olive oil

⅛ cup tamari

1 tablespoon Worcestershire sauce

⅓ cup lemon juice

1 teaspoon grated lemon zest

THIS marinade simply enhances the natural beef flavor of well-marbled rib-eye steaks. Peppercorns are one of the most popular spices used the world over to season thousands of dishes. There are four main varieties of peppercorns— black, pink, white, and green. We use black peppercorns on our rib-eye steaks, which yield the strongest flavor of the four. Make sure you crack the peppercorns coarsely to enhance the peppery character. Just place the peppercorns in a small plastic bag, and crush them with a meat mallet or the bottom of a heavy skillet, or pulse them in a spice grinder or clean coffee mill before adding them to your marinade.

P lace the rib-eye steaks in a glass or ceramic dish just large enough to hold them.

TO PREPARE THE LEMON PEPPER MARINADE Combine the peppercorns, honey, olive oil, tamari, Worcestershire sauce, lemon juice, and lemon zest.

Pour the marinade over the steaks, and rub it into both sides, making sure that both surfaces of the steaks are coated well. Marinate the steaks in the refrigerator for at least 3 hours, or overnight. Grill the steaks to desired doneness in a gas or charcoal grill. A large steak will normally take 4 to 5 minutes per side to reach a medium doneness on a grill. You may also broil steaks on a drip pan rack approximately 3 inches from the broiler for 4 to 6 minutes per side for a medium doneness.

PER SERVING: CALORIES 360; CALORIES FROM FAT 160; CALORIES FROM SATURATED FAT 70; PROTEIN 43 G; CARBOHYDRATE 3 G; TOTAL FAT 18 G; SATURATED FAT 7 G; CHOLESTEROL 120 MG; SODIUM 190 MG; 44% CALORIES FROM FAT

 Tip from the Team: When marinating, place all of the meat or vegetables with the marinade in a large zipper-closure plastic bag. This is a great way to make sure your food marinates evenly, as you can keep turning the bag over to make sure the liquid gets everywhere.

main attractions

253

Pastel de Choclo

SERVES 6

PASTEL *de Choclo* means "casserole of corn." This authentic Chilean beef dish is eaten on festive family occasions. It's sort of a picadillo or ground beef hash with a golden, sweet corn crust baked over the top and is often baked in a clay pot. Juicy plumped raisins absorb the flavors of cumin and fresh basil. The sweet corn crust and fragrant cinnamon mellow the bold flavor of the beef filling. This dish may be frozen in an oven-ready dish for future dinners. Serve this piping hot with tomato sauce or salsa.

2 cups frozen corn, thawed and drained, or 3 ears fresh corn, shucked, kernels cut from the cob
1 teaspoon cinnamon
1 teaspoon salt
1½ teaspoons sugar
½ cup milk, or soy or oat milk
2 large eggs, beaten

1 tablespoon butter
1 tablespoon olive oil
3 cups chopped yellow onion
2 cloves garlic, minced (1 teaspoon)
1 pound ground beef
⅓ cup chopped pitted ripe black olives
¼ cup raisins, plumped in hot water for 10 minutes and then drained
3 tablespoons chopped fresh basil
½ teaspoon cumin
½ teaspoon paprika
½ teaspoon salt

3 large eggs, hard-boiled and sliced
¼ cup chopped parsley

Preheat the oven to 350°F. Place the corn, cinnamon, salt, sugar, and milk in the bowl of a food processor fitted with a metal blade, and blend to a wet paste. Place the corn mixture in a saucepan, and cook it over medium heat, stirring constantly, until the mixture is cooked to mashed-potato consistency, about 10 minutes.

Cool the corn mixture slightly, and stir in the beaten eggs.

In a large sauté pan, melt the butter with the olive oil over medium-high heat. Add the onion, and cook, stirring often, for about 10 minutes. Add the garlic; sauté 1 minute more, stirring often. Crumble the ground beef into the onions. Add the olives, raisins, basil, cumin, paprika, and salt. Sauté until the meat is cooked, stirring occasionally, for 4 to 5 minutes.

Lightly butter a 9 × 9-inch baking dish. Spread the ground beef mixture on the bottom of the dish in an even layer. Top with the sliced hard-boiled eggs. Spoon the corn mixture on top of the eggs. Bake in the oven until the corn topping is golden brown, 20 to 25 minutes. Cool slightly before serving. Cut into squares. Sprinkle with the chopped parsley.

PER SERVING: CALORIES 330; CALORIES FROM FAT 150; CALORIES FROM SATURATED FAT 50; PROTEIN 21 G; CARBOHYDRATE 27 G; TOTAL FAT 16 G; SATURATED FAT 6 G; CHOLESTEROL 220 MG; SODIUM 650 MG; 45% CALORIES FROM FAT

Carne Asada with Jalapeño Cilantro Pesto

SERVES 4

Spicy Mexican Marinade (page 335)
1½ pounds skirt or flank steak
Jalapeño Cilantro Pesto (page 337)

CARNE asada is barbecued or grilled beef. It is commonly served at family gatherings or as street food in various regions of Mexico. Carne asada is normally sliced thin before grilling; however, in our recipe we marinate the beef in whole pieces, grill it, and then thinly slice it after cooking. It's much juicer this way. Serve the beef hot or chilled. When cold, beef can be sliced very thinly across the grain. Serve on a platter with a bowl of Jalapeño Cilantro Pesto and lime wedges. This lime-scented spicy pesto is the perfect match for this bold-flavored beef dish. Slice the marinated cooked steak, and serve draped across hot rice pilaf or on a flour tortilla. This steak makes a delicious sandwich, too, on your favorite bread. Try it on corn muffins or jalapeño corn bread.

Place the Spicy Mexican Marinade in a shallow dish large enough to hold the steak. Marinate the steak, turning occasionally, for at least 1 hour.

Grill the beef over coals or on a gas grill for 4 to 5 minutes on each side, until cooked to medium doneness.

If you prefer, you may cook the beef in the oven instead. Preheat the oven to 425°F. Heat a cast-iron skillet or heavy-bottom ovenproof pan until smoking hot. Brush the beef with olive oil, and sear the beef on one side for 3 minutes, until browned well. Brush the beef with some of the marinade, turn it, and repeat the process. Place the pan in the preheated oven, and roast for 10 minutes, until the beef is cooked to medium doneness.

Let the beef sit for about 10 minutes; then slice and serve it with the pesto.

PER SERVING: CALORIES 360; CALORIES FROM FAT 160; CALORIES FROM SATURATED FAT 70; PROTEIN 46 G; CARBOHYDRATE 1 G; TOTAL FAT 18 G; SATURATED FAT 7 G; CHOLESTEROL 115 MG; SODIUM 140 MG; 44% CALORIES FROM FAT

main attractions

255

Persian Lamb Roast à la Grand-Mère

SERVES 6

A highly seasoned spice mash gives this lamb roast an intense flavor and spicy kick. Usually reserved for Christmas Eve dinners in Bombay, where it originates, this great roast is suitable for all seasons. Let the lamb marinate for at least four hours, but preferably one or two nights in the refrigerator for the spice mash to permeate the roast.

TO PREPARE THE KASHMIRI SPICE MASH Toast the cumin seeds in a dry pan over moderate heat, shaking continuously for 30 to 45 seconds, until fragrant. Cool the cumin slightly, and combine it in the bowl of a food processor or in a blender with the onion, chilies, garlic, ginger, cinnamon, paprika, salt, light brown sugar, and vinegar. Process well until smooth.

Pierce the lamb randomly with a fork to help the paste permeate the roast. Rub the paste all over the surface of the lamb, and place the lamb in a covered dish in the refrigerator for 1 to 2 nights for best flavor.

When ready to continue, preheat the oven to 500°F. Place the lamb in a roast pan and roast for 25 minutes, uncovered. Lower the oven temperature to 375°F., cover the pan loosely with foil, and continue to roast for 1¾ to 2 hours, basting every 20 to 25 minutes with the juices that accumulate in the bottom of the pan, until the lamb is cooked to desired doneness. When done, a meat thermometer inserted into the thickest part of the lamb will read 145° to 160°F. Remove the lamb from the oven, and allow it to rest for 15 minutes before removing the strings and slicing it. Transfer the lamb to a serving platter, and garnish it with the sliced eggs.

The Kashmiri Spice Mash

2 teaspoons cumin seeds

1 large red onion, cut into 4 pieces

6 dried red Kashmiri chilies, or your favorite dried chili (you may also substitute 1 tablespoon crushed red chili flakes)

6 cloves garlic

1 (2-inch) piece fresh ginger

1 (2-inch) piece cinnamon stick, broken into pieces

1 tablespoon paprika

2 teaspoons salt

2 teaspoons light brown sugar

¼ cup cider vinegar

5 to 6 pounds boneless leg of lamb, rolled and tied (Most lamb roast comes tied with butcher's twine or is sold in a cloth net. This helps the lamb keep its shape during the cooking process.)

4 hard-boiled eggs, peeled and sliced

PER SERVING: CALORIES 800; CALORIES FROM FAT 300; CALORIES FROM SATURATED FAT 100; PROTEIN 112 G; CARBOHYDRATE 6 G; TOTAL FAT 33 G; SATURATED FAT 12 G; CHOLESTEROL 480 MG; SODIUM 930 MG; 37% CALORIES FROM FAT

One-Pot Meals

SPICY MAC AND CHEESE ♠ TUSCAN VEGETABLE SAUTÉ ♠ SMOKY MAPLE BAKED BEANS ♠ ROAST EGGPLANT WITH ORZO AND RICOTTA PILLOWS ♠ LENTIL AND MUSHROOM TAGINE ♠ MUSHROOM TOFU STOGANOFF ♠ HARVEST VEGETABLE SHEPHERD'S PIE WITH ORANGE MASHED YAM CRUST ♠ CHILES RELLENOS CASSEROLE ♠ TURKEY PICADILLO ♠ CHICKEN POT PIE WITH WHOLE WHEAT CRUST ♠ CHICKEN AND DUMPLINGS ♠ THAI-STYLE GREEN CURRY CHICKEN ♠ TUNA NOODLE CASSEROLE ♠ MOROCCAN PAN-ROASTED SEAFOOD ♠ DOUBLE DUMPLING BEEF STEW ♠ SAUSAGE AND MULTICOLORED PEPPERS WITH BASIL

One-pot meals. Casseroles. Pot pies. Powerful words in the

genre of home cooking. At first, the reference may conjure up thoughts of a bubbling cheese crust baked over tender noodles and chunks of tuna. Or there might even be memories of hot pan gravy peeking through cracks of a mashed potato crust caramelized around the edge of an old favorite earthenware casserole dish.

The truth is this: One-pot meals take many culinary forms. We set some guidelines for recipes to include in this chapter. The pan in which our recipes are baked becomes an integral part of the "one-pot" theme. In order to meet the requirements, it needs a bottom and some serious sides to stack ingredients. All the ingredients need to simmer or bake together so the flavors mingle. Even a steaming maple-scented pot of beans and veggie dogs qualifies, as long as they are cooked together in the same pot.

One-pot meals also symbolize something else—food has become complicated in the last twenty years. Casseroles remind us of the days when food was straightforward and more accessible. When that giant glass dish was set down on the dinner table, even if the filling was hidden under some kind of crust, it was so friendly and inviting. These comforting dishes take us back to a simpler time.

Saving valuable kitchen time is yet another benefit of one-pot dinners. They may be prepared ahead, even up to three days in advance, and they're oven ready. Many one-pot dinners can be frozen, ready to make the trip from freezer to oven. They are essentially a complete meal in one dish.

One-pot meals are the modern-day antidote for the frenzied daily routine most of us lead. Put on some relaxing music, place the pot in the oven, pour the wine, put the field greens in a bowl . . . and spend time with your family and your guests. And pick that night to volunteer for dish duty—one pot, less cleanup.

Spicy Mac and Cheese

SERVES 6

3 tablespoons butter

1½ cups onion, chopped

3 cloves garlic, minced
  (1½ teaspoons)

1½ teaspoons cumin

1½ teaspoons coriander

¼ cup unbleached all-purpose flour

2 cups milk

1 large jalapeño pepper, seeded and
  chopped

¼ teaspoon cayenne pepper

1½ teaspoons salt

2 cups canned diced tomatoes,
  undrained

½ cup grated mozzarella cheese

½ cup grated cheddar cheese

½ cup grated Swiss or Jarlsberg
  cheese

1 pound penne pasta, cooked and
  drained

½ cup grated Parmesan cheese

½ cup dried bread crumbs

Vegetable oil for spraying baking dish

THIS is comfort food with a rocket-powered flavor booster made of minced fresh jalapeño chilies. You may enjoy this hot, right from the pan, or make it a day or two before you want to serve it. The flavors blend well and the casserole sets up, making slicing easy. You may cut the mac and cheese into small squares or diamonds to reheat. If you want to add a decorative touch, sauté one or two extra sliced jalapeños or some diced colorful bell peppers and scatter them on the top before baking. Add cooked chicken breast pieces to this casserole for a heartier (but nonveggie) take for extra protein. Change the spicy profile by switching peppers—try this with 3 to 4 tablespoons chopped canned chipotles in adobo sauce or give it an Asian spice twist with 3 to 4 tablespoons of bottled chili sauce with garlic and omit the cumin.

Preheat the oven to 350°F. Melt the butter in a large sauté pan, and add the onion, garlic, cumin, and coriander. Cook for 2 to 3 minutes, stirring often, or until the onion is soft. Mix in the flour, and cook the mixture over moderate heat for 1 minute, stirring constantly. Using a wire whisk, slowly incorporate the milk into the onion mixture until the flour and milk are blended. Bring this to a boil, lower the heat to a simmer, and stir in the jalapeño pepper, cayenne pepper, salt, and tomatoes with their juice. Simmer for 15 minutes.

Remove the pan from the heat, and stir in the mozzarella cheese, cheddar cheese, and Swiss cheese, blending until well mixed. Combine the sauce and cooked pasta in a large mixing bowl. Place the sauced pasta in a 9 × 9-inch greased baking dish. In a small bowl, mix the Parmesan cheese with the bread crumbs. Sprinkle the Parmesan topping over the pasta. Bake for 30 to 35 minutes, until the crumb topping is golden brown.

PER SERVING: CALORIES 420; CALORIES FROM FAT 150; CALORIES FROM SATURATED FAT 90; PROTEIN 22 G; CARBOHYDRATE 46 G; TOTAL FAT 17 G; SATURATED FAT 10 G; CHOLESTEROL 45 MG; SODIUM 1,040 MG; 36% CALORIES FROM FAT

one-pot meals

Tuscan Vegetable Sauté

SERVES 6

A simmering pot of rosemary- and basil-scented Tuscan vegetables forms perfect food for the soul. Make sure to serve this dish in a large bowl; the colors and shapes are sure to be the center of attention when placed on your dinner table. Try this dish over polenta, pasta, or risotto. Top a piece of grilled or broiled fish with this colorful mixture. You may use jarred or canned chickpeas. If you prefer to cook your own, see "Preparing Dried Beans in a Hurry," page 156.

¼ cup olive oil

3 cloves garlic, minced
   (1½ teaspoons)

1 pound red onions, sliced
   1 inch thick

1 pound green peppers, seeded and
   chopped

1 pound red peppers, seeded and
   chopped

½ pound yellow squash, sliced
   ½ inch thick

1 pound zucchini, sliced ½ inch thick

4 large vine-ripe tomatoes, seeded
   and chopped

½ cup pitted and chopped Kalamata
   olives

3 cups cooked chickpeas

⅛ cup whole fresh rosemary leaves

1 tablespoon dried Italian herbs

½ cup chopped fresh basil

2 teaspoons salt

1 teaspoon freshly ground pepper

¼ cup chopped parsley to garnish

Place the olive oil in a large sauté pan, and heat it over medium-high heat. Add the garlic and onions, and sauté them for 1 minute, stirring often. Reduce the heat to medium, and add the peppers, squash, and zucchini. Cook, stirring often, for 4 to 5 minutes, until the vegetables begin to become tender. Stir in the tomatoes and cook, stirring often, for 1 minute. Reduce the heat to low. Add the olives, chickpeas, rosemary, Italian herbs, basil, salt, and pepper. Cook for 1 minute, or until heated through. Place in a serving dish, and garnish with the parsley.

PER SERVING: CALORIES 240; CALORIES FROM FAT 110; CALORIES FROM SATURATED FAT 15; PROTEIN 6 G; CARBOHYDRATE 33 G; TOTAL FAT 12 G; SATURATED FAT 1.5 G; CHOLESTEROL 0 MG; SODIUM 810 MG; 46% CALORIES FROM FAT

Tips from the Team: Try these ideas to get the most out of fresh herbs.

- Take a cup or vase, fill it with water, and immerse the stems of herbs as you would with fresh flowers. Store in the refrigerator.
- Extra herbs you can't use fast enough? Take an ice tray from your freezer. Chop the herbs and split them evenly into a few of the ice compartments. Fill with water and freeze. Remove the "herb cubes" and store them in a marked container or plastic bag. Then, whenever you want a little herb for a recipe, simply grab a cube and add it to the recipe (or thaw it and use the herb as you normally would).

Tuscan Vegetable Sauté

fresh herbs

tomatoes

chickpeas

yellow squash

Kalamata olives

Smoky Maple Baked Beans

SERVES 10

THIS dish is extremely appealing to both vegetarian and nonvegetarian appetites. Made with vegetarian or traditional bacon, this is a modern version of the classic Boston baked beans. The aroma of grated fresh ginger and smoky chipotle chili peppers are mellowed by sweet maple syrup.

If you want this recipe to be vegetarian, leave out the Worcestershire sauce in the Honey Jalapeño Barbecue Sauce. If you do not use Honey Jalapeño Barbecue Sauce, use any barbecue sauce and add one jalapeño, stemmed, seeded, and chopped.

1 pound dried great northern beans
(about 2 cups)
2 cups Honey Jalapeño Barbecue
Sauce (page 305)
1 1/2 cups chopped onions
1 tablespoon grated fresh ginger
(1-inch piece)
2 whole canned chipotle peppers in
adobo sauce, drained
1/8 cup soy "bacon bits"
1/2 cup pure maple syrup
1/4 cup molasses
1/4 cup apple juice
1 cup tomato purée
1/4 cup cider vinegar
1 tablespoon tamari

P lace the beans in a large sauce pot; cover them with water and allow the beans to stand overnight, or for at least 2 hours.

Discard the soaking water, rinse the beans, and cover them with cold water. Add the barbecue sauce, onions, ginger, chipotles, "bacon bits," maple syrup, molasses, apple juice, tomato purée, cider vinegar, and tamari. Bring the mixture to a boil, reduce to medium heat, cover, and simmer until the beans are tender and the sauce has thickened, 1 to 2 hours. Add more water if the beans appear dry. You may also bake the covered dish in a 325°F. oven for the same amount of time, adding a bit of water or apple juice if the mixture looks a little dry.

PER SERVING: CALORIES 180; CALORIES FROM FAT 10; CALORIES FROM SATURATED FAT 0; PROTEIN 7 G; CARBOHYDRATE 38 G; TOTAL FAT 1 G; SATURATED FAT 0 G; CHOLESTEROL 0 MG; SODIUM 330 MG; 6% CALORIES FROM FAT

Recipe Bonus These rich-tasting and mahogany-colored beans form a perfect base for simmering veggie dogs, natural hot dogs, or sausages. After the beans are cooked, take enough out for dinner, place them in a casserole dish, and arrange your favorite meat or vegetable dogs over the top, or slice them in 1-inch lengths and blend in. Cover loosely with foil or with a cover, and bake in a 375°F. oven for 20 minutes, until the whole dish is heated through.

Roast Eggplant with Orzo and Ricotta Pillows

SERVES 4

⅛ cup olive oil

1 cup chopped onion

2 large leeks, washed and sliced about ½ inch thick

1 large eggplant (2½ to 3 pounds), peeled and chopped

2 medium red peppers, seeded and chopped

3 large tomatoes, chopped

½ cup sun-dried tomatoes, thinly sliced

3 large cloves garlic, minced (1½ teaspoons)

½ pound orzo pasta, cooked

½ cup chopped fresh basil

½ cup tomato juice

1 cup ricotta cheese

½ cup pine nuts

½ cup dried bread crumbs

½ cup grated Parmesan cheese

¼ cup chopped parsley

2 teaspoons dried Italian herbs

TINY orzo pasta is baked with vegetables, herbs, and tomato juice in this unusual dish with a rustic Italian feel. The orzo soaks up flavor from the cooking juices as the pasta becomes tender. The ricotta pillows rest on top of this dish, lightly glaze over the vegetables, and resemble a meringue dusted with sharp Parmesan cheese and studded with pine nuts.

Preheat the oven to 375°F. In a large sauté pan, heat the olive oil. Add the onion, leeks, eggplant, and peppers, and cook over medium-high heat for 3 to 5 minutes, until the vegetables are soft; add a sprinkling of water to prevent the vegetables from sticking to the pan. Remove the pan from the heat.

Add the chopped tomatoes, sun-dried tomatoes, garlic, and orzo. Stir in the basil and tomato juice. Mix well. Place the mixture in a 9 × 9-inch greased baking dish. Top with dollops of spooned-on ricotta, forming small pillows over the surface of the casserole. In a small bowl, mix the pine nuts, bread crumbs, Parmesan, parsley, and Italian herbs. Sprinkle this topping over the vegetable-orzo mixture. Bake until the topping is golden brown, about 20 minutes.

PER SERVING: CALORIES 770; CALORIES FROM FAT 250; CALORIES FROM SATURATED FAT 70; PROTEIN 34 G; CARBOHYDRATE 104 G; TOTAL FAT 28 G; SATURATED FAT 8 G; CHOLESTEROL 30 MG; SODIUM 1,060 MG; 32% CALORIES FROM FAT

 Recipe Bonus Try this mixture stuffed into halves of 2 or 3 smaller eggplants. Use the shell from the eggplants by scooping or cutting out the eggplant flesh, leaving a ½-inch-thick shell to fill. Bake the empty shell on a greased baking sheet until soft, about 20 minutes. Fill with roasted eggplant mixture, top with grated mozzarella cheese, and bake or broil until the cheese is melted. Making it this way serves 4 to 6, using half an eggplant per person.

vegan

Lentil and Mushroom Tagine

SERVES 8

A tagine is a traditional Moroccan stew, typically baked slowly in a conical ceramic dish. In fact, the ceramic dish itself is often referred to as a tagine. There are many different kinds of these stews; most are served with couscous. Don't be alarmed by the amount of ingredients: They are simply added to the pot and cooked slowly together while you go about your business. You may make this in a slow cooker if you have one. The mushroom essence cooks into the lentils, which thicken this dish. Fragrant stock, lemon zest, and fennel seed bubble away, adding aromatic spirit to this stew—and to your entire kitchen. Warm pita bread and a drop or two of hot sauce make the perfect accompaniments.

3 tablespoons olive oil

1½ cups chopped onions

3 cloves garlic, minced (1½ teaspoons)

1 cup chopped carrots

1 cup chopped celery

3 cups chopped white button mushrooms

1½ cups chopped portobello mushroom caps

1 cup chopped shiitake mushroom caps

⅛ cup tomato paste

1½ tablespoons cider vinegar

2 teaspoons paprika

1½ teaspoons cumin

2 teaspoons fennel seeds

2 cups lentils

1½ cups vegetable stock

2 cups canned diced tomatoes, with their juice

2 teaspoons salt

1 teaspoon freshly ground pepper

¼ teaspoon cayenne pepper

1 cup sliced assorted bell peppers (red, green, and yellow)

1 pound fresh spinach, washed and stemmed

1 tablespoon grated lemon zest

Place the olive oil in a large sauté pan, and heat it over medium-high heat. Add the onions, and cook them until they are light golden brown, 3 to 5 minutes. Add the garlic, carrots, and celery, and continue to sauté, stirring occasionally, for about 5 minutes, or until the vegetables are tender. Add all the mushrooms and the tomato paste, vinegar, paprika, cumin, and fennel seeds, and cook for 10 to 15 minutes, stirring occasionally. Add the lentils, vegetable stock, diced tomatoes, salt, ground pepper, and cayenne pepper. Simmer covered until the lentils are tender and most of the liquid is absorbed, 20 to 25 minutes. During the last 5 minutes of simmering, add the bell peppers. Add the spinach, and cook until the spinach is wilted, about 1 minute. Stir in the lemon zest. A sauce will form around the lentils; if they appear dry, add a little water or vegetable stock.

PER SERVING: CALORIES 250; CALORIES FROM FAT 40; CALORIES FROM SATURATED FAT 5; PROTEIN 16 G; CARBOHYDRATE 42 G; TOTAL FAT 4.5 G; SATURATED FAT 0.5 G; CHOLESTEROL 0 MG; SODIUM 840 MG; 16% CALORIES FROM FAT

Mushroom Tofu Stroganoff

SERVES 4

1 pound extra-firm tofu, cut into
    1-inch cubes

½ cup Italian Herb Vinaigrette (page
    329), or your favorite vinaigrette

3 tablespoons olive oil

½ large onion, chopped

½ cup burgundy wine

1 pound white button mushrooms,
    sliced ¼ inch thick

2 large portobello mushrooms, diced

¾ cup oat milk or soy milk

3 tablespoons tamari

1 teaspoon freshly ground pepper

2 bay leaves

1 teaspoon dried thyme, or
    1 tablespoon fresh

IT doesn't matter whether one is vegetarian or not—this dish is soul satisfying for all. Baking the tofu dries it out and changes the texture, which then allows it to soak up the pan gravy and mushroom essence. Oat milk (a creamy, dairy-free beverage made from oats) is a healthful substitute for dairy milk or cream because it's rich, and it thickens with cooking. You may substitute vegetable stock for the wine. For a nonvegan version, you may use milk or cream in place of the oat milk.

Serve this over noodles, or use it as a filling for crepes or over polenta. Make this more earthy by varying the recipe with an assortment of other mushrooms in combination (like shiitake, cremini, and porcini).

Marinate the tofu for 30 minutes in the Italian Herb Vinaigrette. Preheat the oven to 450°F. Remove the tofu from the marinade, and place it in a baking dish. Roast the tofu cubes for 20 minutes, until they are lightly browned. Remove them from the oven.

Heat the olive oil over medium-low heat in a large sauté pan. Add the onion, and cook slowly until it's nicely browned, 20 to 25 minutes. Deglaze the pan with the wine as the onion cooks to prevent the onion from burning or getting too brown. Add the white button and portobello mushrooms, and sauté for 1 to 2 minutes, until the mushrooms are limp. Add the oat milk, tamari, pepper, bay leaves, and thyme. Simmer for about 10 minutes, allowing the mixture to thicken slightly. Add the tofu, and heat the stroganoff through. Remove the bay leaves before serving.

PER SERVING: CALORIES 270; CALORIES FROM FAT 120; CALORIES FROM SATURATED FAT 15; PROTEIN 13 G; CARBOHYDRATE 24 G; TOTAL FAT 13 G; SATURATED FAT 2 G; CHOLESTEROL 0 MG; SODIUM 1,120 MG; 44% CALORIES FROM FAT

one-pot meals

Harvest Vegetable Shepherd's Pie with Orange Mashed Yam Crust

SERVES 6

SHEPHERD'S pie was originally created in Canterbury, England, as a means of using up leftover Sunday roast, so it's traditionally made with ground beef or lamb. We created this vegetarian recipe as a hearty vegetable dish suited for holiday gatherings (although beef may be substituted for the tempeh if you like). As it turns out, this dish is popular all year long. The orange mashed potato crust makes a fabulous topping for this pie. If you wish, make a classic mashed potato topping, or use a favorite packaged variety. Both the filling and topping may be made two days prior to assembling. Harvest Vegetable Shepherd's Pie is especially inviting when baked in a ceramic or earthenware dish.

1 pound tempeh

⅛ cup canola oil

1 cup chopped onions

1 cup chopped carrots

½ teaspoon fresh thyme leaves, minced (or ¼ teaspoon dried thyme)

1 pound new potatoes, peeled and diced ½ inch thick

3 cups vegetable stock

3 tablespoons tamari or soy sauce

½ cup frozen peas, thawed

½ cup frozen corn kernels, thawed

½ teaspoon salt

¼ teaspoon freshly ground pepper

1 tablespoon cornstarch

¼ cup water or stock

1½ teaspoons chopped fresh sage, or ½ teaspoon dried

4 cups Orange Mashed Yams (page 302) or mashed potatoes

½ cup sliced almonds

Preheat the oven to 350°F. Crumble the tempeh into pieces that resemble cooked ground beef.

Heat the canola oil over medium-high heat in a large sauté pan. Add the tempeh, onions, and carrots; cook until the onions are translucent, 3 to 5 minutes. Add the thyme, potatoes, vegetable stock, and tamari. Simmer this mixture until the potatoes are cooked but still firm, 15 to 20 minutes. Stir in the peas, corn, salt, and pepper. Bring to a simmer. Combine the cornstarch in a small bowl with the water until smooth. Add the cornstarch slurry to the simmering vegetables, stirring constantly. Stir in the sage.

Place the filling in a 9-inch pie plate or ovenproof casserole dish. Top with 4 cups prepared Orange Mashed Yams. Sprinkle the pie with the sliced almonds. Bake the pie for 25 to 30 minutes, until the yams and almonds are golden brown and the filling is bubbling.

PER SERVING: CALORIES 790; CALORIES FROM FAT 200; CALORIES FROM SATURATED FAT 20; PROTEIN 37 G; CARBOHYDRATE 135 G; TOTAL FAT 22 G; SATURATED FAT 2.5 G; CHOLESTEROL 0 MG; SODIUM 1,130 MG; 25% CALORIES FROM FAT

 Recipe Bonus You may also use this filling to stuff red and green peppers. This works best if the stuffing is chilled first. Prepare the peppers by cutting off the stem end. Leave the peppers whole but clean out the seeds from inside. Cut a small section off the bottom of the pepper if necessary to make it stand up, or slice the pepper in half and fill with equal parts of the tempeh mixture. Place the stuffed peppers in an ovenproof dish. Pour about 1 cup of vegetable stock around the peppers, and bake in a 350°F. oven for 20 to 25 minutes, until the peppers are tender but still firm. Top with a sprinkling of soy or dairy cheese, and let the cheese melt slightly. Or serve with prepared basil-infused tomato or pizza sauce.

Yams versus Sweet Potatoes

SWEET potatoes are native to Central America and come from the same family as the morning glory. The sweet potato is a staple in many Asian and Latin American countries. Sweet potatoes are sweeter and starchier than yams. There are more than four hundred varieties of sweet potatoes, which range from white or yellow in color to deep orange, red, or even purple. Although the terms *yams* and *sweet potatoes* are typically used interchangeably in the United States, true yams are a completely different species. Yams are a staple food in South America and the West Indies, often called batata in the southeastern United States. Yams are starchy, often containing a substance that makes them rather slippery when cut. The flesh cooks up a bit stringy. Yams are good for stews, soups, and casseroles.

Chiles Rellenos Casserole

SERVES 4

MEANING "stuffed peppers," this Mexican dish is made with mild green poblano chilies stuffed with cheese and dipped in an egg batter. Our version is pan-sautéed instead of deep fried, using less oil. We also add some smoky chipotle chilies, which perk up this dish and pair well with the slightly sweet corn topping.

8 poblano chilies

1 cup grated Monterey Jack cheese

1 cup grated cheddar cheese

2 teaspoons chipotle chilies in adobo sauce, chopped, or use 2 teaspoons Adobo Sauce (page 310)

¼ cup unbleached all-purpose flour

4 large eggs, separated

1 teaspoon hot sauce

¼ cup canola oil

1 large egg, beaten

½ cup yellow cornmeal

1 cup sour cream

1 cup frozen or canned creamed corn

Preheat the oven to 450°F. Place the whole poblano chilies on a baking sheet, and roast for about 20 minutes, or until blackened on all sides. Carefully remove the chilies from the baking sheet, place them in a paper bag, and allow them to stand for 15 to 20 minutes. Reduce the oven temperature to 350°F. Remove the chilies from the bag, and rub off their skins. With a sharp paring knife, make a slit in one side of each chili running within ½ inch from the top to the bottom, leaving the chili whole with a pocket for stuffing.

In a medium bowl, combine the cheeses with the chipotle chilies in adobo sauce. Fill the chilies with the cheese mixture, pressing the slit closed after filling. Roll the chilies in the flour to coat all sides.

Beat the egg yolks with the hot sauce, and mix in the remaining flour. In another bowl, beat the egg whites with an electric mixer until stiff; then gently fold the egg whites into the egg yolk mixture.

Heat the canola oil in a large sauté pan. Dip the chilies into the egg mixture, and sauté for 4 to 6 minutes, until golden on all sides. Drain the chilies on absorbent paper towels. Place the chilies in a lightly greased 10 × 12-inch square baking dish, leaving space between each one. In a small bowl, mix the remaining egg with the cornmeal, sour cream, and corn. Pour this mixture over the chilies.

Bake the casserole for 25 to 30 minutes, until the cornmeal mixture is set, firm to the touch, and light golden brown. Serve the casserole immediately.

PER SERVING: CALORIES 390; CALORIES FROM FAT 140; CALORIES FROM SATURATED FAT 70; PROTEIN 27 G; CARBOHYDRATE 38 G; TOTAL FAT 16 G; SATURATED FAT 8 G; CHOLESTEROL 295 MG; SODIUM 680 MG; 36% CALORIES FROM FAT

Turkey Picadillo

SERVES 4

1/8 cup canola oil

1 pound ground turkey

1 medium onion, chopped

2 stalks celery, chopped

1 medium green pepper, seeded and
   chopped

1/2 medium red pepper, chopped

1 medium jalapeño pepper, seeded
   and minced

2 teaspoons dried oregano, or
   2 tablespoons fresh

1 teaspoon cumin

1/4 teaspoon crushed red chili flakes

1 1/2 teaspoons paprika

3 cloves garlic, minced
   (1 1/2 teaspoons)

3 tablespoons tomato paste

1/3 cup cider vinegar

1 teaspoon salt

1/2 cup manzanilla stuffed olives, sliced

1/4 cup raisins

1/4 cup capers, drained

1/2 cup frozen peas, thawed

PICADILLO is a popular Latin American beef hash of sorts. There are many family versions, depending on where the picadillo originates. It may be made with apples, raisins, potatoes, and hot chilies, but it's normally made from beef. Our turkey version is lighter than the original and may be used as a stuffing for peppers, eggplants, or zucchini. Picadillo is traditionally served with white rice, black beans, and fried plantains.

Heat the canola oil over medium heat in a large skillet. Add the ground turkey, breaking up the meat as it cooks until nicely browned. Drain off and discard any excess fat. Add the onion, celery, green and red peppers, jalapeño, oregano, cumin, red chili flakes, paprika, garlic, tomato paste, vinegar, and salt. Cook, stirring often, for 3 to 5 minutes. Add the olives, raisins, and capers, and simmer for 30 minutes, stirring occasionally. Just before serving, stir in the peas; cook for 1 minute more, until the peas are heated through.

PER SERVING: CALORIES 330; CALORIES FROM FAT 160; CALORIES FROM SATURATED FAT 30; PROTEIN 23 G; CARBOHYDRATE 21 G; TOTAL FAT 18 G; SATURATED FAT 3 G; CHOLESTEROL 90 MG; SODIUM 1,070 MG; 48% CALORIES FROM FAT

 Recipe Bonus Use the picadillo as a baked potato topping or to fill empanadas. For quick empanadas, use refrigerated piecrust dough. With a biscuit cutter or a glass, cut 3-inch circles in the dough. Lightly brush the top of each circle with a little water. Place a spoonful of the picadillo filling in the center and fold the circle in half to form a turnover. Seal the edges by pressing them together with a fork or by pinching them with your fingers. Lightly brush the empanada surface with a beaten egg, and bake on a baking pan for 20 minutes in a preheated 350°F. oven until golden brown.

one-pot meals

Chicken Pot Pie with Whole Wheat Crust

SERVES 6

FOR decades, many versions of this classic American dish have appeared on our dinner tables. There are foods that simply fill us up; then there are dishes like pot pies, which elicit memories. For the chicken, the simplest method is to use rotisserie leftovers. If you have more time, cook a whole chicken or boneless skinless breasts in simmering water or stock, which you may use later for soup.

On busy days, use packaged refrigerated prepared piecrust. When time is on your side, try this from-scratch recipe that makes enough for one double-crust pie.

The Whole Wheat Crust

3 cups unbleached all-purpose flour

1 cup whole wheat flour

1 tablespoon salt

1 cup canola oil

½ to ⅔ cup ice-cold water or milk

The Chicken Filling

⅓ cup canola oil

½ onion, chopped

2 large carrots, chopped

2 stalks celery, chopped

⅓ cup unbleached all-purpose flour

1 teaspoon salt

1 cup milk

2 cups chicken stock

2 teaspoons dried Italian herbs

½ teaspoon freshly ground pepper

4 cups bite-size pieces of cooked boneless chicken

1 large egg, beaten with 1 teaspoon water

TO PREPARE THE WHOLE WHEAT CRUST Sift the flours and salt together in a medium bowl. Pour the canola oil and water into a measuring cup without stirring. Add the liquid to the flour all at once. Stir the dough gently with a fork. Form into two balls. Place one large 12 × 12-inch square of waxed paper on a work surface.

Place one of the dough balls in the center of the waxed paper, and top with another 12 × 12-inch square of waxed paper. Using a rolling pin, gently roll the dough out in a circle to the edges of the paper. Peel off the top layer of paper, and place the rolled-out dough in a 9-inch pie plate, waxed paper side up. Remove the waxed paper, and adjust the dough so it fits into the pie plate. Repeat the rolling process for the remaining dough, and use it for the top crust.

TO PREPARE THE CHICKEN FILLING Preheat the oven to 350°F. Heat the canola oil in a large saucepan over medium heat. Add the onion, carrots, and celery, and cook until firm-tender but not brown, 3 to 4 minutes. Blend in the flour and salt.

Cook for 1 minute, stirring constantly. Slowly add the milk, chicken stock, Italian herbs, and pepper. Stir the mixture constantly until it bubbles and thickens slightly; then simmer for 15 to 20 minutes.

Add the chicken and heat until the mixture returns to a simmer. Cook for 1 minute. Remove from the heat and set aside.

Prick the bottom and sides of the piecrust with a fork and crimp the edges. Bake the empty pie shell in the oven for 5 to 6 minutes, until the dough is very light golden brown. Remove the crust from the oven, and cool it for 2 minutes.

Spoon the chicken mixture into the partially baked piecrust. Brush the crimped piecrust edge with about 1 tablespoon of water. Carefully lay the top crust over the chicken filling. Seal and crimp the edges. With a sharp paring knife, cut 2 or 3 slits in the top of the crust. Brush the top crust with the egg mixture. Place the pot pie on a baking sheet, and bake for about 30 minutes, or until the crust is golden brown.

PER SERVING: CALORIES 920; CALORIES FROM FAT 460; CALORIES FROM SATURATED FAT 40; PROTEIN 41 G; CARBOHYDRATE 74 G; TOTAL FAT 51 G; SATURATED FAT 4.5 G; CHOLESTEROL 110 MG; SODIUM 1,700 MG; 50% CALORIES FROM FAT

Variation: For a Parisian twist, substitute fresh thyme for the Italian herbs. During the last 5 minutes of baking, remove the pot pie from the oven, spread about 1½ tablespoons Dijon mustard evenly over the top crust, and sprinkle with ½ cup Gruyère cheese. Return the pot pie to the oven, and bake for 1 to 2 minutes more, until the cheese is golden brown.

Chicken and Dumplings

SERVES 6

PARMESAN-AND-PARSLEY dumplings simmering in rich chicken stock help thicken this sauce. If you don't have the time to make your own stock, use two pounds of boneless skinless chicken breasts simmered for a half hour in three quarts of chicken stock. Just dice the chicken breast when cooked, and save the broth for the body of the dish.

1 whole chicken fryer (about 3½ pounds)

4 quarts water

The Parmesan-Parsley Dumplings

1½ cups unbleached all-purpose flour

½ cup grated Parmesan cheese

¼ teaspoon salt

¼ teaspoon freshly ground pepper

½ cup chopped parsley

1 large egg

½ cup milk

2 cloves garlic, minced (1 teaspoon)

1 cup chopped yellow onion

1 pound carrots, cut into ½-inch slices

1 pound sweet potatoes, peeled and cut into ½-inch pieces

¼ teaspoon crushed red chili flakes

½ pound poultry sausage

4 cups Swiss chard, rinsed and cut into ½-inch pieces

Place the chicken in an 8-quart stockpot, and add the water. Bring to a boil, cover, and simmer for about 45 minutes, or until the chicken is cooked. Remove the chicken from the pot, reserving the stock. There should be about 14 cups of stock remaining. Allow the chicken to cool at room temperature until it's cool enough to handle. Discard the skin; remove all the meat from the bones, and cut it into bite-size pieces.

TO PREPARE THE PARMESAN-PARSLEY DUMPLINGS In a medium mixing bowl, combine the flour, cheese, salt, pepper, and half the parsley. Stir in the egg, mixing well. Slowly incorporate the milk into the mixture.

Bring the reserved stock to a boil. Add the garlic, onion, carrots, sweet potatoes, and red chili flakes. Simmer the stock for 10 minutes. Add the sausage by squeezing marble-size pieces from the casing into the simmering stock. Discard the casings. Add the cooked chicken. Using a spoon, scoop up the dumpling dough into walnut-size pieces. With a spoon, carefully lower each piece of dough into the simmering stock. Cover and simmer for 20 minutes; do not lift the lid. The sweet potato and dumplings will slightly thicken the stock as they cook.

Stir in the Swiss chard, disturbing the dumplings as little as possible. Cover; simmer for 5 minutes, or until the chard is wilted. Garnish with the remaining parsley.

PER SERVING: CALORIES 530; CALORIES FROM FAT 130; CALORIES FROM SATURATED FAT 45; PROTEIN 39 G; CARBOHYDRATE 60 G; TOTAL FAT 15 G; SATURATED FAT 5 G; CHOLESTEROL 135 MG; SODIUM 750 MG; 24% CALORIES FROM FAT

Thai-Style Green Curry Chicken

2 large cloves garlic, minced
   (1 teaspoon)

1 teaspoon galanga powder, or
   1 tablespoon fresh ginger or
   galanga, minced

2 stalks fresh lemongrass, white part
   only, minced, or 1 teaspoon dried
   lemongrass powder

1 to 2 tablespoons Thai green curry
   paste to taste

2 large boneless skinless chicken
   breasts (about 1 pound), cut into
   2-inch pieces

⅛ cup canola oil

1 can coconut milk

⅛ cup lime juice

1 tablespoon tamari or soy sauce

1½ pounds sweet potatoes, peeled
   and chopped into 1-inch pieces

1 cup small tomato wedges

½ cup thinly sliced red onion

¼ cup chopped fresh cilantro

¼ cup chopped fresh mint

¼ cup chopped fresh basil (preferably
   Thai basil)

THIS lovely pale green Asian chicken stew offers incredibly bold flavor and is very easy to prepare. There are many underlying flavors from the intense raw ingredients we've used. Galanga root, or galangal, is a rhizome similar to ginger, with a peppery, spicy taste. It may be found fresh or powdered—either form works well in this recipe. Green curry paste is a mixture of several spices and may be very spicy depending on its freshness. Sweet potato, creamy coconut milk, and cooling mint leaves buffer the heat of the chili paste. Some cooks like to use chicken breast on the bone for this one-pot dinner. You may cut a bone-in chicken breast into two or three pieces following the recipe given. Serve this dish over cooked rice noodles, fresh Chinese egg noodles, or rice. For a visually striking garnish, try surrounding chicken with colorful deep-fried shrimp chips. Galanga root, green curry paste, fresh Chinese egg noodles, and shrimp chips are available in Asian markets.

Mix the garlic with the galanga powder, lemongrass, and curry paste in a large bowl. Add the chicken breasts, and mix well to evenly coat the chicken with the spices. Allow the chicken to marinate for 10 to 20 minutes in the refrigerator.

Heat the canola oil in a wok or large sauté pan over medium-high heat. Sauté the chicken for 5 minutes. Add the coconut milk, lime juice, tamari, and sweet potatoes, and bring to a boil. Simmer the chicken covered for 25 to 30 minutes, until the chicken is cooked through and the sweet potatoes are firm-tender. During the last 5 minutes of cooking, add the tomatoes, red onion, cilantro, mint, and basil.

PER SERVING: CALORIES 730; CALORIES FROM FAT 220; CALORIES FROM SATURATED FAT 110; PROTEIN 71 G; CARBOHYDRATE 56 G; TOTAL FAT 25 G; SATURATED FAT 12 G; CHOLESTEROL 175 MG; SODIUM 420 MG; 30% CALORIES FROM FAT

one-pot meals

Tuna Noodle Casserole

SERVES 6

ALTHOUGH classic tuna noodle casseroles are made with elbow macaroni, our recipe is made with pappardelle noodles, which are wide ribbons of pasta. Here's an action plan that will make this dish easy: Prepare the béchamel sauce up to three days in advance. The pasta may be cooked the day before assembling. On tuna noodle day, just sauté the vegetables and add them to the sauce and cooked pasta, and bake. Even the crumb topping may be prepared in advance. Some cooks use prepared mushroom soup mix for the sauce. The end result is a bubbling, golden brown meal that only needs a salad and warm loaf of sourdough bread to complete a memorable dinner.

B ring a large pot of salted water to a boil. Cook the pappardelle for 6 to 8 minutes, until it is al dente, or follow the directions on the box. Rinse the pasta in cold water, and drain.

Preheat the oven to 350°F.

TO PREPARE THE BÉCHAMEL SAUCE Heat the milk, white pepper, nutmeg, and salt together in a small saucepan over medium-high heat just until it begins to boil. Lower the heat, and keep the milk warm. In a medium saucepan, melt the butter over low heat. Using a wire whisk, blend in the flour, and cook slowly for 2 minutes, stirring constantly and keeping the mixture at a medium simmer. Do not allow the mixture to color or brown. Remove the pan from the heat. As soon as the mixture has stopped bubbling, pour in all of the hot milk at once. Use vigorous strokes with the wire whisk to blend the milk and flour together, making sure to scrape up all bits of the flour from the inside edges of the pan. Set the saucepan over medium-high

1 pound dried pappardelle pasta

The Béchamel Sauce

2 cups milk

Freshly ground white pepper to taste

¼ teaspoon ground nutmeg

¼ teaspoon salt

2 tablespoons butter

3 tablespoons unbleached all-purpose flour

The Tuna Casserole Filling

1 tablespoon canola oil

1 cup chopped onions

½ cup chopped celery

½ cup chopped red pepper

½ cup chopped green pepper

2½ cups sliced white button mushrooms

½ cup frozen peas, thawed

2 (6-ounce) cans tongol tuna, drained

2 teaspoons lemon juice

1 teaspoon hot sauce

The Crumb Topping

1¼ cups dried bread crumbs

½ teaspoon paprika

Salt to taste

1 teaspoon lemon pepper

⅛ cup chopped parsley

1 tablespoon butter

heat, and stir with the wire whisk until the sauce comes to a boil and thickens. Simmer for 10 minutes, stirring constantly. Remove the sauce from the heat.

TO PREPARE THE TUNA CASSEROLE FILLING Heat the canola oil in a medium sauté pan over medium heat. Add the onions, celery, and peppers, and sauté for 2 minutes, stirring occasionally. Add the mushrooms, and cook for 1 additional minute. Transfer the filling to a large mixing bowl. Add the cooked pasta.

Add the béchamel sauce, peas, tuna, lemon juice, and hot sauce to the mixing bowl with the cooked vegetables and pasta; toss lightly to incorporate all ingredients well. Pour into a 2½- to 3-quart greased ovenproof casserole.

TO PREPARE THE CRUMB TOPPING In a small bowl, mix the bread crumbs with the paprika, salt, lemon pepper, and parsley. Sprinkle the topping over the casserole and dot with the butter.

Place the casserole in the oven and bake for 20 to 25 minutes, until the edges of the casserole are bubbling and the bread crumbs are golden brown.

PER SERVING: CALORIES 560; CALORIES FROM FAT 110; CALORIES FROM SATURATED FAT 45; PROTEIN 30 G; CARBOHYDRATE 80 G; TOTAL FAT 13 G; SATURATED FAT 5 G; CHOLESTEROL 40 MG; SODIUM 560 MG; 20% CALORIES FROM FAT

 Recipe Bonus As an alternative, the next time you're grilling or broiling tuna steaks, cook two extra 6-ounce fillets. Then substitute the flaked fresh cooked tuna for the canned tuna, and you'll have a tuna casserole with a just-caught flavor. Try this with leftover rotisserie chicken, as well.

Moroccan Pan-Roasted Seafood

SERVES 6

ROASTING seafood in a very hot oven sears the outside and keeps the inside of the fish and shellfish moist and flavorful. You may use any firm-fleshed fish for this dish, such as halibut, salmon, tuna, grouper, or monkfish. Try adding scallops, also. For extra color and flavor, add ½ cup pitted and roughly chopped Kalamata olives to the combined vegetables and seafood. Try this tossed with pasta, or use it as a taco filling. This dish is also wonderful served at room temperature.

½ cup olive oil

2 cloves garlic, minced (1 teaspoon)

1 tablespoon curry powder

½ teaspoon turmeric

¼ teaspoon cinnamon

1 teaspoon salt

¼ cup lemon juice

¼ teaspoon cayenne pepper

3 tablespoons tamari

1 pound fresh mahimahi or grouper, cut into large chunks

1 pound medium shrimp (41 to 50 per pound), peeled and deveined

1 medium red onion, chopped

1 large red pepper, seeded and chopped

1 large green pepper, seeded and chopped

Combine the olive oil, garlic, curry powder, turmeric, cinnamon, salt, lemon juice, cayenne pepper, and tamari in a small bowl, mixing well. Combine the mahimahi and shrimp in a large mixing bowl. Pour half of the olive oil mixture over the seafood, and toss well. Place in the refrigerator, and allow to marinate, stirring occasionally, for about 30 minutes.

In another large bowl, combine the onion and peppers with the remaining half of the olive oil mixture. Marinate the onions and peppers at room temperature for 30 minutes.

Preheat the oven to 450°F.

Drain all but about 1 tablespoon of the marinade from the vegetables, and place the vegetables in a single layer in a baking dish. Roast them in the oven for 15 to 20 minutes, until the vegetables are tender and golden.

Meanwhile, drain all but about 1 tablespoon of the marinade from the seafood mixture and place the seafood mixture in a single layer in another baking dish. Roast it in the oven for about 10 minutes, or until the shrimp are curled and the seafood is opaque and cooked through.

Combine the cooked vegetables with the seafood. Serve immediately.

PER SERVING: CALORIES 360; CALORIES FROM FAT 180; CALORIES FROM SATURATED FAT 25; PROTEIN 35 G; CARBOHYDRATE 8 G; TOTAL FAT 20 G; SATURATED FAT 3 G; CHOLESTEROL 185 MG; SODIUM 1,020 MG; 50% CALORIES FROM FAT

Double Dumpling Beef Stew

SERVES 6

½ to ¾ cup unbleached all-purpose
flour

1 teaspoon salt

½ teaspoon freshly ground pepper

3 pounds beef top round, trimmed of
excess fat and cut into 1-inch
pieces

3 tablespoons to ¼ cup olive oil

6 carrots, chopped

4 ribs celery, chopped

1 onion, chopped

2 cups tomato juice

4 cups vegetable stock

2 teaspoons minced fresh thyme

1 tablespoon minced parsley

1 cup all-purpose unbleached flour

2 teaspoons baking powder

¼ teaspoon salt

½ cup water or milk

2 tablespoons butter or margarine,
melted

THIS rich and hearty stew forms its own light sauce. You may make this dish up to three days prior to serving. When cooking ahead, make the recipe without dumplings. Just reheat the stew to boiling, add the dumpling dough, and cook as directed below.

In a small bowl, sift the flour with the salt and pepper. Toss the beef in the seasoned flour. Dust off any excess flour, and set the beef cubes aside.

Heat the olive oil over medium-high heat in a large heavy-bottom sauté pan. Add the beef without crowding the pan. Sauté without disturbing for the first few minutes to brown the beef. When the beef browns, begin to stir and turn the beef until it has browned on all sides. This will take about 5 minutes.

Drain off and discard any excess oil. Add the carrots, celery, onion, tomato juice, stock, thyme, and parsley. Cook the beef and vegetables over medium heat for 50 to 60 minutes, until the beef is tender.

While the stew is cooking, prepare the dumpling dough. Sift the flour, baking powder, and salt together. Combine the water with the melted butter, and add it to the dry ingredients. Blend well. After the stew has cooked about 40 minutes, carefully add the dumpling dough, one heaping tablespoon at a time, into the simmering liquid. Cover the pan tightly; bring the stew to a boil. Reduce the heat (don't lift the cover), and simmer for 12 to 15 minutes, until done.

PER SERVING: CALORIES 690; CALORIES FROM FAT 210; CALORIES FROM SATURATED FAT 60; PROTEIN 78 G; CARBOHYDRATE 40 G; TOTAL FAT 23 G; SATURATED FAT 7 G; CHOLESTEROL 200 MG; SODIUM 1,420 MG; 30% CALORIES FROM FAT

 Recipe Bonus Vary the flavor of the dumplings by adding any of these to the raw dough: your favorite fresh herb, chopped pitted olives, chopped red and green peppers, or curry powder.

one-pot meals

Sausage and Multicolored Peppers with Basil

SERVES 8

A classic favorite of Italian street fairs and carnivals, this recipe may be made up to three days before serving. In fact, this recipe benefits greatly from allowing the flavors to meld for a few days. You may even freeze the fully cooked sausage and peppers in an oven-ready dish for future use. Try grilling the sausage instead of roasting it before mixing it into the tomato base. Use any flavored sausage that appeals to you (try garlic-parsley, Italian, sun-dried tomato, and others). There are several varieties in the market. Another option is to substitute a pound of poblano chilies for the bell peppers. This adds an underlying spicy edge.

Serve over polenta, pasta, orzo, or rice. Try a Spanish-style yellow rice or Orange Cashew Rice (page 174) for extra color. You may also use this recipe for a lasagna filling, a hearty hoagie, or an omelette base—cut the sausage smaller, if necessary. Talk about versatile!

2 pounds sausage (poultry, pork, or lamb)
¼ cup olive oil
⅛ cup minced garlic (12 cloves)
3 pounds assorted bell peppers (red, green, and yellow), seeded and cut into 1-inch strips
1 pound onions, sliced about 1 inch thick
3 cups drained canned whole peeled tomatoes, roughly chopped
1 cup chopped fresh basil
½ tablespoon salt
½ tablespoon freshly ground pepper

Cut the sausage into 2-inch lengths. Preheat the oven to 375°F. Heat the olive oil in a large roasting pan or ovenproof sauté pan with raised sides, and brown the sausage, turning frequently, for 4 minutes. Remove the sausage from the pan, and transfer it to a plate. Drain most of the oil from the pan, and add the garlic, bell peppers, and onions; sauté for 3 minutes. Add the tomatoes, and simmer for 5 minutes, stirring often. Return the sausage to the pan, and place the pan in the oven for about 35 minutes, or until the sausage is cooked through and the peppers are tender but not mushy. Add the basil, and season with the salt and pepper.

PER SERVING: CALORIES 350; CALORIES FROM FAT 180; CALORIES FROM SATURATED FAT 45; PROTEIN 23 G; CARBOHYDRATE 21 G; TOTAL FAT 20 G; SATURATED FAT 5 G; CHOLESTEROL 95 MG; SODIUM 1,210 MG; 51% CALORIES FROM FAT

On the Side

GARLIC CREAMED SPINACH WITH ARUGULA ◆ VEGAN CREAMED SPINACH ◆ EMERALD SESAME KALE ◆ ASIAN BRAISED GREENS ◆ MAPLE GLAZED CARROTS ◆ PAN-ROASTED FENNEL ◆ MARDI GRAS JICAMA SLAW ◆ SESAME SUGAR SNAP PEAS ◆ ROASTED BUTTERNUT SQUASH ◆ ROASTED SCARLET PEPPERS ◆ ROASTED BROCCOLI MEDLEY ◆ CRACKLING CAULIFLOWER ◆ SKILLET-ROASTED LIMAS WITH ITALIAN HERBS ◆ SPICY ROASTED EGGPLANT WITH SESAME AND HONEY ◆ SPRING POTATO SALAD WITH TROPICAL HERB DRESSING ◆ GOLDEN POTATO AND AUBERGINE SALNA ◆ APRICOT GLAZED SWEET POTATOES ◆ VERSATILE MASHED POTATOES ◆ PARSNIP MASHED POTATOES ◆ MASHED POTATOES WITH JALAPEÑOS AND CHEDDAR ◆ ANAHEIM CHILI MASHED POTATOES ◆ ORANGE MASHED YAMS

Never underestimate the power of a side dish. Side

dishes are the accessories that add panache to the plate. Stuffings, potatoes, rice dishes, legumes, seasonal vegetables, and grains all contribute distinct personality to our meals. Our vegetable and grain recipes may even outshine the main course.

Side dishes may be made of many different ingredients. Our traditional dinner plate matrix is changing. A square meal is no longer meat, potatoes, and a vegetable. There's a trend to reduce the meat-protein portion size and increase the vegetables, grains, and other accompaniments on our plates. Side dishes, when grouped together, can form a meal full of variety and diverse flavors. You can branch out and select side dishes from other chapters as well. For example, a baked wedge of our Spicy Mac and Cheese (page 259) set over a bed of sautéed Emerald Sesame Kale (page 283) and served alongside Pan-Roasted Fennel (page 286) makes a perfect meal. A balanced combination of side dishes is a great way to make an easy home buffet. Many of the side dish items may be prepared ahead completely while others may be prepped days in advance and finished right before you are ready to serve.

Our collection reflects traditional dishes we grew up with. We have also included some alternative modern methods of preparation to reflect some of our recent dietary concerns. Simplicity is another advantage of many of our side dishes. When you seek out impeccably fresh produce, the pure flavor of those ingredients is easily highlighted with just a few well-chosen additional ingredients and the right cooking methods. Sweet, crunchy fennel exudes a bit of magic when drizzled with extra-virgin olive oil and lemon. Cucumbers, normally so unassuming, flower with personality when tossed with a few ingredients like mirin and tamari (possibly new to your pantry). Many of our side dishes may be converted to entrées by adding your choice of protein. Shrimp, tofu, chicken, or lamb can easily be added to our Golden Potato and Aubergine Salna (page 296) and Crackling Cauliflower (page 292) to create an Indian-inspired entrée.

Mixing and matching side dishes is one of the most appetizing ways to make sure dinnertime is never boring.

Garlic Creamed Spinach with Arugula

1 tablespoon olive oil

1 teaspoon butter

1 large leek, chopped and washed well

2 cloves garlic, minced (1 teaspoon)

10 ounces fresh spinach, washed, or
   16 ounces frozen spinach, thawed
   and chopped

1 tablespoon unbleached all-purpose
   flour

1/2 cup cream

1/2 cup milk

1/8 teaspoon ground nutmeg

Salt and freshly ground white pepper
   to taste

1 cup chopped fresh arugula

CREAMED spinach is a deliciously creamy affair for the palate and the soul. It is comforting to eat and may be served with almost any entrée or simply over pasta, rice, or couscous. We offer two methods of preparing this classic favorite. This one is fairly traditional, with cream, and the other uses oat milk and nondairy soy cheese. We also add some chopped arugula for a nutty, slightly sharp bite. The leeks lend a sweet, mellow flavor and add depth that onions never dreamed of. You may use fresh or frozen spinach for this side dish.

Heat the olive oil and butter in a large sauté pan over medium heat. Add the leek, and sauté for 3 minutes, until soft, stirring often—do not allow the leek to change color. Add the garlic and spinach; sauté for 2 minutes, until the spinach softens. Sprinkle the flour over the vegetables, and stir to combine well. Add the cream, milk, nutmeg, and salt and pepper, combine well, and simmer for 5 minutes, until the sauce thickens and the spinach is tender. Stir in the chopped arugula, and serve.

PER 1/2-CUP SERVING: CALORIES 80; CALORIES FROM FAT 50; CALORIES FROM SATURATED FAT 25; PROTEIN 2 G; CARBOHYDRATE 5 G; TOTAL FAT 6 G; SATURATED FAT 2.5 G; CHOLESTEROL 10 MG; SODIUM 50 MG; 62% CALORIES FROM FAT

 Recipe Bonus If you like puréed creamed spinach, pulse in a food processor for 30 seconds. You may also use a handheld immersion blender. Simply pulse the blender 5 or 6 times, until the spinach is coarsely puréed.

on the side

Vegan Creamed Spinach

SERVES 6 TO 8

THIS version is nondairy but still packed with flavor. You may use soy or oat milk to form the sauce around the spinach. We highly recommend using the addition of soy "bacon bits" in this version.

1 tablespoon olive oil

2 teaspoons margarine

1 large leek, chopped and washed

1 tablespoon soy "bacon bits" (optional)

2 cloves garlic, minced (1 teaspoon)

10 ounces fresh spinach, washed, or 16 ounces frozen spinach, thawed and chopped

1½ tablespoons unbleached all-purpose flour

1½ cups oat milk, or unflavored soy milk

¼ cup grated soy Parmesan cheese

⅛ teaspoon ground nutmeg

Salt and freshly ground white pepper to taste

1 cup chopped arugula

Heat the olive oil and margarine in a large sauté pan over medium heat. Add the leek and soy "bacon bits," and sauté for 3 minutes, until soft, stirring often—do not allow the leek to change color. Add the garlic and spinach; sauté for 2 minutes, until the spinach softens. Sprinkle the flour over the vegetables, and stir to blend. Add the oat milk, soy Parmesan cheese, nutmeg, and salt and pepper, combine well, and simmer for 5 minutes, until the sauce thickens and the spinach is tender. Stir in the chopped arugula, and serve.

PER ½-CUP SERVING: CALORIES 60; CALORIES FROM FAT 30; CALORIES FROM SATURATED FAT 0; PROTEIN 2 G; CARBOHYDRATE 7 G; TOTAL FAT 3.5 G; SATURATED FAT 0 G; CHOLESTEROL 0 MG; SODIUM 65 MG; 50% CALORIES FROM FAT

Recipe Bonus Sprinkle additional soy "bacon bits" and soy Parmesan cheese over the surface of the spinach after preparing. If you eat dairy cheese, place the creamed spinach in an ovenproof dish, sprinkle the spinach with cheddar cheese, and bake the crock for 10 minutes in a preheated 475°F. oven to melt the cheese.

Emerald Sesame Kale

2 teaspoons olive oil

1 teaspoon toasted sesame oil

2 cloves garlic, minced (1 teaspoon)

1 tablespoon minced fresh ginger
   (1-inch piece)

2 bunches kale stems, washed, heavy
   stem removed, leaves chopped

1 tablespoon tamari or soy sauce

1 tablespoon sesame seeds

FRAGRANT cooked ginger and garlic pair perfectly with the pleasant chewy texture of crinkly kale leaves and nutty sesame seeds. It's best to wash the whole kale leaf first before removing the heavy stem that runs through the center. After chopping, allow the water to cling on the leaves. This water prevents the kale from sticking to the pan, allowing the garlic and ginger to brown evenly. A mound of steaming Emerald Sesame Kale makes a great nest for grilled chicken, fish, tofu, or Asian flank steak.

Heat the olive and sesame oils in a large sauté pan over medium heat. Add the garlic and ginger, and sauté for 1 minute, until the garlic just begins to brown. Add the chopped kale, and sauté for 4 minutes, stirring frequently. Sprinkle some water over the kale if it begins to stick to the pan. Add the tamari and sesame seeds, and stir to incorporate well.

PER ¾-CUP SERVING: CALORIES 120; CALORIES FROM FAT 50; CALORIES FROM SATURATED FAT 5; PROTEIN 6 G; CARBOHYDRATE 15 G; TOTAL FAT 5 G; SATURATED FAT 0.5 G; CHOLESTEROL 0 MG; SODIUM 310 MG; 42% CALORIES FROM FAT

on the side

vegan

Asian Braised Greens

SERVES 4 TO 6

GREENS are loaded with both taste and nutrients. Greens were at one time popular only in Southern-style cooking. They were usually cooked with lots of ham or bacon until they were nearly falling apart. In this dish a variety of greens, including red chard, beet greens, and Swiss chard, are left al dente for you to appreciate the herblike, appealingly bitter flavor. You may use a premixed variety, or use your favorite green alone, or in combination. For an added crunchy texture, toss in one cup of whole roasted cashews after adding the dressing.

TO PREPARE THE SPICY ASIAN DRESSING

Whisk together the soy sauce, sesame and canola oils, black and white sesame seeds, lime juice, ginger, garlic, brown sugar, red chili flakes, cilantro, and scallions in a small bowl.

Bring 2 quarts of water to a boil in a large saucepan. Add the chard and bok choy, cooking until just wilted but still bright in color, about 30 seconds to 1 minute. Drain.

Just before serving, pour the dressing over the greens, and toss lightly. Serve immediately. The greens may be cooked, rinsed immediately in ice-cold water, and refrigerated for up to 2 days before serving. When ready to serve, heat the greens for 2 minutes in a microwave, or heat in a large sauté pan in 1/8 cup of water or 1 tablespoon of canola oil. Add the dressing to the heated greens, and serve.

PER 1 1/2-CUP SERVING: CALORIES 100; CALORIES FROM FAT 70; CALORIES FROM SATURATED FAT 0; PROTEIN 3 G; CARBOHYDRATE 4 G; TOTAL FAT 8 G; SATURATED FAT 0 G; CHOLESTEROL 0 MG; SODIUM 690 MG; 70% CALORIES FROM FAT

The Spicy Asian Dressing

1/4 cup soy sauce

1/8 cup toasted sesame oil

1/8 cup canola oil

1/8 cup black sesame seeds

1/8 cup white sesame seeds

1 1/2 tablespoons lime juice

1 tablespoon grated fresh ginger (1-inch piece)

2 large garlic cloves, minced (1 teaspoon)

2 teaspoons brown sugar

3/4 teaspoon crushed red chili flakes

2 1/2 tablespoons chopped fresh cilantro

2 scallions, chopped

8 to 9 cups roughly chopped red chard, heavy stems removed (about 1/2 pound), rinsed and dried (about 1 large bunch)

8 to 9 cups roughly chopped green chard, heavy stems removed (about 1/2 pound), rinsed and dried (about 1 large bunch)

8 to 9 cups roughly chopped bok choy or Napa cabbage (about 1/2 pound), rinsed and dried (about 1/2 large head)

Maple Glazed Carrots

vegan

SERVES 4 TO 6

The Maple Glaze

½ cup pure maple syrup

1 cinnamon stick

¼ cup orange juice

2 oranges, peeled, seeded, and roughly chopped (or 1 cup mandarin oranges, drained)

¼ cup water

1½ tablespoons cornstarch

1 pound carrots, cut diagonally into 1-inch pieces

½ teaspoon salt

¼ teaspoon freshly ground pepper

½ cup chopped parsley

CARROTS are often incorporated into another dish like soup, stew, or a sauce instead of appearing solo, but here they are the stars. Maple syrup and orange juice add a delicate touch to this common root vegetable without camouflaging the honey-sweet natural flavor. Try adding roasted pecans and slivered sun-dried tomatoes at the end for a festive change of pace.

TO PREPARE THE MAPLE GLAZE Place the maple syrup, cinnamon stick, orange juice, and oranges in a sauce pot, and bring to a simmer. Stir together the water and cornstarch until smooth. Stir the cornstarch slurry into the maple mixture, and continue to simmer over low heat, for 30 to 45 minutes, until thickened. Strain the glaze to remove the cinnamon stick and oranges. Cool the glaze.

Steam the carrots for 5 minutes, or boil in salted water for 6 minutes, until firm-tender.

Combine the carrots, maple glaze, salt, pepper, and parsley. Serve immediately. If you prefer serving the carrots steaming hot, put them in a hot saucepan for a few minutes to heat the glaze through.

PER 1-CUP SERVING: CALORIES 140; CALORIES FROM FAT 0; CALORIES FROM SATURATED FAT 0; PROTEIN 1 G; CARBOHYDRATE 34 G; TOTAL FAT 0 G; SATURATED FAT 0 G; CHOLESTEROL 0 MG; SODIUM 190 MG; 0% CALORIES FROM FAT

Tip from the Team: When cooking carrots for soups, sauces, or purées, try adding 1 part ginger ale to 3 parts water. This will help to preserve the color as well as add sweetness.

on the side

Pan-Roasted Fennel

SERVES 3 TO 4

FENNEL, also called anise, is a member of the parsley family and has a sweetly refreshing licorice-like flavor. Embraced in Italy for many years, fennel is just gaining popularity here in the United States. The olive oil helps the fennel turn golden brown during the roasting process, simply accentuating its natural fresh flavor. Serve this dish hot from the oven or at room temperature.

I large fennel bulb, root end trimmed,
 top end removed
 (save some of the lacy green
 fronds for garnish)
3 tablespoons olive oil
Salt and freshly ground pepper to
 taste
I lemon, cut in half

Preheat the oven to 375°F.
 Wash the trimmed fennel bulb well, stand it on a cutting board in a vertical position and cut it into ½-inch-thick slices. The root end will hold the fennel slices together. Sprinkle the fennel with the olive oil, and arrange the slices in a single layer on a baking pan. Try not to overlap the slices, so they can brown evenly. Sprinkle the fennel generously with the salt and pepper. Roast the fennel for 15 to 20 minutes, and then turn carefully to brown the other side. When softened and well browned, 35 to 40 minutes in all, remove the slices from the oven, and squeeze the lemon halves over the fennel, drizzling it with juice. Garnish this dish with the reserved fennel fronds.

PER ½-CUP SERVING: CALORIES 110; CALORIES FROM FAT 90; CALORIES FROM SATURATED FAT 10; PROTEIN 1 G; CARBOHYDRATE 6 G; TOTAL FAT 10 G; SATURATED FAT 1.5 G; CHOLESTEROL 0 MG; SODIUM 40 MG; 82% CALORIES FROM FAT

Recipe Bonus Try topping the fennel with freshly grated Parmesan cheese during the last 5 minutes of cooking. Top a field green or spinach salad with warm roasted fennel and crumbled feta or Gorgonzola cheese.

Mardi Gras Jicama Slaw

SERVES 6 TO 8

1 1/2 pounds jicama

3/4 cup sour cream

1/2 cup chopped scallions

1/2 cup frozen corn kernels, thawed, or 1 ear of fresh corn, shucked, kernels removed

1/2 cup canned black beans, rinsed and drained

1/2 cup chopped parsley

1/8 cup rice vinegar

2 teaspoons cayenne pepper

1 teaspoon salt

A creamy dressing provides the perfect background for crunchy jicama and sweet corn kernels. Allow this salad to marinate for a few hours before serving; the flavors will blend nicely.

Peel and shred the jicama with a cheese grater, using the largest holes or the julienne blade of a food processor, and place in a bowl. Blend in the sour cream, scallions, corn, black beans, parsley, rice vinegar, cayenne pepper, and salt.

PER 1/2-CUP SERVING: CALORIES 60; CALORIES FROM FAT 15; CALORIES FROM SATURATED FAT 10; PROTEIN 2 G; CARBOHYDRATE 12 G; TOTAL FAT 1.5 G; SATURATED FAT 1 G; CHOLESTEROL 5 MG; SODIUM 240 MG; 25% CALORIES FROM FAT

on the side

vegan

Sesame Sugar Snap Peas

SERVES 4 TO 6

SUGAR snap peas were created late in the 1970s, as a cross between snow peas and green peas. We're sure glad someone was dreaming about a sweet completely edible plump pod packed with juicy luscious peas inside. Available year-round, this pea must have its string removed before eating. Start at the bottom tip and pull the string up the front, snap off the stem, and pull the string down the back side. Don't overcook these, as they lose their vivid color and super-sweet flavor rapidly. For a complete meal, toss the cooked vegetables with a 16-ounce package of cooked thin Chinese egg noodles. This side dish brightens any entrée.

1 cup diagonally sliced carrots

1 pound fresh sugar snap peas, strings removed

⅛ cup toasted sesame oil

2 teaspoons grated fresh ginger

½ teaspoon salt

½ teaspoon lemon pepper

⅛ cup white sesame seeds

⅛ cup black sesame seeds

1 scallion, sliced thinly and diagonally

Steam the carrots in a steamer for 3 minutes. Add the sugar snap peas, and continue cooking for an additional 4 minutes, until both vegetables are al dente. While the vegetables are steaming, place the sesame oil, ginger, salt, lemon pepper, white and black sesame seeds, and scallion in a large mixing bowl. Blend well. Add the cooked sugar snap peas and carrots. Toss well. You may serve the vegetables at room temperature or heat them gently in a saucepan.

PER ½-CUP SERVING: CALORIES 130; CALORIES FROM FAT 70; CALORIES FROM SATURATED FAT 5; PROTEIN 4 G; CARBOHYDRATE 12 G; TOTAL FAT 7 G; SATURATED FAT 10.5 G; CHOLESTEROL 0 MG; SODIUM 270 MG; 54% CALORIES FROM FAT

Recipe Bonus As an alternative you may cook the vegetables in a microwave-safe dish in ½ inch of water. Place the carrots in first, lightly cover them with plastic wrap, and cook on high for 2 minutes. Add the sugar snap peas, and continue to cook for 3 minutes longer.

Roasted Butternut Squash

1 medium butternut squash

2 medium onions, cut into small wedges, about 1 inch wide (2 cups)

3 tablespoons canola oil

2 teaspoons salt

½ teaspoon ground nutmeg

½ teaspoon dried, rubbed sage

½ teaspoon freshly ground pepper

½ cup dried cranberries

OVEN roasting squash adds character to this inherently sweet winter vegetable. Sage is an unexpected taste surprise, as squash is normally served with cinnamon and nutmeg. Try adding a cup of toasted walnuts (see page 21).

Preheat the oven to 400°F. Peel the squash. (A sturdy vegetable peeler works best.) Using a heavy knife, cut the squash in half lengthwise. Scoop out and discard the seeds. Cut the squash into 1-inch cubes, and place in a medium mixing bowl. Add the onions, canola oil, salt, nutmeg, sage, and pepper. Mix the vegetables and spices until well coated. Place the squash mixture in a shallow baking pan. Roast until the vegetables are tender and golden brown, about 45 minutes, stirring occasionally. The squash should be firm, not mushy. Remove the pan from the oven and add the cranberries. Toss lightly to blend.

PER ¾-CUP SERVING: CALORIES 150; CALORIES FROM FAT 60; CALORIES FROM SATURATED FAT 5; PROTEIN 1 G; CARBOHYDRATE 21 G; TOTAL FAT 7 G; SATURATED FAT 0.5 G; CHOLESTEROL 0 MG; SODIUM 630 MG; 40% CALORIES FROM FAT

on the side

Roasted Scarlet Peppers

SERVES 4 TO 6

THIS simple dish may be made using red, yellow, and green peppers for a special presentation. For an extra flavor booster, add ⅛ cup balsamic vinegar along with the olive oil. Roasted Scarlet Peppers may be used in many ways. As an appetizer, spread toasted sliced baguettes with a little goat cheese. Top with a small spoonful of the roasted peppers cut into ¾-inch strips. As a condiment, slice or dice the peppers as desired, and serve with grilled steaks, chicken, fish, or fajitas. As a salad, top field greens with roasted peppers, and drizzle with extra-virgin olive oil and balsamic vinegar.

4 large red peppers, stemmed, cut in half, and seeded
2 large cloves garlic, minced (1 teaspoon)
2 teaspoons salt
1 teaspoon freshly ground pepper
¼ cup olive oil
¼ cup large capers, drained
¼ cup chopped fresh basil

Preheat the oven to 400°F. Place the peppers in a large mixing bowl. Add the garlic, salt, pepper, and olive oil. Toss well. Place the peppers in a baking dish. Roast until they are nicely browned and al dente–soft, about 15 minutes. Remove the dish from the oven. Toss the peppers with the capers and fresh basil.

PER ½-CUP SERVING: CALORIES 100; CALORIES FROM FAT 80; CALORIES FROM SATURATED FAT 10; PROTEIN 1 G; CARBOHYDRATE 8 G; TOTAL FAT 9 G; SATURATED FAT 1.5 G; CHOLESTEROL 0 MG; SODIUM 840 MG; 80% CALORIES FROM FAT

Oven-Roasted Tomatoes

SOMEWHERE wonderful in between fresh tomatoes and marinated sun-dried tomatoes lies the realm of the succulent, slow-roasted, semi-dry marinated tomato. With higher residual moisture than a regular sun-dried tomato, roasted tomatoes are tender, sweet, and ready to use. Oven-roasted tomatoes are basically bruschetta waiting to happen: Toast slices of baguette and top each with a roasted tomato half. Drizzle on a little of the oil from the cup, and you've got an instant appetizer. Match it with some fresh mozzarella, and you won't need to worry about an entrée.

Roasted Broccoli Medley

4 cups broccoli florets

2 medium red peppers, seeded and
thinly sliced

2 medium green peppers, seeded and
thinly sliced

1 large red onion, thinly sliced

1/8 cup olive oil

1/8 cup tamari

2 teaspoons dried Italian herbs

1/4 teaspoon freshly ground pepper

Pinch of salt

1 whole head of garlic, cloves
separated and peeled

1 tablespoon olive oil

4 plum tomatoes, quartered

ROASTING vegetables adds a unique flavor that cannot be replicated by other cooking methods. The dry heat seems to intensify the natural sugar of this nutrition-packed vegetable. During the roasting process the peppers and onions begin to caramelize and release their sweet juices, which creates a light sauce. This is a very colorful dish that works well on a buffet or for a special occasion. Try leftover broccoli medley in a pita with melted provolone cheese.

Preheat the oven to 400°F.

Steam the broccoli for 2 minutes, or boil for 5 minutes in salted water; then chill the broccoli by placing it in a bowl of ice water for 2 minutes. Drain the broccoli and dry on paper towels.

In a large bowl, place the broccoli, red and green peppers, onion, olive oil, tamari, Italian herbs, pepper, and salt; toss to combine.

Place the vegetables in a baking pan, and roast for 8 to 10 minutes, until the broccoli is tender yet still firm. In the meantime, toss the peeled garlic cloves with the oil, and roast them in a baking pan on a separate oven rack for 10 minutes, until golden and tender. Add the tomato quarters to the broccoli pan, and roast for an additional 4 minutes, until the tomatoes begin to soften. Remove the vegetables from the oven. Add the roasted garlic cloves, and toss lightly.

PER 1-CUP SERVING: CALORIES 90; CALORIES FROM FAT 50; CALORIES FROM SATURATED FAT 5; PROTEIN 3 G; CARBOHYDRATE 9 G; TOTAL FAT 5 G; SATURATED FAT 0.5 G; CHOLESTEROL 0 MG; SODIUM 270 MG; 55% CALORIES FROM FAT

on the side

Crackling Cauliflower

SERVES 4

IT'S called crackling for a reason. Taste buds are surrounded by lots of powerful spices vying for attention—all successful in the end. Add in a half pound of grilled tofu for a full-meal alternative. Serve with Orange Cashew Rice (page 174) for an Indian-inspired meal. This dish may be served hot from the pan, at room temperature, or chilled the next day.

Preheat the oven to 400°F.

Place the cauliflower, onions, canola oil, curry powder, garam masala, fennel seeds, red chili flakes, salt, garlic, ginger, lemon zest, and pepper in a large bowl. Toss the ingredients together, and blend until each piece of cauliflower is coated with the oil and spices. Place the mixture in a large baking pan, and roast for 25 to 30 minutes, until the cauliflower is crisp-tender, turning the cauliflower every 10 minutes to cook evenly. When done, the cauliflower should be golden brown. Place the cauliflower in a large serving bowl. Mix in the peas and cilantro.

1 large head of cauliflower, cut into florets (about 6 cups)
1 cup diced red onions
¼ cup canola oil
½ tablespoon curry powder
½ tablespoon garam masala
½ tablespoon fennel seeds
¼ teaspoon crushed red chili flakes
2 teaspoons salt
2 large garlic cloves, minced (1 teaspoon)
1 tablespoon grated fresh ginger (1-inch piece)
½ tablespoon grated lemon zest
1 teaspoon freshly ground pepper
½ cup frozen peas, thawed
¼ cup chopped fresh cilantro

PER 1-CUP SERVING: CALORIES 200; CALORIES FROM FAT 130; CALORIES FROM SATURATED FAT 10; PROTEIN 5 G; CARBOHYDRATE 17 G; TOTAL FAT 15 G; SATURATED FAT 1 G; CHOLESTEROL 0 MG; SODIUM 1,010 MG; 65% CALORIES FROM FAT

Skillet-Roasted Limas with Italian Herbs

SERVES 4 TO 6

1 pound frozen lima beans

2 teaspoons olive oil

2 large garlic cloves, minced (1 teaspoon)

¼ cup pitted, chopped green olives

½ teaspoon dried basil

½ teaspoon dried oregano

¼ teaspoon dried sage

¼ teaspoon freshly ground pepper

¾ cup canned diced roasted red peppers, well drained

LIMA beans have been cultivated in Lima, Peru, since about 5000 B.C.—hence the name. Lima beans can be found fresh, frozen, and dried. Fordhooks (also called butter beans) and baby limas are the two most common varieties. Frozen limas work best in this simple dish. This is an unusual recipe because the legumes are herb roasted, which really enhances the delicate bean flavor. It also crisps the surface of the bean, which steams the inside, making the texture more fluffy than boiling.

Preheat the oven to 400°F. Cook the lima beans in enough boiling salted water to cover them, until firm-tender, 6 to 8 minutes. Drain the beans well, and dry them on paper towels. Place the lima beans in a medium mixing bowl. Add the olive oil, garlic, olives, basil, oregano, sage, and pepper. Toss well.

Place the bean mixture in single layer in a baking pan, spreading thinly and evenly. Roast until the beans are softened and golden brown, 10 to 15 minutes, stirring occasionally. Remove from the baking pan and place in a medium serving bowl. Mix in the roasted red peppers.

PER ½-CUP SERVING: CALORIES 110; CALORIES FROM FAT 25; CALORIES FROM SATURATED FAT 0; PROTEIN 6 G; CARBOHYDRATE 17 G; TOTAL FAT 2.5 G; SATURATED FAT 0 G; CHOLESTEROL 0 MG; SODIUM 170 MG; 23% CALORIES FROM FAT

 Recipe Bonus For a change of pace, replace the lima beans with frozen shelled edamame (soybeans), cooked according to package directions.

Spicy Roasted Eggplant with Sesame and Honey

SERVES 4 TO 6

ASIAN-SPICED roasted eggplant is a truly inspired side dish. The warm chunks of roasted eggplant draw in the flavors of ginger, garlic, and crushed red chili flakes from the sesame dressing. Roasted eggplant may be eaten warm, chilled, or at room temperature. As a side dish, it goes well with Asian dishes of any kind. You may serve it over cooked noodles or rice or for a vegetarian entrée. You may also add 1 pound of diced firm tofu to bump up the protein. It makes a flavorful sandwich topping, as well. Try Spicy Roasted Eggplant stuffed into a pita bread with spinach for lunch or a snack. Miso gives the eggplant a smoky, sweet character. To enhance the earthy qualities of this recipe, add two cups shiitake mushroom caps sautéed in ⅛ cup canola oil to the finished recipe.

2 medium eggplants, peeled and cut into ¾-inch cubes (about 4 cups)

⅛ cup white or red miso

¾ cup Roasted Sesame–Honey Dressing (page 334), plus more as needed

½ teaspoon salt

¼ teaspoon freshly ground pepper

1 large red pepper, seeded and diced

½ cup chopped fresh cilantro

Preheat the oven to 450°F. Place the eggplants in a large bowl. In a small bowl, whisk the miso with the dressing until well blended. Add the miso mixture to the eggplant along with the salt and pepper. Toss lightly, and let marinate at room temperature for about 20 minutes. Drain off any excess liquid, and place the eggplant in a large baking pan.

Roast for 15 to 20 minutes, or until the edges of the eggplant have browned. The eggplant should be slightly firm, not mushy. Remove the eggplant from the oven, and cool it in the pan. Place the eggplant in a large bowl. Gently mix in the red pepper and cilantro. You may add some additional Roasted Sesame–Honey Dressing to moisten the eggplant.

PER 1-CUP SERVING: CALORIES 100; CALORIES FROM FAT 15; CALORIES FROM SATURATED FAT 0; PROTEIN 4 G; CARBOHYDRATE 20 G; TOTAL FAT 2 G; SATURATED FAT 0 G; CHOLESTEROL 0 MG; SODIUM 550 MG; 15% CALORIES FROM FAT

Spring Potato Salad with Tropical Herb Dressing

SERVES 4 TO 6

3 pounds red bliss potatoes

1/2 cup chopped parsley

6 scallions, finely sliced

2 teaspoons salt

1 1/2 teaspoons freshly ground pepper

1/4 cup plus 2 tablespoons Tropical
  Herb Dressing (page 326)

TENDER red bliss potatoes have a great quality: When warm, they soak in whatever dressing they are tossed with, here the Tropical Herb Dressing, concentrating the tart citrus flavor.

Spring Potato Salad can lift a hamburger or hot dog to epicurean levels. Roast or grilled chicken is a natural entrée mate for this side. This is a great picnic potato salad.

Rinse the unpeeled potatoes, and place them in a steamer. Steam the potatoes until they're firm-tender, 20 to 30 minutes. You may also boil the potatoes for 35 minutes in salted water if you prefer. Let the potatoes sit until they're cool enough to handle, and cut them into quarters. You will have about 8 cups.

Place the warm potatoes in a large bowl. Add the parsley, scallions, salt, pepper, and Tropical Herb Dressing. Toss the salad together to blend the ingredients. Serve this dish at room temperature, or chill it in the refrigerator and serve cold.

PER 1-CUP SERVING: CALORIES 230; CALORIES FROM FAT 80; CALORIES FROM SATURATED FAT 10; PROTEIN 6 G; CARBOHYDRATE 31 G; TOTAL FAT 9 G; SATURATED FAT 1 G; CHOLESTEROL 0 MG; SODIUM 680 MG; 35% CALORIES FROM FAT

Variation: Try this side dish as an easy country frittata filling. For a 3-egg omelette, chop Spring Potato Salad into bite-size pieces. Add the salad to scrambled eggs while they're cooking, along with 1/4 cup diced plum tomatoes. Cook until the eggs are set into a large thick pancake and the potatoes and tomatoes are warmed through.

on the side

295

vegan

Golden Potato and Aubergine Salna

SERVES 6 TO 8

SALNA is an Indian stew. This Indian dish illuminates any meal because of the brilliant yellow color contributed by turmeric. Spicy chilies, mustard seeds, and ginger provide interesting taste and visual combinations at the same time. The minced cilantro gives an extra punch of freshness when sprinkled over the top for a garnish. This dish actually tastes better the second day when the flavors have had a chance to marry. Use jalapeño or serrano chilies for this recipe.

Preheat the oven to 450°F. Place the potatoes, eggplants, garlic, ginger, garam masala, turmeric, chilies, mustard seeds, and olive oil in a large mixing bowl, and toss until the potato and eggplant quarters are thoroughly covered with the spices and oil.

Place the mixture in a single layer in a large baking dish. Reduce the oven to 375°F. and bake for 40 to 50 minutes, turning at 20-minute intervals, until the potatoes are golden brown on the outside and cooked inside and the eggplant is soft and melting. Serve garnished with the cilantro and scallions.

PER ¾-CUP SERVING: CALORIES 100; CALORIES FROM FAT 35; CALORIES FROM SATURATED FAT 5; PROTEIN 2 G; CARBOHYDRATE 17 G; TOTAL FAT 4 G; SATURATED FAT 0.5 G; CHOLESTEROL 0 MG; SODIUM 350 MG; 35% CALORIES FROM FAT

1 pound Yukon Gold potatoes (about 4 large potatoes), quartered

4 Japanese or Italian eggplants, unpeeled and quartered (about 2 pounds)

4 cloves garlic, minced (2 teaspoons)

1 tablespoon minced fresh ginger (1-inch piece)

1 tablespoon garam masala

½ teaspoon turmeric

2 or 3 fresh green chilies, cut in half lengthwise, seeds removed

1 teaspoon black or yellow mustard seeds

¼ cup olive or canola oil

½ cup chopped fresh cilantro, to garnish

4 scallions, finely sliced, to garnish

Apricot Glazed Sweet Potatoes

3 pounds sweet potatoes, peeled,
cut into 1-inch pieces

The Apricot Glaze

¼ cup water

½ cup pure maple syrup

¼ cup brown sugar

⅛ cup orange juice

¼ cup honey

1 tablespoon lemon juice

1 tablespoon butter

½ teaspoon cinnamon

⅛ teaspoon whole cloves

⅛ teaspoon ground nutmeg

Pinch of salt

Pinch of freshly ground white pepper

¾ cup chopped dried apricots

THIS dish is a family holiday natural, which would normally accompany a large roast, but we think you will enjoy it all year round. Fragrant dried apricots plump up in the maple cinnamon syrup and mix well with the sweet potatoes. Try the sauce on carrots or butternut or acorn squash rings. If you prefer a sweeter version, after pouring the apricot sauce over the potatoes, place the potatoes in an ovenproof dish and bake uncovered for 20 minutes, which allows the glaze to darken and caramelize.

Steam the potatoes for 10 to 12 minutes, until tender; or boil in enough salted water to cover them, for 12 to 15 minutes, until tender.

TO PREPARE THE APRICOT GLAZE Place the water, syrup, brown sugar, and orange juice in a saucepan. Stir over medium heat until the sugar dissolves, about 1 minute. Bring the mixture to a boil, and cook for 5 minutes, or until slightly thickened and syrupy. Add the honey, lemon juice, butter, cinnamon, cloves, nutmeg, salt, white pepper, and apricots. Return the glaze to a boil, lower the heat, and simmer for 5 to 7 minutes. Remove the glaze from the heat, and allow it to rest for about 15 minutes. The mixture will thicken as it rests.

Pour the glaze over the sweet potatoes, and stir to mix well.

PER 1½-CUP SERVING: CALORIES 440; CALORIES FROM FAT 20; CALORIES FROM SATURATED FAT 10; PROTEIN 5 G; CARBOHYDRATE 104 G; TOTAL FAT 2.5 G; SATURATED FAT 1.5 G; CHOLESTEROL 5 MG; SODIUM 35 MG; 4% CALORIES FROM FAT

 Recipe Bonus For extra crunch and a fruitier flavor, add ½ cup diced raw unpeeled pears or Granny Smith apples just before adding the glaze.

Versatile Mashed Potatoes

SERVES 6 TO 8

THESE potatoes are cook-friendly and versatile. They are light and airy with a clean aftertaste sometimes elusive in traditional mashed potatoes that contain lots of butter and cream. You may make these the old-fashioned way or completely nondairy. Oat milk (a creamy, rich, oat-based nondairy alternative to milk) is a great substitute for dairy products because of its velvety consistency and ability to withstand the heat of cooking. Many nondairy milks, like soy or rice milk, separate and become clotted when heated.

3 pounds russet potatoes

4 tablespoons butter (1/2 stick)

2 teaspoons salt, plus extra to taste

1/2 teaspoon freshly ground pepper

3/4 cup milk, half and half, or oat milk, heated

P eel the potatoes. Roughly cut them into small, uniform pieces, about 1-inch dice. Place them in a sauce pot, add enough water to cover them by 1 inch, and bring to a boil. Reduce the heat to medium, and boil uncovered until the potatoes are tender when pierced with a fork, 20 to 25 minutes. Drain off the water, but keep the potatoes in the same pot. Mash the potatoes with a hand mixer or potato masher until all lumps are gone. Add the butter, salt, pepper, and milk, beating until the mixture is smooth and fluffy. Add only as much of the milk as necessary to achieve a velvety creamy consistency. The potatoes should be thick and fluffy, not soupy. Adjust the seasonings to taste.

You may hold the mixture for a while before serving by covering it and keeping it warm. If necessary, just before serving, return the pan to low heat and mix the potatoes with a spoon until heated through. You may need to add some more milk if the potatoes are too thick.

PER 1-CUP SERVING: CALORIES 210; CALORIES FROM FAT 60; CALORIES FROM SATURATED FAT 35; PROTEIN 4 G; CARBOHYDRATE 35 G; TOTAL FAT 6 G; SATURATED FAT 4 G; CHOLESTEROL 15 MG; SODIUM 490 MG; 28% CALORIES FROM FAT

Variations

- For vegan mashed potatoes, substitute 4 tablespoons margarine for the butter and use oat milk instead of dairy milk.

- For extra-virgin olive oil mashed potatoes, substitute 3 1/2 tablespoons extra-virgin olive oil for the butter.

Parsnip Mashed Potatoes

3 pounds russet potatoes

1 pound parsnips

4 tablespoons butter (½ stick)

2 teaspoons salt, plus extra to taste

½ teaspoon freshly ground pepper

¾ to 1 cup milk, oat milk, rice milk,
   or soy milk, heated

PARSNIPS are one of the most neglected vegetables in the plant kingdom. They sometimes make a cameo appearance, served during winter holidays. Appearing like ivory-colored carrots, to which they are related, parsnips have a sweet mild celery flavor and are a great source of fiber. Make sure you cook them until just tender; overcooking dilutes their flavor. They are a perfect match for mashed potatoes because they lend a subtle nutty, almost toffeelike flavor.

Peel the potatoes and parsnips. Roughly cut them into small, uniform pieces, about 1 inch thick. Place them in a sauce pot, add enough water to cover them by 1 inch, and bring to a boil. Reduce the heat to medium, and simmer uncovered until the potatoes and parsnips are tender when pierced with a fork, 20 to 25 minutes. Drain off the water, but keep the vegetables in the same pot. Mash the potatoes with the parsnips using a hand mixer or potato masher until all lumps are gone.

Add the butter, salt, pepper, and milk, beating until the mixture is smooth and fluffy. Add only as much of the milk as necessary to achieve a good consistency; it should not be soupy. Adjust the seasonings to taste. You can hold the mixture for a while before serving by covering it and keeping it warm. If necessary, just before serving, add a bit more milk, return the pan to low heat, and mix with a spoon until heated through.

PER 1-CUP SERVING: CALORIES 260; CALORIES FROM FAT 60; CALORIES FROM SATURATED FAT 4; PROTEIN 5 G; CARBOHYDRATE 46 G; TOTAL FAT 7 G; SATURATED FAT 4 G; CHOLESTEROL 15 MG; SODIUM 500 MG; 23% CALORIES FROM FAT

on the side

Mashed Potatoes with Jalapeños and Cheddar

SERVES 6 TO 8

SHARP cheddar and power-packed jalapeño peppers juice up these mashed potatoes and add a downy consistency and pale peach hue. If you don't feel like grating your own cheese, look for packaged grated cheddar or even a mix of cheddar and Monterey Jack cheeses. These spuds are also multipurpose. If you have leftovers, scoop and form them into small patties. Dredge both sides in fresh bread crumbs. Sauté the patties in a little olive oil until one side is golden brown. Using a wide spatula, carefully turn the patty over and brown the other side. For a cocktail party treat, cut jalapeños in half, scoop out the seeds, and fill them with mashed potatoes (a pastry tube makes this easier). Bake in a 375°F. oven for 25 minutes, until the chili is softened and the potatoes are golden.

3 pounds russet potatoes

½ pound sharp cheddar cheese, grated

3 tablespoons butter

2 teaspoons salt, plus extra to taste

½ teaspoon freshly ground pepper

¾ to 1 cup milk or half and half, heated

2 or 3 jalapeño peppers, seeded and minced

Peel the potatoes. Roughly cut them into small, uniform pieces, about 1-inch dice. Place them in a sauce pot, add enough water to cover them by 1 inch, and bring to a boil. Reduce the heat to medium and simmer uncovered until the potatoes are tender when pierced with a fork, 20 to 25 minutes.

Drain off the water, but keep the potatoes in the same pot and mash them with a hand mixer, immersion blender, or potato masher until all lumps are gone. Add the cheese to the potatoes. Add the butter, salt, pepper, ¾ cup of the milk, and the jalapeño peppers, beating until the mixture is fluffy and most of the cheese has melted into the potatoes. Add only as much of the milk as necessary to achieve a good creamy consistency. The potatoes should be thick and fluffy, not soupy. Adjust the seasonings to taste.

PER 1-CUP SERVING: CALORIES 280; CALORIES FROM FAT 90; CALORIES FROM SATURATED FAT 50; PROTEIN 12 G; CARBOHYDRATE 37 G; TOTAL FAT 10 G; SATURATED FAT 6 G; CHOLESTEROL 30 MG; SODIUM 680 MG; 32% CALORIES FROM FAT

Anaheim Chili Mashed Potatoes

SERVES 6 TO 8

3 pounds russet potatoes

1/8 cup extra-virgin olive oil

2 Anaheim chilies, seeded and chopped

1 large red pepper, seeded and chopped

1 large yellow onion, chopped (about 1 1/2 cups)

1 teaspoon chili powder

1 teaspoon cumin

1 teaspoon dried oregano, or 1 tablespoon fresh

2 teaspoons salt, plus extra to taste

3/4 cup to 1 cup buttermilk

1 1/2 cups frozen corn kernels, thawed and well drained

1/2 cup chopped fresh cilantro

2 teaspoons hot sauce, or to taste

ANAHEIM chilies, named after the city in California, are glossy, dark green chilies, mildly spicy with a long and narrow appearance. They perk up mashed potatoes. When sautéed first with sweet peppers, onions, and southwestern spices, the Anaheim chili taste expands and encourages the mild potatoes to speak up.

Peel the potatoes. Roughly cut them into small, uniform pieces, about 1-inch dice. Place the potatoes in a sauce pot, add enough water to cover them by 1 inch, and bring to a boil. Reduce the heat to medium and simmer uncovered until the potatoes are tender when pierced with a fork, 20 to 25 minutes. Drain off the water.

Heat the olive oil in a medium sauté pan. Cook the chilies, red pepper, onion, chili powder, cumin, and oregano over medium heat until tender. Add the chili mixture to the warm potatoes along with the salt and 3/4 cup of the buttermilk. Mash with a hand mixer or potato masher until well blended. Add only as much of the buttermilk as necessary for a good consistency; it should not be soupy. Add the corn, cilantro, hot sauce, and additional salt, if needed. Mix well.

PER 1 1/2-CUP SERVING: CALORIES 240; CALORIES FROM FAT 40; CALORIES FROM SATURATED FAT 5; PROTEIN 5 G; CARBOHYDRATE 47 G; TOTAL FAT 4.5 G; SATURATED FAT 0.5 G; CHOLESTEROL 0 MG; SODIUM 1,460 MG; 17% CALORIES FROM FAT

on the side

301

vegetarian

Orange Mashed Yams

SERVES 6 TO 8

THESE potatoes are sweetened with brown rice syrup, which is subtle in its level of sweetness and colored with orange juice and zest. If you like, add a drizzle of maple syrup. Use as a topping for Harvest Vegetable Shepherd's Pie (page 266) or as a delicious side vegetable. Make this into an extra-special holiday casserole by adding roasted pecans to the yams and then placing the mixture in an ovenproof casserole dish. Top with spoonfuls of jarred or homemade cranberry relish and heat through. Or stuff the yam into hollowed-out orange shells (cut a little off the bottom so the orange will stand straight), and bake for 15 minutes to heat.

3 1/2 pounds yams or sweet potatoes, peeled, cut into large chunks
1/2 cup brown rice syrup
Juice and zest of 1 large orange (you should have 1/4 cup juice)
1 teaspoon lemon juice
3 tablespoons butter
Salt to taste

Steam the yams for 20 minutes, or boil in water for 25 minutes, until soft. Place the brown rice syrup, orange juice, orange zest, lemon juice, and butter in a saucepan. Place on high heat until the margarine is melted. Bring the mixture to a boil, and cook for about 2 minutes, or until syrupy. Remove the pan from the heat. Mash the reserved yams. You should have about 4 cups. Combine the orange juice mixture with the yams. Add the salt. Mix well.

PER 1/2-CUP SERVING: CALORIES 160; CALORIES FROM FAT 20; CALORIES FROM SATURATED FAT 0; PROTEIN 2 G; CARBOHYDRATE 34 G; TOTAL FAT 2 G; SATURATED FAT O G; CHOLESTEROL 0 MG; SODIUM 45 MG; 13% CALORIES FROM FAT

Sauces, Dressings, Dips, and Salsas

HONEY JALAPEÑO BARBECUE SAUCE ♠ TOMATILLO SAUCE ♠ JAMAICAN JERK SAUCE ♠ EASY MOLE SAUCE ♠ IMPERIAL ORANGE SAUCE ♠ ADOBO SAUCE ♠ RAISIN-ORANGE SAUCE ♠ LEMON TAHINI SAUCE ♠ CREAMY PEANUT SAUCE ♠ CURRY COCONUT PEANUT SAUCE ♠ CREOLE REMOULADE SAUCE ♠ SOY DIPPING SAUCE ♠ THAI DIPPING SAUCE ♠ SPINACH ARTICHOKE DIP ♠ TOASTED PEPITA DIP ♠ WARM HERBED GOAT CHEESE DIP ♠ HABANERO ALE CHEESE DIP ♠ SUPER BOWL CON QUESO DIP ♠ BLACK BEAN HUMMUS ♠ RED PEPPER HUMMUS ♠ RASPBERRY VINAIGRETTE ♠ KIWI AND SATSUMA MANDARIN ORANGE DRESSING ♠ TROPICAL HERB DRESSING ♠ TIKKA SALAD DRESSING ♠ MISO SALAD DRESSING ♠ ITALIAN HERB VINAIGRETTE ♠ CREAMY FETA AND ROASTED GARLIC DRESSING ♠ FETA DILL DRESSING ♠ BUTTERMILK RANCH DRESSING ♠ DECO PINK BEET DRESSING ♠ ENLIGHTENED CAESAR DRESSING ♠ ROASTED SESAME–HONEY DRESSING ♠ SPICY MEXICAN MARINADE ♠ JALAPEÑO CILANTRO PESTO ♠ CRAN-APPLE RASPBERRY CHUTNEY ♠ ONION CHUTNEY ♠ TOMATILLO-CHIPOTLE SALSA ♠ PICO DE GALLO ♠ CUCUMBER RAITA

Because of their versatility, dressings, sauces, and marinades are a cook's best allies. They may be used to flavor salads and lift the natural taste of vegetables, grains, and pasta. When used with poultry, seafood, meat, and soy foods, they add complex character and can tenderize, as well. Dressings and marinades are usually simple to prepare ahead of time and often keep well refrigerated.

Dressings, sauces, and marinades have a rich culinary history. Asian cultures have used soy sauce and tamari (aged wheat-free soy sauce) for five thousand years, and the Babylonians drizzled oil and vinegar on simple vegetable and grain salads more than two thousand years ago. Early Romans preferred plain salt on their salads. In fact, the word *salad* comes from the Latin word for "salt" (*sal*).

Though bottled dressings have been available since the early 1900s, until the turn of the century, cooks always made their own dressings and marinades. However, it's really only in the twentieth century that American cooks began to turn dressing salads into an art form by combining various oils, vinegars, citrus juices, and herbs in countless ways.

Fresh vegetable crudités and crunchy snack foods seem unadorned and lonely without dips and salsas. Salsa, once a mainstay of the Southwestern United States, has become a national treasure. Dips and salsas provide incredible menu diversity—use them to enhance the flavor of appetizers or as a sandwich spread or pizza topping. They can also be used to add panache to many grilled seafood, poultry, beef, or vegetarian entrées. These are one of the few foods that are at home in almost any menu course. Since many dips and salsas can keep well for days in the refrigerator and be ready to serve at a moment's notice, they are great to have on hand.

Most of our dressings also double as marinades. For example, our Roasted Sesame–Honey Dressing (page 334) may be tossed into fresh sliced vegetables for a quick slaw with a twist, or used to marinate chicken, tofu, or beef before roasting or grilling. It's important to note that after marinating any raw meat, poultry, or seafood, you should discard any remaining marinade to avoid contamination, or boil it if you want to use it as a sauce. Our sauces are equally kitchen-friendly. Think of this chapter as a cache of surplus flavor at your fingertips, and explore the possibilities.

Honey Jalapeño Barbecue Sauce

2 cups ketchup

2 cups honey

½ cup Dijon mustard

½ cup seeded and minced jalapeño
pepper

¼ cup rice vinegar

2 teaspoons hot sauce

¼ cup plus 2 tablespoons sugar

⅛ cup curry powder

1 tablespoon paprika

2 teaspoons soy sauce

4 cloves garlic, minced (2 teaspoons)

2 teaspoons canola oil

2 teaspoons Worcestershire sauce
(optional)

2 teaspoons lemon juice

1 teaspoon freshly ground pepper

THIS barbecue sauce from New England has enormous flavor. The combination of honey and jalapeño will have your taste buds in a flurry of hot and sweet. Although the ingredient list looks long, all you need to do is throw everything in a pot and simmer. Try this on unpeeled shrimp, either grilled on a barbecue or broiled in your oven. It's impressive on beef or pork ribs, chicken, and seafood. Try it on slabs of extra-firm tofu, as well. If you want this recipe to be vegetarian, leave out the optional Worcestershire sauce.

Combine the ketchup, honey, mustard, jalapeño, rice vinegar, hot sauce, sugar, curry powder, paprika, soy sauce, garlic, canola oil, Worcestershire sauce, lemon juice, and pepper in a medium saucepan. Bring the sauce to a simmer; cook for 15 minutes, until smooth and thickened.

PER ¼-CUP SERVING: CALORIES 110; CALORIES FROM FAT 10; CALORIES FROM SATURATED FAT 0; PROTEIN 1 G; CARBOHYDRATE 28 G; TOTAL FAT 1 G; SATURATED FAT 0 G; CHOLESTEROL 0 MG; SODIUM 340 MG; 9% CALORIES FROM FAT

sauces, dressings, dips, and salsas

305

vegan

Tomatillo Sauce

MAKES 1¾ CUPS

USE this recipe as a sauce for poultry, beef, pork, or seafood. It's great brushed on an ear of grilled corn, too.

To use as a dip for chips and veggies, garnish with finely chopped red onion and a dollop of sour cream or ⅛ cup finely chopped seeded jalapeño for a little extra heat.

1 tablespoon canola oil
1 medium yellow onion, minced
2 cloves garlic, minced (1 teaspoon)
⅛ cup seeded and minced jalapeños
1½ cups canned tomatillos or 1 cup finely minced husked and washed fresh tomatillos (about 6 medium; see Note)
½ cup minced fresh cilantro
½ teaspoon salt

Heat the canola oil in a medium pan, and sauté the onion, garlic, and jalapeños for 2 to 3 minutes, until the onion is translucent. Add the tomatillos to the onion mixture; continue to sauté for 2 to 3 minutes longer. Cool completely. Purée the mixture in a food processor fitted with a metal blade. Place the salsa in a small bowl. Add the cilantro, season with the salt, and mix well.

NOTE: If you can't find fresh or canned tomatillos, use unripe tomatoes and add a little lime juice to obtain the acidity characteristic of tomatillos.

PER ¼-CUP SERVING: CALORIES 35; CALORIES FROM FAT 20; CALORIES FROM SATURATED FAT 0; PROTEIN 1 G; CARBOHYDRATE 4 G; TOTAL FAT 2.5 G; SATURATED FAT 0 G; CHOLESTEROL 0 MG; SODIUM 140 MG; 57% CALORIES FROM FAT

Tomatillo

TOMATILLO literally means "little tomato" in Spanish. Tomatillos, members of the Cape gooseberry family, have a lemony flavor and are encased in paperlike husks. They are used extensively in salsas, both cooked and raw. Once found only in Latin American grocery stores, tomatillos may now be purchased in many Whole Foods Market stores because of the general interest in ethnic foods. These glossy-skinned little tomatoes are always used in the green state. Look for hard-fleshed fruits and remember, they need to be husked and washed well before you use them in your salsas and sauces. They stay fresh in your refrigerator for 2 to 3 weeks if you keep them dry in a paper bag.

Jamaican Jerk Sauce

MAKES 2 CUPS

1 Scotch bonnet or jalapeño pepper,
 halved and seeded

4 scallions, sliced into 2-inch lengths

3 cloves garlic, peeled (1½ teaspoons)

3 tablespoons freshly grated ginger
 (1 2-inch piece)

4 sprigs fresh thyme, minced

1 tablespoon whole allspice berries,
 ground in a coffee mill, or
 2 teaspoons dried

Juice of 2 limes

½ cup ketchup

½ cup pineapple juice or tomato
 juice

JERKING is actually a method of cooking in Jamaica. Typically chicken, pork roast, or cuts of goat are marinated in jerk seasoning—either dry spices or a wet marinade like this recipe—then roasted in a pit or grilled slowly over wood coals. Scotch Bonnet peppers are some of the hottest chili peppers in the world. You may substitute jalapeños instead. The best flavor for this jerk recipe is from whole allspice berries, which are also called pimientos in Jamaica. Whole allspice berries may be ground in a coffee mill or you may use ground allspice powder.

In the bowl of a food processor or in a blender, process the Scotch Bonnet pepper, scallions, garlic, ginger, and thyme leaves until finely ground. Add the allspice, lime juice, ketchup, and pineapple juice and purée the mixture for 30 seconds, until well combined.

PER ¼-CUP SERVING: CALORIES 35; CALORIES FROM FAT 0; CALORIES FROM SATURATED FAT 0; PROTEIN 1 G; CARBOHYDRATE 8 G; TOTAL FAT 0 G; SATURATED FAT 0 G; CHOLESTEROL 0 MG; SODIUM 190 MG; 0% CALORIES FROM FAT

Recipe Bonus Keep a batch of jerk sauce in your refrigerator; it will keep for up to a month. You may use it to baste everything from tofu chunks to poultry, seafood, or red meat while roasting or barbecuing. It's especially good when you marinate chicken, roast pork, or thick slices of tofu overnight. Grill, roast, or broil the following day. Serve with additional sauce for dipping.

Easy Mole Sauce

MAKES 3 CUPS

MOLE is the national dish of Mexico, and the name literally comes from the Nahuatl word meaning "sauce" or "concoction." It is a concoction indeed, with many ingredients blending together to form a universe of flavor. Mole calls for Mexican chocolate, which has a much grainier texture than other chocolate. The small amount added isn't sweet, and it gives a deep earthy flavor and burnished sienna color to this sauce. You may use mole sauce to season poultry, pork, seafood, tofu, and even portobello mushrooms. It's also great on enchiladas.

1 dried pasilla chili

1 dried New Mexican red pepper chili

1 cup roughly chopped onions

1 cup seeded and diced tomatoes

1 tablespoon tahini

¼ cup sliced almonds

1 (9-inch) corn tortilla, torn into large pieces

¼ cup dark raisins

¼ teaspoon whole cloves

¼ teaspoon cinnamon

¼ teaspoon coriander

½ teaspoon salt

1 tablespoon canola oil

2 cups vegetable stock

½ teaspoon sugar

⅛ cup unsweetened cocoa powder or ground Mexican chocolate

Place the pasilla and red pepper chilies in a dry sauté pan, and toast over medium heat for about 15 minutes, turning often. (Be careful not to inhale the fumes—they may irritate your eyes.) When they're cool enough to handle, remove and discard the stems and seeds. Place the chilies in a medium sauce pot, and add enough water to cover them. Bring to a boil, and simmer uncovered for 15 minutes.

Remove the peppers from the water, and allow them to drain in a colander. Place the peppers, onions, tomatoes, tahini, almonds, tortilla, raisins, cloves, cinnamon, coriander, and salt in the bowl of a food processor fitted with a metal blade, and purée.

Heat the oil in a medium sauté pan; add the puréed pepper mixture. Cook on medium-high heat, stirring often, for 10 minutes. Stir in the vegetable stock, sugar, and cocoa. Lower the heat to a simmer, and cook for 45 minutes, until the sauce turns a dark mahogany color and is thick enough to coat the back of a spoon.

PER ¼-CUP SERVING: CALORIES 40; CALORIES FROM FAT 20; CALORIES FROM SATURATED FAT 0; PROTEIN 1 G; CARBOHYDRATE 5 G; TOTAL FAT 2.5 G; SATURATED FAT 0 G; CHOLESTEROL 0 MG; SODIUM 60 MG; 50% CALORIES FROM FAT

 Recipe Bonus For a "nutty" difference, replace the almonds with pepitas (pumpkin seeds) or white sesame seeds.

Imperial Orange Sauce

MAKES ¾ CUP

1 cup orange juice

2 tablespoons tamari or shoyu

¾ cup water

2 cloves garlic, minced

1½ tablespoons freshly grated ginger

½ teaspoon ground Szechwan peppercorns

2 teaspoons orange zest

2½ teaspoons toasted sesame oil

1 tablespoon honey

1 tablespoon cornstarch

1 tablespoon sherry

THIS sauce certainly lives up to the definition of "imperial"—splendid and lofty. The bold orange flavor and fragrant heat from ground Chinese peppercorns goes well with everything from tofu to rice or grilled shrimp. Szechwan peppercorns may be found in many Whole Foods Market stores and Asian markets. Although the Chinese peppercorns are more lively, you may substitute black peppercorns if desired. Try adding a garnish of fresh julienned snow-pea pods for extra crunch and color.

Place the orange juice, tamari, water, garlic, ginger, peppercorns, orange zest, sesame oil, and honey in a saucepan. Bring to a boil. Lower the heat and simmer for 2 to 3 minutes, stirring occasionally.

In a small bowl, mix the cornstarch with the sherry. Blend into the orange sauce, stirring constantly, until the sauce thickens. Remove from heat.

PER ⅛-CUP SERVING: CALORIES 20; CALORIES FROM FAT 5; CALORIES FROM SATURATED FAT 0; PROTEIN 0 G; CARBOHYDRATE 3 G; TOTAL FAT .5 G; SATURATED FAT 0 G; CHOLESTEROL 0 MG; SODIUM 105 MG; 25% CALORIES FROM FAT

sauces, dressings, dips, and salsas

vegan

Adobo Sauce

MAKES 1½ CUPS

THIS is an all-purpose Southwestern-style tomato-based sauce that works well in lasagnas, casseroles, and one-pot dinners. Ancho chilies are rich, sweet, and milder than most chilies. The ancho chili, which is about four inches long, is known as a poblano when it's fresh. You may use your favorite marinara sauce for the base of adobo. Try this sauce over our Couscous Cakes with Mint and Red Pepper (page 209), Portobello Burgers (page 210), or Eight-Layer Tortilla Pie (page 144).

2 ancho chili peppers
2 cups hot water
⅛ cup canola oil
1 medium yellow onion, chopped
1 teaspoon dark chili powder
1 teaspoon cumin
1 teaspoon dried oregano
¼ teaspoon cayenne pepper
2 teaspoons salt
½ teaspoon freshly ground pepper
1 cup jarred tomato sauce

Soak the chilies in the hot water until they're completely softened, about 30 minutes. Remove the chilies from the water, and reserve 1 cup of the water. Remove and discard the stems and seeds from the chilies. Heat the canola oil in a medium pan, and sauté the onion over medium heat until almost tender, about 2 minutes. Blend in the chili powder, cumin, oregano, cayenne, salt, and pepper. Sauté for 1 minute, stirring often. Add the chilies and the reserved 1 cup water. Simmer uncovered for 5 minutes. Add the tomato sauce; simmer uncovered for at least 30 minutes, until the sauce has a rich brown, ruddy color. Purée the mixture in the bowl of a food processor or in a blender until smooth. You may also use a handheld immersion blender. The sauce should coat a spoon when finished.

PER ¼-CUP SERVING: CALORIES 45; CALORIES FROM FAT 25; CALORIES FROM SATURATED FAT 0; PROTEIN 1 G; CARBOHYDRATE 5 G; TOTAL FAT 2.5 G; SATURATED FAT 0 G; CHOLESTEROL 0 MG; SODIUM 370 MG; 55% CALORIES FROM FAT

 Recipe Bonus Adobo Sauce may be used as a marinade as well as a serving sauce. Try brushing adobo on pork tenderloin while grilling. Whisk a little into your favorite barbecue sauce. For a smoky-flavored variation, replace the ancho chilies with 3 dried chipotle chilies (smoked jalapeños), rehydrating the chipotles in the 2 cups of hot water. If you can't find dried chipotles, use 3 chipotles from a can of chipotles packed in adobo sauce and omit the soaking step.

Raisin-Orange Sauce

MAKES ABOUT 2 CUPS

½ cup orange juice

1 cup rosé wine

2 shallots, chopped

⅛ cup raisins

2 tablespoons butter

⅛ cup chopped parsley

THE tart citrus flavor cuts the richness of roast pork. The raisins add a textural surprise.

Place the orange juice, wine, shallots, and raisins in a small saucepan. Bring the sauce to a boil, and allow to cook until reduced by almost half, for about 30 minutes. Remove from the heat, and whisk in the butter and parsley.

PER ⅓-CUP SERVING: CALORIES 90; CALORIES FROM FAT 35; CALORIES FROM SATURATED FAT 20; PROTEIN 1 G; CARBOHYDRATE 7 G; TOTAL FAT 4 G; SATURATED FAT 2.5 G; CHOLESTEROL 10 MG; SODIUM 5 MG; 39% CALORIES FROM FAT

Lemon Tahini Sauce

MAKES ABOUT 2 CUPS

1 cup tahini

½ cup water or plain yogurt

2 cloves garlic, minced (1 teaspoon)

¼ cup lemon juice

¼ cup finely minced parsley

½ teaspoon cumin

½ teaspoon hot sauce

Salt and freshly ground pepper to taste

A classic sauce drizzled over falafel, try it with our baked, not fried falafel (page 27). This tart sauce made with sesame seed paste and fresh lemon juice is perfectly suited for grilled or steamed vegetables or grilled poultry or seafood.

Place the tahini, water, garlic, lemon juice, parsley, cumin, hot sauce, and salt and pepper in the bowl of a food processor or in a blender. Pulse for 1 minute, until the sauce is smooth and well blended. Add a bit more liquid if the sauce thickens.

PER ¼-CUP SERVING: CALORIES 170; CALORIES FROM FAT 140; CALORIES FROM SATURATED FAT 2; PROTEIN 5 G; CARBOHYDRATE 5 G; TOTAL FAT 16 G; SATURATED FAT 2 G; CHOLESTEROL 0 MG; SODIUM 10 MG; 82% CALORIES FROM FAT

Creamy Peanut Sauce

MAKES 3 CUPS

EVEN though it's Thai-inspired, the peanut butter triggers comforting childhood memories sans jelly. The balance of tart vinegar and lime, pungent ginger, and the mild sweetness of raw sugar are pure joy. Use it as a dipping sauce for grilled chicken, seafood, beef, or pork. Brush a little on as a glaze while roasting meat, poultry, or fish. Try it on grilled skewers, char-grilled eggplant, Udon noodles, and raw vegetable salads, as well. Experiment by making this recipe with freshly ground peanut butter—the flavor is intense. It keeps well in your refrigerator for up to two weeks.

½ cup canola oil

¼ cup toasted sesame oil

1 cup finely chopped yellow onions

⅛ cup finely minced garlic (12 cloves)

1 2-inch piece of ginger, roughly chopped

¼ cup red wine vinegar

1 cup water

3 tablespoons sugar

¼ cup ketchup

½ cup creamy peanut butter

½ cup fresh cilantro leaves

¼ cup tamari

2½ tablespoons lime juice

1 teaspoon hot pepper sauce, or to taste

Heat the canola and sesame oils in a large sauté pan over medium heat; add the onions, garlic, and ginger, and simmer uncovered for 5 minutes, stirring often. Add the vinegar, water, sugar, ketchup, peanut butter, cilantro, tamari, lime juice, and hot pepper sauce; simmer uncovered for 5 minutes. Cool the sauce mixture. In a blender or the bowl of a food processor fitted with a metal blade, purée the mixture until smooth.

PER ¼-CUP SERVING: CALORIES 150; CALORIES FROM FAT 120; CALORIES FROM SATURATED FAT 15; PROTEIN 3 G; CARBOHYDRATE 7 G; TOTAL FAT 13 G; SATURATED FAT 1.5 G; CHOLESTEROL 0 MG; SODIUM 270 MG; 80% CALORIES FROM FAT

Curry Coconut Peanut Sauce

vegetarian

1 teaspoon canola oil

1 small red onion, minced

3 cloves garlic, minced
  (1¹/₂ teaspoons)

1 serrano pepper, seeded and minced

4 teaspoons minced fresh ginger

4 teaspoons curry powder

4 teaspoons cumin

1 (13.5-ounce) can coconut milk

5 tablespoons creamy peanut butter

¹/₄ cup minced fresh cilantro

5 teaspoons tamari

4 teaspoons honey

¹/₈ cup lime juice

¹/₈ cup ketchup

³/₄ cup water

THIS sauce should come with a warning: One spoonful will have you hooked. Fortunately, it complements almost anything from vegtables to poultry and tofu.

Heat the canola oil in a saucepan over medium heat. Sauté the onion, garlic, serrano pepper, and ginger until the onion is translucent. Add the curry powder and cumin; sauté over low heat for 1 minute. Add the coconut milk, peanut butter, cilantro, tamari, honey, lime juice, ketchup, and water. Bring the sauce to a boil, whisking often. Reduce the heat; simmer for 10 minutes.

PER ¹/₈-CUP SERVING: CALORIES 50; CALORIES FROM FAT 35; CALORIES FROM SATURATED FAT 17; PROTEIN 1 G; CARBOHYDRATE 3 G; TOTAL FAT 4 G; SATURATED FAT 2 G; CHOLESTEROL 0 MG; SODIUM 75 MG; 70% CALORIES FROM FAT

sauces, dressings, dips, and salsas

313

vegetarian

Creole Remoulade Sauce

MAKES 1¾ CUPS

A French Caribbean–inspired tartar sauce that enhances any seafood dish. (It also makes a great sandwich topping.) Creamy mayonnaise studded with fragrant minced tarragon, tart capers, and sweet pickles makes this sauce particularly well suited to Cajun Seafood Cakes (page 218). This Creole sauce also pairs well with chilled shrimp, crayfish, lobster, and grilled calamari. Try it as a dressing for a seafood salad, too.

1 cup mayonnaise
½ small red onion, roughly chopped
2 scallions, roughly chopped
3 sprigs fresh parsley
3 sprigs fresh tarragon, or
  2 teaspoons dried tarragon
⅛ cup capers, well drained
¼ cup drained and roughly chopped
  dill pickles, or use bottled dill
  relish
1½ tablespoons lemon juice
1 teaspoon salt
½ teaspoon hot sauce
1 teaspoon Dijon mustard

Place the mayonnaise, onion, scallions, parsley, tarragon, capers, dill pickles, lemon juice, salt, hot sauce, and mustard in the bowl of a food processor fitted with a metal blade. Pulse until the mixture is well combined but retains some chunkiness.

PER ¼-CUP SERVING: CALORIES 110; CALORIES FROM FAT 90; CALORIES FROM SATURATED FAT 20; PROTEIN 0 G; CARBOHYDRATE 4 G; TOTAL FAT 20 G; SATURATED FAT 2 G; CHOLESTEROL 0 MG; SODIUM 550 MG; 82% CALORIES FROM FAT

 Recipe Bonus For a lower fat content, reduce the mayonnaise to ½ cup and add ½ cup low-fat plain yogurt. For a spicier version, add ⅛ cup drained horseradish.

THE WHOLE FOODS MARKET COOKBOOK

Soy Dipping Sauce

vegan

MAKES ¾ CUP

½ cup tamari

1 scallion, sliced thinly and diagonally

Pinch of crushed red chili flakes

5 teaspoons rice wine vinegar

1 teaspoon minced fresh ginger

1 tablespoon minced fresh cilantro

THIS simple dipping sauce yields wonderful flavor. It can be drizzled over pasta or your favorite entrées to impart Asian taste.

In a bowl, combine the tamari, scallion, red chili flakes, rice wine vinegar, ginger, and cilantro.

PER ⅛-CUP SERVING: CALORIES 10; CALORIES FROM FAT 0; CALORIES FROM SATURATED FAT 0; PROTEIN 1 G; CARBOHYDRATE 2 G; TOTAL FAT 0 G; SATURATED FAT 0 G; CHOLESTEROL 0 MG; SODIUM 660 MG; 0% CALORIES FROM FAT

The Immersion Blender

THE best way to make dressings and marinades at home is with a handheld immersion blender. This invaluable tool has a handle attached to a stem housing a small propeller-like blade that you place directly in a bowl of liquid ingredients to purée or blend them. You may even make thicker recipes like hummus with an immersion blender. They are inexpensive, and they enable you to combine all the ingredients in one bowl or jar and mix easily, forming a smooth emulsion.

sauces, dressings, dips, and salsas

315

Thai Dipping Sauce

MAKES ¾ CUP

THIS sauce, also called nuac cham, is made with Vietnamese fish sauce, a pungently flavored condiment available in many Whole Foods Market and Asian grocery stores. The sauce is light and looks unassuming, but it exudes tremendous flavor. It can be used as a dip for Garden of Eva Summer Rolls (page 28) or as a marinade for vegetables, seafood, or poultry.

1 tablespoon fish sauce

Juice of 1 lime

2 teaspoons rice vinegar

1 teaspoon sugar

½ teaspoon red chili paste with garlic

1 clove garlic, minced (½ teaspoon)

1 tablespoon grated carrot

¼ cup water

In a bowl, combine the fish sauce, lime juice, rice vinegar, sugar, chili paste, garlic, carrot, and water. Mix well.

PER ⅛-CUP SERVING: CALORIES 10; CALORIES FROM FAT 0; CALORIES FROM SATURATED FAT 0; PROTEIN 1 G; CARBOHYDRATE 2 G; TOTAL FAT 0 G; SATURATED FAT 0 G; CHOLESTEROL 0 MG; SODIUM 250 MG; 0% CALORIES FROM FAT

 Tip from the Team: A little oil on your hands will keep your skin from absorbing the heat from chili peppers. Wash your hands with soap and water afterward to remove the oil and capsaicin. If you still manage to get it in your eyes, rub hair on your eyes and the fire immediately disappears.

Spinach Artichoke Dip

MAKES 4 CUPS

2 cups grated Parmesan cheese

2 cups grated Monterey Jack cheese

1 cup mayonnaise

1 cup sour cream

1 (14- or 15-ounce) can artichoke
hearts, drained and diced

1 (10-ounce box) frozen spinach,
thawed and squeezed dry

6 cloves garlic, minced (1 tablespoon)

½ teaspoon freshly ground pepper

THIS classic steak house dip may be made nondairy by using soy cheese and soy-based mayonnaise. The spinach retains its crispness and adds contrasting texture to the creamy garlicky dip. Soft chunks of artichoke help smooth the tang of the Parmesan cheese. This mixture may be made up to two days before baking. Just pop in the oven when your guests arrive. Serve hot with chips or fresh raw vegetables or as a great topping for baked potatoes.

Preheat the oven to 400°F. Combine the cheeses, mayonnaise, and sour cream in a large bowl until well blended. Add the artichoke hearts, spinach, garlic, and pepper. Mix well. Place the mixture in a 1- to 1½-quart casserole dish. Bake the dip uncovered for 15 minutes, or until the mixture is bubbling.

PER ¼-CUP SERVING: CALORIES 100; CALORIES FROM FAT 60; CALORIES FROM SATURATED FAT 35; PROTEIN 7 G; CARBOHYDRATE 4 G; TOTAL FAT 6 G; SATURATED FAT 4 G; CHOLESTEROL 20 MG; SODIUM 280 MG; 60% CALORIES FROM FAT

sauces, dressings, dips, and salsas

317

Toasted Pepita Dip

MAKES 2 CUPS

PEPITAS are edible pumpkin seeds. These teardrop-shaped hulled seeds are a beautiful green color and have less fat than most nuts. Toasting brings out the aromatic, nutty flavor. The fragrant pale green color of the nut oil contained in the pumpkin seeds combined with jalapeño and cilantro give this dip a chic elegance with universal appeal. Try toasting corn tortilla wedges in the oven for three minutes until crisp, then use them to scoop this dip.

Serve with warm flour tortillas, tortilla chips, or raw veggies. This dip is also tasty spread on a grilled skirt steak or chicken wrap.

1 cup pepitas (pumpkin seeds), toasted (see Note)
3 scallions
⅓ cup chopped fresh cilantro
1 jalapeño, seeded and roughly chopped
½ cup sour cream
1 teaspoon cumin
⅛ cup lime juice
2 cloves garlic, minced (1 teaspoon)
½ teaspoon cayenne pepper
1 teaspoon salt
½ teaspoon freshly ground pepper
4 plum tomatoes, seeded and finely diced

Place the toasted pepitas in the bowl of a food processor fitted with a metal blade. Add the scallions, cilantro, jalapeño, sour cream, cumin, lime juice, garlic, cayenne, salt, and pepper, and purée. Transfer to a serving bowl; stir in the tomatoes.

NOTE: To toast, place the pepitas in a dry sauté pan over medium heat. Cook, stirring or tossing often, for 3 minutes, until you just begin to smell the pepitas and their color is light golden brown.

PER ¼-CUP SERVING: CALORIES 40; CALORIES FROM FAT 15; CALORIES FROM SATURATED FAT 5; PROTEIN 2 G; CARBOHYDRATE 6 G; TOTAL FAT 1.5 G; SATURATED FAT 0.5 G; CHOLESTEROL 5 MG; SODIUM 140 MG; 37% CALORIES FROM FAT

 Recipe Bonus Shelled pumpkin seeds make a great snack; just toast and salt them or sprinkle them with a bit of Cajun spice or tamari.

Warm Herbed Goat Cheese Dip

MAKES ¾ CUP

2 cloves garlic, finely minced
  (1 teaspoon)
4 ounces plain mild fresh goat cheese
1 sprig fresh rosemary (about
  2 inches long)
¼ cup extra-virgin olive oil

THIS is a soulful appetizer. Use a mild goat cheese and a high-quality extra-virgin olive oil. If you enjoy a bit of heat, lightly dust with freshly milled black pepper or even better, a sprinkling of minced, jarred green peppercorns in brine. Serve with thinly sliced baguettes, crostini, focaccia bread, water crackers, or baked pita chips.

Preheat the oven to 350°F. Spread the garlic on the bottom of a 5 × 9-inch au gratin dish, a ramekin, or a very small casserole, at least 1½ inches deep. Crumble the goat cheese on top of the garlic. Place the rosemary sprig between the cheese and the side of the dish, following the curve of the dish. Tamp the cheese down with the back of a spoon so that the surface is even. Add the olive oil until it reaches about ⅛ inch from the top of the dish. Bake for 10 minutes, until bubbling.

PER ¼-CUP SERVING: CALORIES 230; CALORIES FROM FAT 200; CALORIES FROM SATURATED FAT 70; PROTEIN 6 G; CARBOHYDRATE 1 G; TOTAL FAT 22 G; SATURATED FAT 8 G; CHOLESTEROL 20 MG; SODIUM 150 MG; 87% CALORIES FROM FAT

sauces, dressings, dips, and salsas

319

Habanero Ale Cheese Dip

MAKES 4 CUPS

HABANERO chilies are some of the world's hottest peppers; they originate in the Caribbean and the Yucatán peninsula. This small rounded chili, which ranges from yellow green to red, packs quite a punch. You may substitute Scotch Bonnet chilies, from the same family. Serve this spicy, heat-seeking dip in a round loaf of bread with the center removed and bottom intact to form an edible bread bowl. Sprinkle the top with a little paprika, and accompany with corn or tortilla chips for dipping. The cooling cream cheese soothes the spiciness—but have plenty of cold beverages available for aftereffects. In fact, you can start with the remainder of the ale you will be left with from this recipe.

½ pound extra-sharp cheddar cheese, grated
¾ pound habanero-jack cheese, grated
½ pound cream cheese
1 teaspoon salt
1 cup pale ale
⅓ cup finely chopped fresh chives
⅓ cup finely chopped fresh cilantro

Preheat the oven to 375°F. Mix the cheeses together with the salt in a large bowl. Place the cheese mixture in an ovenproof casserole; spread out the ingredients evenly with the back of a large spoon. Pour the ale over the mixture, and bake uncovered, until the cheese starts to melt, about 15 minutes.

Remove the casserole from the oven, and carefully blend the mixture with a spoon until it's creamy and well combined. Bake uncovered for 15 minutes. Remove from the oven, and mix again. Blend in the chives and cilantro.

PER ¼-CUP SERVING: CALORIES 110; CALORIES FROM FAT 60; CALORIES FROM SATURATED FAT 35; PROTEIN 9 G; CARBOHYDRATE 2 G; TOTAL FAT 7 G; SATURATED FAT 4 G; CHOLESTEROL 20 MG; SODIUM 320 MG; 54% CALORIES FROM FAT

Super Bowl con Queso Dip

1 cup plus 3 tablespoons pale ale

1 clove garlic, finely minced
(½ teaspoon)

½ pound sharp aged cheddar cheese, cubed

1 pound mild cheddar cheese, cubed

¾ cup prepared tomato salsa

1 tablespoon seeded, minced jalapeño pepper

2½ tablespoons cornstarch

1 teaspoon salt, or to taste

½ teaspoon freshly ground pepper, or to taste

¼ cup chopped fresh cilantro

BEER, cheese, and chili peppers. Although it sounds like a three-course bachelor dinner, these ingredients combined make a savory, rich dip appropriate for any gathering. You may use a dry white wine or tomato juice instead of the ale if you prefer.

Pour the 1 cup ale into a stainless-steel sauce pot, add the garlic, and bring to a simmer over medium heat. Add the cheddar cheeses, and stir until melted. Stir in the salsa and jalapeño, mixing well.

In a small bowl, combine the cornstarch with the remaining 3 tablespoons ale, and mix thoroughly. Stir the cornstarch slurry into the cheese mixture, and simmer, stirring constantly, until smooth. Season with the salt and pepper.

To serve, transfer to a fondue pot over a low flame. Top with the chopped cilantro. Serve with tortilla chips, warm flour tortillas, pretzels, or raw veggies.

PER ¼-CUP SERVING: CALORIES 130; CALORIES FROM FAT 80; CALORIES FROM SATURATED FAT 45; PROTEIN 9 G; CARBOHYDRATE 2 G; TOTAL FAT 80 G; SATURATED FAT 5 G; CHOLESTEROL 30 MG; SODIUM 350 MG; 61% CALORIES FROM FAT

 Recipe Bonus For extra protein and to stretch the dip, stir in 1 cup of cooked and drained pinto, kidney, or black beans.

sauces, dressings, dips, and salsas

321

vegan

Black Bean Hummus

MAKES 3 CUPS

A twist on classic hummus, this dip proudly shows off the glossy black beauties called turtle beans. Try to leave them fairly chunky when incorporating them into the dip. The combination of the two legumes—turtle beans and chickpeas (or garbanzos)—produces a nutty flavor and bewitching presentation. Chickpeas are a staple of many cultures and usually end up in soups, stews, and salads. Here they provide a creamy background for this unusual dip. This makes a nice sandwich spread for a chicken or veggie wrap.

1 cup chickpeas, cooked and drained
⅛ cup tahini
2 teaspoons finely minced garlic (4 cloves)
1 tablespoon lemon juice
½ cup water
1 teaspoon cumin
2 teaspoons salt
1 tablespoon finely minced parsley
¼ cup extra-virgin olive oil
½ teaspoon hot sauce, or to taste
1 cup cooked and drained black turtle beans

Place the chickpeas, tahini, garlic, lemon juice, water, cumin, salt, parsley, olive oil, and hot sauce in the bowl of a food processor fitted with a metal blade. Pulse until the mixture is well blended but still slightly coarse. Add the turtle beans, and pulse until the beans are combined but still coarse.

PER ¼-CUP SERVING: CALORIES 50; CALORIES FROM FAT 30; CALORIES FROM SATURATED FAT 0; PROTEIN 1 G; CARBOHYDRATE 4 G; TOTAL FAT 3.5 G; SATURATED FAT 0 G; CHOLESTEROL 0 MG; SODIUM 180 MG; 60% CALORIES FROM FAT

Variation: Try adding a little minced cilantro and fresh sweet corn for another variation. Or give homemade pizza an unusual twist by using creamy hummus instead of marinara sauce. The hummus flavor concentrates when baked and forms a bold flavored base for vegetables. You don't even need cheese, because of the richness provided by the tahini.

Red Pepper Hummus

1 cup cooked chickpeas

⅛ cup tahini

1 tablespoon lemon juice

3 cloves garlic, minced
   (1½ teaspoons)

1 cup jarred roasted red peppers,
   well drained

4 sprigs fresh basil

1½ teaspoons dried Italian herbs

1 tablespoon tomato paste

1 teaspoon paprika

¼ cup plus 2 tablespoons balsamic
   vinegar

1 teaspoon salt

¼ teaspoon hot sauce

¼ cup extra-virgin olive oil

MIDDLE East meets Tuscany in this cross-cultural appetizer made with sweet roast peppers and tart balsamic vinegar. Although unorthodox, the combination of these two ethnic flavor backgrounds blends very well. The intense smoky flavor of roast peppers is tamed by the aged balsamic vinegar.

This sublime dip makes an incredible sandwich spread with grilled vegetables, and is also a colorful and suitable accompaniment for falafel.

Place the chickpeas, tahini, lemon juice, garlic, roasted peppers, basil, Italian herbs, tomato paste, paprika, vinegar, salt, hot sauce, and olive oil in the bowl of a food processor bowl fitted with a metal blade, and purée until smooth. This dip can be stored for up to 4 days in the refrigerator.

PER ¼-CUP SERVING: CALORIES 80; CALORIES FROM FAT 60; CALORIES FROM SATURATED FAT 5; PROTEIN 2 G; CARBOHYDRATE 6 G; TOTAL FAT 6 G; SATURATED FAT 1 G; CHOLESTEROL 0 MG; SODIUM 260 MG; 75% CALORIES FROM FAT

 Tip from the Team: To remove the smell of garlic from your fingers, rub your fingers on a stainless-steel spoon under running water.

sauces, dressings, dips, and salsas

323

vegan

Raspberry Vinaigrette

MAKES 3 1/2 CUPS

THIS vibrant pink dressing is not only the base for our Wild Rice with Pecans and Cranberries (page 173) but is also welcome over any green salad. Try tossing it with raw seasonal vegetables, as well. You may use fresh or frozen raspberries or strawberries in this recipe. Be sure to defrost frozen berries before using. This vinaigrette will keep for up to a week in the refrigerator. This dressing is wonderful drizzled over grilled salmon, tuna, or chicken breasts.

1 pint raspberries or strawberries (2 cups)
2 medium shallots, chopped
1/4 cup Dijon mustard
3/4 cup extra-virgin olive oil
1/3 cup raspberry vinegar
Salt and freshly ground pepper to taste

P lace the raspberries, shallots, and mustard in the bowl of a food processor or in a blender. Purée for 45 seconds, until smooth. With the processor or blender running, slowly add the olive oil until a smooth emulsion is formed, about 30 seconds, and then continue to purée for an additional 30 seconds. Add the vinegar, and combine well. Season with salt and pepper. If the dressing looks too thick, you may add a small amount of water or cranberry juice to thin it to the desired consistency.

PER 1/8-CUP SERVING: CALORIES 80; CALORIES FROM FAT 70; CALORIES FROM SATURATED FAT 1; PROTEIN 0 G; CARBOHYDRATE 2 G; TOTAL FAT 8 G; SATURATED FAT 1 G; CHOLESTEROL 0 MG; SODIUM 70 MG; 87% CALORIES FROM FAT

What Kind of Oil?

MOST dressings call for aromatic extra-virgin olive oil, which has a fruity flavor and a rich ripe olive bouquet. It has the most pronounced olive flavor because it is from the first pressing of the olive. When we are looking for the other dressing or marinade flavors to come through, we use a neutral canola oil instead. Grapeseed oil may also be substituted in any recipe. Remember, if you're using the dressing for a green salad, toss it in immediately before serving, as greens are delicate and will wilt if the dressing is added too prematurely.

Kiwi and Satsuma Mandarin Orange Dressing

MAKES 1½ CUPS

1 tablespoon olive oil

½ medium onion, chopped

2 cloves garlic, minced (1 teaspoon)

2 kiwis, halved, flesh scooped from their skin

½ cup extra-virgin olive oil

2 satsuma or clementine oranges, halved

¼ cup balsamic vinegar

Salt to taste

KIWI fruit and satsuma oranges are at their peak season in December. They are loaded with natural sugar balanced with the right amount of acid to make a tart dressing that may be used on mature lettuces—like hearts of romaine, red oak leaf, or butter lettuce—strong enough to hold up to the creamy dressing.

Heat the olive oil in a small sauté pan over moderate heat, and sauté the onion and garlic for 3 minutes, until tender and lightly browned. Place them in the bowl of a food processor or in a blender.

Add the kiwi pulp, and purée for 1 minute, until smooth. With the processor running, gradually add the extra-virgin olive oil to form a smooth and creamy emulsion. Add the juice from the satsuma or clementine oranges and the balsamic vinegar, and combine well for a few seconds more. Season with the salt.

PER ⅛-CUP SERVING: CALORIES 60; CALORIES FROM FAT 50; CALORIES FROM SATURATED FAT 5; PROTEIN 0 G; CARBOHYDRATE 3 G; TOTAL FAT 5 G; SATURATED FAT 0.5 G; CHOLESTEROL 0 MG; SODIUM 0 MG; 83% CALORIES FROM FAT

sauces, dressings, dips, and salsas

325

vegan

Tropical Herb Dressing

MAKES 1 CUP

THIS versatile dressing may be drizzled over salads, tossed with pasta, or stirred into cooked or raw vegetables. It's also a great marinade for poultry, beef, pork, or lamb because the enzymes in the pineapple juice act to tenderize the meat. Try adding a few spoonfuls to cooked warm red bliss potatoes.

¼ cup Dijon mustard
½ cup extra-virgin olive oil
½ cup pineapple juice
⅛ cup cider vinegar
6 leaves fresh basil, chopped
Salt and freshly ground pepper to taste

Combine the mustard and olive oil in the bowl of a food processor and process on high for 1 minute, until smooth. Add the pineapple juice, vinegar, basil, and salt and pepper, and process for another minute, until smooth and creamy.

PER ⅛-CUP SERVING: CALORIES 100; CALORIES FROM FAT 90; CALORIES FROM SATURATED FAT 10; PROTEIN 0 G; CARBOHYDRATE 2 G; TOTAL FAT 10 G; SATURATED FAT 1.5 G; CHOLESTEROL 0 MG; SODIUM 135 MG; 90% CALORIES FROM FAT

 Tip from the Team: Lots of people make vinaigrettes at home— just extra-virgin olive oil and vinegar for salad dressing. Sometimes it's hard to get the right balance. If the dressing has too much vinegar, or if the flavor is just too harsh, we sometimes soften it with a little bit of real maple syrup. It adds body and sweetness and also serves as an emulsifier.

Tikka Salad Dressing

vegan

MAKES 2 CUPS

1/8 cup lemon zest

1/2 cup lemon juice

2 teaspoons turmeric

2 teaspoons cumin

2 teaspoons coriander

3 cloves garlic, finely minced
(1 1/2 teaspoons)

2 teaspoons sugar

3 tablespoons grated or finely minced
fresh ginger (3-inch piece)

1/2 teaspoon crushed red chili flakes

2 teaspoons salt

1/8 cup chopped yellow onion

2 cups extra-virgin olive oil

THIS East Indian recipe is both a dressing and a marinade. The smooth velvet consistency cleverly conceals a bold, peppery flavor. You may add a teaspoon of garam masala for a sharper flavor. Try this recipe to marinate chicken, pork, lamb, or firm chunks of fresh fish (tuna or salmon) and thread on skewers. You may simply pour Tikka Salad Dressing over mixed greens, cooked warm vegetables, or sliced cucumbers. Tikka will keep for up to two weeks in the refrigerator.

Place the lemon zest, lemon juice, turmeric, cumin, coriander, garlic, sugar, ginger, red chili flakes, salt, and onion in the bowl of a food processor fitted with a metal blade. Process until well blended. With the processor running, slowly add the olive oil in short drizzles until the dressing is well blended and has thickened slightly. Refrigerate.

PER 1/8-CUP SERVING: CALORIES 170; CALORIES FROM FAT 170; CALORIES FROM SATURATED FAT 25; PROTEIN 0 G; CARBOHYDRATE 2 G; TOTAL FAT 19 G; SATURATED FAT 2.5 G; CHOLESTEROL 0 MG; SODIUM 170 MG; 100% CALORIES FROM FAT

vegan

Miso Salad Dressing

MAKES 3 CUPS

OUR Miso Salad Dressing introduced thousands to this rich and versatile soy food with many uses. White miso is the most mild and sweet tasting and here it blends with tofu to form the creamy silken texture of this dressing. The taste becomes somewhat addictive, and you will end up pouring it on steamed vegetables, potatoes, and pasta, as well. It's also great for an Asian cole slaw dressing or as a savory sauce for grilled salmon. This dressing keeps for up to five days, refrigerated.

½ cup roughly chopped yellow onions
½ pound extra-firm tofu, drained
¼ cup white miso
½ cup cider vinegar
¼ cup extra-virgin olive oil
¼ cup chopped parsley
I cup water

Place the onions, tofu, miso, vinegar, olive oil, parsley, and water in the bowl of a food processor fitted with a metal blade. Process until smooth and creamy. Refrigerate.

PER ⅛-CUP SERVING: CALORIES 30; CALORIES FROM FAT 20; CALORIES FROM SATURATED FAT 0; PROTEIN I G; CARBOHYDRATE I G; TOTAL FAT 2 G; SATURATED FAT 0 G; CHOLESTEROL 0 MG; SODIUM 95 MG; 67% CALORIES FROM FAT

Italian Herb Vinaigrette

MAKES 1 1/2 CUPS

1 cup extra-virgin olive oil

1/2 cup red wine vinegar or balsamic
vinegar

2 sprigs fresh rosemary

2 teaspoons dried Italian herbs

1/2 teaspoon freshly ground pepper

1/4 teaspoon crushed red chili flakes

2 sprigs parsley

1/2 teaspoon salt

THIS all-purpose vinaigrette complements any salad but also adds an aromatic herb flavor to chicken breasts, seafood, tofu slabs, or pasta. Try it on 1/2-inch-thick seasonal vegetable "steaks" cut from eggplant, zucchini, or yellow squash. Use a high-quality, fruity extra-virgin olive oil for this recipe. You may add a few sprigs of any of your favorite fresh herbs—we like basil, sage, thyme, or oregano.

P lace the olive oil, vinegar, rosemary leaves, Italian herbs, pepper, red chili flakes, parsley, and salt in the bowl of a food processor fitted with a metal blade, and process for about 30 seconds, or until well blended. Or mix the ingredients in a large bowl with a handheld mixer or by hand with a wire whisk.

PER 1/8-CUP SERVING: CALORIES 150; CALORIES FROM FAT 150; CALORIES FROM SATURATED FAT 20; PROTEIN 0 G; CARBOHYDRATE 2 G; TOTAL FAT 17 G; SATURATED FAT 2.5 G; CHOLESTEROL 0 MG; SODIUM 75 MG; 100% CALORIES FROM FAT

Variation: For a nice tomato twist that uses less oil, reduce olive oil to 1/2 cup and vinegar to 1/4 cup. Add 1 cup tomato juice, and continue with the recipe.

 Tip from the Team: To easily add fresh herbs to your recipe (without a knife, cutting board, and cleanup!), snip fresh herbs with kitchen shears directly into the dish you are preparing. For basil or larger leaves, place several leaves in a stack, roll them up, and then snip.

sauces, dressings, dips, and salsas

329

vegetarian

Creamy Feta and Roasted Garlic Dressing

MAKES 2 1/2 CUPS

THIS thick and creamy all-purpose dressing can also be used as a dip. The sweet flavor of roasted garlic is the perfect mellowing note for the feta cheese base. Try mixing in 1/2 cup pitted and finely minced Kalamata olives, for more of an authentic Mediterranean taste. This dressing benefits from a bit of aging, as the pungent feta mellows alongside the creamy ricotta. The lemon in this dressing makes it a perfect complement to falafel stuffed into pita bread.

1 to 2 whole heads roasted garlic (see page 10)
1 cup crumbled feta cheese
1/2 cup sour cream
1/2 cup ricotta cheese
1/2 cup cottage cheese
1/2 cup cream cheese
1 teaspoon hot sauce
1 tablespoon lemon juice
Salt to taste

Place the roasted garlic, feta cheese, sour cream, ricotta cheese, cottage cheese, cream cheese, hot sauce, lemon juice, and salt in the bowl of a food processor fitted with a metal blade. Pulse until the dressing is smooth but still a little coarse. Refrigerate and use as a dip or sauce for vegetables.

PER 1/8-CUP SERVING: CALORIES 120; CALORIES FROM FAT 80; CALORIES FROM SATURATED FAT 60; PROTEIN 5 G; CARBOHYDRATE 4 G; TOTAL FAT 9 G; SATURATED FAT 6 G; CHOLESTEROL 30 MG; SODIUM 250 MG; 67% CALORIES FROM FAT

Feta Dill Dressing

vegetarian

MAKES 1¼ CUPS

1 cup yogurt

3 tablespoons finely crumbled feta cheese

1 tablespoon lemon juice

1 tablespoon minced fresh dill

2 teaspoons lemon pepper

RICH and tangy feta cheese was traditionally made with goat's or sheep's milk throughout Greece, the birthplace of this versatile and piquant cheese. Today, because of commercial production, much of it is made with cow's milk. It continues to be a great addition to salads. Our dressing marries fresh fragrant dill and feta, a classic combination. This simple dressing has a pure flavor and couldn't be easier to prepare.

Use as a dressing for salads, a dip for raw veggies, or a sauce for steamed vegetables. This is also a savory sauce for cold poached salmon.

Combine the yogurt, feta cheese, lemon juice, dill, and lemon pepper in a large bowl. Refrigerate.

PER ⅛-CUP SERVING: CALORIES 20; CALORIES FROM FAT 0; CALORIES FROM SATURATED FAT 0; PROTEIN 1 G; CARBOHYDRATE 3 G; TOTAL FAT 0 G; SATURATED FAT 0 G; CHOLESTEROL 0 MG; SODIUM 35 MG; 0% CALORIES FROM FAT

sauces, dressings, dips, and salsas

331

vegetarian

Buttermilk Ranch Dressing

MAKES 3 1/2 CUPS

SIMPLE and full-flavored, this dressing balances sweet caramelized garlic with the pleasing tart flavor of buttermilk. Try this dressing over salad greens or mixed into a bowl of sliced cucumber and red onion. This is a great alternative to traditional oil-based dressings. You may also marinate vegetable skewers in this ranch dressing and grill them. Most people are surprised to learn that creamy, rich buttermilk has only a 2 percent fat content.

1 1/2 cups buttermilk

2 cups plain yogurt

1/2 cup roasted garlic (see page 10)

1 teaspoon lemon pepper

2 teaspoons salt

2 teaspoons celery seed

1 teaspoon sugar

2 tablespoons finely minced parsley

Purée the buttermilk, yogurt, garlic, lemon pepper, salt, celery seed, sugar, and parsley in a blender or in the bowl of a food processor fitted with a metal blade. For best flavor, refrigerate for at least 1 hour before serving. You may also use a handheld immersion blender to mix the dressing.

PER 1/8-CUP SERVING: CALORIES 25; CALORIES FROM FAT 0; CALORIES FROM SATURATED FAT 0; PROTEIN 2 G; CARBOHYDRATE 4 G; TOTAL FAT 0 G; SATURATED FAT 0 G; CHOLESTEROL 0 MG; SODIUM 130 MG; 0% CALORIES FROM FAT

 Tip from the Team: If you don't have buttermilk on hand, you can substitute by adding 1 teaspoon lemon juice or 1 teaspoon vinegar to 1 cup milk.

Deco Pink Beet Dressing

MAKES 3 CUPS

2 cups shredded peeled raw beets

1 cup roughly chopped yellow onions

1/2 cup honey

2 cloves garlic, minced (1 teaspoon)

1/4 cup cider vinegar

1 cup mayonnaise

THE first time you glimpse this dressing, the title will make perfect sense. This vivid crimson-colored beet dressing lights up any salad with a sweet and tart flavor. Drizzle Deco dressing over field greens and add the crunch of rye or pumpernickel croutons. Although beets have the highest sugar content of any vegetable, they are low in calories.

P lace the beets, onions, honey, garlic, cider vinegar, and mayonnaise in the bowl of a food processor fitted with a metal blade. Purée until the mixture is smooth.

PER 1/8-CUP SERVING: CALORIES 45; CALORIES FROM FAT 25; CALORIES FROM SATURATED FAT 5; PROTEIN 0 G; CARBOHYDRATE 6 G; TOTAL FAT 2.5 G; SATURATED FAT 0.5 G; CHOLESTEROL 0 MG; SODIUM 65 MG; 55% CALORIES FROM FAT

Enlightened Caesar Dressing

MAKES 3 CUPS

1 cup buttermilk

3/4 cup grated Parmesan cheese

1 tablespoon finely minced garlic
   (6 cloves)

1 cup mayonnaise

1/4 cup plain yogurt

1 teaspoon freshly ground white
   pepper

THIS is a great salad dressing—the kind that sticks to every inch of greens. After chilling in the refrigerator for a few hours, the mixture will be thick enough to use as a dramatic cold contrasting sauce for hot vegetables or as a topping for baked potatoes.

B lend the buttermilk, Parmesan cheese, garlic, mayonnaise, yogurt, and white pepper together in a large bowl. Refrigerate until well chilled.

PER 1/8-CUP SERVING: CALORIES 60; CALORIES FROM FAT 45; CALORIES FROM SATURATED FAT 15; PROTEIN 2 G; CARBOHYDRATE 2 G; TOTAL FAT 5 G; SATURATED FAT 1.5 G; CHOLESTEROL 5 MG; SODIUM 160 MG; 75% CALORIES FROM FAT

vegetarian

Roasted Sesame–Honey Dressing

MAKES 2½ CUPS

THIS is one of our favorite all-purpose marinades and dressings. It's extremely versatile in the kitchen. When tossed in a salad, especially with shredded cabbage or any seasonal vegetable, it creates vibrant flavor harmony. As a marinade for poultry, beef, tofu, eggplant slices, and tempeh, it provides a simple way to prepare grilled or broiled main dishes. It also gives chicken wings new meaning used as either a marinade or a dip. You may use any bottled teriyaki or Szechwan sauce for this recipe.

⅛ cup tamari

¼ cup water

4 cloves garlic, minced (2 teaspoons)

⅛ cup grated fresh ginger (2-inch piece)

1 cup canned pineapple juice

⅛ cup teriyaki sauce

2 teaspoons toasted sesame oil

¼ cup white sesame seeds

¼ cup cider vinegar

3 tablespoons honey

½ teaspoon Szechwan sauce

Place the tamari, water, garlic, ginger, pineapple juice, teriyaki sauce, sesame oil, sesame seeds, cider vinegar, honey, and Szechwan sauce in a large bowl, and mix well. You may also use a handheld immersion blender for a smoother, creamier version.

PER ⅛-CUP SERVING: CALORIES 35; CALORIES FROM FAT 10; CALORIES FROM SATURATED FAT 0; PROTEIN 1 G; CARBOHYDRATE 5 G; TOTAL FAT 1.5 G; SATURATED FAT 0 G; CHOLESTEROL 0 MG; SODIUM 180 MG; 28% CALORIES FROM FAT

Tip from the Team: A little oil in your measuring spoon or cup will keep honey or molasses from sticking, so measure your oil first.

Spicy Mexican Marinade

⅛ cup olive oil

1 teaspoon dark chili powder

1 teaspoon cumin

2 teaspoons dried oregano

2 teaspoons paprika

¼ teaspoon crushed red chili flakes

2 cloves garlic, finely minced
   (1 teaspoon)

½ small yellow onion, chopped

¼ cup seeded, finely chopped
   Anaheim peppers

⅛ cup chopped fresh cilantro

⅛ cup lime juice

1½ cups tomato juice

3 tablespoons tomato paste

½ cup water

A favorite flexible marinade that serves as a dressing, as well. Chili peppers, cumin, and cilantro blend together with the pleasant acidity of tomatoes. Use it to marinate beef, poultry, pork, and lamb, or for a vegetarian entrée it works terrifically with sliced tofu, tempeh, seitan, and any seasonal vegetable. You will begin to notice a spicy flavor when you leave ingredients soaking for at least one hour, but it's best to marinate overnight for it to really kick in. Try grilling some of the items suggested above and serving warm over a Caesar salad.

Place the olive oil in a sauce pot. Add the chili powder, cumin, oregano, paprika, and red chili flakes. Sauté for 5 minutes, stirring frequently; then immediately remove the marinade from the heat, and allow it to cool. Place the garlic, onion, Anaheim peppers, cilantro, lime juice, tomato juice, tomato paste, and water in the bowl of a food processor fitted with a metal blade, and add the flavored olive oil. Blend until smooth.

PER ⅛-CUP SERVING: CALORIES 0; CALORIES FROM FAT 0; CALORIES FROM SATURATED FAT 0; PROTEIN 0 G; CARBOHYDRATE 0 G; TOTAL FAT 0 G; SATURATED FAT 0 G; CHOLESTEROL 0 MG; SODIUM 0 MG; 0% CALORIES FROM FAT

sauces, dressings, dips, and salsas

A Word About Using Marinades

MANY of our marinades can be used to flavor meat, poultry, seafood, and other sources of protein before cooking. Generally speaking, the longer food marinates, the more flavor will permeate the ingredient, producing more taste. The only exception is when marinating delicate seafood, which actually "cooks" with the addition of any acid, such as vinegar or citrus juice. Seafood should be marinated for only 20 to 30 minutes to flavor before it is cooked by any of your favorite methods. Marinating ingredients has a side benefit of tenderizing them.

Red meat, poultry, and tofu, as well as tempeh or vegetable steaks cut from hearty vegetables like eggplant, squash, and onions, benefit from marination before cooking. If you are marinating ingredients, let them sit in the marinade in a covered dish or sealed plastic bag in the refrigerator for at least 2 hours so the flavor can begin to do its job. Most often, overnight marination in the refrigerator is best for optimum flavor. Make sure to discard any marinade that has been in contact with raw meat, poultry, or seafood, as it may contain bacteria. You may also boil extra marinade if you wish to serve it with the cooked dish.

The following dressings all add wonderful flavor to your favorite foods. After marinating, you may grill, bake, steam, or sauté the marinated items, producing bold taste results.

Jalapeño Cilantro Pesto

MAKES 3 1/2 CUPS

4 cups roughly chopped fresh cilantro

4 cups spinach, washed and stemmed

2 cloves garlic, minced (1 teaspoon)

1/2 cup pecan pieces, toasted

1/4 cup plus 2 tablespoons lime juice

1/4 cup plus 2 tablespoons extra-virgin olive oil

1/4 cup plus 2 tablespoons canned chopped tomatillos

1/4 jalapeño pepper, seeded and minced

1/4 cup sour cream

1 1/2 teaspoons salt

1 teaspoon freshly ground pepper

VIVID green cilantro leaves are grown from the coriander plant. They are very pungent, and they're used in Mexican, Asian, and Latin cooking. Combined with spicy jalapeño peppers, they make a very flavorful pesto, which goes well with any Mexican or Asian dish. This pesto may also be used as a sandwich spread or topping for pizza or quesadillas.

Combine the cilantro, spinach, garlic, pecans, lime juice, olive oil, tomatillos, and jalapeño pepper in the bowl of a food processor or in a blender, and purée for 1 to 2 minutes, until well combined.

Add the sour cream, salt, and pepper and blend for 30 seconds more, until smooth. This pesto may be made up to 2 days prior to serving.

PER 1/4-CUP SERVING: CALORIES 110; CALORIES FROM FAT 100; CALORIES FROM SATURATED FAT 15; PROTEIN 1 G; CARBOHYDRATE 3 G; TOTAL FAT 11 G; SATURATED FAT 2 G; CHOLESTEROL 0 MG; SODIUM 180 MG; 91% CALORIES FROM FAT

sauces, dressings, dips, and salsas

337

Cran-Apple Raspberry Chutney

MAKES 6 CUPS

FLAVORS of tart cranberries and apples mixed with sweet apricot preserves make this chutney a great all-purpose condiment for pork, lamb, poultry, or beef. Raspberries give it a bright ruby color that adds interest to any dinner table.

Place the cranberries, apples, sugar, apricot preserves, raspberries, and lemon juice in a medium mixing bowl. Blend well, and chill. Fold in the mint, and serve.

PER ½-CUP SERVING: CALORIES 150; CALORIES FROM FAT 0; CALORIES FROM SATURATED FAT 0; PROTEIN 0 G; CARBOHYDRATE 39 G; TOTAL FAT 40 G; SATURATED FAT 0 G; CHOLESTEROL 0 MG; SODIUM 5 MG; 0% CALORIES FROM FAT

1 pound fresh cranberries, finely chopped
2 tart green apples, peeled, cored, and finely chopped
1 cup sugar
½ cup apricot preserves
1 (10-ounce) package frozen raspberries, thawed and drained well
1 teaspoon lemon juice
½ teaspoon chopped fresh mint

Onion Chutney

MAKES 1 CUP

THIS is a universal condiment with sweet, sour, and spicy depth. It's at home on any dish and can be used as a sandwich topping, as well.

In a medium skillet, heat the olive oil and sauté the onion and green pepper until the onion is translucent. Add the ketchup, hot pepper sauce, vinegar, paprika, and cayenne pepper; cook for 30 seconds more. Combine all the ingredients well; chill.

PER ¼-CUP SERVING: CALORIES 40; CALORIES FROM FAT 15; CALORIES FROM SATURATED FAT 0; PROTEIN 1 G; CARBOHYDRATE 10 G; TOTAL FAT 1.5 G; SATURATED FAT 0 G; CHOLESTEROL 0 MG; SODIUM 190 MG; 38% CALORIES FROM FAT

2 teaspoons olive oil
1 medium red onion, minced
½ green pepper, minced
¼ cup plus 2 tablespoons ketchup
½ teaspoon hot pepper sauce
¼ cup white wine vinegar
1 teaspoon paprika
Pinch of cayenne pepper

Tomatillo-Chipotle Salsa

MAKES 4 CUPS

1 pound tomatillos, chopped

2 poblano chilies, seeded and chopped

1 small yellow onion, chopped

1 clove garlic, minced (½ teaspoon)

2 chipotle chilies in adobo, chopped

½ cup minced fresh cilantro

1 teaspoon salt

USE this salsa for serving with tamales, for dipping chips, or for serving with grilled poultry, pork, or tofu. It's also a great addition to quesadillas.

Blend the tomatillos, poblano chilies, onion, garlic, chipotle chilies, cilantro, and salt together in a large mixing bowl.

PER ¼-CUP SERVING: CALORIES 25; CALORIES FROM FAT 5; CALORIES FROM SATURATED FAT 0; PROTEIN 1 G; CARBOHYDRATE 5 G; TOTAL FAT 0.5 G; SATURATED FAT 0 G; CHOLESTEROL 0 MG; SODIUM 180 MG; 20% CALORIES FROM FAT

Pico de Gallo

MAKES 2 CUPS

2 large tomatoes, diced

1 small red onion, minced

1 scallion, very thinly sliced

1 serrano pepper, seeded and minced

⅛ cup lime juice

⅛ cup chopped fresh cilantro

Salt and freshly ground pepper

PICO de Gallo means "rooster's beak." It's really a salsa that can be made with any ingredient. The odd name came from the fact that salsa was once eaten with the thumb and finger, which resembled a rooster's beak. It's delicious with any grilled meat, poultry, seafood, or tofu.

In a medium bowl, combine the tomatoes, onion, scallion, serrano pepper, lime juice, cilantro, and salt and pepper. You may make this salsa a day prior to using. Fresh pico is best when used within 2 days.

PER ½-CUP SERVING: CALORIES 30; CALORIES FROM FAT 0; CALORIES FROM SATURATED FAT 0; PROTEIN 1 G; CARBOHYDRATE 7 G; TOTAL FAT 0 G; SATURATED FAT 0 G; CHOLESTEROL 0 MG; SODIUM 20 MG; 0% CALORIES FROM FAT

Cucumber Raita

MAKES 2½ CUPS

IN a way, raita was one of the first designer foods. Cooling yogurt, cucumber, and mint quell heat from even the most fiery chili. In some countries it is even used as a chaser following shots of vodka.

I n a large mixing bowl, combine the yogurt, onion, cucumber, tomato, serrano pepper, mint, cilantro, garlic, cayenne pepper, cumin, turmeric, ground pepper, salt, and lemon juice and blend well. Prepare the raita at least 30 minutes ahead of time to allow its flavors to meld.

PER ¼-CUP SERVING: CALORIES 80; CALORIES FROM FAT 15; CALORIES FROM SATURATED FAT 10; PROTEIN 6 G; CARBOHYDRATE 10 G; TOTAL FAT 1.5 G; SATURATED FAT 1 G; CHOLESTEROL 5 MG; SODIUM 170 MG; 19% CALORIES FROM FAT

2 cups plain yogurt

½ small red onion, minced

½ small cucumber, peeled, seeded, and minced

½ medium tomato, seeded and minced

½ serrano pepper, seeded and minced

⅛ cup minced fresh mint

1 tablespoon minced fresh cilantro

1 clove garlic, minced (½ teaspoon)

Pinch of cayenne pepper

¼ teaspoon cumin

½ teaspoon turmeric

¼ teaspoon freshly ground pepper

¼ teaspoon salt

1 teaspoon lemon juice

Beverages, Nectars, and Smoothies

APRICOT ASCENSION ◆ APPLE BERRY FREEZE ◆ CHOCOLATE PEANUT

BUTTER TWIST ◆ MANGO PASSION MONTAGE ◆ CAPPUCCINO SNAP ◆ JUST

SQUEEZED VEGETABLE COCKTAIL ◆ LICUADO ◆ ULTRA REFRESHING TRIPLE

CITRUS LIMEADE ◆ SOOTHING FRESH GINGER TEA ◆ PASSION POTION ◆

SANGRIA ◆ BLOODY MARY COCKTAIL MIX

Beverages, nectars, and smoothies encompass a wide
collection of drinks. Many categories fall into this group, ranging from nutritious smoothies and shakes to calming teas, tonics, and fresh-squeezed juices. We've even included a few party drinks and punches with which you may experiment.

The popularity of blended drinks, or smoothies, has dramatically increased over the past several years. Smoothies are viewed as a portable power food that has it all. Smoothies come in an almost infinite variety of flavors and can act as a base to which nutritional supplements are added.

Drinkable recipes are simple and quick to produce at home. The only special equipment our shakes and fruit drinks require is a blender or food processor. There are a lot of ingredient options with smoothies. With few exceptions, fruit-based smoothies are best when made with frozen fruit. It's the frozen fruit that gives smoothies a creamy, thick consistency and smooth finish. Smoothies make a great outlet for those really ripe bananas or soft berries hanging around your kitchen a bit too long. Bananas form the base for many fruit drinks, as they add natural sweetness and help provide the velvety consistency of many recipes.

Although smoothies are simple to make, there are some rules that will allow you to make the best drinks possible. For example, the best way to prepare ripe bananas for blending is by cutting them into 1-inch slices and freezing them on a plate until well frozen. Then you can lift them in individual pieces from the plate and store them in a covered container. This allows you to add them a few at a time to whatever recipe you are making without their sticking together in a big clump. Berries should be frozen on a plate, as well, then transferred to a container. If they are large, cut them in half before freezing. Some people prefer to sweeten them with sugar before freezing. Any soft fruit such as melons, peaches, plums, or apricots may be cut and frozen for up to three months to use in smoothies. This is a good way to preserve seasonal fruits to enjoy all year round.

Another consideration is which liquids and frozen yogurts to add. There is a variety of fruit nectars and juices available, which range from sweet organic apple juice to more exotic selections like litchi juice, tropical fruit mixes, and wild berry combinations. Many of the juice choices can be interchangeable. If you are making a tropical smoothie, experiment with guava nectar instead of papaya or pineapple. Stay with the overall theme of the drink. You may also substitute nondairy beverages for milk such as soy, rice, oat, or almond milk. Instead of using frozen yogurt, you may use a nondairy rice or soy frozen dessert; a fruit-based sorbet would also be great as a substitute.

Fresh-squeezed juices are also enjoying a renewed appreciation and are a refreshing and nutritious way to start a day. You must have a juicer to squeeze fresh vegetable and fruit juices at home. If you make the commitment to juice regularly, then a juicer is a worthwhile investment.

You'll also find a restorative tea and some party beverages—such as a spicy tomato juice and horseradish-spiked cocktail mix (page 352) and our Ultra Refreshing Triple Citrus Limeade (page 348), also suitable for a memorable margarita.

Apricot Ascension

SERVES 1

LIME juice cuts this sweet blend of apricot and papaya juice. The frozen banana adds a creamy textured base. Try using orange juice instead of papaya juice for a citrus twist.

1 cup apricot juice
¼ cup papaya juice
½ frozen banana, cut into
   1-inch-thick slices
Juice of 1 lime
2 sprigs fresh mint to garnish

Place the apricot juice, papaya juice, banana, and lime juice in a blender, and purée for 30 to 45 seconds, until smooth and creamy. Garnish with fresh mint sprigs.

PER 12-OUNCE SERVING: CALORIES 240; CALORIES FROM FAT 0; CALORIES FROM SATURATED FAT 0; PROTEIN 2 G; CARBOHYDRATE 60 G; TOTAL FAT 0 G; SATURATED FAT 0 G; CHOLESTEROL 0 MG; SODIUM 15 MG; 0% CALORIES FROM FAT

Apple Berry Freeze

SERVES 1

YOU may use any firm crisp apple for this shake—Granny Smith, Gala, Fuji, and Delicious all work well. The dates add sweetness and help form the body of the drink. Try substituting other berry juices for the strawberry—even cranberry is good.

4 or 5 large chunks of unpeeled apple
   (about ½ apple)
4 frozen strawberries
2 pitted dates
¾ cup apple juice
¼ cup strawberry juice
2 strawberries, thinly sliced to garnish

Place the apple, strawberries, and dates along with the apple and strawberry juices in a blender, and purée for 30 to 45 seconds, until smooth and creamy. Garnish with the sliced strawberries.

PER 12-OUNCE SERVING: CALORIES 230; CALORIES FROM FAT 10; CALORIES FROM SATURATED FAT 0; PROTEIN 1 G; CARBOHYDRATE 57 G; TOTAL FAT 1 G; SATURATED FAT 0 G; CHOLESTEROL 0 MG; SODIUM 0 MG; 4% CALORIES FROM FAT

Chocolate Peanut Butter Twist

SERVES 1

⅛ cup chocolate or carob chips

1 tablespoon peanut butter

½ cup milk, or soy, oat, or rice milk

1 cup vanilla frozen yogurt

1 teaspoon chocolate shavings,
  or ½ teaspoon cocoa powder to
  garnish

SILKY and sinful, this dreamy concoction is a special treat. You may use an equal amount of chocolate syrup instead of the chips; however, the chips provide little flecks when puréed, which add character to this shake. You may also use a frozen nondairy-based sorbet for the yogurt.

Place the chocolate, peanut butter, milk, and frozen yogurt in a blender, and purée for 30 to 45 seconds, until smooth and creamy. Garnish with chocolate over the top.

PER 12-OUNCE SERVING: CALORIES 580; CALORIES FROM FAT 200; CALORIES FROM SATURATED FAT 90; PROTEIN 26 G; CARBOHYDRATE 75 G; TOTAL FAT 22 G; SATURATED FAT 10 G; CHOLESTEROL 100 MG; SODIUM 260 MG; 34% CALORIES FROM FAT

Mango Passion Montage

SERVES 1

2 ounces frozen mango or peach
  slices

3 frozen strawberries, sliced

½ cup passion fruit juice

½ cup crushed ice

2 sprigs fresh mint to garnish

PASSION fruit juice is extremely fragrant and bold flavored. The sweet mango pairs well with strawberries and provides much of the creamy consistency for this drink. If you're freezing your own cut mango for this drink, use only a very ripe mango; it will scream with intense flavor. You may also purchase diced frozen mango or peaches.

Place the mango, strawberries, fruit juice, and crushed ice in a blender or in the bowl of a food processor, and purée for 30 to 45 seconds, until smooth and creamy. Garnish with the fresh mint sprigs.

PER 12-OUNCE SERVING: CALORIES 130; CALORIES FROM FAT 0; CALORIES FROM SATURATED FAT 0; PROTEIN 1 G; CARBOHYDRATE 33 G; TOTAL FAT 0 G; SATURATED FAT 0 G; CHOLESTEROL 0 MG; SODIUM 15 MG; 0% CALORIES FROM FAT

Cappuccino Snap

SERVES 1

FROZEN coffee is so refreshing. You can substitute a fruit- or chocolate-based sorbet for the frozen yogurt or frozen soy dessert for a nondairy version. If you like, add a dollop of whipped cream over the top.

2 ounces espresso, chilled or at room
    temperature, regular or decaf
4 ice cubes, crushed
¼ teaspoon cinnamon
1 cup frozen vanilla or coffee yogurt
Sprinkle of grated nutmeg to garnish

Place the espresso, crushed ice, cinnamon, and yogurt in a blender and process for 30 to 45 seconds, until smooth. Garnish with the grated nutmeg.

PER 12-OUNCE SERVING: CALORIES 320; CALORIES FROM FAT 45; CALORIES FROM SATURATED FAT 25; PROTEIN 16 G; CARBOHYDRATE 53 G; TOTAL FAT 5 G; SATURATED FAT 3 G; CHOLESTEROL 90 MG; SODIUM 115 MG; 14% CALORIES FROM FAT

Tip from the Team: When you are preparing iced coffee, a great way to sweeten it without adding a grainy texture is to pour your desired amount of sugar into a small cup and pour a small amount of hot coffee on it, just enough to melt the sugar. Pour your cold coffee into a glass, add the sugar mixture, and add ice. Presto—sweet coffee without the crunch.

Just Squeezed Vegetable Cocktail

SERVES 1

1 small beet, peeled

2 stalks celery

6 sprigs parsley

3 large carrots

1½-inch-thick slice unpeeled ginger
   (optional)

SWEET beets and carrots provide incredible flavor and are a nutritional powerhouse when mixed with earthy celery and fresh parsley. This is a very popular combination. Add a small piece of ginger for a spicy nuance.

Run the beet, celery, parsley, carrots, and optional ginger through a juicer, and serve immediately.

PER 12-OUNCE SERVING: CALORIES 140; CALORIES FROM FAT 5; CALORIES FROM SATURATED FAT 0; PROTEIN 4 G; CARBOHYDRATE 33 G; TOTAL FAT 0.5 G; SATURATED FAT 0 G; CHOLESTEROL 0 MG; SODIUM 210 MG; 3% CALORIES FROM FAT

Licuado

SERVES 1 TO 2

12 ounces milk

1 cup frozen sliced strawberries

½ frozen banana, cut in chunks

⅛ cup light brown sugar

½ teaspoon vanilla extract

¼ cup vanilla ice cream or frozen
   yogurt

1 tablespoon whipped cream to
   garnish

Pinch of cinnamon to garnish

LICUADO is a blended fruit shake and a common beverage in many Latin American cultures where it is served in small drink stands with placards that say JUGOS Y LICUADOS. These stands sell everything from fresh-squeezed carrot juice to creamy tropical fruit–based shakes. Our summer fruit licuado is refreshing and rich in calcium and vitamins.

Pour the milk into a blender or in the bowl of a food processor. Add the strawberries, banana, brown sugar, vanilla, and ice cream. Blend for 45 seconds to 1 minute, until smooth and creamy. Garnish with a dollop of whipped cream and a sprinkle of cinnamon.

PER 11-OUNCE SERVING: CALORIES 230; CALORIES FROM FAT 40; CALORIES FROM SATURATED FAT 25; PROTEIN 10 G; CARBOHYDRATE 39 G; TOTAL FAT 4.5 G; SATURATED FAT 3 G; CHOLESTEROL 26 MG; SODIUM 130 MG; 17% CALORIES FROM FAT

vegan

Ultra Refreshing Triple Citrus Limeade

SERVES 2 TO 3

THE tart flavor of citrus is slightly tamed by sweet maple syrup and rounded out with orange juice, which makes this drink refreshing and light. You may use sugar if you prefer a sweeter end result. Try adding some crushed mint leaves. Some folks like to add a pinch of ground cayenne pepper when they feel like having a warming pick-me-up cocktail; others use it as a base for an all-natural margarita mix.

Juice of 3 limes
Juice of 1 orange
Juice of 1 lemon
¼ to ⅓ cup maple syrup
3 cups water

In a pitcher or bowl, combine the juices from the limes, orange, and lemon. Add the maple syrup and water; then mix well. You may keep the limeade covered in the refrigerator for up to 3 days.

PER 12-OUNCE SERVING: CALORIES 90; CALORIES FROM FAT 0; CALORIES FROM SATURATED FAT 0; PROTEIN 0 G; CARBOHYDRATE 24 G; TOTAL FAT 0 G; SATURATED FAT 0 G; CHOLESTEROL 0 MG; SODIUM 10 MG; 0% CALORIES FROM FAT

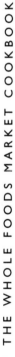

Soothing Fresh Ginger Tea

2 cups cold water

¼ cup sliced fresh unpeeled ginger, washed well

2 dried allspice berries

1½-inch-long piece cinnamon stick

1 tablespoon honey, or to taste

Lemon juice to taste

THIS warming, soothing tea is spicy with the intense flavor of fresh ginger, allspice, and cinnamon. It's lightly sweetened with honey, but feel free to try it with maple syrup. It's delicious chilled, as well.

Place the water, ginger, allspice berries, and cinnamon stick in a small sauce pot, and bring to a boil. Lower to a simmer, and cook gently for 10 minutes. Strain the liquid into a cup, sweeten with the honey, and add a squeeze of lemon juice.

PER 12-OUNCE SERVING: CALORIES 110; CALORIES FROM FAT 5; CALORIES FROM SATURATED FAT 0; PROTEIN 1 G; CARBOHYDRATE 28 G; TOTAL FAT 0.5 G; SATURATED FAT 0 G; CHOLESTEROL 0 MG; SODIUM 25 MG; 4% CALORIES FROM FAT

 Recipe Bonus The aroma from simmering ginger tea is so aromatic and pervasive that it can be used as a potpourri to make your home smell like the holidays. Just double the recipe, leave out the honey and lemon, and simmer slowly until the liquid becomes very reduced and your room is fragrant with spice.

beverages, nectars, and smoothies

349

vegan

Passion Potion

SERVES 1

THERE have been some historical references attributed to this elixir, regarding the potential amorous effects it may have on those who imbibe the sweet clove-scented nectar. Remember, there are no guarantees; just enjoy it for what it is.

Use frozen fruit if you like a more frozen, thickened drink.

½ banana, sliced

½ ripe papaya, seeds removed, cut into chunks

½ cup watermelon or strawberry juice

¼ teaspoon whole cloves

⅛ teaspoon cinnamon

Leaves from 1 sprig fresh mint

Place the banana, papaya, watermelon juice, cloves, cinnamon, and mint leaves in the bowl of a food processor or in a blender, and purée for 45 seconds, until smooth.

PER 12-OUNCE SERVING: CALORIES 150; CALORIES FROM FAT 10; CALORIES FROM SATURATED FAT 10; PROTEIN 2 G; CARBOHYDRATE 38 G; TOTAL FAT 1 G; SATURATED FAT 0 G; CHOLESTEROL 0 MG; SODIUM 10 MG; 7% CALORIES FROM FAT

Sangria

SERVES 8

1 (½-liter) bottle dry red or
white wine

1 (12-ounce) can fruit juice
concentrate

4 oranges sliced in half and cut into
½-inch-thick slices

3 lemons sliced in half and cut into
½-inch-thick slices

3 limes sliced in half and cut into
½-inch-thick slices

2 apples, cored, halved, and cut into
½-inch-thick slices

2 pears, cored, halved, and cut into
½-inch-thick slices

1 pint strawberries, stems removed,
hulled, and thinly sliced

2 cups chopped pineapple

2 cups orange liqueur, such as triple
sec or curaçao

SANGRIA is a festive party-time wine steeped with fresh ripe fruits and combined with fruit juices. Prepare it with red or white wine; each lends its own special flair. Adding lemonade concentrate makes the taste tart, which goes well with a dry white wine. Red wine combines well with a concentrated tropical fruit juice mixture. You may use any fresh fruits in season. Either way, this sangria is good enough to build the rest of the party around. We've added orange liqueur, which imparts a sweet citrus punch. You may leave it out if you wish.

In a large pitcher, combine the red or white wine, fruit juice concentrate, oranges, lemons, limes, apples, pears, strawberries, pineapple, and orange liqueur. Marinate all ingredients together for at least 2 hours (preferably overnight) in the refrigerator. Serve white wine sangria well chilled and red wine sangria not too cold, but with ice.

PER 8-OUNCE SERVING: CALORIES 280; CALORIES FROM FAT 5; CALORIES FROM SATURATED FAT 0; PROTEIN 2 G; CARBOHYDRATE 41 G; TOTAL FAT 1 G; SATURATED FAT 0 G; CHOLESTEROL 0 MG; SODIUM 10 MG; 2% CALORIES FROM FAT

 Recipe Bonus If you prefer a milder and somewhat sparkling punch, add a quart of club soda, lemon-lime soda, or ginger ale just before serving.

beverages, nectars, and smoothies

Bloody Mary Cocktail Mix

SERVES 1

A multipurpose cocktail that can be enjoyed alone or as a mixer. It's equally tasty made with tomato or vegetable juice, and you may even add some fresh-squeezed carrot or celery juice for a stellar flavor booster. Depending on the heat of the Cajun spices, you may want to add a few drops of your favorite hot sauce. If you're a vegetarian, omit the dashes of Worcestershire sauce.

12 ounces tomato or vegetable juice
1 teaspoon prepared white
   horseradish
1 tablespoon lemon juice
2 dashes Worcestershire sauce
¼ teaspoon Cajun spices
¼ teaspoon celery salt
Hot sauce to taste (optional)
1 stalk celery, 8 to 10 inches long,
   with leaves attached, to garnish
Wedge of lemon to garnish

Combine the tomato juice, horseradish, lemon juice, Worcestershire sauce, Cajun spices, celery salt, and hot sauce, if desired, in a shaker or blender, and mix well.

Garnish with a fresh celery stalk and lemon wedge.

PER 12-OUNCE SERVING: CALORIES 70; CALORIES FROM FAT 0; CALORIES FROM SATURATED FAT 0; PROTEIN 3 G; CARBOHYDRATE 18 G; TOTAL FAT 0 G; SATURATED FAT 0 G; CHOLESTEROL 0 MG; SODIUM 550 MG; 0% CALORIES FROM FAT

 Recipe Bonus Use this recipe as a flavorful marinade for seafood, including fish steaks, shrimp, and scallops. Marinate the seafood for an hour; then grill or broil it.

Cooking with Kids

There is something powerful about bringing our kids into the kitchen.

There is something powerful about bringing our kids into the kitchen. Setting up a step stool, handing them a spoon or a handful of peas to shell, and showing them how ingredients are transformed into a meal is one of the greatest experiences you can share with your child. When we teach our kids something that is dear to us, we impart more than just a recipe. Children gain much more than simply learning how to make a favorite family cake or lasagna. Cooking teaches children how to follow directions and how to clean up, and it also gives them responsibility. It also helps children with hand-to-eye coordination and manual dexterity, as well as counting and measuring skills. Most of all, it's a great opportunity to develop teamwork skills and a sense of confidence. We've chosen a variety of simple recipes, many of which can be made entirely by kids. Of course, children should always be guided and taught respect for safety skills like cutting with a knife or using a pan over the high heat of a range top.

This chapter also includes some valuable healthful lunch box tips. The daily routine of making school lunches can become a chore, even though you want your kids to eat healthfully. We offer easy recipes and tips for hollowing a roll and filling it with tuna or chicken salad so it resembles a savory jelly roll of sorts or making a mini chef's salad with dressing on the side to keep it fresh until eaten.

Getting your children to eat healthfully can feel like a continuous battle, but if they are involved in the preparation of their food, they will likely feel a sense of pride and be more apt to want to enjoy the fruits of their labor.

Fluffy Cottage Cheese Pancakes

1 large egg, lightly beaten

⅛ cup cottage cheese

⅛ cup unbleached all-purpose flour

1½ tablespoons sugar

1 tablespoon butter

THESE puffy and light pancakes make a wonderful way to start the morning . . . or end the day. Eat 'em up with your choice of yogurt, applesauce, or sour cream. This recipe is so easy that kids can make the batter themselves. Try dusting the pancakes with cinnamon or vanilla sugar.

In a mixing bowl, combine the egg, cottage cheese, flour, and sugar together with a fork. Heat a nonstick pan over moderate heat, and add the butter. When the butter is hot and begins to sizzle, drop the batter by tablespoonfuls into the buttered pan. You don't want the butter to turn brown, as it will burn before the pancakes are cooked. Cook for 3 minutes, until lightly browned. Flip the pancakes, and brown the other side.

PER SERVING: CALORIES 80; CALORIES FROM FAT 40; CALORIES FROM SATURATED FAT 20; PROTEIN 3 G; CARBOHYDRATE 8 G; TOTAL FAT 4.5 G; SATURATED FAT 2.5 G; CHOLESTEROL 60 MG; SODIUM 45 MG; 50% CALORIES FROM FAT

cooking with kids

vegan

Orange Glazed Sweet Potato Oven Fries

SERVES 8

SWEET and crunchy, these sweet potato fries are loaded with flavor. Use a pastry brush to apply the orange glaze. Try to slice the potatoes as thinly as you can so they will get very crispy.

Olive or canola oil for spraying the potatoes

2 pounds medium sweet potatoes or yams, skin on, well scrubbed, sliced in ¼-inch-thick rounds

¼ cup orange marmalade

Juice of ½ lemon

½ teaspoon salt

Freshly ground white pepper to taste

Preheat the oven to 450°F.

Lightly spray a baking pan with the olive or canola oil, and arrange the sweet potato slices in rows, not overlapping. Mix the marmalade with the lemon juice, and brush on the sweet potato slices. Season with the salt and pepper, and bake for 15 to 20 minutes, until crispy and golden brown.

PER SERVING: CALORIES 160; CALORIES FROM FAT 5; CALORIES FROM SATURATED FAT 0; PROTEIN 2 G; CARBOHYDRATE 38 G; TOTAL FAT 0.5 G; SATURATED FAT 0 G; CHOLESTEROL 0 MG; SODIUM 130 MG; 3% CALORIES FROM FAT

Tomato Clouds

SERVES 4

4 medium tomatoes (firm)

1 cup grated Monterey Jack or cheddar cheese

¼ cup cornmeal

1 clove garlic, minced (½ teaspoon)

½ teaspoon dried oregano

1 large egg, separated, plus 1 large egg white

Olive oil for oiling pan

A golden cheese meringue forms a puffy crown over these juicy, plump stuffed tomatoes. They may be served as a side dish or easily turned into a main course by mixing in some flaked tuna. Have your kids use a teaspoon to hollow out the tomatoes.

Preheat the oven to 450°F.

Core the tomatoes, cut a thin slice off the top of each, and remove the pulp and seeds with a small spoon.

In a mixing bowl, combine the grated cheese, cornmeal, garlic, oregano, and the egg yolk. Blend well.

In a separate stainless-steel mixing bowl, place the two egg whites. Beat the whites until they're firm with a hand mixer or wire whisk. Stir a third of the whites into the cheese mixture; then gently fold in the remainder with a spatula. Spoon about ½ cup of the mixture into the center of each tomato. Lightly oil a baking pan. Place the stuffed tomatoes on the oiled baking pan, and bake them for about 15 minutes, or until puffed and golden. Serve immediately.

PER SERVING: CALORIES 190; CALORIES FROM FAT 100; CALORIES FROM SATURATED FAT 50; PROTEIN 11 G; CARBOHYDRATE 12 G; TOTAL FAT 12 G; SATURATED FAT 6 G; CHOLESTEROL 80 MG; SODIUM 290 MG; 53% CALORIES FROM FAT

 Recipe Bonus When throwing a tea party, cherry tomatoes may be substituted in place of the medium tomatoes for an excellent hors d'oeuvre. Bake for 8 to 10 minutes.

Ginger Ale and Honey Braised Carrot Coins

SERVES 6

THIS colorful side dish shines with bright flavor. The concentrated ginger ale reduces to combine with the natural sweetness of the carrots and forms a light sauce. Try it with Potato-Chip-Crusted Fish Bites (page 362) or Hand to Mouth Chicken Drumsticks (page 363).

1 pound carrots, cut into
   1/2-inch-thick coins
1 cup ginger ale
1 teaspoon minced fresh ginger
1 tablespoon honey
1 teaspoon orange zest
Juice of 1 lemon
Juice of 1 orange
Salt and freshly ground pepper to
   taste

Preheat the oven to 375°F.

Place the carrots, ginger ale, ginger, honey, orange zest, lemon juice, and orange juice in a large heavy-bottom ovenproof sauce pot, and bring to a boil.

Place the uncovered pot in the oven; bake for about 35 minutes, or until the liquid reduces, forming a sauce around the carrots. The carrots should be tender but still retain character. Season with the salt and pepper.

PER SERVING: CALORIES 70; CALORIES FROM FAT 0; CALORIES FROM SATURATED FAT 0; PROTEIN 1 G; CARBOHYDRATE 17 G; TOTAL FAT 0 G; SATURATED FAT 0 G; CHOLESTEROL 0 MG; SODIUM 35 MG; 0% CALORIES FROM FAT

"Eat with Your Fingers" Chinese Vegetable Garden

2 teaspoons canola or peanut oil

½ cup broccoli florets

½ cup sliced carrot (½-inch-thick pieces)

½ cup sliced celery (½-inch-thick pieces)

½ cup snow peas, ends snipped

½ cup sliced red pepper (½-inch-thick matchsticks)

¼ cup water chestnuts, sliced

I ear fresh cob corn, cut in 1-inch-thick wheels (optional)

2 teaspoons tamari or soy sauce

I teaspoon honey

Squeeze of lemon juice

HERE'S the perfect antidote for kids who think eating vegetables isn't entertaining. This dish is full of shapes and colors —and yes, kids can eat this with their fingers. Try mixing the cooked vegetables into noodles or couscous. You may also toss in cooked pieces of chicken, diced tofu, or shrimp.

Heat the canola or peanut oil in a large sauté pan or wok over moderate heat, and toss in the broccoli, carrot, celery, snow peas, red pepper, water chestnuts, and optional corn wheels, and stir constantly to prevent burning for 3 minutes, until the vegetables are firm but begin to cook.

Add the tamari and honey; continue to cook for a moment longer. Don't overcook the vegetables, which will keep them slightly crunchy and easy to hold. Squeeze the lemon over all, and serve.

PER SERVING: CALORIES 70; CALORIES FROM FAT 25; CALORIES FROM SATURATED FAT 0; PROTEIN 2 G; CARBOHYDRATE 12 G; TOTAL FAT 2.5 G; SATURATED FAT 0 G; CHOLESTEROL 0 MG; SODIUM 110 MG; 36% CALORIES FROM FAT

Three Dips and a Shrimp Stick

SERVES 4

MOST kids seem to like food on a stick. Use medium shrimp (21 to 25 per pound) for the skewers. If you prefer, serve these multipurpose dips with chicken or vegetable sticks. All three dips are very colorful, and kids (not unlike adults) enjoy the visual appeal of the bright pink, green, and yellow combination. Any of the dips are great with raw vegetables, as well. They may be made two days prior to serving and will keep for up to five days in the refrigerator.

TO PREPARE THE SPINACH DIP Heat the olive oil in a nonstick pan over medium heat. Add the onion, and sauté for 3 minutes, until well browned. Do not stir initially, to aid the browning process. Add the spinach, and continue to cook for a few more minutes. Transfer the mixture to a bowl, and cool completely. Add the yogurt, and combine well. Season with the salt and pepper.

TO PREPARE THE PINK DIP In a bowl, combine the yogurt, mayonnaise, ketchup, paprika, lemon juice, and hot pepper sauce. Mix well, and reserve in the refrigerator.

TO PREPARE THE HONEY-DIJON DIP In a bowl, combine the Dijon and whole-grain mustards, honey, mayonnaise, and lemon juice. Mix well, and reserve in the refrigerator.

TO PREPARE THE SHRIMP MARINADE Combine the olive oil, lemon juice, garlic, oregano, and parsley in a large bowl.

The Spinach Dip

2 teaspoons extra-virgin olive oil

1/2 small onion, chopped

1/2 cup frozen chopped spinach, thawed

1/2 cup plain yogurt

Salt and freshly ground white pepper to taste

The Pink Dip

1/3 cup plain yogurt

I tablespoon mayonnaise

I tablespoon ketchup

I teaspoon sweet paprika

I teaspoon lemon juice

Dash of hot pepper sauce

The Honey-Dijon Dip

I tablespoon Dijon mustard

I tablespoon whole-grain mustard

1/8 cup honey

1/4 cup mayonnaise

I teaspoon lemon juice

The Shrimp Marinade

1/2 tablespoon olive oil

I teaspoon lemon juice

I clove garlic, minced (1/2 teaspoon)

1/2 teaspoon dried oregano

I tablespoon minced parsley

I pound medium shrimp (21 to 25 per pound), peeled and tails left on

Place 4 to 6 shrimp on a wooden or metal skewer. Pour the marinade over the skewers, and marinate for 1 hour in the refrigerator. Brush the skewers with the marinade, and broil or grill over coals for 4 to 6 minutes on each side, until the shrimp are opaque and cooked through.

PER SERVING WITH SPINACH DIP: CALORIES 190; CALORIES FROM FAT 60; CALORIES FROM SATURATED FAT 10; PROTEIN 26 G; CARBOHYDRATE 6 G; TOTAL FAT 6 G; SATURATED FAT 1 G; CHOLESTEROL 175 MG; SODIUM 220 MG; 31% CALORIES FROM FAT

PER SERVING WITH PINK DIP: CALORIES 170; CALORIES FROM FAT 45; CALORIES FROM SATURATED FAT 10; PROTEIN 24 G; CARBOHYDRATE 4 G; TOTAL FAT 5 G; SATURATED FAT 1 G; CHOLESTEROL 175 MG; SODIUM 260 MG; 26% CALORIES FROM FAT

PER SERVING WITH HONEY-DIJON DIP: CALORIES 230; CALORIES FROM FAT 80; CALORIES FROM SATURATED FAT 15; PROTEIN 24 G; CARBOHYDRATE 13 G; TOTAL FAT 9 G; SATURATED FAT 1.5 G; CHOLESTEROL 170 MG; SODIUM 430 MG; 35% CALORIES FROM FAT

 Recipe Bonus Cut the bottom inch off a melon or grapefruit. Place the grilled shrimp sticks vertically into the melon or grapefruit placed with the cut side flat on a plate. Serve with small dishes of the dips and plenty of napkins.

Potato-Chip-Crusted Fish Bites

SERVES 3

CRUNCHY on the outside, moist and juicy on the inside, these fish bites will have your kids hooked at first bite. Try using tortilla chips for an alternative, and serve the fish bites with salsa. The potato-chip-crusted bites are great when served with Pink Dip (page 360).

The Potato Chip Crust

1 cup potato chips or tortilla chips, crushed

½ cup dried bread crumbs

1 tablespoon chopped parsley

The Egg Dip

¼ cup ketchup

1 tablespoon tamari or soy sauce (low sodium)

1 large egg, lightly beaten

½ pound firm fish such as tuna, salmon, cod, or halibut, cut into 1-inch cubes or fingers

½ cup unbleached all-purpose flour

Vegetable or olive oil for spraying pan

Preheat the oven to 450°F.

TO PREPARE THE POTATO CHIP CRUST In a medium pan or bowl, combine the crushed chips, bread crumbs, and parsley.

TO PREPARE THE EGG DIP In a small bowl or pan, mix together the ketchup, tamari, and egg.

Dredge the fish cubes lightly in the flour, shaking off all excess. Pass the fish pieces from the flour into the egg dip, and then lightly press the fish into the potato chip mixture, forming a coating around each piece. Place the fish pieces on a baking pan lightly sprayed with the vegetable oil, and bake for about 20 minutes, or until crispy and golden outside and cooked through.

PER SERVING: CALORIES 410; CALORIES FROM FAT 110; CALORIES FROM SATURATED FAT 30; PROTEIN 30 G; CARBOHYDRATE 45 G; TOTAL FAT 12 G; SATURATED FAT 3.5 G; CHOLESTEROL 115 MG; SODIUM 740 MG; 27% CALORIES FROM FAT

Hand to Mouth
Chicken Drumsticks

SERVES 6

The Marinade

1 cup plain yogurt

1/8 cup crunchy peanut butter, softened (see Note)

1/2 cup apricot juice

1 tablespoon tamari or soy sauce

6 chicken legs, skin removed

The Crunchy Crust

1 1/2 cups crushed corn flakes

1 tablespoon chopped parsley

1/2 teaspoon salt

1/4 teaspoon freshly ground white pepper

Vegetable or olive oil for spraying pan

THESE flavorful drumsticks go well with Orange Glazed Sweet Potato Oven Fries (page 356). You may marinate the chicken and store it in the refrigerator for up to two days before baking.

TO PREPARE THE MARINADE Combine the yogurt, softened peanut butter, apricot juice, and tamari in a bowl or plastic bag.

Add the chicken legs to the marinade, and allow them to marinate for at least 1 hour, or overnight in the refrigerator.

Preheat the oven to 375°F.

TO PREPARE THE CRUNCHY CRUST Combine the corn flakes, parsley, salt, and pepper in a bowl or plastic bag.

Remove the chicken legs from the marinade, and place them one at a time into the crust mixture, rolling them around to coat evenly. If using a bag, shake them around to coat. Place the chicken legs on a sheet pan lightly sprayed with oil. Bake for about 45 minutes, or until they are crunchy on the outside and cooked through. To test for doneness, stick the thickest portion of the chicken leg with a small knife or skewer. If the juice runs clear, the chicken is cooked. If the juice is pink, cook a few minutes longer.

NOTE: To soften peanut butter, allow it to stand at room temperature for about 1 hour. For faster results, place the peanut butter in a cup, and place for 30 seconds in a microwave on high.

PER SERVING: CALORIES 210; CALORIES FROM FAT 80; CALORIES FROM SATURATED FAT 20; PROTEIN 26 G; CARBOHYDRATE 6 G; TOTAL FAT 8 G; SATURATED FAT 2.5 G; CHOLESTEROL 90 MG; SODIUM 310 MG; 38% CALORIES FROM FAT

cooking with kids

363

Olé Turkey Tacos

SERVES 4

TURKEY taco filling is much lighter than traditional beef. The sweet onions and garden peppers simmered in this mixture add lots of flavor. If your kids are funny about these particular vegetables, you may make this recipe with just the turkey. A great way to throw a party for your children is to make a fiesta theme bash and serve the tacos with Orange Cashew Rice (page 174), broccoli florets, and carrot sticks with dip. Teach them a bit about other cultures through the food you serve.

⅛ cup canola or olive oil
1 pound ground turkey
½ small onion, chopped
½ green pepper, chopped
½ red pepper, chopped
1 clove garlic, minced (½ teaspoon)
1 tablespoon chili powder
1 teaspoon dried oregano, or
   1 tablespoon fresh
½ teaspoon cumin
1 tablespoon unsweetened cocoa
   powder
1 (15-ounce) can kidney beans, well
   rinsed and drained
8 ounces tomato sauce

Heat the canola or olive oil in a nonstick saucepan large enough to hold all the ingredients. Add the ground turkey, and sauté for 5 minutes, until cooked through. Add the onion, peppers, garlic, chili powder, oregano, cumin, and cocoa powder. Continue to cook for 3 minutes longer. Drain off any fat that has accumulated in the pan. Add the beans and tomato sauce. Simmer for about 20 minutes. The mixture should be of fillinglike consistency and hold up to a taco shell.

You may serve the filling with bowls of shredded lettuce, diced tomato, grated cheddar or soy cheese, and salsa. Supply taco shells, and everyone can fill his or her own.

PER SERVING: CALORIES 300; CALORIES FROM FAT 110; CALORIES FROM SATURATED FAT 25; PROTEIN 26 G; CARBOHYDRATE 22 G; TOTAL FAT 13 G; SATURATED FAT 3 G; CHOLESTEROL 90 MG; SODIUM 650 MG; 37% CALORIES FROM FAT

 Recipe Bonus For 3-bean filling, omit the turkey and use a mixture of equal parts kidney, black, and pinto beans. Or you may substitute 1 pound of diced firm tofu for the turkey and prepare following the same directions as above.

Ants on a Log

vegan

SERVES 8

4 stalks celery, well washed

1 cup peanut butter, creamy or crunchy

⅓ to ½ pound raisins

KIDS love to help in the kitchen, especially if what they're making is something they enjoy eating. This old favorite is better than ever these days when you can get organic peanut butter, raisins, and celery. Here's a tip: Try filling the logs using a small pastry bag or cake-decorating bag. Ants on a Log are great for kids to share with friends after school or at a party. Try other "insects" such as craisins, nuts, and small pieces of dried fruit.

Cut the celery into 3- to 4-inch "logs." An adult should do this cutting, but it's good to teach kids how important it is to wash fruits and veggies before eating. Turn the logs over to the kids and let them fill the hollow with peanut butter, and then top with raisin "ants."

PER SERVING: CALORIES 250; CALORIES FROM FAT 150; CALORIES FROM SATURATED FAT 30; PROTEIN 9 G; CARBOHYDRATE 21 G; TOTAL FAT 16 G; SATURATED FAT 3.5 G; CHOLESTEROL 0 MG; SODIUM 25 MG; 60% CALORIES FROM FAT

Olé Turkey Taco

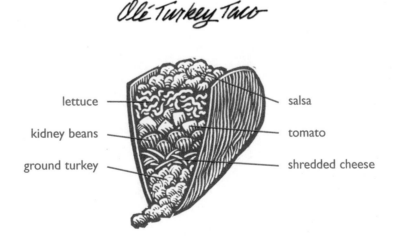

lettuce — salsa

kidney beans — tomato

ground turkey — shredded cheese

Open-Faced Apple Tahini Sandwich

SERVES 2

KIDS never seem to tire of this classic easy-to-make combination. Try Gala or Granny Smith apples, which go well with the nut butter. You may also want to try cinnamon raisin bread.

Core and cut the apple into approximately ⅛-inch slices. Spread your choice of nut butter on each slice of the bread. Lay the apple slices on the bread. Drizzle the tahini on top of the apple slices; then drizzle the honey. Sprinkle the cinnamon on top. Put the slices into a toaster oven, and toast on high. You may need to toast twice—watch the bread to prevent burning.

1 small apple (any variety, peeled or unpeeled)

1 teaspoon peanut, cashew, or almond butter

2 slices whole wheat or multigrain bread

1 tablespoon tahini

1 tablespoon honey or maple syrup to taste

¼ teaspoon cinnamon

PER SERVING: CALORIES 190; CALORIES FROM FAT 60; CALORIES FROM SATURATED FAT 10; PROTEIN 5 G; CARBOHYDRATE 31 G; TOTAL FAT 7 G; SATURATED FAT 1 G; CHOLESTEROL 0 MG; SODIUM 150 MG; 31% CALORIES FROM FAT

Sparkling Orange Gelled Dessert

SERVES 8

2 envelopes unflavored gelatin
($1/8$ cup)

$1/4$ cup cold water

$1 1/2$ cups plus $1/2$ cup orange juice

$1/3$ cup sugar

2 cups ginger ale

4 oranges, peeled and diced

8 strawberries, hulled and sliced, plus
more to garnish

8 sprigs fresh mint to garnish

GELATIN molds have been around for a long time. Our version is made with honest, natural ingredients and doesn't need to glow in the dark to be satisfying. Use any of your kids' favorite seasonal fruits. Try making this on a small dinner plate and have your children make faces with the cut fruit before chilling the dessert.

Sprinkle the gelatin over the cold water in a saucepan. Let it soften for 5 minutes; then heat it gently until the gelatin dissolves. Add the $1/2$ cup orange juice and the sugar. Warm gently until the sugar dissolves. Do not overheat. Place the remaining $1 1/2$ cups orange juice with the ginger ale in a large bowl, and whisk in the gelatin mixture.

Divide the oranges and berries among 8 small serving bowls or glasses. Spoon $1/2$ cup gelatin mixture into each bowl or glass. Allow the dessert to set in the refrigerator for a few hours. Garnish with extra berries and fresh mint.

PER SERVING: CALORIES 260; CALORIES FROM FAT 0; CALORIES FROM SATURATED FAT 0; PROTEIN 3 G; CARBOHYDRATE 65 G; TOTAL FAT 0 G; SATURATED FAT 0 G; CHOLESTEROL 0 MG; SODIUM 5 MG; 0% CALORIES FROM FAT

Chocolate Earth Balls

SERVES 4

THIS easy no-bake recipe makes a sweet and healthful treat for after school or in a lunch box. These rich morsels are like chocolate truffles for children. They offer lots of mouth appeal because they are chewy, crunchy, and smooth all at the same time. Kids can help make them and decorate with raisins and nuts to create their own planet!

1 cup peanut butter

⅓ cup clover or orange blossom honey

2 teaspoons carob powder or unsweetened cocoa powder

½ cup raisins

¾ cup unsweetened shredded coconut, divided

½ cup chocolate chips

¼ cup sesame seeds

¼ cup finely chopped nuts (walnuts or pecans work best)

Before measuring the peanut butter, stir it up well. Mix the peanut butter, honey, and carob powder until well combined. Stir in the raisins and only ⅛ cup of the coconut. Stir in the chocolate chips. Refrigerate for 1 to 2 hours.

Place the remaining coconut, sesame seeds, and nuts into 3 separate bowls. Using a spoon, scoop small heaps of the peanut mixture from the bowl; then roll into 1¼-inch balls. Rolling is easier if you form a rough ball, roll in the coconut, and then continue rolling into a more perfect shape. Roll each finished ball in more of the coconut and in the sesame seeds and chopped nuts. Arrange the balls on a plate, cover loosely with plastic wrap, and refrigerate for at least 30 minutes.

PER SERVING: CALORIES 790; CALORIES FROM FAT 480; CALORIES FROM SATURATED FAT 140; PROTEIN 23 G; CARBOHYDRATE 68 G; TOTAL FAT 53 G; SATURATED FAT 15 G; CHOLESTEROL 5 MG; SODIUM 55 MG; 61% CALORIES FROM FAT

Peanut Butter Play Dough

SERVES 6

1 cup peanut butter, creamy or
crunchy

½ cup honey

¾ to 1 cup powdered soy milk or
powdered milk

TRY this on picky eaters or just for the fun of it. It's like combining arts and crafts with snack time, and you and your children will enjoy the results. Play with it, shape it, and then eat it!

Mix the peanut butter and honey in a mixing bowl. Although it's not necessary, if you heat the mixture in a microwave for 25 seconds first, you may find it a little easier to shape. Gradually add the powdered milk and work it into the peanut butter with a spoon or wire whisk until it reaches the consistency of Play-Doh.

Once the peanut butter mixture is made, you may roll it into small shapes or flatten it with a rolling pin, and stamp out cookie cutter shapes and eat. Your kids will have their own ideas for constructing an edible work of art.

PER SERVING: CALORIES 370; CALORIES FROM FAT 200; CALORIES FROM SATURATED FAT 40; PROTEIN 14 G; CARBOHYDRATE 36 G; TOTAL FAT 22 G; SATURATED FAT 4.5 G; CHOLESTEROL 0 MG; SODIUM 55 MG; 54% CALORIES FROM FAT

cooking with kids

Vegan

Watermelon Spritzer with Free-Form Frozen Fruit

SERVES 8 TO 10

THIS great party drink is easy to make and entertaining for the kids. Honestly, grown-ups will be bobbing for the refreshing frozen watermelon shapes that float in this sparkling beverage, as well. Slice watermelon either from a whole small melon or across a halved melon for greatest surface area.

3 (1-inch) slices seedless watermelon, cut across a small whole melon
2 bottles watermelon juice, chilled
½ bottle sparkling water, chilled

The night before serving, use cookie cutters to stamp out some fun shapes from the seedless watermelon. Place these assorted shapes of watermelon on a plate in the freezer overnight. The frozen melon will act as edible ice cubes. When you are ready to serve, combine the chilled watermelon juice and sparkling water in a clear punch bowl, and drop in the frozen watermelon shapes. You may add other frozen fruits such as seedless grapes, strawberries, raspberries, or blueberries.

PER 1½-CUP SERVING: CALORIES 80; CALORIES FROM FAT 10; CALORIES FROM SATURATED FAT 0; PROTEIN 2 G; CARBOHYDRATE 19 G; TOTAL FAT 1 G; SATURATED FAT 0 G; CHOLESTEROL 0 MG; SODIUM 15 MG; 12% CALORIES FROM FAT

Creative Lunch Box 101

It's difficult to be inspired each day when making box lunches for school. Here are some simple tips and creative ideas to help you beat the box lunch blues.

- Cinnamon raisin pita bread stuffed with cream cheese and grated carrots
- Whole wheat bread with peanut butter, banana, and chopped dates
- Toasted English muffin or bagel with a drop of marinara sauce and melted Swiss, cheddar, or mozzarella cheese (additional toppings of your choice)
- Hollowed red or green pepper stuffed with tuna salad (don't forget a plastic fork)
- Celery stuffed with peanut butter or cream cheese, rolled in sliced almonds (a piping bag works well for this)
- A hollowed apple filled with a mixture of farmer cheese, granola, and raisins
- Scooped-out dinner rolls filled with tuna or egg salad—these resemble a savory stuffed jelly roll doughnut
- Thinly sliced turkey or turkey bologna wrapped around cheese sticks, dill pickles, or carrot sticks
- Small bunches of frozen grapes
- Cooked pasta shapes tossed with cubes of cheese—try cooked alphabet noodles for added fun
- Utilize small plastic soufflé cups (available in party stores or supermarkets) that hold approximately 2 ounces of salsa, ranch dressing, peanut butter, or tahini. They can be sealed with a lid and are leakproof. Serve these with raw vegetable skewers or sticks, chips, bread rounds, or crackers.
- Leftover quesadillas cut into small wedges make a great lunch treat.
- Frozen juice boxes help cool down your child's lunch box. Juice will normally be ready to drink by lunchtime.

Desserts

RUM-PAINTED PINEAPPLE ORANGE BUNDT CAKE ♠ CHOCOLATE ANGEL FOOD CAKE ♠ MIXED NUT AND FLAX SEED BAKLAVA ♠ CINNAMON STREUSEL COFFEE CAKE WITH DRIED BLUEBERRIES ♠ THE NUTCRACKER SWEET CHEESECAKE ♠ LABOR OF LOVE CHEESECAKE ♠ NECTARINE BLUEBERRY JOHNNYCAKE ♠ MAPLE BAKED PEARS OR APPLES WITH ROLLED OAT CRUST ♠ STRAWBERRY COBBLER ♠ PUMPKIN BREAD PUDDING ♠ LEMON LIME BARS ♠ MAPLE BUTTERSCOTCH MACADAMIA BLONDIES ♠ UNBAKED BROWNIES ♠ RASPBERRY ESPRESSO POTS DE CRÈME ♠ FRAGRANT SPICED FUJI APPLE PIE ♠ PEAR BURRITOS ♠ SILKEN TOFU CHOCOLATE MOUSSE ♠ BALSAMIC BERRY DESSERT TOPPING

Some say the dessert is the most important part of a

meal, but not because our culture has an incurable sweet tooth. Dessert is the last morsel of food in our mouths at the end of a meal. It's our taste buds' final remembrance. It is also the area where many of us allow self-indulgence, something of a reward for eating smart in our daily lives. If we make intelligent meal choices on a regular basis, we may reward ourselves with a bit of decadence. That's not to say that all desserts need to be rich and sinful. Again, it's about choices and personal taste. A sweet ending can be as light as a cinnamon-and orange-spiked Pear Burrito (page 392) or as devilish as a rich cream cheese cake (page 381). It may also be as simple as a perfectly ripe wedge of melon.

Most of our desserts are home-style, accessible, and comforting in character. They include a wide spectrum ranging from fruit-based desserts and ice cream toppings to old-fashioned lemon bars (page 386), brownies (page 388), and tart Fuji apple pie (page 390). We've taken a few favorites like baklava and added a new twist by using a variety of nuts, not just the traditional pistachios, and our baked apples (page 383) are encrusted with a crunchy rolled oat and cinnamon crust.

Whole Foods Market's shelves feature many varieties of alternative whole-grain flours, sweeteners, and nondairy beverages that may be incorporated into your desserts (see "Whole Foods Glossary," page 395). We'll even show you how to whip up a rich chocolate mousse from silken tofu . . . really. That's why we offer you choices. Some of our recipes are traditional, and others use products that may not be a part of your pantry (before now, that is). One thing is for sure, they are all brimming with flavor.

It's a good idea to have all your ingredients measured, scooped, and portioned in front of you before you begin to create your dessert. Baking involves much more chemistry and science than the intuitive process of cooking. Also, your oven must be preheated to ensure accurate baking.

Rum-Painted Pineapple Orange Bundt Cake

MAKES 1 (10½-INCH) BUNDT CAKE (SERVES 12)

½ pound (2 sticks) butter, softened

3 cups granulated sugar

6 large eggs

3 cups unbleached all-purpose flour

¼ teaspoon baking soda

½ teaspoon salt

1 cup sour cream

½ cup fresh ripe pineapple, chopped
   very well

1 teaspoon vanilla extract

2 teaspoons orange extract

2 teaspoons grated orange zest

The Rum Paint

¼ pound (1 stick) butter

⅛ cup sugar

¼ cup rum

LIGHT and moist, this citrus cake soaks in the syrupy "rum paint," which gives it a tropical flavor. You may use unsweetened canned crushed pineapple instead of the fresh fruit if you choose. Only use a fresh pineapple if it's really ripe.

Preheat the oven to 325°F. Grease and flour a 10½-inch Bundt cake pan. In a large bowl with an electric mixer, cream the butter and sugar until they're light and fluffy, 1 to 2 minutes. Add the eggs, one at a time, beating well after each addition.

In a small bowl, sift the flour, baking soda, and salt together. In another small bowl, combine the sour cream, pineapple, vanilla, orange extract, and orange zest until well mixed. By hand, add some of the sour cream mixture to the butter mixture alternately with the sour cream mixture, blending well after each addition, until all the flour and sour cream mixtures have been added and the batter is well blended.

Bake for 1 hour and 10 minutes, until a toothpick inserted in the center comes out clean. Cool for about 1 hour.

TO PREPARE THE RUM PAINT In a small saucepan, over medium heat, melt the butter with the sugar and rum until the sugar is dissolved. Cook over medium-high heat for 2 to 3 minutes, until the mixture is slightly syrupy.

With a wide pastry brush, paint the mixture onto all surfaces of the cooled cake, repeating until all the rum paint has been used.

PER SERVING: CALORIES 610; CALORIES FROM FAT 270; CALORIES FROM SATURATED FAT 160; PROTEIN 7 G; CARBOHYDRATE 77 G; TOTAL FAT 30 G; SATURATED FAT 17 G; CHOLESTEROL 180 MG; SODIUM 150 MG; 44% CALORIES FROM FAT

desserts

375

vegetarian

Chocolate Angel Food Cake

MAKES 1 (10-INCH) CAKE (SERVES 8)

THIS perfect combination of dark chocolate and slightly bitter orange speaks vibrantly in this light and airy angel food Bundt cake. Serve a slice drizzled with melted chocolate and some fresh orange slices.

1 plus ¼ cup granulated sugar

1 cup unbleached all-purpose flour

½ teaspoon salt

12 large egg whites

1 tablespoon lemon juice

1 tablespoon vanilla extract

1 tablespoon grated orange zest

⅛ cup orange liqueur such as triple sec (optional)

1 (3½-ounce) dark chocolate bar, grated

Preheat the oven to 350°F.

Sift about ¼ cup of the sugar with the flour and the salt. Repeat twice. In another bowl, on the medium-high speed of an electric mixer, beat the egg whites until they're frothy. Add the lemon juice, and beat until soft peaks form. Gradually sprinkle the remaining cup sugar evenly over the egg whites, ¼ cup at a time, beating at medium speed for 1 to 2 minutes. Sift some of the flour mixture over the whites and gently fold it in, using a flexible spatula. Add the vanilla and orange zest. If using liqueur, add now. Alternately, fold in the remaining flour mixture and the grated chocolate until well blended, using gentle strokes to avoid deflating the egg whites.

Carefully pour the batter into an ungreased 1-inch angel food or Bundt pan. Bake until the cake is lightly browned and a knife inserted near the center comes out clean, 40 to 45 minutes. Remove the cake from the oven, and invert the pan over the neck of a bottle to cool for 30 to 45 minutes. This will hasten the cooling process, as the cake pan will be suspended in air without resting on a countertop. Run a knife around the edges of the pan to loosen and remove the cake from the pan.

PER SERVING: CALORIES 290; CALORIES FROM FAT 40; CALORIES FROM SATURATED FAT 25; PROTEIN 7 G; CARBOHYDRATE 52 G; TOTAL FAT 4 G; SATURATED FAT 2.5 G; CHOLESTEROL 0 MG; SODIUM 200 MG; 14% CALORIES FROM FAT

 Tip from the Team: Here is a general "rule of thumb" for high-altitude baking: Slightly decrease sugar, increase oven temperature by 10 to 20 degrees, slightly increase liquid, and slightly increase flour.

Mixed Nut and Flax Seed Baklava

vegetarian

SERVES 15

1 cup chopped cashews

1 cup chopped walnuts

2 cups chopped pistachios

1 cup flax seeds, whole

¼ cup granulated sugar

1 tablespoon essence of rosewater
    (available in Middle Eastern
    grocery stores)

¾ plus ¼ cup melted butter

1 (1-pound) package frozen phyllo
    dough, thawed

The Syrup

3 cups granulated sugar

1½ cups water

⅛ cup lemon juice

TRADITIONALLY made exclusively with pistachios, a variety of nuts gives this baklava an unusual twist and added flavor. Rosewater, a fragrant liquid extract made from rose petals, adds a floral bouquet. You can make the baklava without it if you wish. Both whole wheat or regular phyllo dough may be used.

Preheat the oven to 300°F. Place the cashews, walnuts, pistachios, and flax seeds in a medium bowl. Stir in the sugar and rosewater until well combined.

Brush the bottom of a 9 × 13-inch baking dish with about ¼ cup of the melted butter. Working with 8 sheets of phyllo dough at a time, brush each sheet with a thin coating of melted butter, and carefully stack the sheets on top of each other in the baking dish. When all 8 sheets are in the dish, top with half of the nut mixture.

Brush 8 more sheets of the phyllo dough with the melted butter, and carefully top with the remaining nut mixture. Brush the remaining 8 sheets of the phyllo dough and stack over the nut layer.

With a very sharp knife, cut the baklava into diamond shapes. Wipe the edges of the pan with a damp cloth to clean off any excess butter. Bake for about 1 hour, or until golden brown. Remove from the oven and cool.

TO PREPARE THE SYRUP While the baklava is cooling, combine the sugar, water, and lemon juice in a large saucepan. Bring the syrup to a boil, stirring often; then reduce the heat to medium-low. Cook uncovered, without stirring, until a candy thermometer registers 212° to 218°F., or when syrup dropped from a metal spoon drizzles slowly into thin ribbons. Remove the pan from the heat. Cool.

Pour the cooled syrup evenly over the top of the baklava until all the syrup has been absorbed by the phyllo. Cool for at least 4 hours before serving.

PER SERVING: CALORIES 560; CALORIES FROM FAT 280; CALORIES FROM SATURATED FAT 90; PROTEIN 8 G; CARBOHYDRATE 68 G; TOTAL FAT 31 G; SATURATED FAT 10 G; CHOLESTEROL 35 MG; SODIUM 150 MG; 50% CALORIES FROM FAT

desserts

377

Cinnamon Streusel Coffee Cake with Dried Blueberries

SERVES 10

LIGHT and well spiced with aromatic cinnamon, this coffee cake may be served at any time of day. Feel free to substitute dried cranberries or cherries for the blueberries.

I plus ½ cup granulated sugar
I tablespoon cinnamon
¼ pound (I stick) butter, softened
2 large eggs
I teaspoon vanilla extract
I tablespoon lemon juice
2 cups unbleached all-purpose flour
I teaspoon baking soda
I teaspoon salt
½ teaspoon baking powder
½ pint sour cream
I cup dried blueberries or other dried fruit

In a small bowl, blend the ½ cup sugar with the cinnamon.

Preheat the oven to 350°F. Butter a 9 × 9 × 2-inch pan.

In a medium bowl, cream the butter with the remaining cup of sugar with an electric mixer until fluffy and light in color, about 2 minutes. Blend in the eggs. Add the vanilla and lemon juice. In a third bowl, sift the flour with the baking soda, salt, and baking powder. By hand, add some of the flour mixture to the butter mixture alternately with the sour cream, blending well after each addition, until all the flour and sour cream have been added. Stir in the blueberries.

Pour half of the batter into the prepared pan. Sprinkle with half of the sugar-cinnamon mixture. Pour the remaining batter into the pan, and sprinkle with the remaining sugar-cinnamon mixture. Bake for about 35 minutes, or until the cake tests done. Test the cake for doneness by inserting a wooden or metal skewer in the center. When the cake is done, the skewer will be dry when removed and won't show any sign of wet batter. Serve warm for the best flavor. You may reheat chilled pieces of the cake the following day by heating for 30 seconds in a microwave.

PER SERVING: CALORIES 430; CALORIES FROM FAT 140; CALORIES FROM SATURATED FAT 90; PROTEIN 6 G; CARBOHYDRATE 72 G; TOTAL FAT 16 G; SATURATED FAT 9 G; CHOLESTEROL 80 MG; SODIUM 370 MG; 32% CALORIES FROM FAT

Tip from the Team: Applesauce can replace some of the oil or butter in baked goods recipes. For example, when making chocolate chip cookies that call for 1 cup of melted butter, use $\frac{1}{2}$ cup applesauce and $\frac{1}{2}$ cup butter. Not only is it a lower-fat, heart-healthy option, this is an easy way to convert many baking recipes to vegan!

Sifting Flour

BECAUSE baking involves much more chemistry and accuracy in measurement than any other cooking process, it is essential that all ingredients be measured carefully. One cup of sifted flour weighs 4 ounces, while 1 cup of unsifted flour weighs 5 ounces. This is another reason why bakers weigh ingredients instead of measuring— it's much more accurate.

The Nutcracker Sweet Cheesecake

MAKES 1 (9-INCH) CHEESECAKE (SERVES 8)

ROASTED nuts, coconut, and chocolate make this a very intense cheesecake.

TO PREPARE THE CRUST Preheat the oven to 350°F. In a medium bowl, blend the butter with the graham crackers, almond extract, and chopped almonds. Press onto the bottom of a 9-inch springform pan. Bake the crust for 10 minutes. Remove the pan from the oven. Reduce the oven temperature to 325°F.

TO PREPARE THE FILLING In a medium bowl, beat the eggs with the sour cream, vanilla, almond extract, and salt. Set aside. In a large bowl, with an electric mixer, blend the cream cheese with the sugar until well combined. Stir in the reserved egg mixture. Stir in the coconut and chocolate chips.

Pour the filling into the prepared pan, and bake for 1 hour and 10 minutes, until set. Remove from the oven, and cool at room temperature for 45 minutes. Place in the refrigerator, and chill for at least 6 hours.

TO PREPARE THE CHOCOLATE ICING After the cheesecake has chilled, place the chocolate chips in a small bowl. In a small saucepan, heat the half and half just to boiling. Immediately remove the saucepan from the heat, and pour the half and half over the chocolate chips. Allow to sit for 1 minute, without stirring. Stir with a spoon until the chocolate and cream are smooth.

Frost the top and sides of the cheesecake with the icing. Decorate the cake with the toasted whole almonds. Refrigerate until the chocolate has set.

PER SERVING: CALORIES 940; CALORIES FROM FAT 520; CALORIES FROM SATURATED FAT 270; PROTEIN 18 G; CARBOHYDRATE 87 G; TOTAL FAT 58 G; SATURATED FAT 30 G; CHOLESTEROL 170 MG; SODIUM 580 MG; 55% CALORIES FROM FAT

The Crust

6 tablespoons butter, melted

1½ cups crushed graham crackers

⅛ cup almond extract or almond liqueur

¼ cup slivered almonds, toasted and finely chopped

The Filling

3 large eggs

1½ cups sour cream

1 teaspoon vanilla extract

⅛ cup almond extract or almond liqueur

½ teaspoon salt

3 (8-ounce) packages cream cheese or Neufchâtel, softened

¾ cup sugar

1 cup shredded unsweetened coconut

1 cup semisweet chocolate chips

The Chocolate Icing

1½ cups semisweet chocolate chips

⅓ cup half and half

¾ cup whole almonds, toasted

Labor of Love Cheesecake

¼ pound (1 stick) butter, melted

2 cups graham cracker crumbs

1½ teaspoons cinnamon

½ teaspoon ground nutmeg

4 large eggs, separated

1½ cups plus 1 cup sour cream

½ cup granulated sugar

⅔ cup packed light or dark brown sugar

½ teaspoon salt

2 teaspoons vanilla extract

3 (8-ounce) packages cream cheese, softened

THIS is one of those creamy, dreamy, velvety cheesecakes. Just a small piece is rich and satisfying. Serve it with sliced seasonal fruits such as berries, peaches, pears, or kiwi. You may also use reduced-fat cream cheese and sour cream for this cheesecake.

In a small bowl, blend the melted butter, graham cracker crumbs, cinnamon, and nutmeg until well combined. Press the mixture into the bottom and slightly up the sides of a 9-inch springform pan. Refrigerate the crust for 1 hour.

Preheat the oven to 325°F. In a medium bowl, beat the egg yolks with an electric mixer, until thick. Add 1 cup of the sour cream, half the granulated sugar, the brown sugar, salt, and vanilla, and mix until well combined. Blend in the cream cheese, one package at a time, until creamy and smooth.

In a separate bowl, beat the egg whites with an electric mixer, until foamy, for 1 to 2 minutes. Using a spoon or spatula, stir the egg whites into the cream cheese mixture until combined, and pour into the prepared pan. Bake for about 1 hour, or until the cheesecake is set. Remove from the oven and cool for 1 hour. Refrigerate overnight.

Just before serving, blend the remaining granulated sugar and sour cream, and spread them over the top of the cheesecake.

PER SERVING: CALORIES 650; CALORIES FROM FAT 330; CALORIES FROM SATURATED FAT 190; PROTEIN 17 G; CARBOHYDRATE 64 G; TOTAL FAT 37 G; SATURATED FAT 22 G; CHOLESTEROL 210 MG; SODIUM 660 MG; 51% CALORIES FROM FAT

desserts

vegetarian

Nectarine Blueberry Johnnycake

SERVES 8

JOHNNYCAKES originated back in the 1700s, long before the onset of the pancake. They were traditionally made from a corn dough, which was unleavened and cooked on a griddle. This modern version is lighter and fluffier than the original. Serve warm for the best flavor.

6 cups pitted and sliced nectarines or peaches (¼-inch-thick pieces)
1 pint blueberries or blackberries
¼ cup sugar, or to taste

The Cornmeal Biscuit
1½ cups unbleached all-purpose flour
½ cup medium-grain cornmeal
3 tablespoons sugar
1 tablespoon baking powder
½ teaspoon baking soda
1 teaspoon salt
4 tablespoons (½ stick) cold butter, cut into 12 pieces
1¼ to 1½ cups heavy cream or milk

Preheat the oven to 375°F.

In a small bowl, toss the fruit with the sugar. Set aside.

TO PREPARE THE CORNMEAL BISCUIT In the bowl of a food processor fitted with a metal blade place the flour, cornmeal, sugar, baking powder, baking soda, and salt. Pulse a few times to mix. Add the butter, and pulse in short spurts just until there are no butter lumps remaining and the mixture resembles coarse meal.

Place the cornmeal mixture in a large bowl, and with a large spoon make a well in the center. Pour 1¼ cups of the heavy cream or milk into the well. With a fork, mix the ingredients into the cream, blending well but taking care not to overmix. If necessary, add more cream to moisten the batter.

Place the fruit in a 10-inch pie pan. Top with the cornmeal mixture, spreading the batter out evenly to cover all the fruit. Place the pan on a baking sheet, and bake for 30 to 45 minutes, until the mixture is bubbly and the biscuit is a light golden brown.

PER SERVING: CALORIES 300; CALORIES FROM FAT 70; CALORIES FROM SATURATED FAT 40; PROTEIN 6 G; CARBOHYDRATE 54 G; TOTAL FAT 8 G; SATURATED FAT 4 G; CHOLESTEROL 20 MG; SODIUM 620 MG; 23% CALORIES FROM FAT

Tip from the Team: To get a light, airy biscuit, after adding the liquid ingredients handle the dough gently and as little as possible. Stir in the liquid quickly to moisten, turn out the dough onto a floured board, and gather together. Gently pat out with your hands and cut. Too much handling will spoil the height!

Maple Baked Pears or Apples with Rolled Oat Crust

SERVES 8

4 medium pears or apples
1 teaspoon lemon juice

½ cup maple syrup
¼ pound (1 stick) plus 2 tablespoons
  butter, melted

1 cup rolled oats
½ cup unbleached all-purpose flour
1 cup firmly packed brown sugar
1 teaspoon cinnamon

NUTRITIOUS, sweet rolled oats combine with brown sugar to form a crispy nutty crust over apples or pears. You may use this crust over summer fruits, as well, following the same recipe. Make sure to use only rolled oats that are the steamed, slightly flattened whole oat groats. They are full of flavor and retain a comforting texture that cut oats won't have.

Preheat the oven to 375°F.

Cut the unpeeled pears or apples in half, and remove and discard the seeds and stems. Cut into ½-inch-thick slices. Place the fruit in a large bowl, and toss with the lemon juice.

Place the pears or apples in a 9 × 12-inch baking dish. Pour the maple syrup and the 2 tablespoons melted butter over the sliced fruit, and gently mix in with a fork.

In a medium bowl, combine the oats, flour, brown sugar, cinnamon, and remaining melted butter. Mix with a fork until crumbly. Sprinkle over the fruit. Bake uncovered for 45 minutes, until the crust is golden brown and the fruit is tender. Serve warm for best flavor.

PER SERVING: CALORIES 400; CALORIES FROM FAT 140; CALORIES FROM SATURATED FAT 80; PROTEIN 3 G; CARBOHYDRATE 66 G; TOTAL FAT 15 G; SATURATED FAT 9 G; CHOLESTEROL 40 MG; SODIUM 15 MG; 35% CALORIES FROM FAT

 Recipe Bonus At holiday time, give this dish a celebratory flair by mixing 1 (16-ounce) can of whole cranberry sauce to the cut fresh fruit before baking. If you like nuts, add ½ cup chopped pecans or walnuts to the oatmeal crumb mixture before baking.

desserts

383

vegetarian

Strawberry Cobbler

SERVES 8

ALTHOUGH no one really knows the true origin of this dessert's name, it's thought to have been created because the rustic crust that encases fresh seasonal fruit looks like a cobblestone street when baked. Some cobblers are crusted with more of a biscuit dough, but ours is a bit softer. Cobblers can be made in dishes of any shape. Use one of your favorite old ceramic crocks if it's the right size. You may add some spices such as cinnamon, cardamom, nutmeg, or allspice to the fruit. Vanilla rounds out the flavor of berries, as well.

The Dough

1¾ cups unbleached all-purpose flour

1 teaspoon salt

1 tablespoon baking powder

⅛ cup sugar

6 tablespoons cold butter

¾ cup milk

The Filling

2 quarts strawberries, stemmed and
   cut in half

1 cup sugar

⅓ cup unbleached all-purpose flour

1 teaspoon salt

½ cup water or apple juice

3 tablespoons lemon juice

⅛ cup brown sugar

2 tablespoons butter

P reheat the oven to 400°F.

TO PREPARE THE DOUGH Combine the flour, salt, baking powder, and sugar in a medium bowl. Cut in the cold butter by hand or in the bowl of a food processor fitted with a metal blade, until the mixture is the consistency of coarse sand. Add the milk, and process just until a ball is formed. Refrigerate the dough.

TO PREPARE THE FILLING Place the strawberries in a large bowl.

In a small bowl, combine the sugar, flour, and salt. Slowly whisk in the water and lemon juice, and stir into the strawberries. Place the mixture in a 9 × 9-inch glass baking dish. Bake for about 15 minutes, or until the fruit bubbles. Stir once. Remove from the oven.

Using your fingers, pinch off pieces of the dough about the size of half-dollars and ¼ inch thick. Place the dough on top of the hot berries, covering the entire surface. Sprinkle with the brown sugar; dot with the butter. Return the cobbler to the oven, and bake for 30 minutes, until golden brown.

PER SERVING: CALORIES 400; CALORIES FROM FAT 120; CALORIES FROM SATURATED FAT 70; PROTEIN 5 G; CARBOHYDRATE 67 G; TOTAL FAT 13 G; SATURATED FAT 8 G; CHOLESTEROL 35 MG; SODIUM 670 MG; 30% CALORIES FROM FAT

Pumpkin Bread Pudding

SERVES 15

5 cups canned puréed pumpkin

2 large whole eggs plus 2 large egg yolks

3 cups half and half

¼ cup packed dark brown sugar

1¼ cups granulated sugar

¾ teaspoon cinnamon

¼ teaspoon ground nutmeg

¼ teaspoon cardamom (optional)

⅛ cup water

¾ plus ¼ cup heavy whipping cream

10 cups 2-inch cubes of slightly sweet soft whole wheat bread or challah

WITH a consistency between a pudding and loaf, this is a dense, sweet, and spice-filled dessert. Pumpkin bread pudding is wonderful warm or chilled, and it may be served in a wedge or square with whipped cream, vanilla, or cinnamon ice cream. Sliced pears tossed in a bit of lemon juice and orange liqueur would also be a delicious topping.

Preheat the oven to 350°F.

In a large bowl, mix the pumpkin with all the eggs, the half and half, brown sugar, ¼ cup of the granulated sugar, cinnamon, nutmeg, and optional cardamom.

In a small saucepan, combine the water and the remaining 1 cup sugar, and place on high heat. As the sugar melts, swirl the pan often to ensure even melting. Do not stir with a spoon, because it will slow the melting process and cause uneven browning. Cook for 3 to 4 minutes, until the sugar has a deep caramel color, and remove from the heat.

Carefully whisk about ¼ cup of the heavy cream into the caramel, stirring until well combined. Whisk in the remaining cream.

Pour the caramel mixture into a 2½-quart oblong casserole dish. Add half the bread cubes on top of the caramel. Pour in half the pumpkin mixture. Top with the remaining bread and then the remaining pumpkin mixture, making sure to soak all the bread. Allow to sit for 30 minutes. Bake in the oven for 30 to 45 minutes, until set.

PER SERVING: CALORIES 320; CALORIES FROM FAT 120; CALORIES FROM SATURATED FAT 70; PROTEIN 7 G; CARBOHYDRATE 43 G; TOTAL FAT 14 G; SATURATED FAT 8 G; CHOLESTEROL 95 MG; SODIUM 170 MG; 37% CALORIES FROM FAT

 Recipe Bonus Don't care for pumpkin? Try substituting cooked hubbard or acorn squash for the pumpkin in this recipe. If you don't feel like cooking the squash, it's normally available precooked in the frozen food section of the grocery store.

desserts

vegetarian

Lemon Lime Bars

MAKES 18 BARS

WHEN we first put out the call for favorite desserts, several versions of old-fashioned lemon bars arrived. We selected a few, spun them together, and came up with the best of lemon and lime in one bar. These bars are tart and satisfying.

2 cups unbleached all-purpose flour, sifted, plus 1/4 cup

1/2 cup powdered sugar

1/2 pound (2 sticks) butter

4 large eggs, beaten

2 cups granulated sugar

3 tablespoons lemon juice

3 tablespoons lime juice

1 teaspoon grated lemon zest

1 teaspoon grated lime zest

1 teaspoon baking powder

Powdered sugar for dusting

Preheat the oven to 350°F. Sift the 2 cups sifted flour and powdered sugar together. Cut the butter into the flour and sugar until the mixture looks like coarse meal. Press into a 13 × 9 × 2-inch pan. Bake for about 20 minutes, or until lightly browned. Remove the pan from the oven.

In a medium bowl, beat the eggs, granulated sugar, and lemon and lime juices and zests for 1 to 2 minutes, until frothy. Sift the remaining 1/4 cup flour and baking powder together, and stir it into the egg mixture. Pour over the baked crust. Bake for 20 to 25 minutes, until set. Remove from the oven, and allow it to cool. Sift the additional powdered sugar over the top, and cut the lemon-lime dessert into squares.

PER SERVING: CALORIES 260; CALORIES FROM FAT 100; CALORIES FROM SATURATED FAT 60; PROTEIN 3 G; CARBOHYDRATE 38 G; TOTAL FAT 11 G; SATURATED FAT 7 G; CHOLESTEROL 75 MG; SODIUM 45 MG; 38% CALORIES FROM FAT

 Tip from the Team: To keep your homemade cookies moist, tear bread slices (any kind) in quarters and lay them on top of your cookies in an airtight container (approximately 3 slices per dozen). The bread will soak up the air and become extremely hard, and the cookies will become ultimately moist.

Maple Butterscotch Macadamia Blondies

MAKES 12

¾ cup chopped macadamia nuts

1½ cups unbleached all-purpose flour

1 teaspoon baking powder

½ teaspoon salt

1½ sticks butter, softened

1 cup packed light brown sugar

⅔ cup granulated sugar

2 large eggs

1½ teaspoons maple extract

1½ cups butterscotch chips

THINK of these as a kinder, gentler brownie. Macadamia nuts are so buttery and rich, they make a perfect partner to the creamy flavor of butterscotch. You won't miss chocolate in this version.

Preheat the oven to 350°F. Place the macadamia nuts on a baking sheet, and roast them until they are nicely toasted, 4 to 6 minutes. Remove them from the oven.

Grease a 9-inch square cake pan. In a medium bowl, stir the flour, baking powder, and salt with a fork to blend. In another bowl, blend the butter, brown sugar, and granulated sugar with an electric mixer on medium speed until light and fluffy, 2 to 3 minutes. Beat in the eggs and maple extract. By hand, stir in the flour mixture until just combined. Stir in the butterscotch chips and toasted macadamias. Pour the batter into the prepared pan, spreading it evenly. Bake for 50 to 60 minutes, until golden brown. Cool, and cut into squares.

PER SERVING: CALORIES 480; CALORIES FROM FAT 260; CALORIES FROM SATURATED FAT 120; PROTEIN 4 G; CARBOHYDRATE 52 G; TOTAL FAT 29 G; SATURATED FAT 13 G; CHOLESTEROL 65 MG; SODIUM 160 MG; 54% CALORIES FROM FAT

Unbaked Brownies

MAKES 16 (2-INCH) SQUARES

THIS unbaked brownie is rich without containing chocolate. This very simple recipe has a velvet texture when chilled. For an alternative to square brownies, after blending in the coconut and sesame seeds, form the mixture into balls and roll each ball in chopped peanuts or pecans, sesame seeds, or coconut.

1 cup creamy or smooth peanut butter
1 cup honey
1 cup soy powder
1 cup noninstant dry milk powder
1 cup flaked unsweetened coconut
1 cup sesame seeds

In a large saucepan, over medium heat, melt the peanut butter with the honey, stirring often. Remove from the heat as soon as the peanut butter has melted. Add the soy powder, and stir well. Stir in the dry milk powder until well combined. Blend in the coconut and the sesame seeds.

Spread the mixture into an 8 × 8-inch baking pan. Refrigerate until firm, about 2 hours. Cut into 2-inch squares.

PER SERVING: CALORIES 280; CALORIES FROM FAT 150; CALORIES FROM SATURATED FAT 40; PROTEIN 15 G; CARBOHYDRATE 26 G; TOTAL FAT 16 G; SATURATED FAT 4.5 G; CHOLESTEROL 10 MG; SODIUM 100 MG; 53% CALORIES FROM FAT

Raspberry Espresso Pots de Crème

SERVES 6

3 tablespoons ground espresso beans

2 cups half and half

½ cup sugar

1 tablespoon seedless raspberry jam

6 large egg yolks, beaten lightly with a fork

1 tablespoon raspberry liqueur

CREAMY custardlike texture flavored with espresso and berries.... What more can we say? There are a lot of options to explore with this silken dessert. You may substitute dairy, oat, or rice milk for the half and half. Try adding some fresh raspberries to the serving dishes before pouring in the custard mix. You may also add a few tablespoons of melted chocolate to the custard.

Place the espresso beans, half and half, and sugar in a small saucepan. Over medium-high heat, bring to just underneath a boil, but do not let the mixture actually boil, stirring occasionally. Remove from the heat. Cover and cool for 45 minutes.

Preheat the oven to 350°F.

Pour the mixture through a cheesecloth or fine sieve. Discard the coffee grounds. Stir the raspberry jam into the cream mixture. Return the cream mixture to the heat, and heat to scalding, stirring occasionally. Remove from the heat, and, using a fork, slowly beat the cream mixture into the beaten egg yolks. Stir in the liqueur. Strain the mixture through a fine sieve into 6 ½-cup oven-safe serving dishes. Cover each dish with aluminum foil.

Place the dishes in a shallow baking pan and pour 1 inch of boiling water into the pan. Bake for about 25 minutes, or until the center of the custard just slightly jiggles when shaken. Immediately remove from the hot water, remove the lids (saving the foil), and cool.

When cooled, re-cover each dish with the reserved foil, and refrigerate until ready to serve.

PER SERVING: CALORIES 250; CALORIES FROM FAT 130; CALORIES FROM SATURATED FAT 70; PROTEIN 6 G; CARBOHYDRATE 24 G; TOTAL FAT 14 G; SATURATED FAT 7 G; CHOLESTEROL 240 MG; SODIUM 40 MG; 52% CALORIES FROM FAT

desserts

Fragrant Spiced Fuji Apple Pie

MAKES 1 (9-INCH) PIE (SERVES 8)

FUJI apples originated in Fujisaki, Japan, back in the 1950s. They have a juicy, sweet golden flesh and hold up well to cooking and baking. Fresh ginger balances the flavor of the Fuji apples, adding a spicy nuance. Grinding the allspice berries and coriander seeds in a coffee grinder will add intense flavor to the pie filling. If you grind your own spices, use two allspice berries and ¾ teaspoon whole coriander seeds. You may also grate fresh nutmeg. Either way, this is not your typical apple pie.

Preheat the oven to 400°F.

TO PREPARE THE CRUST Blend the flours, sugar, and salt together. Chop the frozen butter into small pieces, and cut it into the flour mixture with a pastry blender or two knives until a fine meal is achieved. Slowly blend in the ice water until the flour mixture has moistened into a ball. Chill for 30 minutes. Using a lightly floured rolling pin, roll out a circle larger than the pie tin by about 2 inches, and place it in a 9-inch pie pan. The rolled-out dough should be wider than the pan and the edges should hang over the pie pan.

TO PREPARE THE FILLING Place the sliced apples in a large bowl. Squeeze the lemon juice over the apple slices, and add the ginger, nutmeg, coriander, allspice, brown sugar, and flour. Toss the apples until all the ingredients are mixed and the apples are coated well.

Mound the filling inside the crust; flip up the sides of the dough to partially cover the apples, which will give you a rustic look. Dot the top with the butter. Bake for 45 minutes, until the crust is golden brown and the apples are tender.

PER SERVING: CALORIES 470; CALORIES FROM FAT 230; CALORIES FROM SATURATED FAT 140; PROTEIN 5 G; CARBOHYDRATE 59 G; TOTAL FAT 25 G; SATURATED FAT 15 G; CHOLESTEROL 65 MG; SODIUM 250 MG; 49% CALORIES FROM FAT

The Crust

1 cup unbleached all-purpose flour
1½ cups whole wheat flour
1 tablespoon sugar
1 teaspoon salt
½ pound (2 sticks) butter, frozen
½ cup ice water

The Filling

4 to 5 large Fuji apples, peeled and
  sliced ½ inch thick
Juice of 1 small lemon
1 tablespoon finely grated fresh
  ginger (1-inch piece)
¼ teaspoon ground or freshly grated
  nutmeg
1 teaspoon coriander
½ teaspoon allspice
⅔ cup packed light brown sugar
3 tablespoons flour

1 tablespoon butter

Tip from the Team: When making pastry for a pie that uses a dense shortening like butter, it is really important to make sure that your shortening is cold. Use a pastry blender or two knives to blend the fat into the flour. Never mix with your hands—the heat from your skin will partially melt the fat into the flour, causing the pastry to be tough.

You should also refrigerate the pastry dough for at least a half hour prior to rolling it out. Handle the dough as little as possible. The more a pastry dough is kneaded or worked, the tougher it will be when it bakes.

Pear Burritos

SERVES 6

THIS is a perfect dessert for autumn or winter. Warm flour tortillas keep the fragrant cinnamon- and clove-spiked juice of cooked pears wrapped inside. You may use apples as a substitute if you prefer.

4 medium ripe pears, peeled, cored, and cut into ¼-inch-thick slices
1 cup apple cider
¼ cup granulated sugar
3 whole cloves
1 cinnamon stick
1 (2-inch) slice of orange peel
8 ounces fromage blanc, like triple crème or mascarpone
6 (10-inch) flour tortillas
Fresh mint leaves to garnish

Place the pears, apple cider, sugar, cloves, cinnamon stick, and orange peel in a large saucepan, and bring to a boil. Reduce the heat, and simmer until the pears are crisp-tender, 4 to 5 minutes.

With a slotted spoon, remove the pears, and set them aside. Discard the cinnamon stick, cloves, and orange peel. Bring the reserved liquid to a boil, and cook until the mixture reduces by half and is thick and syrupy.

Preheat the oven to 350°F. Line a baking sheet with parchment paper or aluminum foil. Place about ⅛ cup of the fromage blanc in the center of each tortilla, and, with a flat-edged knife or spatula, spread the cheese into a 3-inch circle. Top with 3 or 4 pear slices; then carefully roll up the burrito. Place seam side down on the prepared baking sheet. Bake for about 10 minutes, or just until the tortillas begin to brown. Remove to serving plates, and spoon some of the reduced sauce over the burritos. Garnish with the mint leaves. Serve immediately.

PER SERVING: CALORIES 520; CALORIES FROM FAT 210; CALORIES FROM SATURATED FAT 100; PROTEIN 9 G; CARBOHYDRATE 71 G; TOTAL FAT 23 G; SATURATED FAT 11 G; CHOLESTEROL 50 MG; SODIUM 370 MG; 40% CALORIES FROM FAT

 Tip from the Team: To ripen fruits faster, put them in a small paper bag along with a near-ripe to overripe banana. The excess natural ethylene gas from the banana accelerates the ripening process.

Silken Tofu Chocolate Mousse

vegan

12 ounces silken-style tofu, drained well

¼ cup plus 3 tablespoons unsweetened cocoa powder

⅓ cup maple syrup (barley malt or rice syrup may be substituted)

1 tablespoon orange zest

1 tablespoon instant coffee granules (decaf or regular)

1 tablespoon vanilla extract

Pinch of salt

1 ounce almond liqueur (optional)

SILKEN tofu is soft and creamy in texture. It gives this dessert a mousselike quality when chilled overnight in the refrigerator. Because the silken tofu is so neutral in taste, the chocolate and orange emerge as the major flavors. You may use carob powder instead of chocolate if you prefer.

Process the tofu, cocoa powder, maple syrup, orange zest, coffee granules, vanilla, salt, and optional liqueur in the bowl of a food processor or in a blender for 1½ minutes, until smooth. Pour the mousse into wine or champagne glasses or dessert-type serving dishes, and chill overnight. Serve the mousse with fresh orange sections, toasted almonds, or shaved chocolate garnish over the top.

PER SERVING: CALORIES 240; CALORIES FROM FAT 40; CALORIES FROM SATURATED FAT 15; PROTEIN 13 G; CARBOHYDRATE 35 G; TOTAL FAT 4.5 G; SATURATED FAT 1.5 G; CHOLESTEROL 0 MG; SODIUM 70 MG; 17% CALORIES FROM FAT

desserts

vegan

Balsamic Berry Dessert Topping

SERVES 6

DARK, sweet, and juicy berries make an incredible topping for ice cream, sorbet, angel food cake, or shortcake. The unusual combination of tart vinegar and a few grindings of black pepper really forms an unorthodox background for seasonal berries. Allow the berries to stand at room temperature for at least 20 minutes for the flavors to marry. Try these over vanilla bean ice cream. If the color doesn't wow you, the flavor certainly will.

1 pint blackberries
1 pint raspberries
1 pint strawberries, sliced
⅛ cup aged balsamic vinegar
¼ cup sugar
Freshly ground pepper to taste
¼ cup cassis (black currant liqueur)
   (optional)

Combine the berries, vinegar, sugar, pepper, and optional cassis in a large mixing bowl, and stir gently with a spoon. Let stand at room temperature for at least 20 minutes before serving.

PER SERVING: CALORIES 90; CALORIES FROM FAT 5; CALORIES FROM SATURATED FAT 0; PROTEIN 1 G; CARBOHYDRATE 23 G; TOTAL FAT 0.5 G; SATURATED FAT 0 G; CHOLESTEROL 0 MG; SODIUM 0 MG; 6% CALORIES FROM FAT

Whole Foods Glossary

The natural and organic world is diverse and continually evolving. At Whole Foods Markets, we have thousands of delicious recipes using great-tasting, pure ingredients. We simply couldn't include everything within the pages of this book, although we surely tried to address all the basics. Check out www.wholefoodsmarket.com for more recipes and a wealth of information about natural and organic foods.

How to Build the Natural Foods Pantry

Key components of a natural foods lifestyle are balance and eating a variety of foods. A natural foods diet should be diverse and flavorful, with an abundance of grains, beans, fresh fruits, vegetables, and your choice of protein sources. A wealth of ethnic cuisine is reflected within a natural foods diet—including Mediterranean, Indian, Hispanic, and Asian culinary traditions. Our pantry is full of many unusual ingredients that come from a variety of cultures. Although some of these ingredients were once rather obscure, they are now much more readily available because of the demand and increased awareness of eating for great health.

Specific ingredients in the glossary that we recommend keeping on hand are highlighted with a leaf icon next to their listings. Don't feel the need to buy all of them at once—essentially these are a good foundation for a natural foods pantry.

AGAR-AGAR is a jellylike thickening agent derived from several varieties of red seaweed. Agar has no flavor, color, or smell of its own. Agar is also called kanten, and it comes in the form of bars, flakes, or granules. It's a great substitute for animal-based gelatins. It can be used to thicken puddings, pies, desserts, mousses, and jellies. To use, agar is mixed with cold water and then brought to a boil. The resulting thick liquid is incorporated into recipes that need to be thickened.

ARROWROOT, a powdered tropical root, is used just like cornstarch but has the advantage of being unrefined and is a perfect alternative for people with corn allergies. One tablespoon dissolved in a cup of cold water bathes stir-fries in a glossy sauce with the consistency of Chinese-style sweet and sour.

BEANS

Aside from grains, beans and legumes are the most consumed food in the world. Beans are high in protein, yet they contain none of the cholesterol found in many animal protein sources. Beans are the perfect complement to whole grains and are abundant in energy-producing complex carbohydrates. They are also an excellent source of soluble fiber, the type that has been shown to help lower serum cholesterol.

Beans are available either dried, canned, or jarred. Make sure you check the labels; when purchased in some stores beans may contain sugar or artificial additives.

Adzuki are small, dark-red beans with a mellow flavor, traditionally used in Asian cooking. Adzuki beans are high in protein and contain good amounts of calcium, iron, and vitamin A. (See Adzuki Bean Loaf, page 160.)

Black-eyed peas are the hallmark of American Southern cooking, with good reason. Named for the distinctive black dot that graces each cream-colored bean, black-eyed peas cook up soft and rich tasting. Nothing goes better with cooked greens.

Black turtle beans, compact oval beans, are essential to most Mexican and Hispanic meals. They are delicious prepared with cumin, hot chilies, and lime. Shiny, ink-black turtles have an assertive, almost nutty flavor.

Chickpeas or garbanzo beans are round beans featured in cooking from Africa, India, the Middle East, and Italy. Known as the main ingredient in the spread hummus, they are also at home in stews, salads, and hearty entrées.

Edamame are fresh green soybeans. Excellent quality organic soybeans are available frozen with or without the shell. Steam them lightly before using, and serve them as a snack. Their delicate sweetness is addictive.

Fava beans, also known as *broad beans,* date back to ancient Europe, and their hearty earthy taste retains a hint of their untamed past. Nevertheless, favas are gaining in popularity among both natural foods and gourmet cooks for the depth of flavor and silky texture they acquire when properly cooked.

Kidney beans are a large oval-shaped reddish brown bean used often in chili and other Southwestern and Mexican recipes, as well as in some Italian dishes. They are mild in flavor.

Lentils are named for the French word meaning "lens," and they're one of the quickest-cooking and most versatile beans. Aside from making a fabulous soup (see page 87), lentils are the basis of the savory Indian sauce dahl. Cooked with less water, lentils make a scrumptious bed for poached fish or stewed meat.

Mung beans are surprisingly versatile considering their unusual appearance—dark green and perfectly round. They are the source of the familiar Chinese bean sprouts used in chow mein, and they're also used in India for dahl and as flour. Mung beans are also the origin of clear cellophane noodles. (See Spicy Mung Bean Soup, page 71.)

Navy beans and their larger cousin *great northern beans,* are the familiar white beans used for baked beans and warming soups. Mild and very digestible, navy beans are a good choice for someone new to beans.

Pinto beans are the rich, light-brown bean of Tex-Mex fame. Their uniquely substantial texture is what makes them hold up so well in burritos, enchiladas, and refried beans. (The original Spanish *refrito* actually implies "well-fried," not "fried twice.")

BURDOCK ROOT looks like a long brown-skinned carrot and can be cooked like one— by boiling, braising, or sautéing. A staple of macrobiotic cuisine, burdock root tastes like a cross between carrots and sunflower seeds.

BUTTER in a natural foods cookbook? Of course. Although butter is higher in saturated fat than vegetable oils, it should be used in moderation. Save butter for what it does best— create the lightest piecrusts, pastries, and cookies. High-quality pure dairy butter is so flavorful that only a bit is needed to enrich sauces, soups, or vegetables. This is where great butter really shines.

CAROB can replace cocoa in recipes. Derived from the pods of the Mediterranean locust tree, carob lends a smooth, chocolate-like taste without the bitterness or caffeine. It is a good source of calcium. (See Chocolate Earth Balls, page 368.)

CHILIES

Chilies are grown the world over and take many forms, colors, and sizes. Most chili species grow between ½ inch and 6 inches long and can range in diameter from ½ inch to about 2 inches. Normally speaking, the smaller the chili the more of a wallop it packs. It's fair to say that, behind salt and pepper, chilies are one of the most important seasonings in today's kitchens, adding excitement to many recipes.

Chili Pepper Primer

TYPE	DESCRIPTION	DRY (heat level)	FRESH (heat level)
Anaheim	Long and rather thin chilies with a fairly mild flavor. They can be found in green and red versions. The red ones are dried many times and strung on cords called ristras, which can be found throughout the Southwest. They are one of the chilies used for chiles rellenos.	Hot	Mild
Ancho	Technically these are dried poblano peppers but are sometimes marketed fresh and look like little flattened pattypan squash. These are also fairly mild, with a fruity flavor. Great in Mexican or Southwestern cooking.	Hot	Medium
Bird Chili	Also called Thai bird or pequín chilies. These spicy peppers are great in Asian dishes.	Hot	Hot
Cayenne	Most of us are familiar with ground cayenne pepper made from this spicy chili. It is from chilies that are long and slender with pointy tips. These are very hot and make a great fiery marinara sauce.	Very Hot	Hot
Chipotle	Dried, dark red to brown smoked jalapeño peppers with a rich, slightly sweet flavor. Chipotle chilies are available dried, which must be reconstituted in water before incorporating into most recipes, or canned in a thick tomato-based sauce called adobo.	Hot	N/A
Habanero	Also called Scotch Bonnets. These chilies are really, really, really spicy and should be used with care. They're shaped like little hats or slightly flattened lanterns and come in yellow, orange, red, and green. Great for Caribbean or Latin American dishes.	Very Hot	Very Hot

TYPE	DESCRIPTION	DRY (heat level)	FRESH (heat level)
Jalapeño	One of the most common chili peppers, they range from green to red in color. About 2 inches in length, they are medium spicy on the chili scale. You can find them fresh, pickled, canned, and in many processed foods. Great in Mexican, Southern, and Southwestern cuisine.	Hot	Medium
Pasilla	Also called chile Negro because of its dark brown color, this is a medium-hot dried chili about 6 to 8 inches long. It's excellent in sauces, spice rubs, and stews. A fresh pasilla is called a Chilaca chili.	Medium	Medium
Poblano	These are ancho chilies in the fresh green stage. These chilies, which almost look like pointed green peppers, are hit-and-miss regarding spiciness. Sometimes they're really hot, sometimes mild. You never know by looking. Have a little spoon of sugar ready just in case. Great for stuffing, making chiles rellenos, or for a sandwich, salad, or pizza topping, simply roasted and peeled.	Medium	Medium
Red Savina	This new entry into the exotic chili-head arena is a member of the habanero family. They are laboratory tested and certified at over 570,000 Scoville units, making them the spiciest peppers on earth.	Very Hot	Very Hot
Serrano	Popular in the Southwest, these small pointed green chilies are quite spicy. They can sometimes be found in the less pungent ripe, red stage. Great for salsas and sauces.	Very Hot	Very Hot

CONDIMENTS—With the ever-increasing interest in ethnic foods, there are many more condiments available today. Experiment with them, and keep your favorites in your pantry. Some good ones to try are hoisin sauce, chili paste with garlic, Thai curry pastes, and chipotle peppers in adobo sauce.

DAIKON is a large white radish, a distinctly Japanese vegetable used in miso soup and brine pickles. (See Japanese Kale Salad with Shiitake Mushrooms, page 118.)

FLAX SEEDS are an outstanding source of omega-3 essential fatty acids and soluble fiber. Flax devotees often grind the seeds and use a tablespoonful a day on cereal. They may also be added whole to baked goods for a nutty crunch as well as a fiber boost. (See Mixed Nut and Flax Seed Baklava, page 377.)

FLOUR

Experimenting with different flours can transform your recipes and add a wide variety of nutrients.

Buckwheat flour can substitute for some of the wheat flour in recipes such as waffles, pancakes, and muffins. Its deeply nutty flavor may be habit-forming. Because buckwheat is low in gluten, it is not recommended for bread baking.

Chickpea flour, since it is made from a bean, is higher in protein and calcium than grain flours. It adds a rich, sweet flavor to crepes and is the basis of the crisp Indian wafer papadum.

Durum (semolina) is the variety of wheat that has the highest protein content and is the ideal pasta flour. Be sure to buy whole wheat semolina; nothing makes tastier or more nutritious whole wheat pasta. It can also be mixed with whole wheat bread flour for dense Italian bread.

Rice flour is a good gluten-free alternative flour for people with wheat sensitivity. Its delicate taste lends itself to muffins, crepes, and desserts. For best results, use recipes that are specifically developed for rice flour.

Rye flour is low in gluten, so it should be mixed with wheat flour for bread baking. Breads made with rye flour are moist and dense; they make delicious sandwiches.

Soy flour can be substituted for a small portion of other flours in recipes to boost protein. Because it has no gluten, it does not rise well on its own.

Spelt flour, from an ancient relative of wheat, is high in protein and creates breads that are light, sweet, and nutty. When substituting spelt for wheat, reduce liquid in the recipe by 25 percent.

🌿 *Unbleached all-purpose wheat flour* is the most commonly used flour in baking and cooking.

🌿 *Whole wheat flour* comes in two basic versions: bread flour and pastry flour. Both are high in gluten and ideal for baking. Bread flour is characterized by its high protein content and works best in yeasted baked goods. Pastry flour is higher in starch, lower in protein, and lends itself to quick breads, cookies, muffins, pancakes, and other goods that rely on baking powder rather than yeast.

FREE RANGE is a term used to describe the method in which poultry is raised for production. It signifies to consumers that the chickens are allowed to roam freely within the poultry house while also having access to the outdoors.

GENETICALLY ENGINEERED FOODS—Biotechnology is a broad term describing processes such as crossbreeding, plant hybridization, and fermentation. While biotechnology has been used by humans for thousands of years, genetic engineering is a relatively new and rapidly developing form of biotechnology that has raised public questions and concern regarding its impact on the environment, the safety of food made from genetically modified plants and animals, as well as the ethical implications of the technology. Unlike traditional breeding techniques, genetic engineering focuses on recombinant DNA technology—the manipulation (blocking, adding, or scrambling) of the genetic material (the DNA) inside the cells of living organisms to block or add desired, selected traits. The result is often referred to as a genetically engineered product, commonly abbreviated as GE (genetically engineered) or GMOs (genetically modified organisms).

GHEE is the preferred (and revered) cooking fat in India, and it's often the oil of choice for gourmet chefs, who know it as clarified butter. Ghee has a higher smoking point than butter, making it a good choice for sautéing and frying.

GRAINS

Amaranth is one of the smallest grains in the world—about the size of a poppy seed. This highly nutritional grain has a mildly spicy, earthy flavor and a sticky gelatinous texture. Amaranth is gluten-free and tastes good when combined with other grains, such as brown rice or millet.

Barley, an ancient cultivated grain, is available whole and hulled or pearled, a description of the remaining grain after a process of refining. Barley, often used in soups and stews, is also a welcome addition to grain-based salads and hot breakfast cereals. (See Barley Primavera, page 105.)

Buckwheat, despite its name, is not related to wheat. It is actually the edible fruit seed of a plant related to rhubarb and is gluten-free. Roasted buckwheat, called kasha, has an assertive flavor and dried texture when cooked. Unroasted whole white buckwheat has a mild flavor and soft texture.

Bulgur is a form of wheat that has been partially steamed and dried before being ground or cracked into smaller pieces. Bulgur has a nutty flavor perfect for pilafs, soups, and salads.

Couscous—available in whole wheat or refined wheat versions, couscous looks like a grain, but it's actually a tiny pasta made from durum (semolina) wheat flour. Traditionally, couscous is used as a bed for savory Moroccan stews. Because of its ability to absorb and enhance flavors, couscous has won favor among natural foods cooks. It can be cooked with broth or even fruit juice with delicious results. Increased demand for this delicate pasta is helping other sizes of couscous to enter our American market. Israeli couscous is a large pearl of traditional couscous. It has a slightly milder flavor than regular couscous. Also, large pearls of Lebanese couscous, Syrian couscous, and French whole wheat couscous can be found in most Middle Eastern grocery stores and through the mail. For information on cooking couscous, please see page 180.

Kamut is a rediscovered high protein "grandfather wheat" cultivated in Egypt around 4000 B.C. Kamut is larger than regular wheat with a rich buttery flavor and a pleasantly chewy texture. It is excellent in cereals, breads, and pastas.

Millet, a gluten-free grain, is a tiny round yellow seed high in protein. Its delicate flavor and soft, cohesive texture make millet an excellent choice for soups, pilafs, cereals, and baked goods. (See Millet and Yam Burgers, page 216.)

Oats, originally used for medicinal purposes, are a valuable food source that can be incorporated into many recipes far beyond the limits of breakfast cereal. Uses of oats include whole oat groats in pilafs and salads, oat bran added to breads or casseroles, oatmeal in cookies and dairy-free soups, and steel-cut oats in hot cereal or added to baked goods. (See "Feel Your Oats" Burgers, page 208.)

Polenta is simply yellow cornmeal that is cooked into a thick porridge. It can be served simply spooned onto a plate and topped with cheese or sauce or pressed into a pan or mold. Slices of polenta may be served as is or grilled and, when substituted for other grain, they add a warm sense of comfort to any meal. (See Savory Tomato Pesto Polenta, page 198.)

Quinoa, native to the South American Andes mountains, has been cultivated for nearly five thousand years. Quinoa was a staple food of the Andean people, regarded as a sacred food by the Incas. Spanish conquerors destroyed the Incas' crops and prohibited the Indians from cultivating it by penalty of death. Quinoa disappeared for centuries until it was restored by a couple of Americans who saw the potential for a nourishing source of food and started recultivation in Colorado. Although regarded as a cereal, botanically, quinoa is really the fruit of a plant that belongs to the same family as beets, chard, and spinach. Quinoa seeds are tiny and round with one flattened side. The seeds have a light yellow color, although black quinoa can sometimes be found, as well. (See Quinoa Stuffed Peppers, page 168.)

Rice—Although there are more than 7,000 rice varieties grown in the world, here are the ones that find their way into our kitchens most frequently.

Arborio—This round rice is essential in the making of the classic Italian dish risotto. This is considered an elegant rice with an unusual quality of being able to absorb large quantities of liquid without becoming mushy or losing its bite.

Basmati—This aromatic long grain rice is originally from India and Pakistan. The grains are long and slender. Basmati rice is extremely fragrant when cooked and has a strong nutty flavor. Basmati rice comes in white and brown; the brown basmati has more fiber and takes longer to cook than the white. This rice is excellent in a variety of ethnic dishes and can be made into many side dishes or salads. (See Cilantro Lime Rice, page 172, or Orange Cashew Rice, page 174.)

Brown—This is unpolished rice with the outer bran intact. It is more nutritious than white rice and takes longer to cook. It's excellent in pilaf and stuffing. With its pleasing chewy texture and earthy taste it stands up well to other flavors. Medium-grain brown rice is plump, contains a bit more starch, and has a fluffy texture when cooked. Short-grain brown rice has a sweet flavor, is sticky when cooked, and is excellent in sushi or rice puddings.

Japonica—Meaning "Japanese," this Asian domesticated rice variety is distinguishable by its shorter, rounded grains, which tend to stick together when cooked. This rice is a red mahogany to black color. The flavor is buttery and nutty, and it makes an excellent side dish, pilaf, and salad.

Sweet—Sweet rice is also called glutinous rice. These grains are plump and short and look white with a waxy finish. Sweet rice becomes very sticky when cooked, which makes it a great choice for desserts, puddings, and rice molds.

Thai black—This is a short-grain black rice from Asia, Indonesia, and the Philippines. It cooks up very sticky with a mild nutty, sweet flavor. It has a striking look on the plate and lends itself well to exotic desserts and rice pudding. (See Thai Black Rice Salad, page 108.)

Wehani—A reddish brown, short-grain rice with the flavor of walnuts. With the outer bran intact, this rice is cooked much like brown rice. It's wonderful in soups, casseroles, stuffing, and side dishes. Wehani is particularly delicious when combined with nuts and dried fruit like cherries, raisins, or cranberries.

White—White rice has been hulled and polished, which strips many of its nutritional attributes. Although it may look attractive because it is white and shiny, it is quite neutral in flavor and character. Some white rice is enriched with iron and vitamins to restore some of its nutritional value.

Wild—Not really a rice, although many cooks consider it a rice species, it's the seed of an aquatic plant native to the Great Lakes area of the United States. Wild rice is great to mix with other rice varieties as it has a strong hazelnut flavor and can be quite domineering by itself. It has a chewy texture, and the dark color contrasts attractively with other foods. It's great in stuffings and salads. Always wash well before using to remove any debris or dirt. (See Wild Rice with Pecans and Dried Cranberries, page 106.)

Rye kernels are typically hulled and ground into flour for use in bread and cracker baking. Yet rye's hearty flavor, either whole, flaked, or cracked, is a welcome addition to pilaf dishes, salads, and hot cereals.

Spelt—An ancient type of wheat, spelt provided several cultures sustenance in the form of cereal, bread, and pilafs. For centuries spelt was popular in Egypt, Europe, and throughout the Mediterranean; however, by 1900 it was hard to find. Spelt has since been resurrected and can be found in many specialty and natural foods stores. The kernels are oval and dark brown. It has a nutty taste and chewy texture and can be ground like any other grain into flour and then used in breads, cakes, pastries, and pastas. It's also used in hot cereals and soups. Spelt seems to be accepted by some people who cannot tolerate wheat. However, since spelt contains gluten, individuals allergic to wheat should first check with a health professional for guidance.

Teff is an extremely tiny gluten-free grain. When cooked, it remains crunchy on the outside with a sticky texture inside and a sweet and malty flavor. Commonly used in Ethiopia, teff is appropriate for porridge, soups, or prepared like polenta.

Wheat berries, the whole grain of wheat, are short rounded kernels of varying shades of brown. Berries have a pleasant, chewy texture and nutty flavor. Soak them overnight before cooking and use in salads, pilafs, breads, casseroles, and stuffing. (See Wheat Berry Waldorf Salad, page 175.)

GRAIN MILKS

Oat milk has a smooth, sweet quality that makes it a perfect foil for cereal.
Rice milk is the lightest of all—a good choice for shakes and smoothies.

HUMMUS is a classic Middle Eastern vegetarian specialty made from puréed chickpeas with garlic, olive oil, and lemon. Try it in a whole wheat pita pocket with tomatoes, sprouts, and your favorite grilled or raw vegetables.

IRRADIATION is a method of food preservation in which foods are treated with ionizing radiation from Cobalt 60, Cesium 137, X rays, or high-energy electron beams from machine sources. Irradiation is also referred to as "ionizing radiation" because it produces energy waves strong enough to dislodge electrons from atoms and molecules, thereby converting them to electrically charged particles called ions. Other terms commonly used to identify ionizing irradiation are "cold pasteurization" and "irradiation pasteurization." Ionizing radiation reduces the number of disease-causing organisms in foods by disrupting their molecular structure and killing potentially harmful bacteria and parasites. However, when food is irradiated, some nutrients are destroyed, and untested compounds, referred to as URPs (unique radiolytic products), may be created. While irradiation of food has been shown to kill or inactivate a number of food-borne pathogens, it will not eradicate all pathogens. Additionally, irradiation can be used only on a limited number of foods. Foods that the U.S. Food and Drug Administration (FDA) have approved for irradiation include wheat, flour, red meat, poultry, pork, fresh shell eggs, vegetables, and spices as well as refrigerated and frozen uncooked meat, meat by-products, and certain other meat food products.

KEFIR, originally made from camel's milk high in the Caucasus Mountains, is now a sour liquid yogurt-tasting beverage made from cow's milk. Usually found in the dairy section, it also comes in several flavors.

KUDZU, derived from a plant root, is a more powerful thickener than arrowroot and is used in one third the quantity. Its pure white chunks dissolve instantly in cold water and its silky texture lends itself to soups and homemade puddings.

LEMONGRASS—A central ingredient in Thai and Vietnamese cooking, this long and slender yellow green stalk looks like a thin scallion and has a sharp citrus flavor.

Lemongrass is highly aromatic and only the bottom three to four inches of pale white stem are used when cooking. It can be used in stir-fries, soups, sauces, and stocks. It's also called fevergrass, and many cultures make tea from the stalks believing that it can quell fever when ill. It can be found fresh, powdered, or chopped and frozen in most Asian grocery stores.

MIRIN is a sweet cooking wine made from brown rice. Be sure to buy a natural variety. Mirin turns soy-based Asian sauces into lively, sweet glazes. Use it also to sweeten salad dressings for a change of pace.

MOCHI is made from glutinous rice that is pounded and formed into flat cakes. Mochi is one of the quickest and tastiest ways to eat whole grain. Always look for brown rice mochi to get the richest flavor and greatest health benefits. Slice the hard cake into small squares, and watch them puff up and become light and chewy when baked, pan-toasted, or heated in a waffle iron.

MUESLI is a cold cereal made from rolled oats, dried fruits, and nuts. It is traditionally mixed with milk (or a nondairy alternative) and served with sliced or chopped fruit after the grains have absorbed the liquid.

MUSHROOMS

The mushroom family encompasses many shapes and forms. The best way to clean mushrooms is to use a mushroom brush or a clean cloth to gently clean the surface of the mushroom, or if there is noticeable dirt, rinse well in cold water and drain immediately. Never soak mushrooms; they are already predominantly water, and they will soak up excess water easily.

Always choose mushrooms that are fresh and not wrinkled, spongy, or spotted. Look for mushrooms that aren't split and without dark, separated gills. Although mushrooms are available canned and frozen, we recommend fresh unless you are using dried mushrooms for a specific dish. Dried mushrooms should be soaked in warm water for 30 minutes and then rinsed before using. Some cooks save the mushroom soaking liquid for sauces and soups.

Some more commonly available mushrooms include:

Chanterelle—Chanterelles are golden, yellow mushrooms with a cup-shaped, indented cap ranging from 3/4 inch to 3 inches across. They have a peppery, fruity flavor and make an incredible omelete, crepe, or garnish for stews.

Enoki—A delicate mushroom, it is thin and cream-colored with a tiny cap and long stem. Enokis are mild in flavor.

Morel—These mushrooms have a conical-shaped cap that is usually brown or golden colored. Morels are highly prized for their strong woodsy flavor and aroma. They are hard to clean because of the honeycomb caps, which get quite dirty. Make sure you rinse them several times, as quickly as possible and dry them immediately on paper towels.

Oyster—This mushroom has a mild flavor with a tender white flesh. It's served best simply sautéed in olive oil or butter and lightly seasoned with salt and pepper.

Portobello—The familiar large round cap has become the king of mushrooms, not so much for the size but for versatility and flavor. This is a great mushroom to use in vegetarian dishes because of its meaty texture and strong flavor.

Shiitake—This mushroom is dark brown with a chewy, meaty texture and a strong, earthy flavor. Available fresh and dried, they are used in Asian-inspired dishes such as stir-fries, soups, and stews.

MUSTARD—A pungent condiment made from ground mustard seeds and spices. There are many flavors and textures, the most common varieties being Dijon style and stone-ground mustard. Great for sauces, glazes, marinades, and dressings.

NUT BUTTERS add versatility to the natural foods kitchen. Natural nut butters substitute for less healthful spreads and may be used to thicken sauces. If you like peanut butter, you'll love an almond butter and fruit spread sandwich. Spread nut butter on whole-grain cakes or quick breads as an alternative to sugary frosting, or mix with hot cereals for extra protein. Stir in cashew butter to create a creamed soup without the cream.

NUT MILKS have gone way beyond being dairy substitutes for people with allergies to being appreciated for their own unique flavors and textures. Almond milk is rich and sweet.

NUTS

Although in our country nuts and seeds are predominantly eaten as snacks, they are a highly nutritious food. Most nuts are essentially the seeds or dried fruits of trees, with a hard outer casing or shell. The outer hulls of these seeds are softer than their nuts and are sometimes edible. Although peanuts are classified as a legume, they are commonly viewed as a nut.

Nuts are a good source of protein. Most nuts and seeds contain 8 to 25 percent of their calories from protein. Some nuts such as Brazil nuts, almonds, and filberts also are a good source of calcium. Most nuts also provide some potassium and iron.

Nuts, although nutritious, are also high in calories and fat and should be enjoyed in moderation.

Here are some favorite nut varieties and some simple ways to prepare them at home:

Almonds—After roasting, they can be tossed in salads or cooked couscous. Make a simple dessert by plumping couscous in apple juice or ginger ale. Add toasted almonds, cinnamon, and raisins. Serve this warm; drizzle a little cream or yogurt over the top.

Brazil nuts—Chop these large nuts and sauté in some butter or olive oil with sliced carrots, quartered brussels sprouts, or sliced zucchini.

Cashews—Roasted cashews add tremendous flavor to wild or brown rice. Add toasted cashews to cooked rice; sprinkle some tamari and a squeeze of lemon over all.

Pecans—Roasted pecans make a delectable topping for oatmeal and other hot cereals. Also use in pies, cookies, muffins, and granola. Top off bitter greens and savory grain pilafs.

Pine nuts—You may brown them in a sauté pan with a tablespoon of olive oil. Try adding the pine nuts and oil to cooked green beans or asparagus.

Pistachios—Try chopping shelled pistachios and mix with some bread crumbs. Use this as a crust for tofu, eggplant steaks, or tempeh. Dip the tofu, tempeh, or vegetables in some beaten egg first or soak in buttermilk; then press into crumbs. Bake in a 375°F. oven until golden brown, about 15 minutes.

Walnuts or Black Walnuts—Excellent for baking, walnuts also liven up rice pilaf dishes and vegetable stews. Try cooking some basmati rice and then adding toasted walnuts, lightly sautéed peas, and mushrooms.

OILS

Mass-market cooking oils have often been extracted using solvents such as hexane, or high heat, which damages the flavor and nutritive value of the oil. Look for oils marked "expeller pressed" to ensure that they have been obtained only by mechanical extraction. In general, monounsaturated oils, such as olive and canola, are more likely to promote healthy cholesterol levels and less likely than polyunsaturated oils to cause free-radical damage. However, polyunsaturated oils do supply essential fatty acids and have a place in healthful cuisine.

Avocado oil has a nutty flavor that does wonders for homemade salad dressings. Monounsaturated.

Canola oil, created in Canada from a special variety of rapeseed, is an ideal all-purpose oil because it has very little flavor of its own and has a medium-high smoking point. It allows the other ingredients in recipes to shine through. Monounsaturated.

Corn oil has a buttery flavor that makes it ideal for baking and for sautéing vegetables. Do not use it for deep-frying, as it will foam and smoke at high heat. Polyunsaturated.

Flax seed oil is generally used as a nutritional supplement for its high content of omega-3 essential fatty acids. Fans take a tablespoon per day, on salads or hot cereal. Flax seed oil is very fragile and must never be heated; add it to cooked foods after cooling.

Olive oil, virgin and extra-virgin—A wide variety of handcrafted olive oils from Italy, Spain, Greece, and other countries have made olive oil sampling as sophisticated as wine tasting. Some are more fruity; others spicy or tannic. Buy small bottles at first until you've found the ones you like best. Extra-virgin olive oil comes from the first crushing of the olive fruit and is the finest grade. It is bright green and has a stronger olive flavor than the more refined olive oils. Try it in homemade vinaigrette dressings, as a dip for whole-grain bread, or drizzled over white meat.

Peanut oil is a favorite for stir-frying and deep-frying because of its high (450° F.) smoking point—as long as it is refined. Monounsaturated.

Safflower oil is mild flavored and good for general cooking. Like most polyunsaturated oils, it should not be used for deep-frying, as it oxidizes readily.

Sesame oil gives Asian cuisine a distinctive flavor. Refined, it is an excellent choice for stir-frying. Toasted sesame oil has a deep, roasted-nut flavor that is ideal in small amounts for flavoring Asian vegetable dishes, sauces, and soups. Typically, dark roasted sesame oil is used as a flavor drizzle after stir-frying vegetables. Don't use it to sauté the vegetables, because of the low smoke point. Monounsaturated.

Unrefined oils—Refined oils have been highly filtered and distilled and lack the deep, rich color and flavor of unrefined oils, as well as most of the nutrients. However, unrefined oils have too low a smoking point to be used for deep-frying and other high-heat cooking methods, and they become rancid more quickly and easily than refined. For most purposes, cooks prefer oils that are expeller pressed and refined. Unrefined olive oil is referred to as virgin or extra-virgin (see Olive oil, above). Always refrigerate unrefined oils.

Walnut oil is a little hard to find, but the fresh, nutty flavor it lends to salad dressings can't be beat. Polyunsaturated. Hazelnut oil is a good alternative.

OLIVES—Ask at a well-stocked grocery store or cheese shop for naturally cured olives. They are often sold in bulk and in an increasing variety of types and origins. Olives that are naturally cured and offer delicate flavor nuances that would otherwise be destroyed. Canned black olives are actually unripe green olives that have been darkened by lye-curing. A few olives add interest and a bit of healthful oil to many dishes.

ORGANIC FOODS—Organic foods are grown without the use of potentially harmful synthetic pesticides, herbicides, and fungicides. Organic agriculture is specifically designed to promote and enhance soil biodiversity by using earth-friendly agricultural methods and practices. The "organic" label denotes the use of materials and practices that enhance the earth's natural ecological balance. Organic food handlers, processors, and retailers adhere to strict standards and guidelines that maintain the integrity of organically grown products. According to the National Organic Standards Board, established under the Organic Foods Production Act of 1990, the primary goal of organic agriculture is to optimize the health and productivity of interdependent communities of soil life, plants, animals, and people by seeking to restore, maintain, and enhance ecological harmony. The term *Certified Organic* indicates that the product you purchase has been certified by either a private certifying agency or a state government agency that is fully accredited by the United States Department of Agriculture (USDA). All certifying agencies must act consistently, competently, and impartially in the certification process. This ensures consumers that production and handling practices always meet national organic standards.

PASTA—Be creative in selecting pasta. A host of new colors, shapes, and types of pasta is available. Those with wheat allergies may choose from delicious pastas made from kamut, quinoa, or spelt. Once you get used to whole-grain pasta, the white-flour kind may seem pale and bland in comparison. (See pages 179 to 181 for more information and cooking times.)

SEA VEGETABLES OR SEAWEED

Seaweed and sea vegetables come in many different shapes and sizes. Sea vegetables have been eaten for hundreds of years in various parts of Asia, the British Isles, Canada, and the Caribbean. Most of us are familiar with nori, the wrapper that holds sushi together. At one time or another, you may have also eaten sea vegetables, never knowing they were a hidden ingredient in sauces, ice creams, puddings, and convenience foods in the form of carrageen or Irish moss. Nutritionally, sea vegetables are a good source of minerals such as

The Top 10 Reasons to Buy Organics

1. Support the environment: Organic production systems support natural ecosystems by using long-term farming solutions. This restores, maintains, and enhances ecological harmony, and positively affects the health of the environment.

2. Support our future needs: Organic farming embraces the principle that agriculture must meet the needs of the present without compromising the needs of future generations.

3. Build a biologically diverse agriculture: Organic agriculture respects diversity within the environment, including the protection of plant and wildlife habitats.

4. Help protect our water resources: Environmentally friendly farming solutions contribute to the overall quality of our lakes, rivers, estuaries, and ground and drinking waters.

5. Increase productivity of the land: Organic agriculture builds productive nutrient-rich soil that resists topsoil erosion.

6. Help protect our health: Organic production systems limit inputs of toxic and persistent chemicals into the environment. Choosing organic foods improves our own health, the health of our children, the health of farm workers, and the health of future generations.

7. Help small farms: Although more large-scale farms are making the conversion to organic practices, most organic farms are small independently owned and operated family farms.

8. Support a true economy: Buying organic is a direct investment in the long-term future of our planet. The choices we make now can free us from costly pesticide-related environmental cleanups in the future.

9. Save energy: Organic farming is less reliant on nonrenewable energy sources, substituting renewable sources or labor to the extent that is economically feasible.

10. Organic food tastes great: Chefs across the country are committed to using organic ingredients because plants from healthy soils and organically fed livestock provide us with more flavorful food. Organic foods allow true flavors to shine through!

potassium, calcium, phosphorous, iron, and iodine. Because sea vegetables spend their life in the ocean, the sodium content is also rather high.

Sea vegetables are sold in dried strands, sheets, and powdered forms. With the exception of dulse and nori sheets, most sea vegetables must first be soaked in water or boiled to plump up before serving in a variety of dishes. They may be added to salads or soups, made into marinated relish, served as a sandwich topping, or cooked with seafood. When planning your recipe, remember that most sea vegetables increase in volume three to five times when they are reconstituted. (See Essential Sea Vegetable Salad, page 112.)

Arame is one of the more mild-flavored sea vegetables. Arame looks like thin black shreds and is slightly sweet. It makes a beautiful garnish for dishes. This sea vegetable is normally soaked in warm water for twenty minutes to plump up before being used in recipes.

Dulse is a red sea vegetable that is normally available in whole stringy leaves or sometimes powdered as a condiment. It has a somewhat chewy texture with a slightly salty aftertaste. It is also available smoked. Dulse is harvested off the northeast coast of Maine and in the British Isles. It is delicious mixed into cole slaw with shredded cabbage, carrots, scallions, and olive oil.

Hijiki, a black strand thicker and fatter than arame, has a delicate flavor and must also be soaked before using. Hijiki adds a lot of character to soups, chowders, noodle dishes, and stir-fries.

Kombu is a thick, dark brown sea vegetable that lends itself toward flavoring soups and broths. Many cooks put a small piece in the water for cooking dried beans to enhance flavor. To make a kombu broth, soak a ribbon of kombu overnight in water. The next day, heat the soaking liquid to boiling with a sliced onion and carrot. Simmer for twenty minutes, and after cooling, reserve the broth for further use.

Nori gives fast food a whole new meaning. Start with a pot of cooked short-grain rice, a package of nori sheets, and your imagination. Cooked or smoked salmon, well-drained steamed spinach, pickles of all kinds, and spears of carrot and cucumber all make wonderful sushi fillings. Toast the nori according to the package directions before use.

Wakame is a tender, deep-green sea vegetable that goes into miso soup (for the beginner) or seaweed salad (for the die-hard fan). (See Miso Broth, page 60.)

SEITAN (wheat gluten is commonly known by this Japanese name) can be substituted for meat in stews, kebobs, paella, and a host of other dishes. Well-seasoned, it is perhaps the "meatiest" of the meat substitutes. (See Spicy Mexican Marinade, page 335.)

SESAME SEEDS are one of the oldest known seasonings, dating back to 3000 B.C. Originally brought to our shores and incorporated into American cuisine by African slaves, these small flat oval seeds come in colors ranging from light brown to black. Always look for the dark brown seeds, which have part of the outer hull intact, making them more nutritious. Sesame seeds have a high oil content and should be purchased in small quantities, as they can quickly turn rancid. Keep the seeds in a sealed jar in a cool place in your kitchen for up to two months or store in your refrigerator for four to six months.

SOY

The soybean contains isoflavones (plant components) that support heart health, strong bones, and balanced female hormones. Soy is available in veggie burgers and dogs, and an increasing number of ready-made meat substitutes. (See also: *tempeh* and *tofu*.)

Miso is a versatile seasoning paste made from fermenting soybeans with a grain starter and sea salt. The traditional seasoning of Japanese soup, miso may also be used in dips and sauces. Once you start experimenting with miso, it's hard to stop. There are several varieties of miso, ranging from mild white miso to more pungent red and brown miso. Try beginning with mellow white miso, which is sweet and mild. (See Miso Salad Dressing, page 328.)

Soy milk is a great alternative for those with dairy allergies and is an easy way to get soy isoflavones into the daily diet. It comes in a variety of flavors, and in both sweetened and unsweetened versions.

Soy sauce—Don't settle for less than naturally brewed soy sauce, which is also known as shoyu or tamari. The only ingredients listed should be soybeans, wheat, water, and sea salt. Tamari is the same as shoyu, but does not contain wheat. Use these delectable liquids sparingly, for their sodium content is high. The advantage of genuine, naturally brewed soy sauces is that they are so flavorful, a little goes a long way. Always read the label when buying soy sauce, as many times cheap versions are nothing more than water, salt, and caramel color. Tamari and soy sauce are also available in low-sodium form.

Tamari is a traditional Japanese soy sauce made with water, soybeans, and sea salt. Tamari is normally aged in wooden casks for months, which produces a rich winelike flavor much more complex than soy sauce. Tamari can be used as a seasoning in soups, stews, salads, entrées, and dressings.

Tempeh is a traditional Indonesian soy food made by culturing cooked, cracked soybeans with the starter *Rhizopus oligospous*. Its meaty texture and flavor work well in vegetarian burgers, casseroles, and stir-fries.

Tofu, the now-familiar white block of soy curd, is one of the most versatile ingredients in the natural foods pantry. There are essentially three varieties of tofu with regard to texture. Firm, extra-firm, and silken tofu are the most commonly available. Try firm and extra-firm tofu by cutting it into chunks and adding cooked to a meatless stir-fry. These firm varieties may be grilled, sautéed, and broiled because they hold up well to handling.

Marinate cooked firm tofu in flax seed oil and lemon juice in the refrigerator overnight; then toss with chopped vegetables for a salad or sandwich stuffing. Silken tofu is delicate, similar in texture to custard, and may be used for sauces, dressings, and dessert recipes.

SPICES are usually the whole or ground dried seeds of aromatic plants. Consider investing in a spice grinder or coffee mill and buying whole spices to grind yourself. The following spices are the most commonly used: cumin, chili powder, turmeric, curry, garam masala, crushed red chili flakes, cayenne pepper, paprika, white and black peppercorns, Cajun seasoning, cinnamon, cloves, nutmeg, and allspice.

SUMAC is a dark red spice that comes from the berries that grow on bushes throughout the Middle East. It is usually sold ground and has a tart, lemony flavor and is used in Middle Eastern, Mediterranean, and Persian food. It's delicious on rice and sprinkled on shish kebabs. It can be found in most Middle Eastern groceries.

SUPER GRAIN—A nickname for grains such as quinoa and amaranth that are noted for their high concentration of lysine, the amino acid usually found in limited proportions in grains. Since the extra lysine give them a high quality of protein, supergrains can be combined with beans and other grains to boost their protein values.

SWEETENERS

According to the USDA, in 1998 the average American consumed nearly 140 pounds of sugar. Although some of these sugars were from naturally occurring sources such as fruit and vegetables, most were contained in prepared, packaged convenience foods or added to the food we prepare at home. There are many more sweeteners now available on the market. Most sugars contain little more than calories, but many alternative unrefined sugars contain trace elements, minerals, and vitamins. There is no way to claim which sugar is best for you, because most nutritionists will say that regardless of whether it contains minerals or vitamins, during digestion all sugars break down into simple glucose, the basic body fuel, essential to the function of all cells. Most of the nutritionists feel the amount of

trace minerals, vitamins, and elements contained in unrefined sugars are too small to benefit from nutritionally.

Unrefined sweeteners are typically more expensive than white sugar, because of the
growth and processing considerations. Almost all of these alternative sweeteners are available in both organic and conventional varieties.

Amasake is made by culturing cooked rice with fermented rice called koji. Enzymes
convert the rice starch to simple sugars, mainly maltose and glucose. Traditional
amasake is very thick and is typically used for cooking. Ready-to-drink varieties have
consistencies ranging from thin to milk shake–thick.

Barley malt is a thick, dark-colored sweetener made from sprouted barley that is
dried, mixed with water, and cooked until a thick syrup forms. A good whole foods
sweetener, high in complex, slow-digested sugars, barley malt lends itself toward
baking, muffins, chocolate sauces, fruit breads, and desserts. Use it in baked beans,
legume casseroles, and jerk marinades and dressings. Substitute barley malt one for
one with white sugar. Reduce the liquid in your recipe by $1/4$ cup for every cup of
barley malt used.

Brown rice syrup is a mild, minimally refined sweetener. Substitute it one to one for
sugar, but reduce the total amount of liquid in the recipe by $1/4$ cup per cup of brown
rice syrup used.

Date sugar is an intensely sweet powder produced by drying and grinding dates. It
boasts all the nutrients of dates, but it should be used in moderation: Substitute $2/3$
cup of date sugar to 1 cup of sugar in recipes. Dissolving date sugar in hot water before
adding is a must; reduce other liquids accordingly.

Demerara and Muscovado sugars are evaporated cane juice sugars that have been left
minimally processed. The coarse crystals are sticky and dense with molasses and
caramel flavors. These sweeteners are great for desserts, pies, puddings, cakes, and
wherever a caramelized sugar flavor is desired.

Evaporated cane juice is a term for sugars that are made by squeezing sugarcane juice,
drying it, and then milling or grinding it to various degrees of granulation. These
sugars have a mellow, molasses-like flavor and underlying flavor nuances of spice and
vanilla.

Fruit juice sweeteners are often made with apple or grape juice concentrates as the
base with other juice concentrates added to adjust the flavor and sweetness. You may

use the same amount as a substitute for white sugar but must reduce the recipes liquid content by a third.

Honey is one of the least-refined sweeteners, ranging in flavor and color depending on the particular plant from which the bees extracted flower pollen. Since it raises the blood sugar quickly, it should be used in moderation. Always look for raw honey, which has its natural nutrients and enzymes intact. (Do not give honey to babies under 12 months of age because it may contain *Clostridium botulinium.* These spores can cause botulism in an immature immune system; they are harmless after the first year of age.)

Rice syrup is made from slightly polished whole grains of rice. This syrup is lighter colored and more mild flavored than barley malt. It is less sticky, as well. Rice syrup is hypoallergenic, making it a good ingredient for people who are sensitive to wheat or corn. It's less sweet than honey and can be used in baking, cookies, pies, and puddings. Use it to roast root vegetables and allow the flavor of the vegetable to shine through.

Sucanat™ is a minimally refined, evaporated organic sugarcane juice. It has a pleasant, granulated texture and measures just like sugar. It lends a distinct molasses-like taste to whatever it sweetens, so bear that in mind when adding it to recipes.

TAHINI is a smooth sesame paste available raw and roasted. Try it on toasted bread in place of butter or on a vegetarian sandwich. It adds protein, beneficial fats, and a rich, savory flavor. (See Black Bean Hummus, page 322.)

VEGAN—A diet excluding all animal products (such as honey or dairy products) and meats, fish, or fowl.

VEGETARIAN—A diet including plant foods and animal products, such as dairy and eggs, but no meats, fish, or fowl.

VINEGARS

Balsamic Vinegar—In the United States, any dark, sweet vinegar can be labeled "balsamic," but in Italy the regulations determining what can be called *aceto balsamico tradizionale* are many and strict. To make sure yours is authentic, look for a bottle with a wax seal and an insignia of the producer's origin. A limited number of Italian families produce balsamic vinegar, using the same time-intensive methods they did in the Middle Ages—and in some cases, the same casks! The resulting vinegar can be as thick as syrup and costs hundreds of dollars a bottle. For most uses—in salad dressings and sauces—a much less expensive balsamic will do. Italians use balsamic vinegar with dessert: a few drops on berries instead of sugar, or on a sliver of cheese.

Brown rice vinegar is a favorite of natural foods cooks. Rice vinegar is mellow and less acidic than other vinegars. It is great on salads or as a condiment in Asian-inspired dishes. (See Thai Cucumber Salad, page 114.)

Cider vinegar is a great all-purpose vinegar with a faint apple flavor. There are many different acidic strengths and qualities of cider vinegar on the market. The traditional method of vinegar manufacturing is referred to as the Orleans method, which involves apple cider or wine first being fermented with unpasteurized vinegar and then aged in wooden casks for up to six months before it is ready for use. This process yields a much more complex flavor and aroma than the quick method, which is much more mechanized and accomplished in just a few weeks from start to finish.

Infused vinegars—You may make herb- and spice-flavored vinegars at home easily by marinating favorite herbs such as thyme, rosemary, oregano, or tarragon in rice, wine, or cider vinegar. Place four or five lightly crushed fresh herb stalks in a jar with two cups of vinegar and allow to marry for five to six days, until flavors blend. If you like a little zip in your dishes, add some fresh chilies of your choice, along with the herbs or a few cloves of fresh garlic.

Specialty vinegars—Fruit-flavored vinegars, made by infusing raspberries, figs, cherries, and other fruits, are used for salads and sauces. The strong earthy flavor of sherry vinegar is used on salads and to finish sauces. Malt vinegar has a sharp, unusual flavor that goes well with fried foods and potato dishes.

Umeboshi vinegar, also known as ume, is another favorite ingredient of natural foods cooks, especially people who enjoy a macrobiotic lifestyle. Ume vinegar is not a true vinegar. This very tart and somewhat salty condiment is made from liquid from fermented Japanese umeboshi plums and the Asian herb shiso leaf. This is a very strong seasoning and should be used sparingly in dressings, in soups, and on salads.

WASABI is Japanese mustard paste. It is intensely pungent and usually eaten in tiny dabs on sushi. Add a touch to Asian sauces for extra bite. Look for natural, dried wasabi powder and make your own paste; the ready-made pastes often contain artificial green coloring.

YOGURT contains active cultures that contribute beneficial bacteria, along with helpful enzymes, to the digestive system. To avoid overdoing sugar, buy plain yogurt and add fresh fruit. Organic yogurt is also available. Low- or nonfat yogurt is an ideal substitute for sour cream and is even tastier. For the dairy abstainer, soy yogurt is now made with the same beneficial cultures and has the added plus of soy isoflavones. (See: *soy foods.*)

Menu Suggestions

Eating three square meals isn't what it used to be. Although the importance of eating a nutritionally balanced diet has not diminished, the rules have changed. In some ways our culture has become more experimental. Today, grazing or eating small meals more frequently is common to many of us. We are also experiencing a huge interest in ethnic foods and many of our dinner tables reflect a modern global cuisine approach to dining. Multi-ethnic taste samplings served on small plates, such as Spanish tapas, Asian dim sum, and Mediterranean meze, enable us to be more playful and daring with our food choices. Combinations of dishes once considered unusual now fall into the norm, provided they make sense to our taste buds.

Time has also affected our dinner decisions. We want to eat right and want dinners that taste like they took all day to prepare—as long as they take us under a half hour to make.

In order to free up some of your kitchen time, we have put together some menus for you. Here are some everyday, special occasion, and favorite suggestions that may begin a new tradition around your dinner table.

WARMING EVERYDAY DINNERS THAT CAN BE PREPARED AHEAD
Creole Rice and Bean Soup (page 68)
Jamaican Jerk Chicken Wrap (page 139)

Spicy Mac and Cheese (page 259)
Southern-Style Power Slaw (page 119)

Teriyaki Chicken Wings (page 44)
Pad Thai (page 204)
Emerald Sesame Kale (page 283)

Chicken Breast Piccata Florentine (page 231)
Fettuccine with Garlic, Parsley, and Parmesan (page 184)
Serve with a green salad

GLOBAL FLIGHTS OF FANCY
Garden of Eva Summer Rolls (page 28)
Thai-Style Green Curry Chicken (page 273)
Asian Braised Greens (page 284)

Samosas (page 36)
Firecracker Shrimp (page 242)
Orange Cashew Rice (page 174)
Sesame Sugar Snap Peas (page 288)

Grilled Marinated Artichoke Hearts (page 31)
Chicken Toscana with White Beans (page 229)
Roasted Scarlet Peppers (page 290)
Balsamic Berry Dessert Topping over ice cream or biscotti (page 394)

Spicy Chicken and Tortilla Soup (page 85)
Chiles Rellenos Casserole (page 268)
Cilantro Lime Rice (page 172)

Tandoori Stuffed Lettuce Leaf Cups (page 47)
Persian Lamb Roast à la Grand-Mère (page 256)
Yellow Split Peas with Fresh Dill and Crispy Garlic (page 163)

Piquillo Peppers with Goat Cheese (page 38)
Cubano-Style Pork Loin (page 252)
Anaheim Chili Mashed Potatoes (page 301)
Havana Black Beans (page 166)
Rum-Painted Pineapple Orange Bundt Cake (page 375)

Baked Falafel Balls (page 27)
Fattoush (page 111)
Moroccan Pan-Roasted Seafood (page 276)
Mixed Nut and Flax Seed Baklava (page 377)

INSPIRED VEGETARIAN MEALS

Spicy Chickpea Patties with Cilantro, Lime, and Chilies (page 30)
Algerian Eggplant Salad (page 115)
Quinoa Tabbouleh (page 109)

"It's Alive" Salad (page 113)
Chunky Garden Vegetable Chili (page 90)
Orange Cashew Rice (page 174)

Thai Cucumber Salad (page 114)
Kung Pao Tofu (page 223)
Cilantro Lime Rice (page 172)

Seitan Lasagna (page 194)
Pan-Roasted Fennel (page 286)
Serve with a green salad

Portobello Burgers (page 210)
Whole Wheat Linguine with Broccoli (page 189)
Silken Tofu Chocolate Mousse (page 393)

Tomato Bruschetta (page 40)
Tuscan Vegetable Sauté (page 260)
Garlic Spinach Stellini Pasta (page 195)

Essential Sea Vegetable Salad (page 112)
Adzuki Bean Loaf (page 160)
Vegan Creamed Spinach (page 282)

AT HOME FOR THE HOLIDAYS

THANKSGIVING

Here are some alternatives to the traditional turkey:
Pomegranate Glazed Chicken (page 238)
Caramelized Onion Turkey Roulade (page 240)
Red-Chili-Rubbed Salmon (page 246)
Hazelnut Crusted Pork Loin (page 250)

Serve with:
Garlic Creamed Spinach with Arugula (page 281)
Maple Glazed Carrots (page 285)
Roasted Broccoli Medley (page 291)
Versatile Mashed Potatoes (page 298) or Parsnip Mashed Potatoes (page 299)
Pumpkin Bread Pudding (page 385)

VEGETARIAN THANKSGIVING

Spinach, Beet, and Walnut Salad (page 110)
Harvest Vegetable Shepherd's Pie with Orange Mashed Yam Crust (page 266)
Skillet-Roasted Limas with Italian Herbs (page 293)
Wild Rice with Pecans and Cranberries (page 173)

HOLIDAY OR SPECIAL-OCCASION BUFFETS THAT WILL IMPRESS YOUR FRIENDS AND ALLOW YOU TO BE A GUEST AT YOUR OWN PARTY

These buffet combinations look extremely beautiful when combined. The colors and shapes are wonderful, and in most cases all the dishes can be made a day or two prior to serving. Nobody likes to be busy scurrying around cooking while friends and family are in the house.

A MED FEST

These dishes combined form a Mediterranean meze theme. These recipes can all be served at room temperature.

Red Pepper Hummus (page 323)

Spinach Artichoke Dip (page 317)

Fattoush (page 111)

Ligurian Chicken Breasts (page 232) or Athenian Chicken Roll-Ups (page 234)—serve them cut into 1-inch-thick medallions.

Chickpeas Florentine with Roasted Peppers (page 162)

Orzo and Feta with Lemon-Caper Dressing and Kalamata Olives (page 186)

Mixed Nut and Flax Seed Baklava (page 377)

FAMILY FIESTA

Chili Cheese Tamales (page 37)

Red-Chili-Rubbed Salmon (page 246)—leave one side of salmon whole and serve guests from the intact side; it's very impressive.

Chipotle Potato Salad (page 116)

Cilantro Lime Rice (page 172)

Serve with a green salad

Pear Burritos (page 392)

SPECIAL-OCCASION ASIAN

Asian Tuna Dumplings with Soy Dipping Sauce (page 48) or Thai Fish Cakes (page 219)

Thai-Style Green Curry Chicken (page 273)

Spicy Asian Flank Steak Submarine with Szechwan Slaw and Peanut Sauce (page 142)

Pad Thai (page 204)

Thai Black Rice Salad (page 108)

Szechwan Slaw (page 120)

WISHING WE WERE IN TUSCANY

Grilled Marinated Artichoke Hearts (page 31)

Tomato Bruschetta (page 40)

Chicken Toscana with White Beans (page 229)

Sausage and Multicolored Peppers with Basil (page 278)

Tuscan Vegetable Sauté (page 260)

Pan-Sautéed Portobello Pasta with Roasted Garlic and Sun-Dried Tomatoes
    (page 188)

Balsamic Berry Dessert Topping over gelato (page 394)

ECLECTIC TAPAS MENU FOR NEW YEAR'S OR ANY SPECIAL OCCASION

Raspberry-Stuffed Brie Wrapped in Phyllo (page 32)

Turkey, Sage, and Pine Nut Meatballs (page 45) with Cucumber Raita (page 340)

Firecracker Shrimp (page 242)

Quesadilla assortment (pages 148–152)

Crispy Garlic Tofu Bites (page 34)

Cajun Seafood Cakes, made in small silver-dollar style (page 218)

GREAT SUNDAY-NIGHT SUPPERS

Thai Cucumber Salad (page 114) or a green salad

Tuna Noodle Casserole (page 274)

Strawberry Cobbler (page 384)

Grilled Lemon Pepper Rib-Eye Steaks (page 253)

Mashed Potatoes with Jalapeños and Cheddar (page 300)

Southern-Style Power Slaw (page 119)

Nectarine Blueberry Johnnycake (page 382)

Double Dumpling Beef Stew (page 277) or Mushroom Tofu Stroganoff (page 265)

Parsnip Mashed Potatoes (page 299)

Maple Glazed Carrots (page 285)

Lemon Lime Bars (page 386)

Tomato Bruschetta (page 40)

Sausage and Multicolored Peppers with Basil (page 278)

Fettuccine with Garlic, Parsley, and Parmesan (page 184)

Pan-Roasted Fennel (page 286)

Wine Recommendations

When selecting a wine to match your dinner—whether a simple pasta or an elaborate paella—there are literally thousands of options. When wine and food meet at the dinner table, the intensity of the food can cancel the flavor of the wine and vice versa. For example, a simple white wine could be overwhelmed by a heavy red meat. While there are no rules set in stone, here are a few guidelines:

- Drink what you like. Recommendations made by wine experts mean nothing if the wine does not appeal to your taste buds.
- Drink dry wines before you eat sweets. Just like saving your dessert until after your meal, a sweet wine will make everything else taste tart.
- Match texture with texture. Drink a light wine with a light meal. Enjoy a full-bodied wine with a full-bodied meal.

Here are some suggestions:

Wine	Flavors	Food Pairings	Herb/Spice Pairings
REDS			
CABERNET SAUVIGNON [cab-er-NAY SO-vin-yohn]	Currant, plum, black cherry, spice; or herb, olive, mint, tobacco, cedar, and anise with ripe, jammy notes	Roasted red meats, game, lamb, pasta with red sauce, full-flavored cheese, and chocolate desserts	Marjoram, thyme, allspice, and nutmeg
MERLOT [mur-LO]	Currant and cherry flavors with firm tannins	Roasted red meats, game, lamb, pasta with red sauce, pheasant, duck, goose, and full-flavored cheeses	Basil, oregano, rosemary, thyme, allspice, and nutmeg
PINOT NOIR [PEE-no NWAHR]	Black cherry, spice, raspberry, and currant with notes of wilted roses, tar, earth, herb, and cola	Great with Thanks-giving turkey, beef, game, lamb, pork, veal, pheasant, duck, goose, pasta with red sauce, and full-flavored cheeses	Rosemary, thyme, and allspice
SYRAH or **SHIRAZ** [sir-RAH or shih-RAHZ]	Pepper, spice, black cherry, tar, leather, and roasted nut flavors with smooth, supple texture	Beef, small game, poultry, and full-flavored cheeses	Parsley, sage, rosemary, thyme, black pepper, and garlic
ZINFANDEL [zin-fahn-DELL]	Full-bodied, ripe, cherry, black pepper spices, pretty oak shadings	Game, pizza, ham-burgers, barbecued ribs, and tomato-based sauces	Rosemary, thyme, bay leaf, basil, black pepper, and garlic

Wine	Flavors	Food Pairings	Herb/Spice Pairings
WHITES			
CHARDONNAY [shar-doh-NAY]	Intense flavors of apple, fig, melon, pear, pineapple, and lemon with spice, honey, butter, butterscotch, and vanilla	Cream-based sauces, shellfish, poultry, pork, veal, salmon, and full-bodied cheeses	Mustard seeds, rosemary, tarragon, cloves, and fresh ginger
CHENIN BLANC [say-NAN blahnk]	Subtle melon, peach, spice, and citrus notes; made in dry, medium dry, and slightly sweet styles	Asian food, poultry, clams, mussels, shrimp, crab, lobster, and mild cheeses	Dill, fennel, allspice, and cloves
GEWÜRTZ-TRAMINER [geh-VERTS-trah-nee-ner]	Spicy fruity flavors of peach, apricot, and melon	Asian and other spicy, hot food, pork, veal, poultry, duck and mild cheeses	Cilantro, mint, black pepper, and fresh ginger
PINOT GRIS (France) **PINOT GRIGIO** (Italy) [PEE-no-GREE/GREE-zhoh]	Medium-bodied flavors of citrus, spice, figs, and toasted almonds	Pasta with cream or red sauce, veal, poultry, and full-bodied cheeses	Basil, rosemary, thyme, garlic, fresh ginger, and green peppercorn
RIESLING [REES-ling]	Complex fruit flavors of peach, apricot, and green apple; made in a dry to off-dry and sweet style	Asian food, poultry, grilled fish, smoked salmon, shrimp, crab, lobster, fruit, and mild cheeses	Chervil, sage, chili powder, and curry
SAUVIGNON BLANC [SO-vin-yohn BLAHNK]	Tropical fruits such as melon, pineapple, and citrus	Seafood, salads, light pastas, poultry, appetizers, and goat cheese	Basil, oregano, cumin, and fresh ginger

WHAT'S IN A GRAPE?

Wines are named for the region of the world in which the grapes were grown or for the variety of grape.

- A varietal wine is one named after the grape variety from which it is made (or the principal grape if more than one is used). The same variety of grape can taste differently depending upon the soil, the sun, the rain, the temperature, and other factors.
- Alternatively, most European wines are named for the region in which the wine is made. Bordeaux is made in Bordeaux; Chablis in Chablis; Champagne in Champagne. The bottle will not usually tell you what variety of grapes is in the wine.

STORING WINE

If you plan to store the bottle for a month or two, keep the bottles lying down on a rack away from direct heat and sunlight.

If you will be serving the wine soon, follow these guidelines:

- Chill white wines for at least four hours in the refrigerator—champagne for a while longer. Remove white wine from the refrigerator 30 minutes before serving.
- Ideally, red wines should be served at a cool cellar temperature (about 60°F.). If your red wine is at room temperature, chill the bottle in the refrigerator for 10 minutes before serving.

UNCORKING THE BOTTLE

When removed, examine the cork. It should be in good condition. Did it pop when the bottle was opened? If the cork slides out too easily or if it is thin or broken, you may have a bad bottle of wine. Oxygen can make wine oxidize or deteriorate.

Sniffing the cork will not tell you anything about the wine, though. The cork can have an "off" odor and be crusted with tartaric acid crystals, yet the wine can still taste delicious. Nonetheless, you should make sure the cork is not dried out. Wine should be stored on its side or cork down to keep the cork moist and assure a good seal. If the wine is red and old, the cork may become soaked and colored from the wine.

CHECKING WINE

Pour a small amount of wine. Carefully swirl the glass. This allows the wine to "breathe" or open the fruit flavors. Bring it to your nose, inhale deeply, and release. The best indication of taste and quality is if you smell it before it reaches your nose. If the wine smells like sherry, it is oxidized. If it has an off odor, then something was wrong with the way the wine was made or stored.

Look at the wine in the glass from the center to the edge against a white background. A white wine should have a clean, attractive edge—not a watery edge. For reds, a consistent color indicates a younger wine while an amber hue suggests a more aged variety. If white wine has turned brown, the wine has spoiled.

Now it is time to taste the wine. Remember, you are tasting the wine to see it is sound, not to see if you like it. There are thousands of wines to choose from and no one likes them all, but you want to ensure the wine is not past its prime.

Organic Wines

Organic wines do more than taste great—they also help protect and rebuild the earth's natural resources and maintain healthy soil. Organic farming requires vineyards or farms to use and document specific growing practices for three years prior to receiving certification. Healthy soil is the true foundation of organic wine production. Instead of using synthetic pesticides and herbicides, organic vintners encourage biodiversity. This technique helps to regulate and maintain the health of the soil by attracting beneficial insects (the natural predators of harmful insects), encouraging the growth of cover crops other than grape vines in the vineyard, and using natural fertilizers such as composted animal manure. Healthier soil produces a healthier plant.

You'll find wines produced from organically grown grapes labeled several ways:

* *Made from organically grown grapes.* Grapes are grown according to organic standards. Though sulfites occur naturally in wine, many vintners recognize the extreme difficulty of producing a wine that will keep well without including at least some sulfites in addition to those that occur naturally. Sulfites added during fermentation keep the wine's flavor stable for a longer period of time.

* *Organically grown and organically processed.* Grapes are grown according to organic standards. No postharvest sulfites are added and the wines naturally contain lower levels of sulfites. Most organic wines are also labeled "no added sulfites."

* *Biodynamic.* This farming technique supplements methods used by organic producers with homeopathic-like preparations, infusions, and sprays produced on the farm to enhance and regulate plant growth, compost production, and soil fertility. Some biodynamic wine producers add sulfites while others do not.

Today, many of the organic wines taste just as great as conventional wines. The prices are affordable, too. The commitment by organic wine producers not only to producing the highest quality product but also to maintaining the health of the environment is something we can all raise our glass to.

PREPARING FOR A PARTY

Here are answers to the most common questions about preparing for a party:

- *How much wine should I buy?* A standard 750 ml bottle equals approximately five glasses of wine. Determine how many of your guests will drink wine, and expect each to drink two to three glasses each. Some will have more, some less.

- *How much should I spend?* Determine your budget, but don't go overboard. There are great values for less than $12 per bottle and, of course, many wonderful wines that are more expensive.

- *Red or white?* Serve both if your party is more than just a few people. If you would like to stick with just one choice, white may be more appropriate for an afternoon party with lighter foods. Red is a good choice for a heavier menu.

- *What about Champagne?* While people enjoy Champagne, generally your guests won't drink a lot. One glass each can add a festive touch. When serving Champagne, pour less than you would for wine.

The Cheese Course

A BRIEF HISTORY OF CHEESE

Cheese is the oldest known method of preserving milk. The existence of cheese dates back more than one thousand years when nomads traveled with milk stored in pouches made of animal hide. The liquid milk was exposed to heat, which led to the separation of the milk solids (curds) and the milk liquids (whey). The result was solidified milk—cheese!

All cheese is, in simple terms, a separation of the curds and whey of milk product. The manipulation of the curds into various forms or molds in addition to the use of various milks have resulted in the many styles and varieties of cheese we have available today.

TYPES OF CHEESE

There are literally hundreds of varieties of cheese today. Here are some of the basic varieties available domestically and around the world:

- *Fresh cheese* has gone through the cheese-making process and is offered for consumption at a very young age, usually in less than 30 days. These are typically very moist and often spreadable. An example is fresh chevre.
- *Soft ripened cheeses* refer to those with edible bloomy rinds. An example is brie. The cheese ripens from the outside into the middle. The exterior, the bloomy rind, is white. The interior is the chalk; it is hard when the cheese is young and will soften as the cheese ripens.
- *Trappist or monastery cheeses* were originally made by monks in the fourteenth century in Belgium. The cloistered life of a monk offered unique opportunities to develop food and beverages based on the needs of the commune. The monks developed a specific style of cheese usually described as a semi-soft variety with washed rinds. The rinds were typically "washed" by the ales the monks were fermenting in the abbey. Typical of this style is today's Chimay cheese.
- *Whey cheese,* such as ricotta, is produced during the heating of the whey. Basically, the whey that remains from an initial cheese production still contains enough proteins to form other products. When the whey is reheated, these proteins solidify to form another style of cheese.
- *Hard cheese* has either a solid age or is produced using very small curds. An example is Parmigiano-Reggiano, which is aged for a minimum of 18 months according to the Italian law that governs the country's cheese production.

THE FLAVORS

There are as many flavors of cheese as there are varieties. The following items have an effect on the flavor of cheese:

- *Milk.* The most popular milks used in cheese production today come from cows, goats, sheep, and water buffaloes. The animals' milks vary in protein, fat, mineral, and vitamin content. Using raw instead of pasteurized milk also has an effect. Milk has more flavor in its natural, raw state.

- *The animal's diet.* The grass and feed the animal consumes while producing the milk affect the flavor of the final product. For example, Swiss cows eating rich alpine grass produce the nutty flavor in Switzerland's traditional cheeses.

- *Cheese rinds.* Some rinds are natural, which means the cheese hardens naturally from the outside and the rind *is* the cheese minus the moisture content. A natural rind is edible. Also, natural molds on cheese rinds provide unique flavors. Some cheese is washed in a brine, or salty, solution twice a week to prohibit mold growth. Other cheese is washed less frequently to encourage the growth.

- *The age of the cheese.* As a very complex food, cheese continues to develop flavor and complexity with time.

- *The size of the curd.*

RENNETS

Rennet is an enzyme added to the milk that begins the coagulating process that turns milk into cheese. There are different types of rennet: animal, microbial, and vegetarian. Rennetless cheeses, or "acid precipitated cheeses," are created using their natural acidity and do not require the addition of a coagulating enzyme. Cottage cheese, ricotta, and some varieties of mozzarella are examples of rennetless cheeses.

CHEESE FOR VEGETARIANS

More and more cheese products are available in vegetarian varieties. Vegetarians should look for the terms "microbial rennet," "vegetarian rennet," or "made without rennet" when purchasing a cheese product.

ORGANIC CHEESE

Organic cheese production begins with the animals that produce the milk. They must be raised in an organic environment and be fed organic grains. Also, these animals cannot receive antibiotics or growth hormones.

In the cheese-making facilities, all machines used must be designated for the production of certified organic products only. No genetically modified organisms (GMOs) are allowed in organic cheese. Additional strict standards are enforced, including specific guidelines for cleaning equipment.

STORING CHEESE

Cheese will continue its development in your refrigerator if allowed to breathe. Store your cheese wrapped in paper, which allows for moisture retention as well as circulation. Place it in a part of the refrigerator, like the vegetable drawer, where it will not be exposed to light or heat.

SERVING CHEESE

A good rule of thumb is to remove the cheese from the refrigerator approximately 30 to 45 minutes prior to serving, depending on the weight of the cheese. Softer cheese will require less time out of the refrigerator. This time allows the cheese to "open up" and develop, similar to opening a bottle of wine.

The texture of a cheese also contributes to its best form for serving.

- Serve all soft ripened cheeses in wedges.
- Fresh cheeses can be served whole to be spread on bread or crackers.
- Cut semi-soft cheeses into any form desired.
- Semi-hard cheese should be served in wedges or cubes to expose the cheese to the air.
- Hard cheese should be served in large chunks.
- Blue cheese should be served in chunks.
- Aged goat cheese should be presented on its own.

SELECTING CHEESE FOR A PARTY

If you want to satisfy and delight a group of people with different tastes, offer a nice variety of cheeses. A good variety to start with is a blue cheese, a soft ripened cheese, a fresh cheese, a hard cheese, and a unique regional cheese. You may also try selecting a combination of cheeses made from various milks—goat, sheep, and cow. A typical serving at a party is two ounces per person per variety of cheese.

PAIRING WINE WITH CHEESE

If you wish to highlight a particular wine or cheese, create a simple pairing. Your wine merchant and cheesemonger are valuable sources of information and inspiration—ask them for their opinions and favorite combinations. Pick one distinct wine and one cheese that pair together well. For example, for a good winter pairing, pick a Syrah and serve it with a ripened chevre from France such as Puligney St. Pierre. You may also pair cheese and wine

Cheese in Recipes

Cheese is a flavorful addition to many recipes. Since cheese contains a fair amount of salt, you may wish to reduce the amount of salt in your recipe. Try adding cheese to:

- *Oven-roasted potatoes.* Shred an aged Gouda or Parmigiano Reggiano over the top immediately prior to serving.
- *Mashed potatoes.* Add grated Pepato Romano to spice up the flavor.
- *Casserole dishes.* Add grated Romano and omit any salt.
- *Apple pies.* A classic! Shred cheddar on top prior to serving.
- *Soup.* Almost any cheese in the refrigerator will create a new and exciting recipe.
- *Pasta.* Many different cheeses will enhance your pasta dishes, or for an interesting change try a blue Gouda macaroni and cheese.

by focusing on the products' area of origin. Try selecting a cheese and a wine that are both produced in southern France. A nice Cotes du Rhone, full of flavor with fruity components, will pair well with a lovely goat's milk selection from Perigord called Soreda.

A good cheese and wine pairing takes some thought, and the unique flavor characteristics of both the wine and the cheese need to be considered to create a perfect match. Try these ideas:

- For a stronger cheese such as Reblochon or aged Cheddar, select a strong and more flavor-filled wine such as a Chardonnay, Merlot, Zinfandel, or Syrah.
- Creamy cheeses such as brie or St. Andre pair well with effervescent wines such as Champagne or a sparkling wine.
- Fresh cheeses such as Brin D'Amour or Livarot pair well with fruity wines like Chenin Blanc and Riesling.
- Blue cheeses pair well with sweeter wines. Select a late harvest Riesling, Moscato, French Sauterne, or Porto.
- Goat cheeses pair well with crisp wines such as Sauvignon Blanc.
- Hard cheeses such as Parmigiano-Reggiano or year-old Manchego pair well with young red wines such as Cabernet Sauvignon, Merlot, or Chianti.

WHAT'S IN A NAME?

Many cheeses that date back centuries are named for the city or the region of production. Some cheeses are strictly regulated and a cheese produced in a different region of the world could never share an exclusive name. For example, the cheese known as Romano can only be produced in Rome, Italy. Emmentaler is made only in Emmental, Switzerland. Several countries—including Spain, France, and Italy—have regulations applying to the production of name-controlled cheeses. The regulations govern the type of milk, its source, the specific breed of the animal producing the milk, the aging process, and the physical characteristics of the cheese. These rules vary from product to product and country to country, but they are an earnest effort to keep the product quality consistent over time and to maintain the names associated with specific products.

This exclusivity of name and production location is not shared among all cheeses, however. Cheddar, for example, is now produced around the world, yet the cheddar made in Wisconsin tastes much different from the cheddar produced in England. As you taste different types of cheeses from different origins, you may notice you enjoy cheese from a certain area of the world and want to further explore the products of that region.

Resources

There were many books used while writing this book, both for historical reference and for anecdotal entertainment. Here is a list of books that you might find amusing, informative, and even inspirational.

Bricklin, Mark, and the editors of *Prevention* magazine. *Prevention Magazine's Nutrition Advisor.* Emmaus, Pa.: Rodale Press, 1993.

D'Amico, Serge, ed., and François Fortin, ed. *The Visual Food Encyclopedia.* Montreal, Quebec: Quebec/Amerique Inc., 1996.

Domine, Andre. *Organic & Wholefoods— Naturally Delicious Cuisine.* Cologne, Ger.: Culinaria Koneman, 1997.

Herbst, Sharon Tyler. *The Food Lover's Tiptionary.* New York: Hearst Books, 1994.

———. *The Food Lover's Companion.* Hauppauge, N.Y.: Barron's, 1995.

Madison, Deborah. *Vegetarian Cooking for Everyone.* New York: Broadway Books, 1997.

Margen, Sheldon, M.D., and the editors of the University of California at Berkeley. *The Wellness Encyclopedia of Food and Nutrition.* New York: Rebus Publications, 1992.

Roehl, Evelyn. *Whole Food Facts.* Rochester, Vt.: Healing Arts Press, 1996.

Sass, Lorna J. *The Pressured Cook.* New York: William Morrow & Co., 1999.

Shaw, Diana. *The Essential Vegetarian Cookbook.* New York: Clarkson Potter, 1997.

Sonberg, Lynn. *The Health Nutrient Bible.* New York: Simon & Schuster, 1995.

Wittenberg, Margaret M. *Good Food—The Comprehensive Food and Nutrition Resource.* Freedom, Calif.: The Crossing Press, 1995.

PRODUCTS

Delicious food is one of life's few dependable pleasures. Just as Whole Foods Market is different from conventional supermarkets, our private label products are also different. Instead of the same ordinary stuff, Whole Foods Market's own labeled products are made of the highest quality ingredients and offer exceptionally flavorful items from around the world. Many are made by small producers who possess a passion for delicious, quality food as well as a knowledge of traditional methods of preparation. While each recipe and each product includes the highest quality ingredients, many are also certified organic.

All of Whole Foods Market's private label products are free of artificial sweeteners, colorings, flavorings, and preservatives. These all-natural products meet all of our Quality Standards (see page 4) and also taste great. The Whole Kids™ line was the United States' first certified organic product line developed just for children's taste buds.

At Whole Foods Market, our customers can be confident they will find the same high standards of quality and value in our private label products as they do in all the products we carry throughout our stores.

INFORMATION

In our hectic world, it is often difficult to find the time to research and investigate all of the issues affecting our lives. On our website, www.wholefoodsmarket.com, we share our research into natural and organic foods, health, nutrition, food safety, and environmental issues. As an added bonus, we have a recipe section filled with many recipes that didn't fit in this book. A visit to our site will help you stay up to date with important information about the world around us, as well as what affects you and your family in your own home and kitchen.

About Whole Foods Market

Whole Foods Market, a Fortune 1,000 company, is the world's largest chain of natural and organic foods supermarkets. At the end of our 2001 fiscal year we had sales of $2.3 billion and 126 stores in twenty-three states and the District of Columbia. Our stores averaged 28,500 square feet in size. We had more than twenty additional stores in development, with an average size of about thirty-five thousand square feet. There are more than 23,000 Team Members currently working with Whole Foods Market. We are a public company with common stock trading on the Nasdaq Stock Market (symbol: WFMI).

The stores are supported by regional distribution centers, bake houses, commissary kitchens, a seafood processing facility, a produce procurement and field inspection office, and a coffee roasting operation.

According to *Fortune* magazine, Whole Foods Market ranks as the 21st-largest food and drug company in the United States, and the 827th largest company overall. Even with rapid growth, Whole Foods Market remains a uniquely mission-driven company—highly selective about what we sell, dedicated to our Core Values and stringent Quality Standards, and committed to the principles of right livelihood, Team Member empowerment, community service, conscientious retailing, and support for sustainable agriculture.

Our customers can be confident they will find the same high standards of quality and service from all Whole Foods Market stores. You'll find our retail stores and our subsidiary location operating under the names:

Whole Foods Market®
Bread & Circus®
Wellspring®
Fresh Fields®
Harry's Farmers Market®
Allegro Coffee Company®

The Whole Foods Market family of stores is constantly growing. Please visit our website at www.wholefoodsmarket.com for updated store locations and addresses, or call 1-888-SHOP-WFM.

Index

About the Coauthor

Chef STEVEN PETUSEVSKY is a pioneer in the marriage of taste and health, successfully pairing traditional ingredients from the natural foods industry with creative cooking techniques. Petusevsky previously worked for Whole Foods Market, Inc., Unicorn Village, in North Miami, Florida, and for several international hotel corporations, including Inter-Continental Hotels, Meridien Hotels, and Rockresorts (owned by the Rockefeller family).

Petusevsky is a graduate of the prestigious Culinary Institute of America in Hyde Park, New York, where he was awarded a fellowship and served as chef instructor. He is also a widely published food journalist with a reading audience numbered in the millions and has been contributing editor for *Cooking Light* magazine for the past four years, writing a monthly column called "Inspired Vegetarian." He currently writes special features for the magazine. Moreover, Petusevsky is a syndicated columnist for *Chicago Tribune* news service; his column entitled "Vegetarian Today" appears in hundreds of newspapers nationally. His articles also appear in *Natural Health, Vegetarian Times, Fine Cooking,* the *Los Angeles Times* Syndicate, *Supermarket Business,* and *Restaurant Hospitality.* Petusevsky is the author of the Ten Speed Press grains poster.

Conversion Chart
EQUIVALENT IMPERIAL AND METRIC MEASUREMENTS

American cooks use standard containers, the 8-ounce cup and a tablespoon that takes exactly 16 level fillings to fill that cup level. Measuring by cup makes it very difficult to give weight equivalents, as a cup of densely packed butter will weigh considerably more than a cup of flour. The easiest way therefore to deal with cup measurements in recipes is to take the amount by volume rather than by weight. Thus the equation reads:

1 cup = 240 ml = 8 fl. oz.   ½ cup = 120 ml = 4 fl. oz.

It is possible to buy a set of American cup measures in major stores around the world.

In the States, butter is often measured in sticks. One stick is the equivalent of 8 tablespoons. One tablespoon of butter is therefore the equivalent to ½ ounce/15 grams.

LIQUID MEASURES

Fluid Ounces	U.S.	Imperial	Milliliters
	1 teaspoon	1 teaspoon	5
¼	2 teaspoons	1 dessertspoon	10
½	1 tablespoon	1 tablespoon	14
1	2 tablespoons	2 tablespoons	28
2	¼ cup	4 tablespoons	56
4	½ cup		110
5		¼ pint or 1 gill	140
6	¾ cup		170
8	1 cup		225
9			250, ¼ liter
10	1¼ cups	½ pint	280
12	1½ cups		340
15		¾ pint	420
16	2 cups		450
18	2¼ cups		500, ½ liter
20	2½ cups	1 pint	560
24	3 cups		675
25		1¼ pints	700
27	3½ cups		750
30	3¾ cups	1½ pints	840
32	4 cups or 1 quart		900
35		1¾ pints	980
36	4½ cups		1000, 1 liter
40	5 cups	2 pints or 1 quart	1120

SOLID MEASURES

U.S. and Imperial Measures		Metric Measures	
Ounces	Pounds	Grams	Kilos
1		28	
2		56	
3½		100	
4	¼	112	
5		140	
6		168	
8	½	225	
9		250	¼
12	¾	340	
16	1	450	
18		500	½
20	1¼	560	
24	1½	675	
27		750	¾
28	1¾	780	
32	2	900	
36	2¼	1000	1
40	2½	1100	
48	3	1350	
54		1500	1½

OVEN TEMPERATURE EQUIVALENTS

Fahrenheit	Celsius	Gas Mark	Description
225	110	¼	Cool
250	130	½	
275	140	1	Very Slow
300	150	2	
325	170	3	Slow
350	180	4	Moderate
375	190	5	
400	200	6	Moderately Hot
425	220	7	Fairly Hot
450	230	8	Hot
475	240	9	Very Hot
500	250	10	Extremely Hot

Any broiling recipes can be used with the grill of the oven, but beware of high-temperature grills.

EQUIVALENTS FOR INGREDIENTS

all-purpose flour—plain flour
baking sheet—oven tray
buttermilk—ordinary milk
cheesecloth—muslin
coarse salt—kitchen salt
cornstarch—cornflour

eggplant—aubergine
granulated sugar—caster sugar
half and half—12% fat milk
heavy cream—double cream
light cream—single cream
parchment paper—greaseproof paper

plastic wrap—cling film
scallion—spring onion
shortening—white fat
unbleached flour—strong, white flour
zest—rind
zucchini—courgettes or marrow